The Letters
of Henry Venn

The Letters of Henry Venn

WITH A MEMOIR
BY JOHN VENN

The Banner of Truth Trust

THE BANNER OF TRUTH TRUST
3 Murrayfield Road, Edinburgh EH12 6EL
PO Box 621, Carlisle, Pennsylvania 17013, USA

*

First published 1835
First Banner of Truth edition 1993
ISBN 0 85151 653 X

*

Printed in Great Britain at
The Bath Press, Avon

THE

LIFE

AND

A SELECTION FROM THE LETTERS

OF THE LATE

REV. HENRY VENN, M.A.

SUCCESSIVELY VICAR OF HUDDERSFIELD, YORKSHIRE, AND

RECTOR OF YELLING, HUNTINGDONSHIRE,

AUTHOR OF " THE COMPLETE DUTY OF MAN," &c.

———

THE MEMOIR OF HIS LIFE

DRAWN UP

BY· THE LATE REV. JOHN VENN, M.A.

RECTOR OF CLAPHAM, SURREY.

———◆———

EDITED BY THE REV. HENRY VENN, B.D.

PERPETUAL CURATE OF ST. JOHN'S, HOLLOWAY;

LATE FELLOW OF QUEEN'S COLLEGE, CAMBRIDGE.

FOURTH EDITION.

LONDON:

JOHN HATCHARD AND SON,

187, PICCADILLY.

—

1836.

CONTENTS.

PART I.

CONTENTS.

PART II.

CORRESPONDENCE, IN CHRONOLOGICAL ORDER.

CONTENTS.

CONTENTS.

SECTION II.—LETTERS WRITTEN FROM HIS ACCEPTANCE
OF YELLING, TO THE COMMENCEMENT OF HIS
CORRESPONDENCE WITH HIS SON.

1770.

1771.

1772.

CONTENTS.

CONTENTS.

CONTENTS.

1780.

Section IV.—LETTERS WRITTEN FROM THE TIME OF HIS SON'S ORDINATION, TO THE YEAR 1788.

CONTENTS.

CONTENTS.

1785.

CONTENTS.

CONTENTS.

1791.

1792.

1793.

1794.

1795.

1796.

CONTENTS.

PART III.

LETTERS ON PARTICULAR SUBJECTS, TOO LONG FOR INSERTION IN THE PRECEDING SECTIONS.

ADVERTISEMENT

TO

THE SECOND EDITION.

———

THE sale of the First Edition, within a few months after its appearance, has sufficiently justified the Editor in submitting this volume to the public.

The corrections and additions introduced into this Edition are very few and unimportant. There are, however, two points which seem to require explanation.

A regret has been expressed, in many quarters, that a second volume of the Correspondence has not been added, out of the stores which are still in the Editor's hands. But it must be remembered, that the range of topics in Mr. VENN's Letters is not extensive, and that the events of his life were, comparatively, few: so that a second volume would consist, for the most part, of the repetition of sentiments, arising from circumstances and occasions similar to those already recorded.

It has been suggested, also, that the Memoir should have been intermingled with the Letters, instead of standing by itself, in the First Part of the Work. The Editor, however, adheres to his original plan, from a wish to keep the matter, which was prepared by the Rev. JOHN VENN, unbroken, and distinct from the rest;—not only because it was originally intended to stand in such a form, but, also, because its value, as a sketch of the progress of Mr. VENN's mind in religious knowledge, would be impaired by a different arrangement.

The Editor, in again committing this volume to the Public, begs to express his gratitude to the Giver of all good, for the blessing which has already crowned his labours, and to renew his earnest prayers for the continuance of the same Divine grace.

HOLLOWAY,
    7th Feb. 1835.

PREFACE BY THE EDITOR.

The Memoir which composes the First Part of the present volume was drawn up by the late Rev. John Venn, with the intention of its being prefixed to a new edition of his father's works. He had also written the following paragraph, as the commencement of a Preface.

"The Compiler of this Memoir deeply feels the impropriety of troubling the public with the lives of those who have little claim to public notice. But he trusts that every person, who feels the influence of filial piety, will justify his breaking through this rule, when he is told that a Life of his honoured and excellent father has been already given to the public, full of misrepresentations, and calculated to produce a most injurious impression respecting his character and principles; and that this Life has been extensively circulated, inserted into biographical histories, and even prefixed to an edition of his principal work, without any public denial or indignant refutation.

"In the Memoir which follows, which exhibits the real character of one, by whose writings the

Church has been edified, and by whose example
many have been animated, the author can truly say,
that he has endeavoured to free himself entirely
from partiality . . . . ."

The Memoir, which the preceding fragment was
intended to introduce, was left in an unfinished
state. It had been commenced by Mr. Venn soon
after his father's death; but, when a few of the
first pages had been written, it was laid aside till
his own last illness; so that the greater part of it
was dictated by him from his death-bed. This circumstance will doubtless increase the interest with
which it will be read; and it will also account for
any degree of haste or abruptness which may be
apparent in the composition. It has now devolved
upon one of the third generation to put the finishing
hand to the work, and to present it to the public.

I have presumed to incorporate some additional
matter with the original Memoir, in order to complete the narrative; distinguishing such additions,
by including them within angular brackets. I have
also given a large collection of Letters, which will
form the domestic annals of the greater part of my
grandfather's life.

It may be expected that I should offer some apology, for having thus enlarged my father's design,
and departed still further than he had contemplated
from the rule laid down by him in the preceding
fragment. It is hoped, however, not only that

the intrinsic excellence of the Letters will justify
their publication ; but, also, that they may claim an
additional interest, as presenting a lively portrait
of one of the earliest Preachers who obtained the
name of *Evangelical**, and who bore a conspicuous
part in the revival of religion in this country during
the latter part of the eighteenth century.

The following pages exhibit the life and labours,
the principles, and temper of mind, of one who has
been universally known as a zealous advocate of
Evangelical sentiments.

I will not enter upon any formal description of
these sentiments ; because I believe that the difference between the Clergy usually denominated
Evangelical, and many of their brethren, from whom
they are thus distinguished, consists not so much

* I am aware that there is an apparent impropriety in using a
term as the exclusive designation of one class, which ought to
belong to all the professed Preachers of the Gospel of Christ. I
trust that the exclusive application of the term among the Ministers of the Established Church is daily becoming unnecessary and
improper. Yet, the most superficial knowledge of the state of
religion in this country will shew, that in the early part of the
eighteenth century the tone of Christian Doctrine and Practice was
lamentably depressed, both in the Church and among the Dissenters ;
and that about the year 1740 there was a revival of light and
energy among some of the Ministers of the Church, which was
gradually diffused throughout the land, and has materially raised
the tone of religious sentiments even among those who are
strangers to the power of godliness. It was natural, therefore,
that in the early days of this revival, when the light and energy of
a few stood out in bold relief from the surrounding mass, this exclusive designation should have been generally attributed, assumed,
or allowed.

in their systematic statement of doctrines, as in
the relative importance which they assign to the
particular parts of the Christian System, and in
the vital operation of Christian Doctrines upon the
heart and conduct. Under this view, I persuade
myself that the difference in question will be best
understood from the perusal of such a Life as
I here present to the reader.

The Character before us stands distinguished
from the devout but inefficient profession of orthodox principles which characterized the High Church
School in which Mr. Venn was brought up. All his
early prepossessions, and the notions which he imbibed from education and filial respect, were in
favour of that school—all his worldly hopes of preferment were connected with it: for some time he
conscientiously and zealously strove to fulfil his ministry upon that scheme; but he failed to acquire
solid peace and satisfaction in his own mind, or to
accomplish any great good in the souls of others;
till he had discovered, by diligent study of the
Bible, those views which were accompanied with
such blessed results to himself and to thousands of
his hearers throughout the rest of his life. The
accurate description given by his son, in the Memoir,
of the steps by which he was gradually led to those
views (pp. 17—21) appears to me, in this light,
most important, and worthy of attention.

On the other hand, the character here delineated is equally distinguished from that exhi-

bited by too many, in former and present times, who have assumed or acquired the name of Evangelical, without any other pretension to that name than the adoption of a doctrinal Shibboleth. The nature of Evangelical Religion is here shewn, in an entire devotion of heart to the Lord Jesus Christ—an evident victory over the world—abounding love and good-will towards men, and the other fruits of the Spirit manifest in the life and conduct; and is thus essentially distinguished from a worldly, self-indulgent, lukewarm, and unsubdued temper of mind, whether cloked under an Evangelical or any other profession of religion.

Another point, which I think the present volume will illustrate, is the Rise and Diffusion of Evangelical Religion in the Established Church during the period over which the succeeding Memoir extends. For we are here furnished with the case of Mr. Venn, and with many incidental notices of the names and labours of his early coadjutors among the Clergy. And I apprehend it may be shewn, that, for the most part, these men derived their views of the Truth directly from the Word of God; that their labours were chiefly devoted to the revival of true religion in the Church; and that those labours were, under God, the main cause of the revival which followed.

I am aware, that a different view of the case is often given; and that the labours of Mr. Whitfield and the Wesleys are regarded not only as the

means of the revival of religion among persons
connected with their societies, but also of that
which took place among the Clergy. A Preface,
and more especially a Preface to a somewhat bulky
volume, is not the place for entering at large into a
question which may be controverted ; but I may be
permitted, perhaps, to point out how far the present
volume seems to support the view of this question,
which I have ventured to suggest.

The case of Mr. Venn himself is clearly stated in
the Memoir, in these words :—" This change of his
sentiments was not to be ascribed to an intercourse
with others : it was the steady progress of his
mind, in consequence of a faithful and diligent application to the Holy Scriptures, unbiassed by an
attachment to human systems. It was not till
some years afterwards that he became acquainted
with any of those preachers who are usually known
by the name of Evangelical ; though his own views
now agreed with theirs, and were strictly, and in
a proper sense, Evangelical; that is, in conformity
with the motives and hopes held out to us in the
Gospel of Christ." (*Memoir by Rev. John Venn.*)

Here, let it be observed, is the case of a minister
of the Church, engaged in the discharge of his
office, whose mind is thus led to the full and cordial reception of these sentiments, by the blessing
of God on prayer and the study of the Bible. He
next discovered, that the Articles and Liturgy of
the Church fully agreed with the more enlightened

and elevated tone of his own newly-adopted views;
and became more than ever attached to her constitution and services, and laboured with more abundant zeal and success in the various offices which
were assigned to him as one of her ministers. In
the West Riding of Yorkshire he was the means of
exciting the zeal of many active friends of the
Church, and of bringing several ministers like-
minded with himself into that neighbourhood.
Upon his removal to the vicinity of Cambridge, his
influence was exerted with signal effect upon many
of the students, who came forward, from year to
year, to consecrate their services to the same cause
in which he was labouring.—From this brief sketch,
it is easy to perceive how greatly the character and
influence of Mr. Venn tended to the revival of vital
religion in the Established Church.

I shall still further trespass upon the patience
of my readers, by selecting and placing together the
names of a few of those fellow-labourers of Mr.
Venn to whom I have already alluded.

The earliest of this class was William Grimshaw,
B.A., educated at Christ's College, Cambridge. The
change of his sentiments was contemporaneous
with, if it did not precede, that of the Wesleys.
And we learn, that, after he had been for some time
engaged in preaching upon these views, "he was
an entire stranger to the people called Methodists;
whom afterwards he thought it his duty to countenance, and to labour with, in his neighbourhood.

He was an entire stranger, also, to all their writings, except a single sermon on Gal. iii. 24., and 'A Letter to the people of England,' published by the Rev. Mr. Seagrave; in which he was surprised to find the divinity, in all material points, of the very same kind with what he now saw with his own eyes in the Word of God, and from which all his peace had flowed." (See Sketch of the Life of Grimshaw, by the Rev. H. Venn, annexed to his Funeral Sermon.)

The next in chronological order is the well-known name of William Romaine, M.A. I am not aware that any account has been preserved of the precise steps by which his mind was led in this respect; but he was a disciple of the Hutchinsonian school; and retained to the last, in common with the members of that school, very strict views respecting Ecclesiastical conformity, and the evil of schism.

The Rev. William Talbot, grandson of a Bishop of Durham, and nephew to Lord Chancellor Talbot, was another preacher of whom Mr. Venn was accustomed to speak, as an early and eminent advocate of Evangelical views. The last scene of his labours was at St. Giles's, Reading; where he died in 1774, aged fifty-seven.

The short career of usefulness, and the admirable writings of the Rev. Samuel Walker of Truro, were of very extensive service to the cause of real Christianity in his own day; and are still held in honour, by multitudes, at the present time. A particular account is given of the progress of his mind, in the search of religious truth, by the Rev. James Stillingfleet, prebendary of Worcester, in a short sketch prefixed to Mr. Walker's " Sermons on the Church Catechism."*

The Rev. Thomas Adam, rector of Wintringham, Lincolnshire, was led to the adoption of the same views, at a comparatively late period of his life, by the independent exercise of prayer and the study of the Bible; of which an interesting account is given in a Memoir prefixed to his " Private Thoughts," by the Rev. James Stillingfleet of Hotham. Mr. Adam also printed, in his life-time, " Lectures on the Church Catechism," and other works, which materially aided the cause of vital religion in that day.

The Rev. Richard Conyers was the college-contemporary of Mr. Venn : and upon Mr. Venn's removal into Yorkshire, their friendship was renewed, upon the higher ground of a perfect similarity in their views of the Gospel, and the spirit in which they laboured for its advancement. Into these views Mr. Conyers had been led by the diligent study of the sacred text. He was first Vicar of Helmsley, and afterwards Rector of St. Paul's Deptford.

The six clergymen whom I have now mentioned,

---

* Since the First Edition of this Work, " The Life and Remains of the Rev. S. Walker " have been published by the Rev. E. Sidney.

together with my grandfather, were all led into similar views, within about ten years after the time from which Mr. Wesley dates the final adoption of his own religious sentiments. I have not included the name of James Hervey, of Weston Flavel, which appears in this volume with highest admiration; because his mind was directly influenced by intercourse with Mr. Charles Wesley. But I think I have stated enough to prove, that there was a body of Evangelical Labourers, who were independent of the Methodists, and nearly contemporaneous with them, and whose labours had an immediate and remarkable influence upon the Clergy of the Church of England.

After this period, the list might be considerably augmented, from the pages before us.—Amongst the names of early and frequent occurrence would be, Jones (of St. Saviour's, Southwark), Burnett (of Elland, one of the early friends of Walker of Truro), Powley, the two Stillingfleets, Fletcher, Berridge, Maddock, Newton, Joseph Milner, Riland, Robinson, Scott, Simeon, &c. &c.

Some idea of the rapid increase which took place in the numbers of the Evangelical Clergy may be formed from the fact, which has been recorded, that when Mr. Romaine first began his course, he could only reckon up as many as six or seven who were like-minded with himself: in a few years, the number was increased to tens; and before he died (1795), there were above five hundred whom he regarded as fellow-labourers with himself in word and doctrine. At what rate the increase has proceeded since that time, I will not take upon myself to say : but, assuredly, it has been such as to fill the heart of every intelligent observer with praise and gratitude to God.

The conclusion to which I think we are led, by a review of the whole case, is this ; —That when it pleased God, in a day of extreme darkness, to "cast His bright beams of light upon the Church"— according to the beautiful Prayer of our Liturgy —He kindled in the minds of many ministers of the Church, in various places and under various circumstances, a revival of genuine and primitive Christianity. By their efforts, and by the large measure of success vouchsafed to them, and by the continual accession of fresh Labourers—who, no less than the first promoters of the revival, had received their views of the Truth, under the teaching of the Holy Spirit, from the independent study of the Word of God, and prayer—the work was carried on to the glorious extent to which it has reached at the present day. The Methodists and the Evangelical Clergy were the chief instruments employed in this work ; and these two bodies of Labourers had a mutual and important influence upon each other*. But, as far as we can trace the

---

* Having reason to fear that this statement has been misapprehended, I take advantage of a new edition, to disclaim the idea, that

operation of human agency, it seems to me, that
the effects of the labours of the Wesleys, and their
immediate coadjutors, were chiefly manifest in the
extension of Methodism; as the effects of the labours of the Evangelical Clergy were in the improved tone of religion in the Established Church;—
that there were, thus, two kindred, but separate and
independent, streams of light, penetrating the gloom
which brooded over the Christian community. That
which flowed in the channel of Methodism burst
forth, indeed, in a more resplendent and sudden
blaze : the other proceeded by a more gradual and
quiet, but progressive, course.

H. VENN.

DRYPOOL, *May* 29, 1834.

that I attribute the revival of which I speak *exclusively* to the
labours of the two religious bodies mentioned above. I fully
allow that the work was promoted, both directly and indirectly, by
many whose names stand deservedly high in the veneration of
the Established Church, who were never classed with the Evangelical Clergy; as well as by many excellent men amongst the
Dissenters.

PART I.

—

MEMOIR.

—

DRAWN UP BY THE LATE REV. JOHN VENN,

AND COMPLETED BY THE EDITOR

B

MEMOIR,

&c. &c.

HENRY VENN was born at Barnes in Surrey, on the
2d of March 1724.

* [His ancestors were clergymen of the Church
of England, in an uninterrupted line, from the
period of the Reformation. The first, of whom
any particular information has been preserved, was
WILLIAM VENN, B.A., Vicar of Otterton, Devonshire, who died in the year 1621. He had two
sons, who afterwards became beneficed clergymen,
and were sufferers, during the time of the com-
monwealth, for their attachment to the King and
the established form of worship; namely, RICHARD
VENN, M.A. (the ancestor of HenryVenn,) who was
presented, in 1625, to the vicarage his father had
held; and Robert Venn, M.A., Vicar of Thelbridge,
Devonshire. Some account of the persecutions
these ministers endured is given in Walker's
" Sufferings of the Clergy." Mr. Walker states, respecting Richard Venn, that " he was dispossessed of
his living by the Parliamentary Commissioners.—
The accusations brought against him, before the
Committee, consisted chiefly of matters which had
passed some years before, relating to his loyalty, and
disaffection to the Parliament.—The witnesses who
appeared against him could not but give an attesta-

---

* The parts included between angular brackets, throughout
this Memoir, have been added by the Editor.—See the Preface.

tion to his worth and honesty, and more particularly to his diligence in the discharge of his ministerial function.—After wandering from place to place, to avoid persecution, he lived to re-possess his vicarage, after the Restoration.—He was a man of worth and learning, a good Christian and a good preacher, well beloved in his parish, and spoken of with honour amongst them to this very day."— Richard Venn had a numerous family of children; one of whom was DENNIS VENN, M.A., Vicar of Holbe ton, Devonshire, who died in 1695, leaving an infant son, RICHARD, who was the father of Henry Venn. This son was brought up under the vigilant superintendence of his mother. Under such tuition, amiable manners and sweetness of disposition might be expected, rather than firmness and resolution : these latter qualities were, however, cultivated by Mrs. Venn, with no small success, in the education of her son, and were striking features of his character in after-life. In illustration of this remark, it is recorded, that being asked when she intended to send her son to college, she replied, " When I have taught him to say ' No', boldly." He completed his education at Sidney College, Cambridge ; where he sustained the character of a diligent student, an able scholar, and a person of strict morals and piety. He became Rector of St. Antholin's, London, and was also possessed of some sinecure preferment. He was distinguished as an exemplary and learned minister, very zealous for the interests of the Church of England, which he conceived to be the grand support of Christianity in this nation. He was also remarkable for great liberality towards the poor, and especially towards distressed clergymen. He enjoyed the friendship and society of Bishops Gibson and Hare, Doctors Berriman, Stebbing, and other learned divines of that day. In the year 1734 he was brought into public notice, and incurred obloquy from certain quarters, in consequence of the determined opposition he made, in conjunction with Bishop Gibson, to the promotion of Dr. Rundle to the bishopric of Gloucester; Dr. Rundle having used expressions in his hearing, which he conceived to be of a deistical tendency.* Mr. Richard Venn married the daughter of Richard Ashton, esq., Paymaster of the Pensions to King Charles II., and Privy Purse to James II. This gentleman was apprehended in 1690, in an attempt to pass over to France, in a small boat, with Lord Preston and Mr. Elliott; and a packet of papers being found upon him, which contained intelligence for the deposed king, he was tried and executed on the charge of high-treason.

Mr. Venn died in 1739, aged 48, leaving three sons—Dr. Edward Venn, of St. John's College, Cambridge, who settled as a physician at Ipswich; Richard, and HENRY; and one daughter Mary, who married Mr. W. J. Gambier, of London. After his death, a volume of his works was published by his widow, containing several of his sermons, and a few papers which had appeared in a periodical work.]

Henry Venn discovered, from a child, such activity and energy of mind, such decision and zeal in whatever he undertook, that all who observed him

---

* See Letters of Dr. Rundle, Lord Bishop of Derry, with Introductory Memoirs, by James Dallaway, M.A.

expected he would one day become an extraordinary character. A few anecdotes of his boyish years will serve to illustrate this.

Whilst he was yet a child, Sir Robert Walpole attempted to introduce more extensively the system of the Excise. A violent opposition was excited, and the popular cry ran strongly against this measure. Our young politician caught the alarm, and could not sleep in his bed, lest the Excise Bill should pass; and, on the day on which it was to be submitted to Parliament, his zeal led him to leave his father's house early, and to wander through the streets, crying " No Excise !" till the evening; when he returned home, exhausted with fatigue, and with his voice totally lost by his patriotic exertions.

A gentleman, who was reported to be an Arian, called one day upon his father. The child (for such he then was) came into the room, and, with a grave countenance, earnestly surveyed him. The gentleman, observing the notice which the child took of him, began to shew him some civil attentions, but found all his friendly overtures sternly rejected. At length, upon his more earnestly soliciting him to come to him, the boy indignantly replied, " I will not come near you; for you are an Arian."

As he adopted, with all his heart, the opinions which he imbibed, he early entertained a most vehement dislike of all Dissenters. It happened that a dissenting minister's son, two or three years older than himself, lived in the same street, in London, with his father; and young Henry, in his zeal for the Church, made no scruple to attack and fight this seceder from it, whenever he met him. It was a curious circumstance, that, many years afterwards, he became acquainted with this very individual, who was then a dissenting minister; and who confessed to him how much he had been the terror of his life; and acknowledged, that he never durst leave his father's door till he had carefully looked on every side, to see that this young champion of the Church was not in the street.

It could scarcely be expected that such vehemence of mind would be restrained within due bounds: it accordingly increased into an inordinate ambition, attended, as is usually the case, with the fever of impatient jealousy. A singular instance of this was exhibited upon his hearing a gentleman very highly commend some of the Latin Exercises of his elder brother. His passions were so agitated by this commendation, that, though he suppressed them so far as to conceal his jealousy, his exertion to do so actually threw him into a convulsion-fit, to the great alarm of the family.

I mention these incidents merely to shew the strong feelings, and decision of character, which he inherited from nature. He possessed powers which could not but be active; but how these powers should be determined, whether to good or evil, whether to the benefit or the injury of society, remained yet a question. Great energy of character is a dangerous quality: it is a power which must do much good or much evil. Hence, Dr. Gloucester Ridley, after attentively observing his character, when young, said, " This boy will go up Holborn, and either stop at Ely Place (the then palace of the

Bishop of Ely), or go on to Tyburn." Happily, his energy was exerted in a right direction!

Let it not, however, be supposed that energy was the only prominent feature of his boyhood. His generous kindness and affection were equally conspicuous ; and he had a natural frankness and vivacity of manner, which won upon all who knew him; so that he was soon the favourite, not only of his parents, but of his brothers, of the servants, and of the whole neighbourhood.

In his early years he experienced several re- markable escapes from danger ; one of which, on account of its singularity, deserves to be recorded.

There was a small court between St. Antholin's church and that part of the rectory-house in which his father's study was situated. This had been roofed and tiled over ; and here he used to play, when he was able to say his lessons, till his father was at leisure to hear him. One day, being perfect in his lesson, he, as usual, asked leave to play, but was refused. As this leave had rarely before been denied, and his father did not appear to be at leisure to hear him, he concluded that his request had been misunderstood, and again asked permis- sion to play, but was immediately and peremptorily refused. Soon after, his mother came into the room; and seeing him looking out of the window, while his father appeared deeply engaged in writing, she asked, of her own accord, whether he might not be allowed to play: but her request was also refused. She thought this extraordinary ; but her surprise was changed into astonishment and gratitude, when, a few minutes after, the whole roof fell in ; and

would have crushed her child to death, had he
been playing there, as was requested. His father
acknowledged that he had no particular reason, at
the moment, for denying the wonted permission;
but, having once refused, thought it proper to persist in the refusal.

It may be here said : ' You produce a miracle, in
order to exalt your hero into a saint.'—I by no
means do this. I do not argue in behalf of any
man's excellence, from such providential inter-
ferences in his favour. I believe that remarkable
instances of preservation from peril, such as can
only be ascribed to the particular interposition of
Divine agency, are experienced by all persons, and
by the bad as well as the good. The inference
which I draw from these facts is this—That they are
intended to demonstrate, not the particular favour
which God bears to an individual, but His general
mercy and care over all his creatures : they are
designed as sensible and striking manifestations,
rendered necessary by the grossness and dulness of
our faculties, of the presence and continual agency
of our Creator : they serve to set the presence of
God more immediately before us. Nor are such
interpositions, I believe, unfrequent. Every person
can probably recollect several, in his own case ; and
he has had opportunities of observing the same
in the case of others. The world, which studiously
excludes from view the supreme cause, attributes
them to accident; but the Scripture, which removes the veil, and explains the agency of the
Almighty, after describing several such instances of
preservation in the 107th Psalm, adds this con-

clusion : " Whoso is wise, and will observe these
things, even they shall understand the loving-kindness of the Lord."

In the year 1737, being twelve years old, he was
sent to school at Mortlake, a neighbouring village
to Barnes, at which he remained two years.   From
this school he was removed to the care of Mr.
Crofts, of Fulham; where he had not been long,
before his father died (Feb. 16, 1739), and he was
deprived of the benefits which he would have derived from the care and superintendence of a pious,
affectionate and learned parent.

He continued at Mr. Crofts' several months after
his father's death; and his quitting this situation
was at his own request—a request which indicated
an energy of mind, and a right turn of thinking,
uncommon in a boy of fourteen.   He told his mother, that, though he was treated with the highest
degree of tenderness at Mr. Crofts', yet the very
indulgence which was shewn to him and the rest of
the boys was an impediment to their improvement.
He requested her, therefore, to send him to a school
where the discipline was more strict, and where the
chief stress was laid upon improvement in learning :
for he considered even severity to be preferable, on
this account, to too much indulgence.

Such a school was found, at the Rev. Mr. Catcott's,
of Bristol, author of a Treatise on the Deluge, and
other Tracts.   He was a man of remarkable strictness, and even sternness of discipline, imposing
large tasks upon his pupils, and very sparing in
his commendations : I however always heard my
father speak of him with the highest respect.   He

gained his master's good opinion, by great diligence, and by a steady desire of inprovement; so
that he never once suffered correction from him, or
incurred his displeasure.

I know not what occasioned his removal from
Mr. Catcott's, where he continued about a year;
but, in 1741, he was placed at the Rev. Dr. Pitman's
Academy, Market-street, Hertfordshire, where he
finished his school education.

In June 1742, being seventeen years of age, he
was admitted of St. John's College, Cambridge,
where his elder brother had already resided some
years. But having obtained a Rustat Scholarship
in Jesus College, he removed in September to that
society, of which he continued a member for seven
years.

Going to college with the advantage of an acquaintance already established with several respectable members of the University, who had been
intimate friends of his father, and having also a
brother who had been resident there upwards of
five years, he was soon surrounded by a numerous
circle of friends. These he increased by qualities
which made his company much sought after;
namely, a never-failing fund of high spirits, a natural hilarity and gaiety of manner, an engaging
sweetness of temper, and a memory stored with
anecdotes, which he related in a manner peculiarly
interesting. Besides this, he captivated all whose
good opinion he wished to gain, by a delicate attention, arising from a happy mixture of benevolence,
modesty, and respect: there were therefore, perhaps, very few men in the University who were so

generally esteemed and beloved. He was, however, very select in the choice of his society, never keeping company either with profligate men or with persons of mean talents. The rule he laid down was, to be acquainted only with those from whom he could gain improvement.

In the year 1745 he took the degree of B.A. In 1747 he was appointed, by Dr. Battie (who had been a ward of his father's), to one of the University Scholarships, which he had just founded, and the nomination to which he reserved to himself during his own life; and in June, the same year, he was ordained Deacon, by Bishop Gibson, in the chapel of Fulham Palace, without a title, from the respect which the Bishop bore to his father's memory. In 1749 he became M.A.; previous to which he had been elected Fellow of Queen's College, chiefly through the recommendation of Mr. Owen Manning, the Tutor of Queen's, who had formed an intimate friendship with him. He would have been chosen Fellow of his own College, had there been a vacancy during the time he was capable of holding that station. He continued Fellow of Queen's till his marriage, in 1757.

It was about the time of his entering into Holy Orders that his first religious impressions commenced: and as the life of a retired and pious clergyman, distinguished neither by rank nor preferment, nor by interesting incidents, can be useful only by tracing accurately his religious progress, it is to this part of his history that I shall now chiefly direct my attention.

Hitherto, religion had made no particular impression on his mind. He was moral and decent in his conduct, regular in his attendance on public worship, and had accustomed himself chiefly to read books of Divinity, after he had taken his degree of B.A.; but he was a stranger to that influence of religion which gives it a predominancy in the mind over every thing besides, and to those views of the benefits and excellence of the Christian dispensation which render the Saviour the object of the highest affection and regard. He possessed, however, high ideas of clerical decorum, and scrupulous conscientiousness in doing faithfully whatever he was convinced to be right: and so highly did he rate a strict regard to conscience, in acting up to the light received, that he often used to say, in his own forcible way of expressing himself, that he owed the salvation of his soul to the resolute self-denial which he exercised, in following the dictates of conscience in a point which of itself seemed one only of small importance.

The case was this :—He was extremely fond of cricket, and reckoned one of the best players in the University. In the week before he was ordained, he played in a match between Surrey and All England: the match had excited considerable interest, and was attended by a very numerous body of spectators. When the game terminated, in favour of the side on which he played, he threw down his bat, saying, "Whoever wants a bat, which has done me good service, may take that; as I have no further occasion for it." His friends inquiring the reason, he replied, " Because I am to be ordained on Sunday ; and I will never have it said of me, ' Well

struck, Parson!'"—and to this resolution, notwithstanding the remonstrances of his friends, and even
of the Tutor and Fellows of his college, he strictly
adhered: nay, though his health suffered by a
sudden transition from a course of most violent
exercise to a life of comparative inactivity, he could
never be persuaded to play any more. Thus, being
faithful in a little, more grace was imparted to him.

The first considerable religious impression made
upon his mind arose from an expression in the
Form of Prayer, which he had been daily accustomed
to use, like the world in general, without paying
much attention to it—" That I may live to the
glory of Thy name!" The thought powerfully
struck his mind :—" What is it, to live to the glory
of God? Do I live as I pray? What course of life
ought I to pursue, to glorify God?" After much
reflection on this subject, he came to this conclusion—That to live to the glory of God required that
he should live a life of piety and religion, in a degree in which he was conscious he had not yet
lived ;—that he ought to be more strict in prayer,
more diligent in reading the Scriptures and pious
books, and more generally holy in his conduct :—
and, seeing the reasonableness of such a course of
life, his uprightness again discovered itself in immediately and steadily pursuing it. He set apart stated
seasons for meditation and prayer, turning his reading chiefly into a religious channel, and kept a strict
account of the manner in which he spent his time
and regulated his conduct. I have heard him say,
that it was his custom at this period to walk almost
every evening in the cloisters of Trinity College,

during the time that the great bell of St. Mary's was
tolling at nine o'clock; and, amidst the solemn
tones and pauses of the bell, and the stillness and
darkness of the night, he would indulge in impressive and awful reflections, on Death and Judgment, Heaven and Hell.

[In a letter, written late in life to one of his
children, he alluded, in the following beautiful manner, to this early stage of his religious progress :—

" (*Yelling, Sept.* 2, 1785.)—How do I feel more than
requited for all the pains I have taken, and the prayers
I have offered, when I read your earnest desires that you
may glorify God! Supernatural is that desire : it is the
bud and the blossom, which bring forth all the fruit the
Church of God bears. Well I remember, when, in the
midst of great darkness respecting the Person, the work,
and office of my adored Redeemer—in the midst of utter
ignorance of the Law and my own total corruption—I felt
this desire, strong and urgent, from day to day : and it
hath never departed from me, and never will! This
supreme desire to glorify God is like a friendly clue in a
labyrinth, which guides us out of all perplexities, and excites an earnest cry, which, in time, brings us to the
enjoyment of our God and Saviour, gives us increasing
views of His excellency and glory, and ripens us for the
vast assembly of perfect spirits, who are swallowed up in
love and adoration of God, and are perfectly one with
each other."]

In this frame of mind, Law's " Serious Call to a
Devout and Holy Life," a book which has been the
means of exciting many to a life of holiness, was
particularly useful to him : he read it repeatedly,
with peculiar interest and advantage; and immediately began, with great sincerity, to frame his life

according to the Christian model there delineated. He kept a diary of the state of his mind ; a practice from which he derived great benefit, though not exactly in the way he expected : for it chiefly made him better acquainted with his own deficiency. He also allotted the hours of the day, as far as was consistent with the necessary duties and employments of his station, to particular acts of meditation and devotion. He kept frequent fasts ; and was accustomed often to take solitary walks, in which his soul was engaged in prayer and communion with God. I have heard him mention, that, in one of these retired walks, in the meadows behind Jesus College, he had such a view of the goodness, mercy, and glory of God, as elevated his soul above the world, and made him aspire towards God, as his supreme good, with unutterable ardour and enjoyment.

So great a change in his taste could not but produce a great alteration in his general mode of life. The sprightly Harry Venn, who was always in company, and himself the gayest of the circle, was now seldom to be met with in mixed parties. He was indeed so entirely engrossed by the things which are spiritual and eternal, that, when he found none of his companions inclined to converse with him on these subjects, he gradually withdrew from their company, and confined himself only to the ordinary intercourses of society. One person only, of all his former numerous friends, appeared willing to listen to his conversation on religious subjects.

For about six months after he was elected Fellow of Queen's, he served the curacy of Barton, near

Cambridge; where he distributed Religious Tracts
and conversed with the poor in a manner that several of them affectionately remembered after an
interval of above thirty years. He afterwards
assisted different friends, by officiating for them, at
Wadenhoe in Northamptonshire, Sible Hedingham
in Essex, and other places; where, besides the regular duty on the Sunday, he used to instruct the
people at his own house, in the week. In July
1750, he ceased to reside in college, and began to
devote himself entirely to ministerial services;
accepting the curacy of a Mr. Langley, who held the
livings of St. Matthew, Friday-street, in London,
and West Horsley, near Guildford, in Surrey. My
father's duty was, to serve the church in London,
during part of the summer, and to reside the remainder of the year at Horsley; and in this employment he continued four years.

At Horsley he instructed many of the poor, during
the week, at his own house. His family prayer
was often attended by thirty or forty of his poorer
neighbours. The number of communicants was
increased, while he was curate, from twelve to
sixty. His activity and zeal, however, offended
some of the neighbouring clergy, who took no pains
in their parishes, and occasioned them to stigmatize
him as an enthusiast and a methodist; though, in
truth, he had no knowledge whatever, at that time,
of the persons usually distinguished by the latter
name. Once, at a meeting of some clergymen, his
character being thus rudely treated, he met with
a singular defender in an old fox-hunting clergyman :—" Hush!" said he; " I feel a great respect

for such men as Mr. Venn, and wish there were
more of the kind! They are the salt of our order,
and keep it from putrefaction. If the whole body
of the clergy were like ourselves, the world would
see that we were of no use, and take away our
tithes; but a few of these pious ones redeem our
credit, and save for us our livings."

While he continued curate of Horsley, he had an
opportunity of shewing a very remarkable instance
of disinterestedness. Sir John Evelyn was patron
of the living of Wotton, in that neighbourhood; a
living then worth between 200*l*. and 300*l*. a year.
He was a gentleman very anxious to keep up the
due knowledge and worship of God in his parish,
and used to maintain the most friendly intercourse
with the clergyman of that and the neighbouring
parish (to which he also presented); being accustomed to drink tea with them, alternately, on a
stated day in the week. It was an object, therefore,
of importance to him to have at Wotton a clergyman
of exemplary character, and a man of knowledge and
learning. As soon as the living was vacant, the
Squire of Horsley, unknown to my father, applied
earnestly in his favour, for the living, to Sir John;
assuring him, that he was the very kind of clergyman who would suit his views: and Sir John himself seemed already disposed to accede to his wishes.
The only reason which made him hesitate was the di-
lapidated state of the parsonage, which, he thought,
would require a person of some private fortune to
put and keep in proper repair. My father having
learnt these circumstances, while the patron's mind
was still wavering, turned the scale against himself.

Having long been acquainted with Mr. Bryan Broughton, Secretary to the Society for Promoting Christian Knowledge, and having a high respect for his virtues, he considered him as exactly the kind of man who would suit Sir John; and, judging that he stood more in need of the preferment than himself, he wrote an anonymous letter to Sir John, giving a full and faithful account of his friend's character, and recommending him to the living : and Sir John, after making inquiry into Mr. Broughton's character, presented him; nor had he ever reason to repent of following the advice of his anonymous correspondent.

Whilst he lived in this retirement, his books and his devotions afforded him a fund of never-ceasing pleasure. He was accustomed to ride upon the fine Downs in that neighbourhood, and to chant to himself the *Te Deum ;* and in this devotional exercise he used to be carried far above terrestrial objects. His plan of life was very methodical, realizing, as far as he was able, that laid down by Mr. Law, in his " Christian Perfection." Mr. Law was, indeed, now his favourite author ; and, from attachment to him, he was in great danger of imbibing the tenets of the mystical writers, whose sentiments Mr. Law had adopted in the latter periods of his life. Many writings of this class discover, indeed, such traces of genuine and deep piety, that it is not at all wonderful that a person of exalted devotional feelings should admire them.

From a too fond attachment, however, to Mr. Law's tenets, he was recalled by the writings of Mr. Law himself. When Mr. Law's " Spirit of

Love," or "Spirit of Prayer," (I am not sure which) was about to be published, no miser, waiting for the account of a rich inheritance devolving on him, was ever more eager than he was to receive a book from which he expected to derive so much knowledge and improvement. The bookseller had been importuned to send him the first copy published. At length, the long-desired work was received, one evening; and he set himself to peruse it with the utmost avidity. He read till he came to a passage wherein Mr. Law seemed to represent the blood of Christ as of no more avail, in procuring our salvation, than the excellence of his moral character. "What!" he exclaimed, "does Mr. Law thus degrade the death of Christ, which the Apostles represent as a sacrifice for sins, and to which *they* ascribe the highest efficacy in procuring our salvation! Then, farewell such a guide! Henceforth I will call no man master!" From that moment he laid aside his overweening esteem for human productions, and applied himself chiefly to the study of the sacred writers.

His preaching was, however, still of the strictest kind. He required (according to the ideas which he had imbibed from the mystical writers) a measure almost of perfection in man; and exalted the standard of holiness to a degree to which it was scarcely possible that the frail children of men could ever reach.

It is true, he was himself striving, with the utmost assiduity, to reach that point. He kept a diary, in which he endeavoured to record the very slightest alienation of thought from the love or fear of God—

every rising of irregular desires and passions—
every thought which seemed to be contrary to the
spirit of our Holy Religion. This he deeply lamented before God, and, with fervent prayer, requested that every thought of his heart might be
brought into captivity to the Law of Christ.

Still, however, as must be the case where a man
cannot attain the object he has proposed to himself,
he was not happy : he did not overcome sin in the
degree in which he had hoped; and, as he was
conscious of no deficiency of endeavour on his
part, he began to feel religion to be a hard service,
rather than one which was perfect freedom : he
deeply felt for the rest of the world, who neither
did, nor, generally speaking, could, make such exertions as himself: and the question often forcibly
occurred to him in the pulpit, "Why do you im-
pose upon others a standard, to which you are
conscious you have not yourself attained?"

Such reflections induced him to study the Scriptures more attentively : and then he began to
perceive that his attachment to mystical writers
had hitherto led him to overlook the particular provision which is made for *fallen* and *sinful* man in the
Gospel of our blessed Lord and Saviour Jesus Christ.
He now saw that it was not upon the perfection
of our obedience, but upon the all-sufficient merits
and the infinite mercies of a Redeemer, that we are
to rely for our justification. He saw that sinners
are brought, through the Gospel, into a new state—
a state of reconciliation to our Heavenly Father—
a state of adoption into his family—a state of grace
and mercy. Hence the religion of Christ now

became to him a religion of hope, and peace, and joy : he saw that our sins are taken away by the blood of Christ, and that, being justified by faith in Him, we have peace towards God, through our Lord Jesus Christ, and rejoice in the hope of the glory of God, and joy also in God, by whom we have received the atonement. He beheld with wonder the infinite tenderness, compassion, and love of the Saviour; upon whose care and providence he now relied, to sanctify him by His Spirit, and to make him meet for the kingdom of glory above. The desire of his heart had been already towards holiness ; but it was with a view to render himself acceptable to a holy God by his own excellence. He now felt the same desire : but it sprang from a different motive : it was an earnest wish to shew forth the praises of Him who had called him out of darkness into his marvellous light. He did not conceive himself, any more than formerly, at liberty to sin against God ; but that which before had been a servile fear was changed into a spirit of filial attachment to his Heavenly Father. Love to God, and to the greatest of all benefactors, his blessed Saviour and Redeemer, now became the ruling principle of all his devotion and all his conduct ; and he entered fully into the meaning of the Apostle, when he exclaimed, " God forbid that I should glory, save in the cross of our Lord Jesus Christ ! " " I count all things but loss for the excellency of the knowledge of Christ Jesus my Lord ;—that I may win Christ, and be found in Him; not having my own righteousness, which is of the law,—but the righteousness which is of God, by faith."

This essential change in his views produced an important change in his feelings and in his preaching. He now enjoyed a peace and cheerfulness of mind, which he had not done before; which he could not do whilst he looked chiefly to himself and his own qualifications for heaven. His preaching, also, set forth a new object, and took a new direction. He now more fully explained to his hearers " the unsearchable riches of Christ"; he set before them the love of God, in making " Him, who knew no sin, to be sin for us, that we might be made the righteousness of God in Him." He entreated them, in the name of Christ, to be reconciled to God; assuring the penitent of a gracious reception, and urging him to flee to the hope set before him—to that Great Deliverer, who would supply all things needful for him ; who would impart to him the sanctifying influences of the Spirit; who would bless him with His grace here, and conduct him to glory hereafter. The effect of his preaching became now much more manifest. The view of so great a salvation, offered so freely to mankind, filled the hearts of many with fervent love to their Saviour, and with earnest desire to be numbered among His Disciples. From that time his preaching became highly useful to many, who gladly devoted themselves to the service of a Saviour, by whom they expected the burden of their sins to be removed, and from whom they hoped to derive grace to help in time of need, comfort in the hour of affliction, peace in the midst of an evil and turbulent world, support in the season of death, and a holy preparation for the life to come.

It is observable, that this change of his sentiments was not to be ascribed to an intercourse with
others : it was the steady progress of his mind, in
consequence of a faithful and diligent application to
the Holy Scriptures, unbiassed by an attachment
to human systems. It was not till some years
afterwards that he became acquainted with any of
those preachers who are usually known by the
name of Evangelical; though his own views now
agreed with theirs, and were strictly, and in a proper
sense, Evangelical ; that is, in conformity with the
motives and hopes held out to us in the Gospel of
Christ.

In 1754, he accepted the curacy of Clapham, in
Surrey, where he resided five years ; officiating at
the same time, during the week, in three different
churches in London, where he held Lectureships.
[His regular duties consisted of a full service at
Clapham on the Sunday morning ; a sermon in the
afternoon at St. Alban's, Wood-street ; and in the
evening at St. Swithin's, London-stone. On Tuesday
morning, a sermon at St. Swithin's ; on Wednesday morning, at seven o'clock, at St. Antholin's ;
and on Thursday evening at Clapham.] At Clapham
he became intimately acquainted with the late John
Thornton, esq., of that place, who was then a young
man of deep piety, and whose views of Divine Truth
soon became congenial with his own. Between
them was formed a friendship of the strictest kind,
which continued till Mr. Thornton's death. Here
also he became intimate with Sir John Barnard*,

* Sir J. Barnard represented the city of London, in seven successive Parliaments ; and was also Lord Mayor in the year 1737.

who was spending the latter days of his life in that village; and of whom he published some interesting Memoirs. Here he first began to experience, from those who disliked the restraints of religion, and from those who wished to be satisfied with a merely formal profession, that opposition which every preacher of vital Christianity must expect. On the other hand, however, he met with many persons to whom his preaching was highly acceptable and useful.

In 1756, he laboured under a severe illness, which incapacitated him for duty, for more than eight months. This, however, was a most useful season to him. He had time to reflect upon his principles and his conduct; and he used to observe, that after that period he was no longer able to preach the sermons which he had previously composed. His views of eternal things had now become clearer—his meditations on the attributes of God more profound—his views of the greatness of the salvation of Christ more distinct; and the whole of his religion had received that tincture of more elevated devotion which rendered his conversation and his preaching doubly instructive.

In May 1757, he married Miss Bishop, daughter of the Rev. Thomas Bishop, D.D., minister of the Tower Church in Ipswich, a gentleman of high eminence as a scholar and a divine, who preached the sermons in St. Paul's, for Lady Moyer's Lecture, in 1724-25, which were afterwards published, together with some other valuable Theological Treatises. In this lady Mr. Venn found a mind congenial with his own,—the most sincere and exalted piety, directed by a sound judgment, and enriched by a sweetness of disposition and animation, which rendered her particularly interesting, as a companion and a friend.

In 1759, he accepted the vicarage of Huddersfield, in Yorkshire, the grand scene of his labours in the Church. He was induced to accept this living, not from any desire of increasing his income; for, in fact, his income was diminished by it materially; the living of Huddersfield not amounting to 100*l.* per annum, and the collection of the income (consisting chiefly of the smallest sums) being made in a way the most disagreeable to his feelings. But he conceived that he should be far more extensively useful in a parish, the population of which consisted of many thousand souls, than in that of Clapham, where he had not experienced the success of his labours in the degree that he had hoped.

As soon as he began to preach at Huddersfield, the church became crowded, to such an extent, that many were not able to procure admission. Numbers became deeply impressed with concern about their immortal souls; persons flocked from the distant hamlets, inquiring what they must do to be saved. He found them, in general, utterly ignorant of their state by nature, and of the redemption that is in Christ Jesus. His bowels yearned over his flock; and he was never satisfied with his labours among them, though they were continued to a degree ruinous to his health. On the Sunday, he would often address the congregation from the desk, briefly explaining and enforcing the Psalms and the Lessons. He would frequently begin the Service with a solemn and most impressive address, exhorting them to consider themselves as in the presence of the Great God of Heaven, whose eye was in a particular manner upon them, whilst they drew nigh to Him, in His own house. His whole soul was engaged in preaching: and, as at this time he only used short notes in the pulpit, ample room was left to indulge the feelings of compassion, of tenderness, and of love, with which his heart overflowed towards his people. In the week, he statedly visited the different hamlets in his extensive parish; and, collecting some of the inhabitants at a private house, he addressed them with a kindness and earnestness which moved every heart. Opposition, however, followed him here: for, what integrity of mind, what excellence of conduct, what purity of zeal, can shield a man from it, when our Blessed Lord, immaculate as He was, and His Apostles endued with His Spirit, were not exempted from it? He was assailed with the old and slanderous insinuation, that he preached the doctrine of Faith alone, and neglected to enforce works; though his whole life was a practical confutation of such a falsehood; and the lives of those who received the doctrines he preached became so strict and exemplary, that they were immediately accused of carrying holiness to an unnecessary length.

An instance occurs to me here of the effect and success of his preaching, which deserves to be recorded. A club, chiefly composed of Socinians, in a neighbouring market-town, having heard much censure and ridicule bestowed upon his preaching, sent two of their body, whom they considered the ablest to detect absurdity, and the most witty to expose it, to hear this strange preacher, and to furnish matter of merriment for the next meeting. They accordingly went; but could not but be struck, when they entered the church, to see the multitude that was assembled together, to observe the devotion of their behaviour, and to witness their anxiety to attend the worship of God. When Mr. Venn ascended the reading-desk, he addressed his flock, as usual, with a solemnity and dignity which shewed him to be deeply interested in the work in which he was engaged : the earnestness of his preaching, and the solemn appeals he made to conscience, deeply impressed them; so that one of them observed, as they left the church, " Surely God is in this place! there is no matter for laughter here!" This gentleman immediately called upon Mr. Venn, told him who he was, and the purpose for which he had come, and earnestly begged his forgiveness and his prayers. He requested Mr. Venn to visit him without delay, and left the Socinian congregation; and from that time, to the hour of his death, became one of Mr. Venn's most faithful and affectionate friends*.

The deep impression made by his preaching, upon all ranks of people, was indeed very striking.

* This gentleman was James Kershaw, esq., of Halifax. A letter written to him by Mr. Venn, soon after the circumstances here recorded, and alluding to them, is given in the series of Correspondence, under the date April 2, 1767.—EDITOR.

A gentleman, highly respectable for his character, talents, and piety — the late William Hey, esq., of Leeds, who frequently went to Huddersfield, to hear him preach—assured me, that once returning home with an intimate friend, they neither of them opened their lips to each other till they came within a mile of Leeds, a distance of about fifteen miles ; so deeply were they impressed by the very important truths which they had heard from the pulpit, and the very impressive manner in which they had been delivered.

But, whilst he was thus listened to by the most crowded auditories, and blessed with an unusual degree of success in his ministry, he was himself suffering under the sharpest trials. He had expected, when he came into Yorkshire, that the cheapness of the country would counterbalance the diminution of his income : he found, however, the case to be otherwise : the hospitality which it was necessary for him to maintain, and the number of visitors who flocked to him, even from distant parts of the country, rendered his expenses very great. He had a wife and an increasing family ; and was separated from his former connexions and friends, by whose interest he might have obtained an accession to his income. But what could he do ? To return back to London, was to abandon a flock, over which God seemed, in His providence, to have placed him ; where his labours were blessed with unusual success ; and where the name of his Lord and Master now began to be generally honoured, and His word obeyed. On the other hand, all the difficulties of embarrassed circumstances, from which he saw no way of deliverance, presented themselves to him. In this state, the faith of his excellent wife was of great use to him. She had, at first, been very averse to his accepting his present situation; but when she now saw the vast extent of the field in which he was to labour, and the uncommon success with which he was blessed, she told him that he was in the path of duty, which he must not, on any account, desert. She exhorted him to throw himself upon the care and providence of that God who will never forsake His servants who faithfully call upon him.—The event answered her expectations: he was at length enabled to live in continual reliance upon the care of Providence, and, from various sources, unexpected at the time, his wants were remarkably supplied.

I will here mention a striking instance of the wonderful manner in which God will sometimes supply the wants of his servants, when they duly trust in Him; though the occurrence did not take place till several years after the date of which I am now speaking. At a period of very pressing difficulty, when a tradesman was importunate for the payment of his bill, he had no resource left, but, with earnest supplication, to make his wants known unto God; and, whilst he was upon his knees, a letter was brought, inclosing a bank-note of 50*l*., with an anonymous address, saying, " Having received great benefit from your ' Complete Duty of Man,' I beg you to accept this small acknowledgment."—He never could discover to whom he was indebted for this seasonable benefaction.

During the severe trials with which he was exercised, a change took place in his sentiments respecting some particular points in Divinity. He had hitherto been a zealous Arminian, hostile to the principles of Calvinism, which he thought equally repugnant to reason and to Scripture; but the experience he now had of the corruption of his nature, of the frailty and weakness of man, of the insufficiency even of his best endeavours, led him gradually to ascribe more to the grace of God, and less to the power and free-will of man.

No one had taken more pains than he to subdue entirely every principle of corruption in his mind; but he now found such a want of faith and confidence in God—such a distrust of His providence—such a disposition to murmur against Him—such an inadequate view of spiritual blessings and religious privileges—such ingratitude to that Saviour who was making him an instrument of the greatest good to his fellow-creatures—that he became more deeply humbled than he had ever been before. He now saw, in a stronger light than ever, the truth of those words, "The heart is deceitful above all things, and desperately wicked"; and felt more sensibly, that, if he was saved at all, it must be by the mere grace of God, since he had done nothing, and could do nothing, to merit so great a salvation. He now, therefore, began to place less confidence in man and in all human endeavours, and to exalt more that grace of Christ which worketh in us effectually, and which quickeneth us according to His sovereign will.

Thus he was prepared to receive the fundamental doctrines of that system which is called Calvinistic, from a practical sense of his own unworthiness, and from the necessity which he found of relying wholly upon the infinite mercy and the free grace of God in Christ Jesus.

This change of sentiment gave a tincture to his preaching; leading him to exalt, in higher strains, the grace and love of God in Christ Jesus, and to speak less of the power and excellence of man. But his Calvinism stopped here. It was not the result of a theory embraced by reading books of that class; he did not attempt to reconcile the difficulties which are found in that system; he did not enforce, as necessary, upon the conscience of others, those particular views which he had himself imbibed; he did not break the bond of brotherly love and union with those of his friends who were still zealous Arminians; and, above all, it did not lead him to relax in his views of the necessity or the nature of holiness. On the contrary, he urged the practice of it most effectually, from what he conceived to be stronger and purer motives.

With respect to others, he candidly left every person to determine for himself what system he should adopt; well convinced, that if a man entertained a supreme love to God, and a steadfast faith in Jesus Christ, he would be a very good Christian, whether he leaned to the views of Calvin or Arminius. He dreaded young men hastily adopting Calvinistic views : and, when once asked, respecting a young minister, about whom he had been much interested, whether he was a Calvinist or an Arminian, he replied, " I really do not know: he is a sincere disciple of the Lord Jesus Christ; and that is of infinitely more importance than his being a disciple of Calvin or Arminius."

[The following extracts from letters written to his friends, at different periods of his life, will serve to confirm the remarks already made :—

Let those who fear the tendency of the doctrines of grace sift and canvass the conduct of those who *live* by them, and then say what ground there is to fear licentiousness. I daily see that the Inspired Writers are never afraid of affirming that the salvation of real believers is secured: all their aim and labour is, to shew that none are believers, none are Christ's, but they that have crucified the flesh with the affections and lusts thereof. For my own part, I profess I could not look upon salvation as nigh to me, but suspended on so many precarious things, as greatly damped my hope, and prevented my joy in the Lord, till I saw that by two immutable things—the Word and the Oath of God—He had provided strong consolation for them that have fled for refuge to the hope set before them. Nevertheless, I could wish almost that the change in my sentiments were never named; for I hate opinions, and would not give a pin's point to have any one believe as I do, till the Scriptures, by the Spirit's teaching, open his understanding."—(*7th April*, 1763.)

"As to Calvinism, you know I am moderate. Those who exalt the Lord Jesus Christ as all their salvation, and abase man, I rejoice in ; and would not have them advance farther, till they see more of the plan of sovereign grace, so connected with what is indisputable, that they cannot refuse their assent. Difficulties, distressing difficulties, are on every side, whether we receive that scheme or no: we must be as little children—we must be daily exercising ourselves in humble love and prayer—we must be looking up to our Saviour for the Holy Ghost. And, after this has been our employment for many years, we shall find how much truth there is in that divine assertion, ' If any man

D

think that he knoweth any thing yet as he ought to know,
that man knoweth nothing.' I used to please myself with
the imagination, fifteen years since, that by prayer for the
Holy Ghost, and reading diligently the Lively Oracles, I
should be able to understand all Scripture, and give it all
one clear and consistent meaning. That it is perfectly consistent, I am very sure ; but it is not so to any mortal's
apprehension here. We are so proud, that we must always
have something to humble us; and this is one means to
that end."—(15th Feb. 1772.)

" Though the doctrines of grace are clear to me, I am
still no friend to high Calvinism. A false, libertine Calvinism stops up every avenue : sin, the Law, holiness,
experience, are all nothing. Predestination cancels the necessity of any change, and dispenses at once with all duty."

" What difficulties surround us ! what rocks on each
hand ! Were not our Pilot infallible, it were impossible to
steer through the narrow pass which lies between Antinomian abuse of the doctrines of grace, and self-righteous
renunciation of the blood of the Cross."

" O Prince of Peace, heal our divisions ! diffuse thy
patient, loving Spirit ! give discernment to distinguish
aright between what is essential and what is not, and to
bear with each other's differences, till the perfect day discovers all things in their true proportions ! "]

In the year 1763, my father published " The
Complete Duty of Man." This work had been un-
dertaken before he left London, and was nearly
finished soon after his arrival at Huddersfield ; but
the increasing engagements of that situation delayed its publication till this period. Of this work,
above twenty editions have been sold : it has proved
highful useful to many. Several remarkable instances of the good which it has produced, fell, in

a very unexpected manner, under the author's own observation. A year or two after its publication, travelling in the West of England, he observed, while sitting at the window of an inn, the waiter endeavouring to assist a man who was driving some pigs on the road, while the rest of the servants amused themselves only with the difficulties which the man experienced from their frowardness. This benevolent trait in the waiter's character induced Mr. Venn to call him in, and to express to him the pleasure which he felt in seeing him perform this act of kindness. After shewing him how pleasing to the Almighty every instance of good-will to our fellow-creatures was, he expatiated upon the love of God, in sending His Son, from the purest benevolence, to save mankind. He exhorted him to seek for that salvation which God, in His infinite mercy, had given as the most inestimable gift to man. He promised to send him a book, which he had himself published; and taking down the direction of the waiter, who was very anxious to give it, he sent him, upon his return to London, a copy of " The Complete Duty of Man." Many years after this, a friend, travelling to see him, brought him a letter from this very person, who then kept a large inn, in the West of England; having married his former master's daughter. His friend told him, that coming to that inn on Saturday night, and proposing to stay there till Monday, he had inquired of the servants whether any of them went on a Sunday to a place of worship. To his surprise, he found that they were all required to go, at least one part of the day; and that the master, with his wife and family, never failed to attend public worship; that they had family prayers, at which all the servants, who were not particularly engaged, were required to be present. Surprised by this uncommon appearance of religion, in a situation where he little expected to find it, he inquired of the landlord by what means he possessed such a sense of the importance of religion. He was told, that it was owing to a work which a gentleman had sent to him several years ago, after speaking to him, in a manner which deeply interested him, of the goodness of God, in giving His Son to die for our sins. On desiring to see the book, he found it to be " The Complete Duty of Man." Rejoiced to find that his guest was going to pay a visit to Mr. Venn, he immediately wrote a letter to him, expressing, in the fulness of his heart, the obligations which he owed him, and the happiness which himself, his wife, and many of his children and domestics, enjoyed daily, in consequence of that conversation which Mr. Venn had had with him, and the book which he had sent him, which he had read again and again, with increasing comfort and advantage.

Another instance occurred at Helvoetsluys, whilst he was waiting for a fair wind to convey the packet to England. Walking upon the sea-shore, he saw a person who, from his dress and manner, he supposed to be an Englishman, and addressed him therefore, in English, as such. The gentleman informed him, that he was a Swede, though he had lived many years in England, and was well acquainted with the language and manners of that country. This circumstance induced him to enter

into conversation with him. The subject of religion was soon introduced; when, to my father's
great pleasure, he found that his companion was a
decidedly religious character. The stranger invited
Mr. Venn to sup with him; and then, after much
interesting conversation, took out of his port-
manteau a book, to which he said he owed all his
impressions of religion; and, presenting it to him,
asked if he had ever seen it. This was his own
work;—and it cost Mr. Venn no little effort to sup-
press those emotions of vanity which would have
induced him at once to discover that he was himself
the author of it.

When he was once in London, he received a note
from the Countess of ——, who, though a stranger
to him, requested to see him. When he waited
on her ladyship, she informed him that her husband,
who had lately died abroad, had put that work
into her hands, and with his dying breath requested
her carefully to read it; adding, that for the last six
months it had been his constant companion, and
that he owed to it that blessed hope, which then
cheered him, of an admission, through the merits
and atonement of Christ, into the kingdom of heaven. He requested her also, upon her return to
England, to see the author, and express his obligations to him.

These were incidental and extraordinary instances
of the good which Mr. Venn's work had been the
means of effecting. It would be needless to recite
all the instances of the benefits obtained from its
perusal, which fell continually under his own observation. From Scotland, Ireland, and America, as

well as in England, he received numerous testimonies to its usefulness.

In 1767, he was visited with the severest domestic calamity—the loss of his affectionate wife; whose prudence had guided him, whose zeal had animated him, whose sound judgment had directed him, and whose kindness and affection had been his great stay and support, amidst all the trials with which he had been surrounded. A heavier trial than this could not have been laid upon him; and nothing supported him under it, but that perfect confidence in God, and that blessed hope of immortality, which it was his great employment to make known to others.

He was now left with the sole charge of five young children; and immediately began to discharge assiduously the duties which he owed to them, and to supply, if possible, the place of the most prudent and affectionate of mothers. The writer of this Memoir remembers, and ever will remember, while memory shall last, the affectionate and judicious manner in which he endeavoured to turn the minds of his children to the contemplation of the highest subjects.

During a thunder-storm, when his children expressed some alarm at the loudness of the thunder and the vividness of the lightning, he took them up with him to a window, where they could observe most distinctly the progress of the storm. He then expatiated to them upon the power of that God, whose will the thunder and the lightning obeyed. He assured them, that the lightning could injure no one, unless with the express permission of that God who directed it. He taught them to fear His power, and adore His Majesty; and finished his address to them, by kneeling down and solemnly adoring that God, whose perfections they had seen so signally displayed.

At another time, he informed them that in the evening he would take them to one of the most interesting sights in the world. They were anxious to know what it was; but he deferred gratifying their curiosity till he had brought them to the scene itself. He led them to a miserable hovel, whose ruinous walls and broken windows bespoke an extreme degree of poverty and want. "Now," said he, " my dear children, can any one, that lives in such a wretched habitation as this, be happy? Yet this is not all: a poor man lies upon a miserable straw-bed within it, dying of disease, at the age of only nineteen, consumed with constant fever, and afflicted with nine painful ulcers."—" How wretched a situation!" they all exclaimed. He then led them into the cottage, and, addressing the poor dying young man, said, " Abraham Midwood, I have brought my children here, to shew them that it is possible to be happy in a state of disease and poverty and want; and now, tell them if it is not so." The dying youth, with a sweet smile of benevolence and piety, immediately replied, " Oh yes, Sir! I would not change my state with that of the richest person upon earth, who was destitute of those views which I possess. Blessed be God! I have a good hope through Christ, of being admitted into those blessed regions where Lazarus now dwells, having long forgotten all his sorrows and miseries. Sir,

this is nothing to bear, whilst the presence of God
cheers my soul, and whilst I can have access to
Him, by constant prayer, through faith in Jesus.
Indeed, Sir, I am truly happy; and I trust to be
happy and blessed through eternity; and I every
hour thank God, who has brought me from a state
of darkness into His marvellous light, and has given
me to enjoy the unsearchable riches of His grace."

The impression made by this discourse upon his
young hearers will never be effaced. Other instances, of the like improvement of the various
events of life, may be seen in his " Complete Duty
of Man," in his admirable chapter upon the Education of Children.

In the year 1771, having accepted the rectory of
Yelling, in Huntingdonshire, which was offered to
him by his friend, the Lord Chief Baron Smythe,
who was then one of the Commissioners of the
Great Seal, he finally quitted Huddersfield. It was
not for the sake of greater emolument that he took
this step; for the income of Yelling was, at that
time, little superior to that of Huddersfield; but it
was solely on account of the declining state of his
health, which was so exhausted by his continual
labours, that he required a long and absolute ces-
sation from all exertion. He had a cough and
spitting of blood, besides other symptoms of an
approaching consumption. He was only able, in
general, to preach once in a fortnight; and the
exertion rendered him incapable of rising from his
couch for several days after. He was deeply wounded
in his feelings at leaving a flock, amongst whom he
had laboured with so much success. The last two

or three months of his residence were peculiarly affecting. At an early hour the church was crowded when he preached, so that vast numbers were compelled to go away. Many came from a considerable distance, to take leave of him, and to express how much they owed to him for benefits received under his ministry, of which he had not been aware. Mothers held up their children, saying, " There is the man who has been our most faithful minister and our best friend!" The whole parish was deeply moved; and when he preached his Farewell Sermon, neither could he himself speak without the strongest emotions, nor the congregation hear him without marks of the deepest interest and affection. Nor did the impression soon wear away: twenty years afterwards, a stranger, passing through that place, and inquiring about their former pastor, heard blessings showered down upon him and his family, with deeply-affected hearts, whilst they deplored their own loss.

[In the year 1824, the Editor of this volume visited Huddersfield, with the view of ascertaining how far the recollection of Mr. Venn's labours had survived the lapse of fifty years. The result of his inquiries will be seen in the following particulars, which were written down at the time, and which preserve, for the most part, the very words in which the information was given.

Through the previous inquiries and kind assistance of Benjamin Hudson, esq., surgeon at Huddersfield, I saw all the old people, then living in that town and neighbourhood, who had received their first religious impressions under Mr. Venn's ministry, and still maintained a religious character. They were all in the middle or lower ranks of life: none of a superior class had survived. What I am about to record must, therefore, be received as the genuine and unstudied testimony of persons of plain unpolished sense.

Mr. William Brook, of Longwood, gave me the following account of the first sermon he heard at Huddersfield Church: — " There was a meeting, every Saturday night, of the most pious people, at Thomas Hanson's, sometimes near twenty, who sang and prayed together. I was first led to go to Huddersfield Church, by listening, with an uncle of mine, W. Mellor, at the door of the house in which this meeting was held: we thought there must be something uncommon, to make people so earnest. My uncle was about nineteen; I was sixteen; so we went together to the church, one Thursday evening. There was a great crowd within the church—all silent—many weeping. The text was, ' Thou art weighed in the balances, and art found wanting.' W. Mellor was deeply attentive; and when we came out of church, we did not say a word to each other till we got some way into the fields. Then W. Mellor stopped, leaned his back against a wall, and burst into tears, saying, ' I can't stand this !' His convictions of sin were from that time most powerful; and he became quite a changed character—a most exemplary person, as you will hear from all the old people, even if they did not like his religion: he died some years after. I was not so much affected at that time; but I could not, after that sermon, be easy in sin; and I began to

pray regularly; and so, by degrees, I was brought
to know myself, and seek salvation in earnest. The
people used to go from Longwood, in droves, to
Huddersfield Church, three miles off: scores of
them came out of church together, whose ways
home were in this direction : and they used to stop
at the Firs' End, about a mile off, and talk over, for
some time, what they had heard, before they separated, to go to their homes. Oh! that place has
been to me 'like a little heaven below!'

" I never heard a minister like him. He was most
powerful in unfolding the terrors of the Law : when
doing so, he had a stern look, that would make you
tremble : then he would turn off to the offers of
grace, and begin to smile, and go on entreating till
his eyes filled with tears."

The next person I saw was George Crow, aged
eighty-two, of Lockwood, a hamlet about a mile
from the town. When I asked him whether he ever
thought of old times, he answered, "Ah! yes; and
shall do to the last. I thought, when Mr. Venn
went, I should be like Rachel, for the rest of my
days, weeping and refusing to be comforted. I was
abidingly impressed the first time I heard him, at an
early period of his ministry. He was such a preacher
as I never heard before nor since : he struck upon
the passions like no other man. Nobody could help
being affected : the most wicked and ill-conditioned
men went to hear him, and were deeply impressed*,

* The expression actually used, conveyed a very striking though
homely illustration : "They fell, like slaked lime, in a moment."
When water is thrown upon hard lumps of lime, their nature is
at once changed, and they fall into a soft powder.

even though they were not converted. I could have heard him preach all night through."

I visited this aged person at night, and sat with him, over the fire, without a candle : he kindled with animation as he spake of these things; and his deeply-rugged features, with brilliant eyes, seen by the occsional blaze from the hearth, presented a picture, such as I never can forget. He was an intelligent man ; and, even at that advanced age, his faculties were lively and perfect. He said further : " There were many used to go from Lockwood every Sunday and Thursday : we had a meeting of the most pious at William Scholefield's, about twenty of us, where a subject given out one time was discussed the next : one of us was the leader, and opened with prayer : afterwards, he asked all round their opinions, and then concluded with prayer. It is kept up to this day, though now but a few of us. The Meeting at Longwood had more than ours. There was another at Berrybrow; and one, a kind of general one, at the town.

" I was one of those who went to Mr. Venn with a large body of people, just before he left Huddersfield, to persuade him to stay. There were more than two rooms could hold. Mr. Stillingfleet and Mr. Riland were present : many talked strongly to him, and told him it was his duty to stay, and such like. I and my brother went to him afterwards, alone ; and he said, if the rest had spoken to him as mildly and affectionately as we did, he should have found it more difficult to withstand. After Mr. Venn left, the people were all squandered* away from the church: so some of us determined to begin a subscription for a chapel. I was one of the three first who put their names down. I had only 5*l.*, and I gave that; and I query whether I have ever had so much in my pocket since.

"I knew Mr. Riland well: he was an excellent man: he used to visit much among the poor: he often came to me, whilst I was at work, and sat down upon the block or any thing, and would say, ' Well, George, how are you? Either ask me something, or tell me something. Be quick! for I have much to do, and little time.' "

The religion of this poor man was of a very advanced and mature character. He quoted passages from Swedenborgh's writings, which he said he had read a good deal of; but, though there were some good things, "it was chiefly random stuff."

I also visited Ellen Roebuck, aged eighty-five, living upon parish allowance, at Almondbury: she was very deaf and infirm; but when once she understood the object of my visit, she talked with great energy, and quoted Scripture with uncommon readiness and propriety. " I well remember his first coming to Huddersfield, and the first sermon he preached. It was on that text, ' My heart's desire for Israel is, that they may be saved'; and it was as true of himself as of St. Paul. I was always attentive to my Bible, and had read it through when I was but a child; but I have reason to thank him for saving me from hell. He took every method for instructing the people: he left nothing

* A provincial expression for " dispersed ".

unturned. Always at work!—it was a wonder he had not done for himself sooner. The lads he catechized used to tell him that people said he was teaching a new doctrine, and leading us into error ; but he always replied, ' Never mind them—do not answer them—read your Bibles, and press forwards, dear lads! press forwards! and you cannot miss of heaven.' " With respect to herself, she said : " They tell me I am old, and must soon be gone ; but I say, God gave me life ; He has preserved my life ; and He will take away my life whenever He sees best."

Upon my asking her if she had seen much trouble, she replied : " Trouble! aye, plenty of it! But what signified trouble! I would always down upon my knees directly, and I never wanted for comfort. I used to think how all things were appointed by God, and nothing could happen but as He pleased. Man may shoot an arrow, but God will direct it. I could always turn the Scriptures to my use, whatever happened."

Sally P——, aged seventy-four, spoke of my grandfather with great reverence, but with deep emotion. I asked her whether she often thought about him : she replied : " Ah, Sir! I have often thought about him, and the pains he took with us ; but it was all lost upon some of us. He had a most piercing tone ; and things that he said have ever since stuck to my mind." I asked her what she particularly alluded to : she said, " I remember that, just before he went, he told us all, that he had broken up our fallow ground, and sown good seed ; but that, if we did not watch over it, and it

did not become fruitful, it would be so much the
worse for us. And so it has been with me! It is
very sorrowful to think of these things; and sometimes it makes me very low."

I trust, however, that this poor woman has
been for many years recovered from the backslidings which she so touchingly confessed; and
will maintain to the end the humble and contrite
frame of mind she now possesses, united, as it is,
with reliance upon her Saviour for pardon and
grace. By a remarkable coincidence, she had been
reading, two days before I called upon her, " Lewis's
Explanation of the Catechism," which my grandfather had given her when a child.

I also saw John Starkey of Cawcliff, aged eighty.
He is past work, but maintained by the family of
J. Whitaker, esq., in whose employment he has been
from youth. As I conversed with him, he seemed
gradually to wake up, till his countenance glistened
with joy. His faculties are still perfect, and his
recollection ready and distinct. There was in him
an uncommon warmth of affection and benevolence.
He said: " I esteemed Mr. Venn too much for
a man; I almost forgot that he was only a creature, and an instrument. His going away went
nearer to my heart than any thing since. I was
very wild and careless when a lad, and would not
go to church; so Mr. Whitaker promised me
sixpence if I would go three times; but I don't
know whether I earned it, I was so careless about
every thing: however, soon after, I heard one
sermon, which made me begin to think. The text
was, ' God is no respecter of persons,' &c.; and

he shewed that it was neither money nor learning,
nor any thing else of that kind, which could make
us happy; but that, without holiness, we were
under God's frown and curse. I then saw something of my real state; and from that time I did
not want hiring to go and hear him. I don't
think any thing would have kept me from him. He
was a wonderful preacher. When he got warm
with his subject, he looked as if he would jump out
of the pulpit. He made many weep. I have often
wept at his sermons. I could have stood to hear
him till morning. When he came up to the church,
he used to go round the church-yard, and drive us
all in before him. About seven or eight of us, who
lived at Cawcliff, used to meet at each other's
houses, once a week, for reading the Scriptures
and prayer: but all my companions are now gone;
and I often think I am left alone, as David says,
' like a sparrow upon the house-top.' It is a
grief to me that I have now no one to talk
with about spiritual things; but then, I think, I
am almost turned eighty, and God has helped
me hitherto, blessed be His name! I cannot be
much longer here, and I must not faint at last.
That text has often cheered my spirits, ' Be content with such things as ye have; for He hath
said, I will never leave thee nor forsake thee.'
These words give me comfort; for He has not forsaken me:—and then there is another, 'With loving-
kindness have I drawn thee.' Oh, blessed, blessed
be His name, for His great loving-kindness! I often
think time is too short to praise Him! Eternity
alone will be long enough! I have found it to

be, as the Scripture says, 'We must through great tribulation enter into the kingdom of heaven.' I have been tried in many ways."

In answer to some remark, he said, "Ah, Sir! I hope I never forget that it is the character which has a right to the promise. If I have not the character, how can I claim the promise. I continually pray to God to search me, and try the ground of my heart. I try to keep up a jealousy over myself; for I often think what a dreadful thing it would be, if I were to fall away at the last. Yet I hope I shall be kept; though I do not always feel so comfortable as I could wish; and I often desire to have the advice of some one more learned than myself. I well remember going over the hills to hear a preacher, and his sermon had a great effect on me; for he preached upon that Scripture, 'My sheep hear my voice, and I know them, and they follow me; and I give unto them eternal life; and they shall never perish, neither shall any man pluck them out of my hand.' Blessed be God! I hoped I was one of those sheep.—'My Father is greater than all.' Ah! that He is; or else I should have been plucked out long since."

He said he had gone to Highfield Chapel ever since it was built, upon Mr. Venn's removal: he rejoiced at the sight of the new churches at Huddersfield: he had much rather have pious ministers in churches than in chapels; for many more would hear them:—he was waiting for death, in a good hope that God would receive him, for Christ's sake, into heaven: he would rather go than stay; but he desired to wait God's time.

E

I conversed with four other persons, who received their first serious impressions under Mr. Venn's ministry, and have since maintained a consistent religious profession.   The substance of their recollections, though not perhaps of equal interest with what I have already recorded, yet no less strongly evinced their gratitude and affection for their revered pastor, and the extraordinary blessing which rested on his labours.*

I will add only a few more scattered recollections, which I received from different quarters, and which seem worthy of preservation.

Mr. Venn made a great point of the due observance of the Sabbath in the town and parish.   He

* Since the publication of the First Edition, I have learned that all the persons whose testimony is recorded above have died in the faith and peace of the Gospel.   The minister who attended Sally P., in her last illness, writes in the following terms respecting her: —" She was generally more ready to speak of her own sinfulness and imperfections, than of the goodness of God and an assurance of His love; but still her hope was fixed on the sacrifice and righteousness of the Redeemer; and sometimes she would speak confidently, and say, though she felt herself to be a most unworthy and sinful creature, yet she believed that God, for Christ's sake, had forgiven her.   She was a fearful Christian; but yet she knew in whom she believed.   The name of Jesus was to her as ointment poured forth; and when, from various causes, she was disposed to be irritable, a conversation with her, on the character and offices of the Saviour, would compose her mind, so that (her friends remarked) the effect of it would remain for several days. From the constant use of our beautiful Liturgy, many parts of it were deeply impressed on her mind, and, to her dying hour, supplied her with the language of prayer: and she said, when she could not bear to read, and could remember nothing else, portions of the Liturgy would recur to her mind, and comfort her, enabling her to lift up her heart in prayer."

induced several of the most respectable and influential inhabitants to perambulate the town, and, by persuasion, rather than by legal intimidation, to repress the open violation of the day. By such means, a great and evident reformation was accomplished.

He endeavoured to preserve the utmost reverence and devotion in public worship, constantly pressing this matter upon his people. He read the service with peculiar solemnity and effect. The *Te Deum*, especially, was recited with a triumphant air and tone, which often produced a perceptible sensation throughout the whole congregation. He succeeded in inducing the people to join in the responses and singing. Twice, in the course of his ministry at Huddersfield, he preached a course of sermons in explanation of the Liturgy. On one occasion, as he went up to church, he found a considerable number of persons in the church-yard, waiting for the commencement of the service. He stopped to address them, saying, he hoped they were preparing their hearts for the service of God—that he had himself much to do to preserve a right frame, &c. He concluded by waving his hand for them to go into the Church before him, and waited till they had all entered.

He took great pains in catechizing the young persons in his congregation, chiefly those who were above fourteen years old. The number was often very considerable; and he wrote out for their use a very copious explanation of the Church Catechism, in the way of Question and Answer.

Such were the vivid and affectionate recollections

of their revered pastor, cherished by the few remaining members of Mr. Venn's flock at Huddersfield, after the lapse of above half a century. What, then, must have been the extent and importance of the impression produced by his labours at the time! When I visited Huddersfield, I found it like the Prophet's olive-tree, after the harvest was over. There remained only "two or three berries on the top of the uppermost bough." How rich and plentiful must the harvest itself have been!]

When my father came to Yelling, his feelings were most deeply excited by the striking contrast between the church at that place and at Huddersfield. Twenty or thirty rustics composed the congregation, who seemed to be utterly void of every just view of religion; but, when his strength was recruited, he laboured in that humble sphere with at least a proportionable degree of success.

Soon after his removal to Yelling, he married a second time. The lady was the widow of Mr. Smith of Kensington, and daughter of the Rev. James Ascough, Vicar of Highworth, Wilts. In the object of his choice, Mr. Venn found an interesting companion and a faithful friend; and his children received the benefit of a maternal care; to the value of which they are anxious, to this day, to give testimony. She lived with him twenty-one years, and was buried at Yelling.

There was an advantage attending the situation of Yelling, which rendered my father's usefulness in retirement much greater than it would otherwise have been. As Yelling is only twelve miles from Cambridge, many of the younger members of that

University, and particularly pious young ministers, were accustomed to repair to him, to be instructed by his counsel, and animated by the views he possessed of the Gospel they were to preach.

His powers of conversation were so admirable, his knowledge of religion so extensive, his acquaintance with the world so instructive, and his vigour of mind so great, that, wherever he was, and in whatever company he was placed, every one silently hung upon his lips, and enjoyed the richest feast from his conversation. I lately met with a clergyman, who came over, with two others, to pay him a visit, without any previous acquaintance with him, or any introduction but that which arose from community of sentiment. He told me, that, to the latest hour of his life, he should never forget that conversation; that it made so deep an impression on him, that he did not forget one single sentence; that, after hearing him converse almost during the whole day, he returned with his companions to Cambridge at night; and each determined, with an earnestness they had never felt before, to devote themselves unreservedly to the promotion of the Gospel of Christ. The party wrote down the heads of that interesting conversation: but, added my friend, I had no occasion to write it down, for it was impressed indelibly upon my memory; and that day stands distinguished amongst all the other days of my life, like a day spent in Paradise. *

* [The narrator of this interview was the Rev. Charles Jerram, Vicar of Witney, Oxon.; and one of his companions was the late Rev. Thomas Thomason, of Calcutta.]

My father continued his ministerial labours till he began to find his faculties impaired by age. He then had wisdom and fortitude enough to retire from that work, which, he said, required all the highest and noblest faculties of man. He used to observe, that the Levites, under the Old Testament, were dismissed from their service at the age of fifty; and collected from it, that God, who is the most gracious and tender of masters, did not require that His servants should exert themselves any longer than while their full powers and faculties continued.

———

Here the Memoir prepared by the Rev. John Venn abruptly terminates. Much as this circumstance must be deplored, it will be some relief to reflect that his main object had been accomplished; namely, that of tracing accurately the progress of his father's mind in religious knowledge and attainments.

The last twenty years of Mr. Venn's life were marked by no peculiar or striking events. His intercourse with the young men at Cambridge, which has been already described, is to be regarded, I conceive, as his chief sphere of usefulness during this period. Several of the most eminent and laborious ministers of the generation which is now well nigh passed away might be mentioned as having been visitors at Yelling, during their residence in Cambridge. One of the earliest amongst the number was the late Rev. Thomas Robinson, Vicar of

St. Mary's, Leicester; who, as his biographer informs us, took Mr. Venn for his "*prototype*," in the discharge of his ministerial duties.

And here I cannot refrain from alluding to the still more important advantages which his society afforded to some who remained in the University; and who have been honoured, in their turn, as the instruments of fostering, directing, and establishing the piety of a multitude of young men, who have, each successive year, left college, to enter upon the duties of the ministry. The Rev. Charles Simeon, Fellow of King's College, and the Rev. William Farish, Jacksonian Professor, are names which will already have occurred to several of my readers. The time is not yet arrived, in which I might be permitted to review the influence of the labours of these excellent men upon the cause of Religion in general, and of that Church in particular of which they have ever been amongst the most firm and efficient friends. But, whatever value may be attached to their labours will reflect an importance upon Mr. Venn's connexion with Cambridge; for they willingly acknowledge how much they owed, under God, to his judicious and animating counsel. On this point I am furnished with the following striking testimony, received from Mr. Simeon, when the foregoing Memoir was submitted to his perusal.

" I most gladly bear my testimony, that not the half, nor the hundredth part, of what might have been justly said of that blessed man of God, is here spoken. If any person now living, his surviving children alone excepted, is qualified to bear this testimony, it is I; who, from my first

entrance into Orders, to his dying hour, had most intimate
access to him, and enjoyed most of his company and conversation. How great a blessing his conversation and
example have been to me will never be known till the
Day of Judgment. I dislike the language of panegyric;
and therefore forbear to expatiate upon a character which
is, in my estimation, above all praise. Scarcely ever did I
visit him, but he prayed with me, at noon-day, as well as
at the common seasons of family worship: scarcely ever
did I dine with him, but his ardour in returning thanks,
sometimes in an appropriate hymn, and sometimes in a
thanksgiving prayer, has inflamed the souls of all present,
so as to give us a foretaste of Heaven itself: and, in all the
twenty-four years that I knew him, I never remember
him to have spoken unkindly of any one, but once; and
I was particularly struck with the humiliation which he
expressed for it, in his prayer, the next day.

" C. SIMEON."

The leisure which Mr. Venn enjoyed at Yelling
enabled him to keep up a very extensive correspondence; and the present volume will sufficiently
prove how much advantage his numerous distant
friends derived from the labours of his pen.

After he left Yorkshire, he generally spent a few
weeks in each year in London. On these occasions
he preached many times in the week, as well as on
the Sundays. Numerous audiences were collected:
his sermons were listened to with the deepest attention; and he received many testimonies of their
usefulness. His own spirit was much refreshed by
these visits; and his clerical friends were accustomed to hail his arrival amongst them as a season
of peculiar pleasure and advantage. When he
visited London in the spring of 1791, he declined,

for the first time, appearing in the pulpit. In the autumn of the same year he engaged a permanent curate for Yelling, the Rev. Maurice Evans; and, after that period, seldom officiated, even in his own small and retired church.

In other places, upon one or two particular occasions, he was prevailed upon to address a congregation; and the partiality of friends would have persuaded him that he could still speak with power and effect, and that he ought not to desist from preaching; but he replied, that, in his better days, it had been his decided judgment that ministers should retire from the public discharge of their office " when they had lived to the dregs of life," and that he would now abide by his former judgment.

The age of sixty-eight may seem a very early period for withdrawing from the public duties of his office; but his constitution had never recovered from the effects of excessive exertion at Huddersfield; and old age came prematurely upon him.

The many temporal mercies which surrounded Mr. Venn in these evening hours of his life were the theme of his constant gratitude and praise. His family consisted of a son and three daughters; one daughter having died in childhood. He was peculiarly happy in his children, who all exhibited, as they grew up, the good effects of a wise education, and those Christian graces which were, in his sight, of supreme and inestimable value. The character of the son is not unknown to the public: I will only therefore add the words which were a thousand times on Mr. Venn's lips : — " A wise son maketh a GLAD father." His eldest daughter, Eling, was

married, in 1785, to the late Charles Elliott, esq., of
Brighton; who, at the time of his marriage, was
engaged in business in London. Mr. Venn's correspondence with this new member of his family
will supply several valuable letters in the following pages: for in Mr. Elliott, fervent piety was
united with great intelligence and activity of mind;
his veneration for Mr. Venn was truly filial; and
he enjoyed a full return of parental regard and
affection. In 1789, Mr. Venn's son was married to
Miss King, of Hull. In 1790, his youngest daughter,
Catherine, married the Rev. James Hervey, M.A.
His second daughter, Jane Catherine, remained un-
married. She was his sole and inseparable companion during the last few years of his life, and
watched over his declining health with devoted
and tender assiduity. A strong understanding and
a well-furnished mind rendered her society an ever-
failing source of satisfaction and entertainment;
and her judicious and active benevolence supplied
his lack of service, when he was no longer able to
inquire into the wants and necessities of his parishioners: so that he had still the gratification of
seeing the poor and sick and wretched flocking to
the Parsonage-house for relief, as to a well-known
asylum.

Even after Mr. Venn was disabled from the exercise of his ministry, he knew not, as he often remarked, what it was to have a tedious or vacant
hour. He found constant employment in reading
and writing, and in the exercises of prayer and meditation: he declared that he had never felt more
fervency of devotion than whilst imploring spiritual

blessings for his children and friends, and especially
for the success of those who were still engaged in
the ministry of the blessed Gospel, from which he
was himself laid aside. For himself, his prayer was,
that he might die to the glory of Christ. " There
are some moments," he once said, " when I am
afraid of what is to come in the last agonies;
but I trust in the Lord to hold me up. I have
a great work before me—to suffer, and to die, to
His glory." But the spread of the Redeemer's kingdom lay nearer his heart than any earthly or per-
sonal concerns: even when the decay of strength
produced an occasional torpor, this subject would
rouse him to a degree of fervency and joy, from
which his bodily frame would afterwards materially
suffer. I have understood that nothing more powerfully excited his spirits than the presence of
young ministers, whose hearts he believed to be
truly devoted to the service of Christ.

About six months before his death, he finally left
Yelling, and removed to Clapham, where his son
was now settled as Rector. His health, from this
period, became very precarious: he was often upon
the brink of the grave, and then unexpectedly restored. A medical friend, the late John Pearson,
esq., who frequently visited him at this time, observed, that the near prospect of dissolution so
elated his mind with joy, that it proved a stimulus
to life. Upon one occasion, Mr. Venn himself
remarked some fatal appearances; exclaiming,
"Surely these are good symptoms!" Mr. Pearson
replied: " Sir, in this state of joyous excitement
you cannot die."

At length, on the 24th of June 1797, his happy spirit was released, and entered into the long-anticipated joy of his Lord.

———

The duty of a Biographer seems to require that some general sketch should be given of the character of the man whose life is presented to the public. But, in the present instance, I am persuaded that I shall be excused from attempting this task; since the most striking features of the character before us have already been portrayed in the Memoir, in far more vivid and attractive colours than the hand, into which the pencil has now fallen, can command. At the same time, I present a Collection of Letters, which will reflect so genuine an image of that character, that my readers will need no further help in obtaining an intimate acquaintance with the mind and feelings of this great and good man.

The following is a List of the Works of Mr. Venn,
published in his life-time, with the dates at which
they first appeared.

1759.—A volume, comprising Fourteen Sermons, published upon his removal to Huddersfield, and dedicated
" To the Gentlemen of Clapham, as an acknowledgment
of the very many civilities and marks of friendship received by him during the time of his residence amongst
them."

1763.—" The Complete Duty of Man." Of this well-
known and popular work mention has already been made
in the Memoir. But it may be proper to notice, that it
was originally divided into fourteen chapters. These
portions were thought too long; and therefore, in the third
edition, a new division was made, into fifty-two chapters,
to correspond with the number of Sundays in the year :
but, by this arrangement, the subjects were inconveniently
broken. A middle plan was therefore adopted in the fifth
edition, and the number of chapters reduced to forty : very
considerable improvements were also made in the style
and language. Some late editions have unfortunately
been printed from the earlier copies of the work : it is
therefore important to observe, that those editions are the
best, which adopt the division into forty chapters.

1769.—" An Examination of Dr. Priestley's Free Address on the Lord's Supper." 8vo. pp. 91. In this work,
various passages in Dr. Priestley's Address are examined,
and the deistical tendency of them detected.

1774.—" Mistakes in Religion exposed ; an Essay on
the Prophecy of Zacharias." In this work, Mr. Venn
takes occasion, from the words of the Song of Zacharias,
in the first chapter of St. Luke's Gospel, to expose several

capital mistakes relating to the doctrines and precepts of religion. The mistakes thus selected are such as he judged most important, " from long observation of their bad effects, in the course of more than twenty years' exercise of his profession, first in London and its near neighbourhood, afterwards in the large and very populous parish of Huddersfield." This work has passed through many editions, and is still kept in print.

1786—" Memoirs of Sir John Barnard, Knt., M.P. for the City of London." 4to. pp. 22. This brief memorial was drawn up immediately after the death of Sir John, which took place in 1764. " It was at length published, from an impulse of affectionate reverence for his memory, no longer to be resisted; and, as a signal instance, that one of the first men of his age, and the glory of London, attained this pre-eminence from the best principles which can govern the human mind." Copious extracts from these Memoirs are inserted in Chalmers's Biographical Dictionary—" Barnard."

The following single Sermons were also published :

1758—" Popery a perfect Contrast to the Religion of Christ:" on James iii. 17.

1759.—" The Variance between Real and Nominal Christians considered ; and the cause of it explained :" on Matt. x. 35, 36.

1760.—" The Duty of a Parish Priest : his obligations to perform it; and the incomparable pleasure of a life devoted to the cure of souls." A Visitation Sermon at Wakefield, on Col. iv. 17.

" An earnest and pressing Call to keep holy the Lord's Day :" on Ezek. xx. 13.

1762.—" Christ the Joy of the Christian's Life; and
Death his Gain :" on Phil. i. 21.   " A Funeral Sermon on
the Death of the Rev. W. Grimshawe, A. B., Minister of the
Parish of Haworth, Yorkshire; with a Sketch of his Life
and Ministry."

1769.—" Man a Condemned Prisoner, and Christ the
Strong-hold to save him:" on Zech. ix. 12.   An Assize
Sermon, at Kingston, Surrey.

1770.—" A Funeral Sermon on the Death of the Rev.
George Whitfield :" on Isaiah viii. 18.

1779.—" The   Conversion   of Sinners   the   greatest
Charity :" on Ps. cxix. 136.   A Sermon on behalf of the
Society for Promoting Religious Knowledge among the
Poor.

1785.—" The Deity of Christ : the practical benefit of
believing it with a true heart, and the pernicious consequences which follow the denial of it proved :" on Matt.
xxii. 41, 42.   A Visitation Sermon at Huntingdon.

PART II.

—

CORRESPONDENCE.

—

IN CHRONOLOGICAL ORDER,

CORRESPONDENCE.

LETTERS WRITTEN FROM MR. VENN'S FIRST APPOINTMENT TO
HUDDERSFIELD, TILL HIS REMOVAL TO YELLING.

In presenting to the public the following Selection from
Mr. Venn's Correspondence, it will be necessary to make
a few preliminary remarks.

Mr. Venn never preserved copies of the letters he
wrote. I have therefore been indebted to the kindness of
numerous friends, to whom I beg to offer my most grateful acknowledgments, for a very large Collection of Original Letters, amounting to above a thousand in number,
and extending over a period of above forty years. Out
of these, I have selected about one fourth part for publication. In making this selection, I have been guided by
two considerations: First, I have chosen those which appeared to possess the greatest intrinsic excellence; and,
in the next place, those which might serve to exemplify
the character of an eminently pious minister in his family
and parish. The latter consideration must plead my
apology for preserving the mention of many domestic circumstances, which would otherwise be utterly unworthy
of public notice. However trivial and unimportant such
circumstances may appear in themselves, the sentiments
and feelings, to which they gave rise, will, I trust, find a

response in the breast of every pious parent and faithful minister.

With the view of sustaining the interest with which the letters will be read, I have preserved, in general, a chronological arrangement. I have also ventured to intersperse explanatory and connecting remarks; avoiding, however, the repetition of matter which has already appeared in the Memoir.

Many of the letters have been reduced in length, by the omission of unimportant passages, or of such as have been judged unsuitable for publication; and, where this has been done without affecting in any degree the sense of the context, marks of omission have not been preserved: on the other hand, where only a part of a letter seemed sufficiently interesting, it has been inserted in the form of an extract.

The Selection commences with letters relating to Mr. Venn's removal from the curacy of Clapham to the vicarage of Huddersfield. The patron of that living was Sir John Ramsden, bart., to whom Mr. Venn was a perfect stranger: but, upon its vacancy, by resignation, in 1759, the Earl of Dartmouth earnestly recommended him, without his knowledge, to Sir John Ramsden, who immediately offered the presentation to him: he hesitated, however, for several weeks, about accepting the offer; and at length determined to visit the place, and make his decision on the spot. He travelled into Yorkshire on horseback: and the following letters were written in the course of the journey.

TO MRS. VENN.

My dear E——,   *Newport Pagnell, April* 3, 1759.

I can, through the great and tender mercy of God, give you joy, by assuring you I am at present much the better for my journey hither, which is more than fifty miles. I have a good appetite, fine weather, and good roads : but what are these, united, if God is absent ? if we are left to our poverty of nature—left to our own vain unsatisfying thoughts—left destitute of that sweet intercourse which is the proper happiness, nay, the very life, of the immortal spirit ? In vain is it for the sun to shine, the landscape to smile, the roads to encourage our journey ;—still must the soul, in such a case, be heavy and dispirited. But quite the reverse has been my happy experience these two days. Every hour on the road has been a sacrifice of prayer or praise. God has marvellously brought forth the spear, and stopped the incursion of rude unhallowed thoughts, and filled me with thoughts excellent and purifying—with intense desires after the knowledge of Himself, His Son, His Gospel, and His promises ; so that, were it not for my dear wife, all on earth would be forgotten in the joyous contemplation of God, and the earnest going-forth of my soul after Him. When I have thus been engaged for myself, I am employed in entreating for you, that you may be supported and comforted in spirit, refreshed and strengthened in body ; that my absence may not be tedious ; nor the presence of a sinful creature be deemed essential in such a degree to your peace and happiness, that you should not enjoy them without me. With you I am mindful of our two sweet babes; that, as the wife of Manoah prayed for Sampson, we may be taught how to order and what to do to them, that the guardian power of a Covenant God, and the heritage of His faithful servants, may be their heritage. I then proceed to remember our noble friends, and our most generous benefactors*, according as I understand their respective necessities. In the intervals, I sing a song of Zion; such as becomes the ransomed of the Lord; such as His boundless love has put into their mouths. From this account, you will understand that I suffer no loss, even of present pleasure, from travelling alone. When God fulfils that promise, as He ever will to them that ask it, " I will dwell in them, and walk in them;"—when, I say, the reality of this promise is experienced, the company of a Christian friend would even disturb and distress me: and whilst that grace, which has been vouchsafed me since I set out, continues, there is not that highly-favoured Child of God upon earth whose company I would covet. But, to make us know how undeserved the gift is, how entirely out of our power to preserve or keep, the Lord adjusts " the times of refreshing from His presence," and, as seemeth Him good, gives light and joy, or withholds and diminishes. But this is our sure foundation, that our abiding trust is in the Lord; and whilst that

* Alluding to Lord Dartmouth's exertions in procuring him the offer of Huddersfield.

abides, the love of God to the soul is unchangeable
and eternal.   Be sure you send me an exact account of your health.   My stages to Huddersfield
will be very easy, this road ; and almost every night
I shall stop at the house of a friend.   I suppose
before my dearest creature receives this letter, she
will have a line from Mr. Harvey, whom I met a
few miles off, and desired him to let you know
I was well.   When I am separated and absent
from you for a season, I feel more sensibly, than
when at home, my union in love with you.   So it is
in spiritual things : the silent complainings of the
faithful soul—" Lord! wherefore art Thou absent
so long? why is the light of Thy countenance
withdrawn ?"—far from being any evidence of want
of faith, do abundantly prove its reality and strength.

The God who is love—love in all His provi-
dences, in all His dealings towards them that fear
Him and believe in the name of His only-begotten
Son—bless you with all blessings!   My best affection to Mr. Daw and my sister.   May you all be
one in Christ!

H. VENN.

TO A FRIEND.

—— Though I travel alone, my mind, and the
mind of every believer, has employment enough.
He looks within ; and sees the plague of his own
heart—self-conceit, and self-will—much darkness in
his understanding, and much depravity in his affections—much of unbelief, and of unsuitable behaviour
from a creature to its Creator, from a sinner to His
Redeemer.   He can look upwards ; and break forth

with fervent desire after the things which are above
—God—the Father, the Son, and the Spirit—obedience to His will, and love to all men for His sake.
He can look on every side, and find matter for
prayer—for converted and unconverted relatives,
friends, benefactors. He can look backward, to the
day when he hung upon the breast ; and forward,
to the endless ages of eternity ; and hear the loud
call of mercy upon mercy, to gratitude and praise.
Thus is the believer furnished, wherever he goes :
from this rich fund he draws a pure and lasting
satisfaction, which strengthens and establishes his
mind in the good ways of the Lord ——

TO MRS. VENN.

Nottingham, April 5, 1759.

God has most graciously brought me, my dearest
E., in increasing strength, to this town, within seventy miles of my journey's end ; to perform which,
I have before me two days and a half. I have
been still highly favoured with the presence of our
adorable Covenant God. This has cheered the way,
and made my time pass delightfully, though without
company. Oh ! how ought we to pray for those
who live without God in the world ! How forlorn
their condition, in many circumstances ! How irksome to travel, as I shall, five or six hundred miles,
a burden to themselves, if they turn their eyes
inward ; not able to have their own enjoyments,
mean as they are, and no Invisible God, to hold
sweet intercourse with by the way !

Immediately upon my arrival here, I received

your letter of good news; which was doubly acceptable, as I could not but be under many fears lest your concern for me might throw you back. How does our God abound in the most tender expressions of His favour towards us! How does He embrace us with mercy on every side!

You will believe me, when I assure you, it gives me great pleasure to find you love me so tenderly. But you have need to beware, lest I should stand in God's place; for your expressions, "that you know not how to be from me an hour without feeling the loss, &c." seem to imply something of this kind. My dearest E., we must ever remember that word which God hath spoken from Heaven: "The time is short: let those who have wives be as if they had none; and those who rejoice, as if they rejoiced not." Both for myself and you, I would always pray that God may be so much dearer to us than we are to each other, that our souls in His love may "delight themselves in fatness," and feel He is an all-sufficient God. By this means we shall be most likely to continue together, and not provoke the stroke of separation by an idolatrous love to one another. By this means we shall love one another in God, and for God; and be armed with the whole armour of God, for all events.

Write me word, in your next—which you will direct to me at Huddersfield—how you find the state of your immortal soul. Surely God has abounded in loving-kindness to us, more than to others! Let us stir up each other, to return sincere and vehement love for all His benefits.

I can discover the horrible pride of my desperately

wicked heart, in the disagreeable feeling the meanness of the towns I pass through gives me, upon
supposition I am to be fixed in one like them. What
deep root have worldly lusts in my soul! And how
easy is it to have the name of having overcome the
world, yea, to flatter ourselves we really have done
it by faith, when, still, love to comfortable accommodations, and to *have things handsome about us,*
prevails.

Dinner is just coming upon table.   I have also to
see my horse fed ;—and therefore, without filling
the other side, I must conclude ; praying that the
Eternal God may be your refuge, the redemption
which is in Jesus your portion, and the Holy Ghost
your comforter. Grace be with you, and all in
our house !

H. VENN.

The answer of Mrs. Venn to the foregoing letter has
fortunately been preserved.   I therefore insert it in this
place, in the confidence that it will be deemed sufficiently
interesting in itself, and shew how worthy she was of the
partner to whom she was united.

FROM MRS. VENN.

Clapham, April 7, 1759.

A THOUSAND thanks to you, my dear, for your
early care to let me hear of your welfare ! I do not
forget to return my thanks and praise to Him who is
the Author of the blessings bestowed on us both.

What joy did it give me, to hear the account you give! how abundantly the want of an earthly companion was made up! it brought to my eyes tears of joy.   Certainly, far sweeter is such intercourse than any earthly communion, even with the most advanced Christian, can possibly be: and when such favours are vouchsafed, all troubles are light, all wants vanish.   This the believing soul is sensible of; but a strange enthusiastic mystery it appears to others.   Yet, blessed be my adorable Redeemer! my own experience has oftentimes confirmed this truth to my soul.   I well know what it means; though I do not enjoy it at all times, nor in that exalted degree to which some favoured Christians attain. However, I trust I shall be satisfied; because I know the earnest desire of my soul, and my constant cry to my God, is, for more love, more light, more zeal, and more holiness of every kind.

In yours from Nottingham, you fear for me, lest my love for you should be carried too far.   But, indeed, I believe you need not fear.   I do not think I love you more than God has commanded me. What love ought the Church to have for her Head, how to feel His absence, how to seek and desire the return of her Beloved!   Submission only, and a steady perseverance in all the commands and ordinances left her, are required, as her part to perform, while she waits and longs for the return of her beloved Head.   Now, I am very sure I do not carry the matter further than this: so pray answer me to it!

And now to give you an account of myself:— I do not remember that I have shed a tear since the day you left me; but am cheerful and easy.   A sigh, or so, on Friday, which was a very wet day ; but no further : so that I think you cannot blame me.

You ask me about the state of my soul: but I hardly know how to give you any satisfactory answer. It is not in the best, neither in the worst, state that I have found it in, since I have been blessed with any knowledge of spiritual concerns. My desires after God, and for actual holiness, are exceeding earnest and strong. A deep and lively sense of the many and late mercies, vouchsafed to me and mine, fills my heart with much praise and thankfulness. I am full of peace. But what have I to disturb my quiet? May not the abounding of temporal blessings satisfy nature; and so give that peace, while grace has no part in the procuring of it ?—I feel a backwardness to talk of God or the things of God, and a sort of easy carelessness creeping upon me ; so that, though in my inmost soul I am breathing after God, I am yet unwilling to discover it, or suffer it to break out into action. I cannot better explain my present state. May God bless our union, by making you a minister of grace to your wife, and causing her soul to be replenished and renewed under your ministry ; that you may be made joyful, by finding yourself a guide and leader of the soul of your Syphe* to the mansions of bliss and glory, which a very short space only keeps us from, and where we shall be perfectly united to all eternity !

I am sorry to hear, the passing through those poor towns occasioned such stirrings of pride. I am very sensible, if the meanness of them has had such an effect on you, it will be far worse with me ; because

* A playful appellation.

my pride is far less subdued than yours : and should our lot be cast, as you observe, where our accommodations are but mean and low, I fear I shall find a great struggle, and a long while before it is overcome. However, I hope to be strengthened according to my trial. Mrs. Knipe begs to be remembered to you, and that you will not forget her at the Throne of Grace, as she daily remembers you. Praying that mercy and peace may abound towards us, I am, with all our love,

Yours,   E. V.

In subsequent letters, Mr. Venn announces his arrival at Huddersfield, and his acceptance of the living. He describes the state of his feelings in the following terms :—

I AM now fully determined that it is the will of God we should come here. I have gone through much perplexity and uneasy suspense ; being one day in this mind, through some favourable circumstance ; another day, in quite a different opinion.— I made earnest prayer to our most loving and gracious Father, that He would look down upon His poor doubting child, unwilling to take a step which there might be cause to repent of; and fearful of doing wrong, either by removing, or by refusing the situation. ——I have since enjoyed an ease of mind and satisfaction, in the prospect of settling at Huddersfield, quite undisturbed. This, joined to the great appearance of my usefulness in Huddersfield, makes me account little of the inconveniences we may meet with.

TO MRS. VENN.

Huddersfield, April 15, 1759.

I SEE, my dearest love, it was the same tender mercy of God, which has embraced me on every side, ever since I was born, that reserved you for my wife. Let those who never knew nor experienced the pleasure of disinterested love, of a union of hearts in the adorable Redeemer, talk of marrying well, and to advantage, when they enrich each other with this world's goods : as for myself, I would again prefer a daughter of faithful Abraham to the heiress of Dives. I never saw so clearly how thankful I should be to God for you, as this day. Upon my return from York, I found your two letters : it was nine days since I had heard of you. I was fearful lest the very violent rains should have made you uneasy on my account, and that uneasiness brought on illness.

Your letter much strengthens me ; and you write as if God had inclined you also to love Huddersfield. But, whatever the event may be, we may be sure we have God for our guide, since we have left nothing undone, which lies in our power, to commit the cause entirely to Him, and to seek direction from Him. If we should go there, I believe, in the most important points it will answer. I trust I shall prosper much more in my own soul, by much reading, meditation, and prayer ; and, which fills me with delight in the thought, shall have opportunity of praying with you alone ; as often as the great Mr. Bolton with his wife—twice every day.

The house, I am sure, you will like much, when

it is furnished : it will be better than our Clapham
house.   But, what is best of all, such a vast multitude of souls to hear—under my care, fourteen
hundred families!—and out of other parishes, together, my audience this afternoon could not be
less than upwards of three thousand!   One of the
tradesmen has been much affected; and stays two
days, that he may ride up with me to town.   People
seem in general much pleased; and I have preached
every time from notes only.   Oh, the happy life we
should lead, should God be pleased to give us the
hearts of many of this people, and appoint me a
pastor over them, according to His own heart !

> " This one thing will I require ;
>   Nothing on earth, besides, desire."

I am glad there are but two whole days before I
shall be drawing nearer and nearer to my dearest
Syphe.   I am still exceedingly well.   God heareth
prayer, and dealeth bounteously with them that put
their trust in Him.   Tell Mrs. Knipe, that leaving
her and her dear brother will be a bitter ingredient
in my cup.   You must assure her there shall be a
Mrs. Knipe's room at the Vicarage-house.   Has
P. come to a determination ?—and will she accept
the honour of being first maid in the vicar's family ?
I know not where to direct you to write to me next.

The Lord of life and glory bless and sanctify
you, my dear, wholly! and give you such clear increasing views of His own exceeding great loveliness
and glory, that even your children and your husband may be as nothing, in your eyes, in comparison
of Jesus Christ !

Ever yours,   H. Venn.

Mrs. Knipe, the lady mentioned in the two preceding letters, was sister to John Thornton, esq. I am indebted to Mr. Venn's correspondence with her for some of the earliest letters I have been able to procure, written during his residence at Huddersfield.

TO MRS. KNIPE.

Huddersfield, June 20, 1760.

YOUR letter, dear Madam, which I received this day, was a feast to us and our Christian friends who were with us from Thornhill; though, if it had been the good pleasure of God, we should have rejoiced to have had a better account of my sister. Irregular self-love, and ignorance of the benefits of affliction, make us often impatient to see our dear friends freed from suffering; though the painful operation is all for health, and under the management of the Divine Physician, who bled for us on the cross.

It was a great pleasure indeed to me, to hear that your brother, for whose spiritual welfare I must ever be deeply concerned, did not differ from me in his judgment of those books which I conclude were recommended. The most plausible way that I know, and by far the most successful, of supplanting the Gospel, is, by a pretended or real zeal for the practice of moral duties. To be sober, humane, a good father, husband, master, and neighbour, is what all must wish to attain—is what all will so applaud when attained—that it seems rash and uncharitable to say, " Yet lackest thou one thing." Honour the Saviour of sinners. Let thy heart be ever as an altar, on which the fire of love to Him is kept alive, if it is not, alas! always bright and flaming, as it should be. I was the more rejoiced to find your dear brother approved of my judgment on the books, because certainly the crying abomination of our age is, contempt of Christ. In proof of this, you may hear sermons and religious books much extolled, where there is not so much as any mention of the Prince of Peace, in whom God was manifest, to reconcile the world unto Himself. Mr. Lawrence Sterne, prebendary of York, published, a few weeks since, two volumes of sermons. They are much commended by the Critical Reviewers. I have read them ; and, excepting a single phrase or two, they might be preached in a synagogue or a mosque without offence. O Madam! what reason have you for thankfulness and rejoicing, that you know yourself to be poor and needy, blind and guilty ; that you can hear, as life-giving sounds, that voice of God, " Behold, I lay in Zion, for a foundation, a stone, a tried stone, a precious corner-stone, a sure foundation," that whosoever believeth on Him shall not make haste. For my own part, I daily see more and more, that if I would walk before God, and delight myself in Him, the only possible way is, to behold His glory, as it is manifested in the undertakings and offices of His only-begotten Son.

It was quite reviving to us to hear you intend to visit Huddersfield every year. You will remember, we have it under your own hand ; and, with Christians, promises are sacred. I shall stand in need of

G

the pleasure your company imparts; as I am about to have a severe trial, I fear, in parting with Mr. Burnett*. His friends in Cornwall advise him entirely to leave Yorkshire, under a notion that he has too much duty laid upon him. I am apprehensive he will be persuaded; and where I shall get an Assistant, whose heart is engaged to save souls, and to preach Christ Crucified without unscriptural peculiarities, I know not. But the Chief Shepherd of the flock, I trust, should the case be so, will, in mercy to me and my people, send some one to help me—not for filthy lucre's sake, but of a ready mind.

I bless God you have found such company as those excellent ones of the earth. Ah! what is the chaff to the wheat! what the empty talking of vanity, every one with his neighbour, to speech that is seasoned with salt, such as ministers grace to the hearer! We are all well; and my wife will endeavour to write for herself. You will remember me in your prayers, that I may be bold on the second of July, when I am to preach the Visitation sermon, that I may speak with Christian love to my brethren, and all meekness. I find too much of selfishness, and of a coward's heart, lest I should be despised, and openly admonished. But I trust, when the hour of action is come, I shall find myself supported. My book† advances but slowly; and I must in earnest so apply, that it may be finished by

* The Rev. George Burnett, then Curate of Huddersfield; and afterwards Incumbent of Elland, in the parish of Halifax; a man of sterling worth, eminent holiness, and greatly blessed in his ministry.

† The Complete Duty of Man.

the beginning of next year. If, therefore, my letters to my dear friend and benefactor should not, for the future, be so long, you will ascribe it to my engagements; which, indeed, I must give up more of my time to, than I have yet done. You will remember, that, as you have no book upon your hands, your paper is to be filled, though my epistles fall short of their usual length. I am now sitting, to receive my dues, at Abraham Hall's, in Goldcar; who is, I believe, a faithful disciple. With love from us all, to all Christian friends, and kind inquirers after us, I commend you to God, praying that His love may rest upon you, and those near and dear to you— that you may find God is all-sufficient—that with Him is the well of life: and may the streams of living water make you fruitful in every good word and work! From your ever obliged and faithful pastor in Christ Jesus,

H. VENN.

TO MRS. KNIPE.

DEAR MADAM, *Huddersfield, Dec.* 21, 1760.

THOUGH I cannot give you so pleasing an account as I could wish of my dear wife, yet she is better than might have been expected. The fever has not yet quite left her, though it is much abated. As it is, it sounds an alarm through my heart, uncertain of the issue. On what slender strings are our best earthly comforts fixed! how soon burst in two, and we bereaved of them! For my own part, I cannot conceive that any thing but the grossest stupidity, or a delight in

G 2

God as our portion, can make the present state of things supportable. Can a man love his wife—can he love his child in any measure as he ought, and not be afflicted to think in what slippery places they are living ? Can he think of parting from either without convulsions, unless he can say, " Though Joseph is not, and Benjamin is not, yet God remaineth my exceeding joy ! "

I read of your growth in grace with the highest pleasure; and no one stronger proof of it can you give, than watchfulness against evil-speaking. That is a remarkable scripture, " If any man *offend not in word*, the same is a perfect man, and able also to bridle the whole body." I am sure of two things, respecting myself and my own experience—that I have such a load of guilt on this account alone, that if there was not the blood of Christ for my propitiation, I must perish for ever; and that in proportion as my unruly member, the tongue, is tamed, I enjoy the heart-reviving presence and peace of God. And no wonder it is so ; since, by speaking evil, though it is true, when no good purpose is immediately to be answered, the following hateful tempers are discovered to rule in the heart : 1. Want of regard to the high and loving authority of God, who has positively forbidden it. 2. Want of brotherly love and charity; which would be grieved for the offences we know any one living in the commission of. 3. Want of humility in our hearts ; which would teach us that we are vile, too vile, ourselves, to complain of others and dwell on their faults.

I hope you see dear Mr. Walker as often as you can, now he is at Blackheath. I could wish

Mr. Thornton was with him: he is one of the jewels which is highly polished before it is made up in heaven. Humbleness and spirituality of mind, with extraordinary degrees of wisdom and judgment, distinguish him.

If it were not for dear Mr. Adam's encouraging approbation, I should faint in my book; but this, when I receive it, is a strong incentive to persevere. In a letter, a few days since, he writes me word that he had an opportunity of reading my two chapters, last sent to him, to Archdeacon Basset; and the result was, an earnest desire to have them printed. I keep close to the work now; and hope to bring up with me, if God continues to bless me with health, twelve chapters, out of fifteen.

My love to my sister, to Mr. Thornton, and all my Christian friends: and may much of the power, presence, and love of God in Christ Jesus be your portion, and the earnest of your dwelling in light and glory with God for evermore! So prays your affectionate and much obliged minister in Christ,   H. VENN.

Jan. 1761.

——I continue, blessed be God! in good health; and Mr. Burnett is much recovered. Our work in some degree prospers; but many fall back, and grow lukewarm, that set out well. Those of our friends whom you knew, I trust gain ground, and are much more settled and strengthened. I have begun again my instruction of the young people at the villages: amongst them, there are about sixteen, between the ages of eighteen and twenty-two, of whom I hear an excellent account, and who answer with great discretion and spiritual understanding. Oh, my friend! what want of benevolence and love to my fellow-creatures is there in my heart, that I am not importunate without ceasing that all may come to the knowledge of Jesus Christ;—which is in heaven begun on earth! My defects and failures of this kind would destroy me, if it were not that God justifieth freely, through the redemption that is in Jesus.   H. V.

TO MRS. KNIPE.

MY DEAR FRIEND,   *Huddersfield, Jan.* 11, 1761.

THIS new year was begun by us with the solemn dedication of our little babe to the service and blessing of the God of the Christians—Father, Son, and Holy Ghost.   Miss S—— represented yourself; and Mrs. G——, Lady L——.   Our day was spent in that communion with God for which we were redeemed by the blood of Jesus, and to which we pray all our dear friends may more and more attain.   God is exceeding gracious to my dear wife, and the dear babe, who thrives abundantly.

Your account of Sir John Barnard is very moving. It is remarkable, that he was once very much struck with, and seemed not to agree with me in, an observation I made, one Thursday evening, to this effect;—that if we were without chastening, whereof all are partakers, then are we bastards, and not sons; that is, the God of Heaven and Earth neglects our education, and is provoked to overlook

us, as men are wont to do their base-born children.
I had more than one or two conversations with him
upon the subject; and I suppose the continued
prosperity he had met with, the honour and high
esteem he was always held in, led him to conclude
that he wanted this mark of a child of God. Since
that time, you see, the cross has been his portion;
and a long season of increasing infirmities and pain,
and all the exercises of patience attending a lingering
but mortal malady, have been appointed to him.
I shall be glad to hear of his dismission; for, sure
I am, my eyes have scarce beheld his fellow. Such
constant circumspection and such deep humility,
such unfeigned Christian love, expressing itself in a
total abstinence from evil speaking, is rarely to be
found, even amongst the faithful in Christ Jesus.
Happy saint! to be so near the glorious transformation. What a mighty and unspeakable change in a
moment will he soon feel—from being burdened
with a body full of weakness and disease, to enjoy
the liberty of a pure spirit; and, from being dis-
tracted in the contemplation of his God by a failing
memory and a weakened understanding, to hold
high and inexpressible fellowship with the Father
of Spirits, without end or interruption!

I rejoice that your dear brother visits him. It is
better to go to the house of mourning than the
house of mirth. There he may see what a miserable estate the admired senator, the renowned politician, would be reduced to, if he was not also the
real Christian! There he may see the preciousness
of the Redeemer; since he will hear, as I have
done from the mouth of that singular man, that it

is not all his deeds of virtue, not all his public patriotism or private benevolence, which can afford him hope or joy, in the review, or in the prospect of approaching eternity—nothing but the promises of God made to the humble believer on His dear Son, and ratified in His blood!

You rejoice me much with the news that Mr. Thornton will pay me a visit here. May he find that God is with us of a truth, and the power of the Lord present to heal! It rejoices my soul whenever I hear that any are brought to Christ, or built up more and more in Him : but to hear this of my friends and benefactors, is the highest pleasure I can receive from others on earth.

Wakefield has been visited, though now not so much, with a fever, little better than a plague. It has carried off, in six weeks, one hundred and sixty souls. It has alarmed the whole neighbourhood, and, I hope, will be made profitable to many souls. Lord, prepare us, that, if a fierce disease is to remove us, sudden death may be sudden glory!

Yours, &c.   H. VENN.

TO MRS. KNIPE.

MY DEAR FRIEND,   *Huddersfield, Feb.* 4, 1762.

You are not less frequently in my thoughts, though I have been but a dilatory correspondent of late, than when I was writing to you more frequently. This you know ; that whilst a spark of grace or gratitude remains, you must have a high place in my regard, and a constant remem-

brance in my prayers.   Great weakness and languor
are the effects of my disorder; and the longer
it continues, the more I must expect it to be thus
with me.   There is one advantage I find, even in
the obstinacy of the complaint, and its resisting
the power of all remedies prescribed by the skilful
in medicine;—it is, that I am by this means less
in danger of trusting in creature-help; and taught
to look with a single eye to Him, who saith to His
Church, "I am the Lord that healeth you," and to
wait His will.   It is a just homage required from
me, a sinful creature, to be paid to the God of
holiness and wisdom, of mercy and of grace.   Our
God exercises His most righteous dominion over
our faculties, wills, and affections.   He first requires the Christian to sacrifice the overweening
opinion he has of his own wisdom and reasoning
to the majesty of His revealed Word, and to believe truths most cordially and steadfastly, which
infinitely surpass his power to conceive clearly.
He next requires that the Christian should part
with the beloved idol of his heart, and, instead of
self-indulgence, crucify the flesh with the affections and lusts.   After obedience is habitually performed in these two grand points, and we have
done the will of God, then comes the last and necessary trial—the furnace of affliction : then He
saith, "Ye have need of patience, that, after ye have
done the will of God, ye might receive the promise."
And it is to be observed, that as the two former
submissions are preparatory to the last, so the last
is exceedingly beneficial to the former, and per-
fective of them.   None ever believe so humbly, and

obey so fruitfully, as those who have suffered patiently. Let it therefore be your prayer, my dear friend, for me, (for I stand in need of it,) that I may with thankfulness endure the afflictive as well as receive the prosperous and pleasing dispensations; and that my practice and deportment may be suitable to my light and knowledge, and the expectations of the Church of God concerning me. This I desire, not as if I despaired of any cure for my disease, but I would desire to be ready, and prepared for all events. If I am not worse, I shall set out the week after Easter: and, perhaps, the journeying will be serviceable.

We have still more cause to rejoice in our work. On Sunday last, our Sacrament was solemn and affecting. Our attention, previously to it, was fixed on Lam. i. 12: it was considered as the most moving complaint of the Great Benefactor to ruined sinners. Our hymn was one of Dr. Watts's, of a piece with the subject; and I trust many were admitted into the Lord's "banqueting-house, and that His banner over them was love"; that many of us " sat down under His shadow with great delight, and His fruit was sweet" unto us. I find, with regard to myself, that the benefit of Prayers, Sacraments, and the Means of Grace, bears exact proportion to the care I take to implore the influence and operation of the Spirit in them; that when I am only a little concerned in asking of the Lord the inestimable comfort of His help, my spiritual duties afford me little comfort in the exercise, and leave no lasting impressions. On the contrary, when I am importunate with the Lord to put life and power in the Ordinances, and to make me feel some correspondent affections, I am enabled to say, " Truly our fellowship is with the Father, and with His Son Jesus Christ."

I am sorry to hear dear Mr. Jones is so ill. It is a hard matter to keep the exact medium—to be, in some resemblance of Elijah, very zealous for our God, and not exert ourselves beyond what the mortal body can bear; or to be regardful of health, without degenerating into laziness. It is certainly the better extreme of the two, to spend and be spent, even to the shortening a little a short life at best, in such a manner as to refute lukewarmness by example, than to live a longer life in a manner not so visibly contrary to it.

I pray our gracious Lord to have you and yours in his safe and holy protection, now and evermore! From your much obliged pastor in Christ,

H. VENN.

TO MRS. KNIPE.

MY DEAR FRIEND,   *Huddersfield, July,* 1762.

THE Sermon* you were so kind as to inclose, gave us a most pleasing account of Mr. Jones's death. Most comfortable and animating are such scenes! In them we see how true the Lord our strength is, and that there is no unrighteousness in Him: we may see what manner of support and consolation He imparts in the dying hour; and that having loved His own which are in the world, He loveth them unto the end. Indeed,

---

* A Sermon by the Rev. W. Romaine, on the death of the Rev. T. Jones, Chaplain of St. Saviour's, Southwark.

as the Apostles were a picture of the Church of
Christ throughout all ages, we may certainly collect
from them how tender and compassionate a Friend
we shall find in our Saviour, when most we need
His presence and love.   During the time He was
with them, He rebuked them often, and sharply;
but when He was going to part from them, affection
breathes in all His discourse.   It is then no longer,
"Where is your faith?"   "Why do ye not understand?" but, "My peace I leave with you; my
peace I give unto you."   "Let not your heart be
troubled.   I go to prepare a place for you; that
where I am, there ye may be also."   In the same
gracious manner He now will and does manifest
Himself, to them that believe in Him, and have
obtained like precious faith with the Apostles.   Let
us not then be afraid to trust Him : let us, in confidence, resign our death to Him.   In this respect,
no less than with regard to the world, we are to be
careful for nothing, but in every thing to cast our
care upon God, knowing that He careth for us.

Since you left us, I have been assaulted in the
dark by two venomous papers—a letter, and a piece
of poetry.   The latter is directed to one of my hearers; and supposed to be written by a believer, exhorting him 'to hold fast his faith ; which is so sure
to save him, that, whatever he does, God will impute
nothing to him : if he does but believe, he may cheat,
oppress, lie—all is still well.'   These are good proofs
they have nothing of real guilt to lay to our charge;
and, whilst they blaspheme and revile, they give us a
noble opportunity of shewing our faith by our works;
even by that work, so impossible to flesh and blood

—blessing them that curse us, and loving those that hate us. Dear Mr. Burnett has met with the same bitter spirit; and the only family that was a great encouragement to him is turned against him. But he can say of the Lord, " Thou art my refuge, my fortress, and my portion; in Him will I trust." I am sure, if our cause were no more invigorating than the religion we oppose is, no one could long continue to minister the Gospel. But it is the power of God unto salvation : it is righteousness, peace, and joy ; and therefore worthy parting with all, for its own sake. May the fulness of the blessings of this Gospel be with you, in your new habitation!

From your much obliged friend and minister in Christ, H. VENN.

Sept. 8, 1762.

——I LATELY paid a visit, in company with Mr. Madan, to Helmsley, and spent four days with our dear friend Mr. Conyers. Immediately upon his receiving us into his house, he broke out into a most fervent thanksgiving unto God, who had sent us to him ; as he had never before received under his roof a faithful Preacher of his dear Crucified Master. We had abundant edification from his discourse. Mr. Madan compares him with Mr. Hervey, in spirit and temper. I think he greatly surpasses even that extraordinary saint, in a peculiar talent for edifying the people ; though he is far inferior in point of learning. Mr. Conyers shines with an amazing lustre, from the bowels of mercy and love that dwell so richly in him towards every one, but much more towards his flock. As

a nurse her children, so does he cherish them;—
as a father his sons, so does he exhort and warn
and comfort them.   In the greatest simplicity, he
accosts them by the most endearing names, and
the most loving appellations.   In proof that I am
not exaggerating in this account, I assure you that
Mr. Madan, myself, Mr. and Mrs. Elmsall, and
Miss Hudson, were all of us melted into tears, and
softened, in a most extraordinary manner.

And now you will grieve with us, to hear that
this our dear fellow-labourer has quite impaired
his constitution by his excessive fatigues in preaching to different congregations, in his most extensive
parish, twenty-one times each week.   Many very
bad symptoms lead us to fear for his life.   May what
we have seen of him abide upon us; and stir us up
to be more zealous for our God!   By seeing what
manner of grace He has to bestow upon them that
diligently seek him, may we never rest short, but
covet earnestly the best gifts.

———

It is worthy of remark, that, notwithstanding the great
extent and extraordinary success of Mr. Venn's ministerial labours at Huddersfield, as recorded in the Memoir,
his letters contain very little mention of the great good
which he was the honoured instrument of effecting.   The
deep and genuine humility of his character, and the high
standard which the love and example of Christ placed before him, led him rather to bewail his short-comings, than
to speak of his success.   But, in another respect, his correspondence affords very striking confirmation of his ministerial zeal and faithfulness: for many pastoral letters

still remain, written to particular members of his flock, during temporary absence from them, which testify how tenderly and vigilantly he watched, in private, over the spiritual progress of those who had derived benefit from his public ministry. I have selected the following eight letters, as specimens of this portion of his correspondence.

The three first letters were written to Miss Hudson, who married, in 1768, the Rev. John Riland, then Curate of Huddersfield, and afterwards, successively, Minister of St. Mary's, Birmingham, and Rector of Sutton Coldfield, Warwickshire. This lady was one of Mr. Venn's most valued and faithful friends and correspondents, as many of the subsequent letters will amply testify.

Mr. Thomas Atkinson, to whom the two next letters were addressed, had left Huddersfield for a few years, to reside in London; and afterwards became an extensive manufacturer at Mold Green, near Huddersfield. He was a man of strong powers of mind, great decision of character, and large benevolence of heart; and exhibited, throughout all his transactions in life, the genuine influence of the Gospel of Christ.

TO MISS HUDSON.

MY DEAR MISS HUDSON,   *Kippax, March* 4, 1763.

SINCE I left you, you have never been out of my thoughts. I remember you going out and coming in, rising up and lying down. I remember you, not barely as a friend, but as one of my flock, and of the seals of my ministry, now particularly needing all consolation.* The only reason

* Miss Hudson had very recently lost a brother, two years older than herself; whose piety and affection were her chief earthly stay in the religious course upon which she had just entered.

of my assuring you I do so, is, that you may judge from hence what manner of love the Father of all spirits must bear towards you : for if I, a corrupted creature, full of such selfish and base dispositions by nature as render me very unfeeling, can thus sympathize with you, what must be the bowels of mercy towards you in that God who has called you by His grace, adopted you for His own child, promised in all your afflictions to relieve you, and overrule them all for your greater good ? But your heart is ready to say, ' How can this be the case, when not only the hand of the Lord has smitten me so sharply, but, under the affliction, I behave not as my conscience tells me I ought? I glorify not God in the midst of the fires.' In answer to this objection, you are sufficiently taught to remember, that the love of God, as a reconciled Father, has ever been manifested most in the trials of His dear children. Behold Job!—a few days strip him of his substance, bereave him of all his children (of whose conversion there was but little hope), and he sees himself full of ulcers, so that he became loathsome to the wife of his bosom : yet this is the man, of all upon the face of the earth, dear to God ; and, because he was so, afflicted in this very remarkable manner. Look upon Aaron, the priest of the Lord, distinguished above all the tribes of Israel (excepting Moses, his brother)—in a moment he loses both his sons, consumed by the hot displeasure of God ! And the time would fail to reckon up the dear and most honoured saints of God, who had the bread of affliction, and the water of affliction, given them to drink. So that

you have not the least shadow of reason to suspect
that you are afflicted through any want of love or
pity in the heart of God towards you; but, on the
contrary, knowing what He declares, to all the
afflicted, in His Word, and especially with respect
to the household of faith, you have much cause to
say, 'Of *very faithfulness*, as a part of the new,
everlasting, ever-blessed covenant, into which I am
brought by the blood of Jesus, God has been
pleased to afflict me!'

But you may grieve, not only for your great
loss—a loss which no one can fully estimate who is
not in your place; but as much, possibly, to find
your soul so much oppressed by it. In this case,
consider also the example of some of the most
eminent and approved saints of God. When His
hand pressed them sore, they expressed all the
same sensibility of their heavy cross as you feel in
your heart, for a season: they made their complaint, and felt the risings of corrupt nature, till,
by prayer, divine succours were supplied from the
Throne of Grace. The chastening was grievous to
them, and in no sense, for the present, joyous;
though afterwards, it yielded to them the peaceable
fruits of righteousness, when they had been exercised thereby. In the Psalms, which contain an invaluable collection of the experience of God's saints
in times of trouble, you will observe (and I beg you
will now read them much) how they are vexed, and
complain of themselves, because they find themselves so very unduly affected by their crosses.
'*Take away the rebuke that I am afraid of*, i. e. for
my impatience, for my self-will, under correction!

for *Thy judgments*, Thy chastisements, are good.'
Though, therefore, it argues much corruption, and
is a great reason for humiliation and self-abhor-
rence, to find that, ignorant worms as we are, we
have in us a disposition to blame the All-wise for
His providence towards us; that, hell-deserving
sinners as we are, we can be prone to say, 'My
grief, if it was now weighed, is heavier than can be
borne'; yet this oppression is not to cast us down,
as if we had not the faith of God's elect and dear
children.

Consider therefore, my dear friend, that neither
is your trial any other than such as is common to
the most beloved of God; neither your manner of
bearing it, though clouds and darkness for a season
rest upon your mind, any thing unusual to the
heirs of glory. May the blessed God, therefore,
the Fountain of all consolation, watch over you
whilst you are in the furnace of affliction, and make
it mighty of operation, to purge away all your dross!
May His presence, grace, love, and power, enrich
your heart so abundantly, that you may, though
sorrowful, yet rejoice in the Lord, and magnify the
God of your salvation! My love to all your afflicted family. I daily remember them at the
Throne of Grace. My wife, who is but poorly,
joins with me in praying for your consolation, and
in wishing you every blessing. I remain your sincere friend and minister, to serve your soul in all
things, for Christ's sake,

H. VENN.

TO MISS HUDSON.

MY DEAR MISS HUDSON, *Kippax, March* 7, 1763.

In my last letter, I endeavoured to lay before you, as considerations peculiarly suited to your present distressed state, the manner in which a most gracious God has been used to deal with His most beloved children, and the manner also in which they expressed their feeling of His afflicting hand. I shall now point out some of those views and purposes for which believers in Christ Jesus are often touched in the most sensible part, and much acquainted with grief.

1st : The first reason is, to wean them from all expectations of happiness from any other quarter than God himself. No words are strong enough to paint the proneness there is, in the very heirs of salvation, to set up resting-places here upon earth. And though they are delivered from the base and sordid love of money, or the poor gratifications which can be gleaned from the honours and pleasures of the world, still they are apt to make Christian friends and relations, idols; and so the strength of their affections, which should centre and settle *all* in God, is by this means very much weakened and divided. Though we discern not this ourselves, nor suspect it, our Divine Physician fully sees the growth of the distemper; and, in love, we are separated from our idols. Disappointments meet us at every turn : where we expected we should be particularly favoured with helps and advantages for godly living, we behold ourselves

left destitute; so that we have no more a place of
refuge upon earth, no more a dear counsellor or
friend who is as our own soul. By this means we
are compelled, as Noah's dove was, by the wide
watery waste, which did not afford a single resting-
place, to fly to the Ark, and to take shelter there.
Our gracious Father, with a loving jealousy over us,
thus secures our whole love to Himself, and appears
altogether glorious in our eyes; as the fountain of
living waters, when the cisterns are broken which
we were hewing out for ourselves.

2dly: It pleases God to afflict very heavily those
who are his dear children by faith in Christ, that they
may more value the choice they have made. When
they see the most innocent, nay, the most laudable,
satisfactions they could possibly propose to themselves from any creature-comfort, all shivered in
pieces, as it were, in a moment, and water of gall
spring up from that very person or thing from which
they promised themselves abundance of joy; in such
a situation, how infinitely desirable a connexion with
Jehovah, never to have an end—a union with Him,
which is as far above all the changes of this mortal
life as heaven is higher than the earth! This must be
apprehended as the chief of all blessings—a portion
of itself sufficient. Then the souls of the faithful are
taught experimentally to say—"Vanity of vanities!
all is vanity," but Christ and His love! "Lord,
to whom shall we go?" from whence expect refresh-
ment and consolation, but from Thyself alone?
"All my fresh springs shall be in Thee!"

3dly: The dear children of God are afflicted in
the most sensible part, in answer to their own

prayers. As our Redeemer said to Zebedee's children, "Ye know not what ye ask! Are ye able to be baptized with the baptism that I am baptized with?" so may it be said of all believers. They all pray that they may be delivered from every accursed thing, and be formed and fashioned according to the will of God in all things. This prayer they put up in the integrity of their souls. It is accepted of God; and He answers it. He brings them into various troubles, that these may work in them patience, and patience experience, and experience hope. He thwarts their own will, where it most vehemently sought to be gratified; and so, at length, moulds them into that self-denying spirit, which is the proper state of a sinner before a God infinitely wise and holy.

4thly: The dear children of God are afflicted in the most sensible manner, that they may know more deeply the evil of sin. Of this evil we have, at best, but very slight conceptions. But when we feel the chastening and correction, knowing, at the same time, it is not the stroke of an enemy, nor the wound of a cruel one, but the very medicine to heal our disease; then we are led to confess, sin must be exceeding sinful, since God never willingly grieves nor afflicts the children of men; since He rebukes for sin, and scourges us for our offences; that, being chastened of the Lord, we may not be condemned with the world; that we may go on our way weeping for a season, and in heaviness, if need be, in order that we may return again with joy, and bring our sheaves with us.

Lastly: All the dear children of God are some

time or other grievously afflicted, that they may be conformed to the image of their Saviour. How sorely afflicted and distressed inwardly was your dear brother, before he entered into glory! And there is not a Scripture saint mentioned, but drank, in some degree, of the cup which Jesus drank of, and was baptized with His baptism of sufferings: so that, were any of the faithful to want chastening, it would be almost sufficient to bring their title to Christ in question.

The God of all grace help my dear friend to ponder these things in her heart, and make them of force, to support her mind from utterly failing! Be of good cheer! for, though afflicted and distressed, remember, your warfare is accomplished, your iniquity is pardoned; you have received double for all your sins—in the abundance of the gift of grace, and of justification unto eternal life, by being brought into the bonds of the everlasting covenant.

My dear wife remembers you in your affliction, as well as I do myself, daily, before the Throne of Grace.

From your sincere friend and pastor in Christ,

H. VENN.

TO MISS HUDSON.

Kensington Gore, July 1, 1763.

MY DEAR MISS HUDSON,

MANY thanks to you for your letter! I had not forgotten you. Not a day passes, but I remember my flock, and you in particular, in the best manner I am able, before the Throne of Grace. Be of good cheer: let not either outward crosses or inward trials cast you down : for know, the Lord sitteth above the water-floods : there is nothing that can ever possibly befal them that have fled for refuge to the Redeemer, but it shall work for good to them.   However appearances may be for a time, all the promises of God, and all the perfections of God, are engaged to succour and to save the weakest believer.   Ponder, my dear Miss Hudson, that character of the child of God, in the 2d verse of the 91st Psalm, and I doubt not you will be enabled to perceive your own picture in it : *I will say of the Lord, Thou art my refuge;* i. e. to Thee have I fled, an accused, self-condemned, accursed creature—to Thee, as manifesting Thyself in Christ Jesus, have I fled for salvation, from the Law, from sin, from my own corruptions ; and still Thou art all my refuge.   *Thou art my fortress :* besieged by the world, by Satan, by my own mighty corruptions, I am kept and defended by Thee alone.   Thou holdest me up, and I am safe : if Thou leavest me but a moment, I must fall into the hands of my enemies.   *Thou art my God.*   In all my former vanities, and in all my former pleasures, I see sin, and I fly from them.   I receive not my happiness, nor seek my portion, in the things of sense and time. Thou, O God ! art my delight : in Thy favour is life; and in close communion with Thee, whenever I partake of it, is my highest enjoyment : my soul seeketh after Thee : when Thou art absent, and hidest Thyself from me, I am troubled.

Such is the experience, and such the feelings, of the faithful in Christ Jesus : and cannot you say, I am a witness, though weak and feeble, of this truth,

and in this picture I behold my own experience?
Hear, then, how precious in the sight of the Lord
thy soul is, and what a complete defence is encom-
passing Thee on every side!

"*Surely*"—it is not a peradventure, but an absolute certainty; as such you are to receive it—in
this confidence you are to use His promise, *Surely
the Lord shall deliver thee from the snare of the fowler*
—from every subtle contrivance and malicious design of Satan: none of his attempts to destroy thee
shall succeed, but be overruled to thy greater good:
—*and from the noisome pestilence ;* though the world
is full of infection, and evil communication, which
will corrupt good manners, abounds on all sides;
though thy heart is always of itself disposed to receive the infection, and thou mayest think it almost
an impossibility to dwell in the world, and not to be
hurt in thy soul by it.—*He shall deliver thee. He
shall cover thee with His feathers :* like the hen, all
alarmed and ever intent to protect her little brood;
communicating warmth from her body to cherish
them, and covering them from every evil she
beholds; so shall the Lord bring thy soul near to
Him, and manifest Himself to thee, and make thee
as sensible He is for thee, and nigh to comfort and
protect, as the chickens are sensible they are under
their mother's care. *And under His wings shalt
thou trust.* He will give thee the power to believe
and depend upon Him. He will create in Thee
more and more affiance, in spite of thy natural unbelief of heart. *His truth,* the word of His grace,
the covenant established from everlasting, respecting all that are in Christ Jesus, this shall fight for

thee, and prevail, like the *shield and buckler* which is turned every way by the soldier, when in battle, to ward off the sword from his body. So will the Lord be jealous for His truth ; and, lest one jot or tittle thereof should fail those that trust in him, He will, at all times, and in all places, defend and save unto the uttermost all His people.

Let me entreat you to pray over this Scripture— pray to have it impressed, applied, and fulfilled in you. Make your complaint against yourself, that you cannot believe these weighty promises : and, in thus doing, by degrees the light of life will more and more manifest itself, and you will find God is all-sufficient.

I am very happy in meeting with many in London who stand fast in the Lord, to whom He was pleased to make me an instrument of good. I preach gene- rally three times every Sabbath. Oh! pray for me, that I may be supplied abundantly with matter, with sound speech, and with love to souls.

Mrs. K. and my sister inquire with affection after you : they wish you much of the power, presence, and comfort of Christ. To Him I commend you, praying He may strengthen you mightily, by His Spirit, in your inward man ; and establish you, so that you may always triumph in Him, as your all- sufficient Redeemer.

From your minister always to serve in Christ,

H. VENN.

TO MR. THOMAS ATKINSON.

MY DEAR FRIEND,   *Huddersfield, Sept.* 6, 1763.

BLESSED be the God and Father of our Lord
Jesus Christ, for His great mercy in opening your
eyes, and undeceiving your foolish heart, which,
through its natural pride, was darkened—darkened
in the midst of religious duties and the profession
of Christianity! Great is the joy I feel on your
account: and, as an older traveller in the same
blessed path in which you are now walking, I will
give you some council, praying our gracious God to
command His blessing on it.

The first thing I would press upon you is, to beg
of God more light. There is not a more false
maxim than this, though common in almost every
mouth, that ' men know enough, if they would but
practise better.' God says, on the contrary, " My
people are destroyed for lack of knowledge." And
as, at first, men live in sin, easy and well pleased,
because they know not what they do, so, after they
are alive and awake, they do little for God, or gain
little victory over sin, through the ignorance that
is in them. They have no comfort, no establishment, no certainty that they are in the right path,
even when they are going to God, because the eyes
of their understanding are so little enlightened to
discern the things that make for their peace. Do you
therefore, my dear Thomas, in all your prayers, call
much upon God for Divine teaching. Insist much
upon the very faint, dim perception you have of the
things you already know. Tell God how little you
see of the evil of sin; how far you still are from

feeling yourself always that corrupt, selfish creature, His word declares you indeed are. Tell the Saviour of that which was lost—what poor, low, unaffecting views you have of His work of obedience, though He was God manifest in the flesh ;—how seldom you can feel your heart happy in the persuasion that your sins were purged away by Himself, and that He now sitteth at the right hand of the Father till your enemies become His footstool, though all Scripture is written to assure you and every believer that this is the very truth. Tell Him how little you know of the excellency, strength, and unconquerableness of the Divine promises. By persevering in such confessions, and asking of the Lord such illumination, you will gradually be filled with all knowledge, and be made wise unto salvation; especially if you make request, as you are always to do, for increasing light, only that you may glorify God in your life and conversation, as you are bound to do. I have one thing only to add more, which is, that you remember, if you are either impatient, or cast down under a sight of your great ignorance in spiritual things, the cause is pride and unbelief of heart : for why should we be impatient for *instant* deliverance from our ignorance, when we deserve most righteously to be left in darkness for evermore ? or why should we be cast down in the view of our ignorance, when Christ promises that all who follow Him shall not *abide* in darkness, but have the light of life abiding in them ?

I had purposed giving you more directions for your comfortable walking with God ; but I shall reserve these for some other epistle ; intending, God

willing, to keep up a correspondence with you, as
you really desire to know God, and be happy in
Him. From your sincere and affectionate friend
and servant in Christ Jesus,

H. VENN.

TO MR. THOMAS ATKINSON.

DEAR SIR,   *Huddersfield, Aug.* 10, 1764.

You will be pleased to hear that the work of
the Lord prospers exceedingly in many souls ; and
we have lately had some happy and triumphant
deaths, which are of great use, in the hands of God,
to awaken, and to convince, and to animate, those
who do already believe.

Mr. Ball you have now with you. May you
make good improvement of such a talent entrusted
to your care ! He is one of those who are described,
in God's word, as burning and shining lights : by
their wisdom, and knowledge of the Truth, they
point out the path of life : and by their love and
zeal they warm our hearts, and stir us up to seek,
as they do.

I hope you read your Bible with much prayer. I
can give you a never-failing receipt, to make a complete Christian and an heir of Glory. You will find
the medicine described in the 19th Psalm, 7—11;
and the method of taking it, Prov. ii. 1—6. By
the use of this medicine and this method, you will
as certainly improve, and grow in grace, as any
sensible diligent boy ever got any knowledge at
school. This is our condemnation ; and, alas ! this
is the real cause of our being so weak in faith, so

cold in our love, so confused in our notions;—the Bible, and prayer over it for the true understanding of it, is not our exercise, our constant employment. Any other means of grace than this, which is yet the most profitable of all, is rather chosen. But, as it is written, the kingdom of Heaven suffereth violence, and the violent take it by force; so in nothing do we offer violence to our evil nature more than in studying God's holy word, and earnestly praying that the Divine truth it teaches may sink deep into our hearts, work mightily, and produce all those gracious effects for which it was of old written by inspiration of the Holy Ghost.

My love to all my dear friends in Christ, who have all of them my daily prayers.

From your very affectionate friend,

H. VENN.

TO A LADY.

DEAR MADAM,   *Huddersfield, Feb.* 5, 1764.

To give instruction to any who are inquiring how they may live to the glory of their God and Saviour, is our professed business, as the ministers of Christ, and our greatest joy on earth. Let this, therefore, plead my excuse for the following lines; which I heartily wish may prove effectual, to increase in you every desire that is acceptable in the sight of God.

I find, Madam, you are conscious of your ignorance in the things of God. For ever blessed be His name, that you are so! The very first step to be wise, in any degree, to the good of the soul, is to lament our blindness, our stupidity, our brutishness,

in knowledge.   Your very lamenting this, is the
grace of God working in a heart naturally too
proud to stoop to any confession of ignorance at
all.   Be of good cheer, Madam, and encourage
yourself in the promises of God.   Read the 25th
Psalm.   There see, with your own eyes, that you
have the word and honour of the God of Heaven
and Earth ; that He is good and gracious to *teach
sinners in the way ;* that, *them that are meek*—
ready to submit, and desirous of being taught, and
willing to comply with all they know—*He will guide
in judgment ;* and *such as are gentle, He will learn
His way.*   Read the 32d Psalm, the last verses :
there your God assures you He will inform and
teach you the way in which you should go ; He
will guide you with his eye, protect your person,
order your steps ; just as you have done, with unspeakable pleasure, your dear little babes', when they
began to walk, and you were afraid of their dashing
their foot against a stone.   Read the 72d Psalm—
the whole speaks of Jesus : it is a public proclama-
tion and call to all sinners who will hear it, that
*He will deliver the poor and needy when he crieth,
and him that hath no helper; He shall spare the poor
and needy, and save the souls of the needy ; He
shall redeem their souls from deceit and violence,
and precious shall their blood be in His sight.*   God
help you to believe these blessed Scriptures ! they
are written for your encouragement.   You are burdened with your own corruptions : you are sore
troubled sometimes, that you can be so cold, so
dead : this is part of the battle you are called to
fight, even to contend against a desperately wicked

heart.   Resist evil shame; and when God has given you light, never put it under a bushel, for fear of being nick-named, or talked over with a sneer. " They that confess me before men, will I confess before my Father"; and, " They that are ashamed of me, of them will I be ashamed"; are words left on record, to counteract our selfish and cowardly hearts.   Christ will comfort the brave soldier that fights for Him, in opposition to self and the world; and vouchsafe him new manifestations of glory. I wish you the enjoyment of great knowledge in the things of God, of great peace in the ways of God, and of a great reward in the kingdom of God. I wish God may be with your offspring; and early give them His grace, that they may be a seed to serve Him, and honourable witnesses for His Truth. I beg my respects to Mr. S.   You may always command my pen, if I can be in the least degree of service to you.   From your very humble servant and well-wisher,

H. VENN.

TO A YOUNG FRIEND.

Huddersfield, Nov. 8, 1768.

SEVERAL things, of late, have put me, my dear Sir, into apprehensions for your spiritual welfare; particularly your absenting yourself from the Lord's Table on Sunday.   I feel for your temptations, and pray for you.   But turn not from the God of all grace: give not up the use of the means of grace, whatever may have been your falls, whatever are the accusations of your conscience, however strong and violent you feel your corruptions.   It is the

cruel suggestion of Satan, which tells you there is
no help for you in your God—that so long as you
have striven, and not yet got the mastery over your
besetting sin, it is in vain to strive any longer : for
in Christ Jesus there is plenteous redemption; and
though He often suffers us to be wounded, and terribly too, yet He will heal—He will deliver the
praying soul—those that are bowed down with the
weight and chains of their sin.   If you, alas! fall
into wilful transgression, sad as the case is, do not
make it worse, by rejecting the only possible remedy.
If you are overcome of presumptuous wickedness,
run to Jesus, with your wounds bleeding, your conscience accusing, and under all the aggravations of
guilt which can possibly attend your fall.   He has
a heart to forgive *all* affronts put upon Him, all the
most heinous provocations, and the most shocking
injuries the devil can tempt poor sinners to commit.

Will you then, my dear young man—in whom I
have taken so much pleasure, as one devoting yourself in the flower of youth to Jesus—will you forsake Him ?   When He is the person injured, and yet
waits to be gracious, will you, the *aggressor*, be
such a foe to yourself, as not to go to Him for pardon?   When He, whom your righteousness cannot
profit, promises to love you freely, and heal your
backslidings, and be a covert to you from the wind
of temptation, will you, who stand in absolute need
of these mercies, keep away?   You will say, I cannot
pray; I am a hypocrite : I cannot lament and weep
for my sin : I feel a love to it, and a desire to commit it with greediness.   Go to Jesus with this confession; repeat it again and again, upon your knees,

or as you walk about : not a soul, among the millions he has saved, but has been in this case : tell
Him the worst you feel ; tell Him it is impossible
for you to resist the devil, and your own desperately
wicked heart, in any strength of your own. Present yourself before Him, as a poor destitute, as a
perishing rebel—as one who, against light and love,
is engaging on the side of the enemies of the Lord.
I have no doubt you will be recovered gloriously—that I, and all the Children of God, and
your dear mother, shall praise His name for His
delivering your captive soul out of the enemy's
hand—if you will call upon Him. I have had,
myself, many a sore and dreadful conflict, before
the time of my redemption came. You will even
receive a blessing from all your falls : God will bring
light out of darkness, and good out of this horrible
evil, if you cry unto Him ; for He will teach you,
by it, what depths of wickedness are in your heart,
how much you need a free and a full salvation to be
given by sovereign grace ; and in a little time you
will be able to say, I am a brand plucked out of the
fire ; I am an enemy to God, saved only through
His good pleasure.

On the contrary, my dear fellow-sinner, put the
case, that, uneasy, and galled with the sight and
sense of your own provocations, you fly from Christ,
you leave off receiving the Sacrament, reading God's
word, and prayer. Alas ! I am ready to weep at the
terrible consequences : sin and Satan must then
necessarily prevail ; conscience will become a sharp
accuser, and haunt you as a ghost ; you will expose
the cause of Christ to shame and reproach amongst

I

His enemies; you will discourage the young people who have begun to run well; you will contribute to keep in their revolt from God those who have, alas! turned back to folly; you will be ashamed of seeing your companions in the good ways of the Lord; you will fear death, and be in a manner forced to fly for refuge—(ah! how different a refuge from the loving Jesus!) to those who are of a seared conscience and of the most profligate life, in order to drown convictions;—which yet you will never be able to do; for this is one part of the righteous punishment immediately inflicted on those who forsake the Lord, after setting their hand to the plough; *they* can never enjoy, as the unawakened, the pleasure of sin, poor and perishing as they are. And at home—what I almost tremble to think of, if you forsake the good path—into what a shocking behaviour will you be betrayed! The mother who bore you, who has prayed for you day and night, who with tears of joy spoke of you to me but a little before her late illness, will be an intolerable reproach to your guilty mind: this will excite in you peevishness and anger, and even hatred and malice, so as to grieve her by hard speeches, and embitter the life of one of the dearest children of God; for the same heart which inclines you to forsake God, and the same enemy that urges you to leave off the use of the means of grace, will lead you on from bad to worse, till who can say what you will not be led to do!

Oh, my dear Sir! the Lord give you understanding to ponder these things—to read what I have offered, in the same spirit of love which made me write it;

and in prayer to God for a blessing upon this endeavour of your minister, who watches for your soul as one that must give an account. I should esteem myself obliged to you, if you would come and converse with me for an hour. I trust God would make it a means of grace to your soul. I am, in much affection, your servant for Christ's sake.

H. Venn.

It pleased God to bless this letter, to the recovery and establishment of the young man.

TO A FRIEND.

DEAR SIR, *Huddersfield, Sept.* 22, 1766.

Your letter, which I received this day, I immediately answer; because I know you will much rejoice to hear that I think the state of your dear sister's mind is still very promising. I see her very frequently; and desire to do so, whilst she is going on. What you mention, of my having left off to go to . . . . ., is true. But I act, I judge, entirely according to my Master's will, in giving myself to reading, to doctrine, to meditation, and, as my strength (which is but small) will bear, to visiting the sick. Where there is a taste and enjoyment of the things of God, I go oftener; but when one person only is to speak, and no answer comes from the company, to prove how pleasing the great topic of discourse is, I plainly see it my duty not to visit. For ministers of the Gospel have another and better employment of their time, than to wait and watch for any particular family, in order to say something that God may please to bless. When I come into the pulpit, it is after study, prayers, and cries for the people : I speak as plainly, and enter into all the cases of the congregation as minutely, as I am able. If, after this, there is a love for the Truth, all my hearers know what delight it is to me to converse with them, and exhort them in private. I do not wonder, my dear Sir, that you feel what you do. Blessed be God for it ! The prayers of a son or a daughter have been, and are constantly, the means of blessing to the whole family. May it be so with yours !

I am glad you tire not in the way. Pray for in-creasing discoveries of the evil of your heart, and of the glorious salvation established in the Covenant of grace. Strange as it sounds, and worse than nonsense, in the ears of a carnal man, yet it is most true, that the happiness of man consists in his humbling views of his own sinfulness; and he enjoys the presence and the love of God deeply in his heart, only in proportion as he feels himself deserving of hell.

My love to all your dear society. May the dew of Heaven be upon you! May your growth in grace be like that of the willows by the water-courses, and every one of you be transplanted to flourish for ever in the courts of the Lord's House!

From your sincere friend,

H. Venn.

The next letter will display, in a signal degree, a distinguishing feature in Mr. Venn's character; namely, his superiority to all worldly considerations, where he judged the honour of Religion to be concerned; and his determination to avoid all appearance of the evil of making a gain of godliness. He had recently formed an intimate friendship with an elderly widow-lady of fortune: she had, in the first instance, applied to him under distress of mind; and, obtaining relief from his advice, became a frequent inmate in his family, and a great admirer of his preaching; and was therefore regarded by others as entirely under his influence. This lady inserted in her will a considerable legacy in favour of her new friend: she had no near relations, who had any claims upon her: and Mr. Venn, in the event of his death, would have left his family almost destitute. Yet, as soon as he heard of her intention, he sent her the following letter.

TO A LADY.

MY VERY DEAR FRIEND,   *Huddersfield, Oct.* 28, 1764.

I understand, by my wife, your most kind and generous intention towards us in your will. The legacy would be exceedingly acceptable; and I can assure you the person from whom it would come would greatly enhance the benefit. I love my sweet children as much as is lawful; and, as I know it would give you pleasure to administer to the comfort of me and mine, I should with greater joy accept of your liberality. But an *insurmountable* bar stands in the way—*the love of Him* to whom we are both indebted, not for a transient benefit, for silver or gold, but for an inheritance incorruptible, undefiled, and that fadeth not away, reserved

in heaven for us. His honour, His cause, is and
must be, dearer to His people, than wife, children,
or life itself. It is the firm resolve of His saints,
" Yea doubtless, and I count all things but loss
for the excellency of the knowledge of Christ Jesus
my Lord." To be therefore a stumbling-block in
the way of any that are seeking after Him—to give
the least countenance to any that would be glad to
bring His followers into contempt, and to call in
question their sincere and disinterested attachment
to Him—would grieve me whilst in health, darken
my mind in sickness, and load me with self-condemnation upon my bed of death. How it would
also render all my exhortations feeble, and make
them accounted only pulpit declamations, if, when
I was pressing that solemn truth upon my people,
" Love not the world, neither the things in the
world," they could say, " Our minister, however,
was careful to secure the favour of his rich prose-
lyte, and at length to gain sufficiently by her"! After
the most mature deliberation, therefore, it is our
request, which we cannot permit you to refuse us,
that you will not leave us any other token of your
regard than something of little value more than
what it derives from the giver. If it should please
God that our connexion should be prolonged some
years, we shall in our hearts still more abundantly
enjoy your friendship, when we are sure that we
are in no danger of being influenced by a regard to
our own interest. And if we must soon have the
cutting affliction of losing you, you may depend on
it we shall not less affectionately make mention of
your name, or call to remembrance your unfeigned

love for us both, in Christ Jesus, than if we had
what the world esteems the only substantial proof
of your regard. As for our children, whom many
will think we have not the love for which we owe
them, by refusing your great favour, I would say
only this—we both know of no inheritance equal to
the blessing of God; and the certain way of se-
curing it, as far as means can avail, is, to be found
ready to lose or suffer any thing, sooner than to
incur the appearance of evil.

Wishing you much strength in your soul under
your great weakness of body, and the abundance of
the revelation of peace and truth amidst your fiery
trials, I conclude myself your most indebted and
affectionate friend and pastor in Christ.

H. VENN.

The lady to whom the last letter was written was too
well convinced of the sincerity of Mr. Venn's character,
and the sacredness of his motives, to evade compliance
with his request; and therefore altered her will, and
bequeathed a favourite watch, instead of the original
pecuniary legacy. She died soon afterwards.

TO MISS WHELER, OF KIPPAX.

Berwick, Shropshire, Nov. 1766.

So sudden was my setting out on this tour, with
Sir Charles Hotham, that I was prevented coming,
dear Madam, to see my sick friends (friends in the
love of Immanuel) at Kippax. My weak state of
lungs, which I still labour under, inclined me to
comply with dear Sir Charles's request. But I

knew not what good things God my Saviour designed in this journey to give unto my soul.

At Brighton, I was fired and encouraged by the example of Lady Huntingdon, and dear Mr. Fletcher, who were there.

At———, I was desired by Mr. ——— (who concluded positively that nothing spiritual could have the least connexion with such a countenance as mine)* to give him a sermon ; which I did, in the afternoon : but, so far from thanking me for the favour, he went away the moment the service was ended : and I never saw him afterwards ; though he told me, as we were walking to church, that he would, after service, take me to drink tea in the Rooms. But I trust the hand of the Lord was in the matter, and some of his children were to receive a benefit.

We next came to a Mr. Townshend's, at Pewsey. That dear minister has a single eye and a warm heart. Three young students are in his house, in order to prepare for the ministry. Here I spoke the word of life to a small church-full, and to a large room-full afterwards ; and though the sphere of action in his parish is small, yet round about there are a great number of souls awakened, and some who know the Lord to be their God.

* Mr. Venn alludes to the following circumstance :—The clergyman who thus offered his pulpit to a stranger, being afterwards rallied by his friends for his incautious offer, replied to this effect : " Who would have thought that such a cheerful, open countenance, as his, could have any connexion with Methodism ?"—This sermon was the means of awakening two persons in the congregation to a serious sense of religion, who became from that time intimate and valuable friends of Mr. Venn.

Our next stage was to Bath, where we heard
Mr. Romaine preach, in that most plain but elegant
chapel of Lady Huntingdon. He was very well
attended on the week-days; but on Sundays the
chapel is crowded. My kind friend Miss Gideon
I had both the pleasure and the grief of seeing
with Mr. and Mrs. Romaine;—the pleasure, because she triumphs in the blood of the Cross, and
is indeed an ornament to her Christian faith; but
it was a grief to see her labouring under a compli-
cation of diseases, and one, among these, the dropsy;
so that Dr. Moisey told me he apprehended there
was great danger of her being soon called hence.
Yet, which of her friends can coolly wish her to
stay? as not only a most infirm, afflicted body prevents the full exercise of her mental powers; but,
even in our best estate of body here, how poor,
how sinful is the soul! We cannot possibly be like
Jesus, till we see Him as He is.

From Bath, through Bristol and Gloucester, we
arrived at Trevecka, in Wales. Howell Harris is
the father of that settlement, and the founder. After
labouring for fifteen years, more violently than any
of the servants of Christ, in this revival, he was so
hurt in body as to be confined to his own house for
seven years. Upon the beginning of this confinement, first one, and then another, whom the Lord
had converted under His word, to the number of
near a hundred, came and desired to live with him,
and that they would work and get their bread. By
this means, near one hundred and twenty, men, women, and children, from very distant parts of Wales,
came and fixed their tents at Trevecka. We were

there three days, and heard their experience, which
they spoke in Welch to Mr. Harris, and he inter-
preted to us.   Of all the people I ever saw, this
society seems to be the most advanced in grace.
They speak as men and women who feel themselves
every moment worthy of eternal punishment, and
infinitely base ; and yet, at the same time, have
such certainty of salvation through the second man,
the Lord from heaven, as is indeed delightful to
behold.   My heart received a blessing from them
and their pastor, which will abide with me.

From Trevecka we came to Berwick, just before
Mrs. Powys received your very kind letter ; for
which she heartily thanks you, and desires me to
tell you, she will herself soon answer it.   Here I
have had great delight in a Mr. Lee, a gentleman of
fortune, above forty years of age, and a man of
uncommon parts.   He is much impressed with a
sense of his own absolutely sinful nature, and that
nothing but the blood of Christ can seal his peace ;
the evidence of which he is seeking after, with much
earnestness.

I have met also with a Mr. Fawcet, a Dissenting
minister at Kidderminster.   He read to me one of
the most delightful accounts I ever heard, of the
pouring out of the Spirit in America, from Long
Island to the very neighbourhood of New Jersey ;
and that, under one sermon of Dr. Findlay, Presi-
dent of that college, near fourscore students in
divinity were wrought upon in so wonderful a
manner, that there is reason to believe the greatest
part are savingly called.   " Ride on, thou Most
Mighty, according to Thy worship and renown " !

I beg my most kind respects to dear Mrs. Medhurst. I trust the Lord will stand by her in the hour of difficulty, and grant the desire of your heart. Pray for me, that I may be fully satisfied to be silent whilst I live, if the Lord is pleased so to appoint. When I can speak only once a week, and not even that without suffering from it, soon my legal heart begins to repine, and suggest, " What do you more than others ? Is not your life an idle and slothful one ?" Oh! that Jesus, to whom I am joined, would put an end to that legality, which tends to darken His glory, love, and salvation!— I conclude myself your very sincere and obliged friend,

H. VENN.

Among Mr. Venn's Correspondents about this period, was a widow-lady of fortune, residing in London, whose friends were generally of a worldly character, and opposed to her strict profession of religion. She had also a son just entering life, of independent fortune, who was, unhappily, averse to the religious views of his mother. The following extracts occur in letters written to this lady.

THE account you give of your reception at R——, and the shyness of former acquaintances, do not surprise me. If you read carefully the 119th Psalm, you will see David was regarded with coolness and estrangement, as well as heartily abused, for his strict piety. You will be unspeakably a

gainer by this. You will be much more at leisure
to dig in the golden mines of Scripture, and meditate thereon, to your great and endless comfort.

I have often thought, that, in the day when the
eternal state of man is to be determined, the
greater part of those that are lost will perish, not
through any gross and scandalous iniquity, but
through a deadness to God and His love, and ignorance of their own sinfulness, and, in consequence
of that, through reigning pride and self-sufficiency.
Now, the one great source of all these miserable
disorders, or that at least by which they are maintained and strengthened, is keeping much company
with those whom the Scripture marks out as engaged in talk without sense—company, not with
near relations or chosen friends; not with those for
whom we have any real or sincere regard; but with
those who come to see us, and we go to see them,
only because the Providence of God has brought
us into one town. It is this that devours infinitely
precious time, and engages us in mere trifling, when
we otherwise should be drawing nigh to God, and
growing rich in Divine knowledge and grace. And
such slaves are we naturally to the love of esteem,
so eagerly desirous of having every one's good
word, that we are content to go on in the circle
of fashionable folly, whilst our hearts condemn us,
and a secret voice, as it were, whispers within, "This
manner of spending time can never be right." How
gracious, therefore, is the constitution of things, that
what we are too much in love with the world to do
for ourselves, the world should do for us; and be so
kind as to lead the way in a separation so salutary

to our souls! The time of persecution, it has been universally agreed, has been a time in which the faithful in Christ Jesus have always flourished most, for this reason;—a thousand hurtful connexions with common acquaintances were then broken off; and the condition of the Christian obliged him to be much with his God, and most wisely employing his precious hours.————

————With regard to your son, you certainly judge right not to restrain him from balls, cards, &c.; since a mother will never be judged, by a son at Mr.————'s age, capable of determining for him: and perhaps, after your most strict injunctions to have done with such sinful vanities, he would be tempted even to violate your authority. The duty you are called of God to exercise now, is, bearing the Cross, borne at different times, and in different measures, by *all* the disciples of a Crucified Saviour. True, it is painful to see one's dear child a lover of pleasure more than of God—painful to see a young creature, born for communion with God and acquaintance with heavenly joys, wedded to trivial gratifications, and the objects of sense alone. But such were we! God prevented us with His goodness, and sounded an alarm in our souls, or we had been such to this hour! He expects, then, that your experience should teach you to wait with patience, till mercy —divine and astonishing mercy—apprehend him also. He expects, that after your continual presenting him every day, as the distressed father did his paralytic son, " Lord, have compassion, and help us!" you should tarry the Lord's leisure, be strong, and comfort your heart, in hope that the day will yet come, when, for your dear and tenderly-beloved son, it shall be sounded in the presence of the Living God, and to the additional transport of angels in glory, " He was dead, and is alive again —was lost, and is found!"

As opportunity offers, you will be ready to represent religion, not as duty, so much as the best pleasure; which, wherever it is in reality, rejoices the heart more than wine, and renders tasteless, in comparison of itself, the whole circle of vain amusements. When you have done this—and, by your own meek, humble, self-denied spirit, exhibited before his eyes the power of godliness—you have done all that possibly lieth in you : and, with acquiescence in God's good pleasure, you are to lie at the door of mercy for your poor son.

There is one thing more, perhaps, that should not be forgot. It is what I purpose doing for my own children, with great seriousness; taking proper times for it. I would advise you, in the most solemn manner, to write a letter, explaining to your son what you mean by real religion, as it is set forth in God's word; the fears and sorrows you have felt, to see him destitute of it; and conclude with earnest entreaties that he would lay this matter to heart, as ever he hopes to be able to stand with you before the Throne of God. This letter I would have you seal up, and write upon it, " To be delivered to Mr. ——, as soon as I am dead." Such an awful call is the most forcible thing we can do for our dear,

unbelieving relations. It is what I design for all my
own, if I depart before them. You see I speak
to you about death, without any fear of startling
you, even about your own death : and though I feel,
should that event come to pass before I am taken
hence, that it would be one of the bitterest days I
ever saw, yet I think it profitable, both for ourselves
and our friends, frequently to anticipate such affecting changes.

As to the Sacrament, it is a point of more difficulty. There is a good deal to be said for his receiving it, on account of the preparation he would
use, which might prove a season of awakening :
and much, on the other hand, against it, as it greatly
sears the conscience to be trifling with and mocking
God in such a solemn ordinance. Suppose, therefore, you were to lay before him the danger of receiving it in a careless spirit ; and then, as he is of
age to judge for himself, let him act as he chooses.

From the whole, you see you are to learn two
most important lessons, from the painful situation
you remain in with respect to your son. The one
is, your own weakness and inability to give a single
ray of light, or excite the faintest conviction of sin,
or communicate the least particle of spiritual good,
to one who is dearer to you than life. How ought
this to take away every proud thought of our own
sufficiency, and keep us earnest, importunate supplicants, at the door of Almighty mercy and free
grace ! The other lesson is, that your own conversion, and reception of the Lord Jesus Christ as
your portion and righteousness, ought to be marvellous in your eyes. You have many kind thoughts

and the highest esteem possible for me; for which I desire to retain a due sense upon my mind: but you know I was merely a voice, which said, " Behold the Lamb of God !" The desire and ability to do so, and that blessed peace you enjoy in consequence of your faith in Jesus, was the *operation of God:* for " who is Paul, and who is Apollos, but ministers by whom ye believe, even as the Lord gave to every man ?" All possible adoration and praise, then, be to God, for His unspeakable gift !

You must take care, dear Madam, that you are not hurt in your own soul by the hypocrisy and evil tempers of great professors in religion. It had like to have proved my eternal ruin, when I was first acquainted with the religious world ; and is daily the cause why many stumble and fall: for contempt of godliness is excited by the deceitfulness and wickedness of those who are accounted godly. Yet it ought not to offend us against religion : for it confirms the truth of the Bible, which speaks of self-deceivers, of false professors, of men that have the form of godliness, and deny the power of it. Why, therefore, should I be staggered, when I see all these things come to pass ? It is designed to make us cease from man, to compel us to walk in close communion with God, and hold us fast by Him. Further, it is designed to stir us up to be jealous over ourselves with a godly jealousy, lest we be found in a delusion, and, with much of religion and of Jesus in our mouths, be strangers to His Spirit, life, and nature.

A further use you may make of the sad discovery, that many have zeal to profess whilst they are

nothing, is, to restrain you from *many* religious acquaintances.   This I am, by experience, convinced
is hurtful to our souls, in two ways.   First, it
accustoms us to prate about religion in a general
way, and about the characters of those who profess
it; because we think we must talk of religion, though
far better laid aside than so used.   Secondly, it robs
us of precious time, and that private communion
with God, in prayer and reading His holy word, for
which conversing with all the saints in heaven,
would they give us their company, can never
make up.——

——With what afflicting thoughts have I again
and again pondered on the sad news you sent me, of
Mr. Hume's Essays being recommended for ——'s
reading.   This is the most effectual method of rendering his conversion a double miracle of God's
grace.   I have read the author, and know what his
horrid diabolical principles lead to.   Alas! is not
the state of man in this world full enough of disappointment, vexation, and various wretchedness, but
he must be made completely miserable, by having
all prospect of a better condition taken from him,
and all hope of future happiness destroyed?   Were
Mr. Hume's scheme true, it were the highest cruelty
to have it generally received.   What refuge would
the needy and oppressed have then to flee unto?
Where could the widow, the orphan, the soul divided
from a friend dear as life, then look for consolation?
In short, think what this earth would be, were the
sun no more to dispense its light and heat!—just

K

such would be the world of mankind, were it generally believed there was no God, who would judge it in righteousness; no heaven for them who love His name. But such men and such writings are sent amongst us as a severe judgment, in the high displeasure of our God, for loving darkness rather than light; and for an empty, formal, hypocritical profession of the faith of our dear Lord, when its power and blessings are set at nought. Give such an impious book as Hume's into the hands of a real and experienced Christian, and he will be no more affected with his deceitful arguments than a man of covetousness is moved, by the cries of the poor, to sell all he has and give it to them. What shall I gain by receiving this man's notions? Nothing; only the sad knowledge that I am as a beast, and to perish like one, perhaps, to-morrow. Oh! what a loss is this to a soul entitled to the true riches! How does this base opinion impoverish and bankrupt the man whose hope is full of glory and honour and immortality!———

———

Mention has been already made, in the Memoir, of the recovery of Mr. Kershaw, of Halifax, from the Socinian error, by a sermon which he heard in Huddersfield Church, when he had gone there with the purpose of turning what he heard into ridicule. The following letter was written to him upon this event.

TO JAMES KERSHAW, ESQ.

Bath, April 2, 1767.

I FEEL myself very much indebted to you, dear Sir, for your favour, which I received yesterday. It brought tears of thankfulness and joy into my eyes, and at the same time humbled me to the dust. To hear the goodness of the Lord bestowed upon you, in the midst of your career of scepticism, and of your being called out of that rational religion (as it is boastingly named) which is the most opposite to vital and saving knowledge, excited my gratitude and praise to God. And your very affectionate acknowledgments to me, as used by the Lord Jesus to be an instrument in your happiness, could not but make me sink down in shame; fully persuaded what I am, and what I deserve. Indeed, Sir, this is my joy—this is the thing that I long for —to see my Saviour's arm prevail—to see the poor, deluded, wretched mind of man brought to solid, rational peace—brought to the knowledge of an all-sufficient Friend, an Almighty Helper; and so to a present enjoyment, the earnest and pledge of heavenly felicity.

The world charges us with enthusiasm: but "we speak that we do know"; we "testify that we have seen." Had we not received the benefit ourselves, we should have little appetite to be set in the pillory, and be bespattered, as we know we are sure to be, for preaching *that Name* which man abhors; because in that Name the glory of God, in all His infinite perfections, is displayed. They call us "mad"; but God distinguishes all the world of unawakened sinners by that very appellation.

K 2

"Madness," he says, "is in their heart." "When he
came to himself, he said, I will arise, &c." The truth
is, were not the life of a Christian, in its form as well
as in its principles, mysterious and despicable to all
who are not Christians indeed, the Bible must be a
book of falsehood ; because it always describes this
life to be a very singular, strange, and absurd one, in
the eyes of men. But with what great injustice does
it appear such ? The life of a Christian is a life of
pleasing admiration of the wonderful love of an
Incarnate God, to miserable, hell-deserving crimi-
nals ; a life of confidence in His unutterable, all-
sufficient friendship ; a life of actual enjoyment of
His pardoning grace, by which sinful lusting after
other things is quenched, and a sweet moderation
in the use and fruition of every creature-comfort
becomes the stated temper of the heart. The life
of a Christian is a life of increasing attainments in
a science which is all practical, all transforming ;
which at once humbles and exalts ; gives God the
full honour of His sovereignty, jealousy, holiness,
and justice upon the despisers of His Majesty ;
yet gives also the sinner the full comfort and
triumph that God's mercy, goodness, and grace
can inspire. The Christian's life is a life spent in
a holy contention against sin, as vile, detestable, de-
vilish; but, engaged in obedience, inward, spiritual,
and universal, as well as outward obedience, flowing from the knowledge of Christ and the love of
Christ, in kind the very same as that which saints
in glory offer up :—they without spot ; whilst the
Christian is here imperfect still, and polluted. A
Christian life is habitually employed in contem-

plation, and in discourse, on the grandest subject
the mind shall ever, through all eternity, be con-
versant with—the power, the glory, the mightiness of the Kingdom of God, is the subject, ever
charming and new. The Christian life is a life inoffensive in the tenor of it, to all around; not only
inoffensive, but useful and beneficial : it is the life
of a mild and loving husband or wife; of a meek,
compassionate master ; of a dutiful, obedient child;
of a faithful, honest servant; of a valuable, trusty
friend; of a benevolent, compassionate member of
society; of a companion, whose conversation is so
far from being impure and frivolous, that it is instructive, animating, and pleasing to every creature
that is alive to the feelings of eternity. The Christian life is a life of very frequent delight in devotional exercises; yet, after all, a life of self-abasement and self-lothing, for defilement, for irregularity
of desire or temper, in any degree : this prevails,
and crowns the excellency of the whole.

Now, my dear friend, if this life is madness, what
is a life of reason ? If any thing more than this is
charged upon us as our practice and doctrine, it is
absolutely groundless. If any other principles than
the experimental knowledge of our fall, the nature
and end of the Law, the Godhead of Christ, justification by faith only, the Spirit's influence and fellowship, such as the Apostles had with our Saviour—if
any other principles than these exploded and despised ones can produce *such a life,* I will embrace
them. If all other systems can do nothing of this
kind, neither make men holy nor happy—down with
them—down with them, even to the ground !

I cannot express the pleasure I feel at your being now willing to be vile and reproached for Jesus—in your being made willing to appear " a fool," for His sake, whom the world derided to His face, and then murdered as a liar and a blasphemer. Let others send their congratulations, when estates are left, and riches increase—the glittering bane of man : I bless my God and Saviour that I can salute you, as entered into the fold of Christ, to be taught, and defended, and strengthened, and comforted all your days on earth ; and then, face to face, to behold your Benefactor with gratitude exquisitely delicious, and see His person, and feel His love—beyond all imagination glorious!

I have been enabled to speak of our Jesus here, to the astonishment of the rich and noble. They have behaved with remarkable attention ; and, by the numbers increasing, I trust the Lord will make himself known by this "foolishness of preaching," as he did of old. God willing, I set my face towards Yorkshire on Monday. May I see you, to our mutual edification!

From your affectionate friend,

and servant in the Gospel,

H. VENN.

In August 1767, Mrs. Venn was seized with an alarming illness, which, in the course of a fortnight, terminated in her death. Mr. Venn was at a distance from home when he received the first intelligence of her danger. The following letter from Mrs. Venn will afford an affecting and pleasing evidence of her piety and resignation.

MY DEAREST EARTHLY LOVE,

I think my own hand will less surprise you than any one's else, informing you that I am not quite well, but better than I was last night. Remember, my dear, He doeth all things well. I feel it to be so at this present moment. I trust this loving Father will still give us another meeting here below : if not, you know we have often surrendered ourselves and each other to His all-wise disposal; and He cannot but do right. I feel His love to me at this time, though faintly, through the earthly clogs to which my flesh cleaves fast.

I am kept very still. Mr. S. sat up with me all night; and Dr. A. has just left me; and both give me very good encouragement : so, my dear, do not be unhappy; nor, I beg of you, if you love me, do not travel faster than your health will permit; and may the God of peace and consolation accompany you! I can never praise Him enough for His goodness to me at this time—to me, the very vilest of those who have fallen from Him. I will get Mr. Riland to write to Mrs. Knipe; and I will direct this to Mr. Gambier's, that, wherever you are, you may soon know the worst. I assure you I write the worst, to prepare you, should things be bad; and to increase your thankfulness, should we meet with joy, which I hope will be granted us. I cannot well write longer, as I only lean on one elbow in the bed. May our God preserve us both, by His covenant of everlasting love!—so prays your affectionate Syphe, for herself and the very best of husbands. E. VENN.

The following particulars are extracted from a brief statement, in Mr. Venn's own hand-writing :—

On the 5th of September, when some alarming symptoms appeared, she told me, " I am ready; I am willing to depart; so clear a view have I of my Saviour!" On Tuesday the 8th, when the fever raged, she laid her hand upon the head of her most dear friend, Miss Hudson, saying, " Oh that I could take you up with me to everlasting rest!" Upon my dearest friend, Mr. Riland, asking her whether she could not still bless God, she answered, smiling, " Oh! now is the time for Him to bless me!" meaning, her disease bore down the activity of her mind, and rendered her entirely passive to receive the comforts of His love. Two days before her departure, she desired we would not pray for her recovery, but for some mitigation of her pain, and for an easy passage to her Lord. This request was fully answered; for though her pain increased, till she once said, " I think it is greater than I can bear," yet the very last words she uttered were— " Oh the joy! Oh the delight!"

I was in much pain after I knew we must part, from the fear of what she might suffer in the agonies of death. But, in the midst of judgment, upon me a sinful man, my God remembered mercy: for she appeared insensible from six in the morning till a quarter past two in the afternoon, on the 11th of September 1767; when only drawing in her breath twice, somewhat longer than usual, her spirit took its flight, and left me suffering, under an affliction, which nothing but the presence and love of Jesus, and the clear evidence of her being with Him, could make supportable.

In the following letter, Mr. Venn announces the event to one of his most intimate and attached friends.

TO MRS. MEDHURST.

DEAR MADAM,   *Huddersfield, Sept.* 11, 1767.

Plead for me with our God and Saviour! He has made me very desolate : this day I am become a widower, and have lost as much as could be lost in the name of wife and mother. She testified how true the Lord, her strength, was; and spoke good of His name; and of her readiness and willingness to depart, having seen His great salvation. I know of no one she will greet with greater joy, in Immanuel's land, than Mrs. Medhurst and her sister. Jesus, hold me by thy right hand, till I reach the same blessed haven!—I remain yours, in much affliction,

                                            H. VENN.

TO MRS. MEDHURST.

Huddersfield, Sept. 14, 1767.

MAY my Master, dear Madam, reward a thousand-fold your kind and tender pity for me! What am I, that you should so load me with your unfeigned regards of Christian love and desire that my bleeding wounds may be healed? I can speak good, even now, of my Master's name. I have as certain a view of my wife's glory as if it was a vision. But I must not expect such an amazing support will last long.   If it please Jesus, my God, be it so!   My God, in Gethsemane, and on the Cross, will at once silence and support my helpless soul.

A thousand thanks for your invitation to come to Kippax!   The Divine order is, for the afflicted to sit alone, and keep silence; because He hath borne it upon him.   Mr. Riland weeps for me; and is a blessing, more than I could have conceived, to my wounded heart.   From your greatly indebted,

H. VENN.

TO MRS. MEDHURST.

DEAR MADAM,   *Huddersfield, Oct.* 9, 1767.

Though I make no doubt you have heard of the loving-kindness of my God and Saviour to me, in the midst of his correction; yet I am sure your sympathizing heart will rejoice in hearing that the power of Jesus is displayed as it is towards so sinful a man as I am.

It is said of Israel, returned from Babylon, "When the Lord turned our captivity, then were we like to them that dream." But that one who has lost the wisest counsellor, the ablest guide of his family, the most pleasing companion, the most affectionate wife—lost her, when all that, as a Christian minister, I ought most to love was increasing in her; when her experimental knowledge of the salvation of God had opened her mouth to speak so charmingly of His name; when her children just began to be struck with her excellence;—that in such circumstances as these I should be for joy as one that dreams, is amazing indeed to myself, and must seem absolutely incredible to the world! and had I not precedents and examples of the same rich grace, I should be ready to say, even whilst all my blessed wife's excellencies, and all her love for me, are indelibly impressed on my heart, that I had not a just affection for her.

But when I read the account of a Mr. Tennant, in New England, preaching at the grave of a much-beloved wife—of Mr. Shaw, a minister of the last age, in Leicestershire, who has described his feelings at the time he was committing two most dear children to a grave which he was forced himself to dig in his own garden (they dying of the plague), and hear him say, he desires to leave it upon record, that God is All-sufficient, even at such an hour as that, and in the midst of so great a calamity—when I consider these things, I can only wonder that such grace should ever be conferred on one who has sinned, and does sin, every breath he draws!

My happiness springs from such an evidence of my wife being in glory, as amounts almost to sight; so that I can engage in no religious exercise, but she is, as it were, an additional spur, to engage in it with all my might.

I feel my debt to my God enlarged in all His favours towards that other part of myself. I with gratitude adore Him, for the precious loan of so dear a child of His, for ten years and four months, to be my wife. I think over, with much delight, the many tokens of love from God during the time of her pilgrimage, and the consolations which refreshed and rejoiced her soul upon the bed of death.

I consider her as delivered from the evil to come ;
and in the possession of all I have been begging of
God for her, ever since we knew each other. Every
degree of peace, of light, of joy, I feel in Jesus
immediately suggests the infinitely-exalted sensations of the same kind which enrapture her spirit.
And, above all, I have now to praise my Master,
that I have an experimental proof that He giveth
songs in the night ; that when dearest comforts are
taken away, the light of His countenance, a little
brighter view of His great salvation, a little stronger
feeling of the tenderness of His heart, is more than
a recompence for every loss we can sustain. I can
now say, from proof, " Our light affliction, which
is but for a moment, worketh for us a far more
exceeding and eternal weight of glory; while we
look not at the things which are seen, but at the
things which are not seen : for the things which are
seen are temporal, but the things which are not
seen are eternal." I am not certain, dear Madam,
whether I sent you an account of the grace, mercy,
and peace, which was bestowed on my blessed
wife. If I have not, I will, upon hearing from you.

I beg my Christian love to Mr. M——and all the
family. From your obliged, afflicted, yet rejoicing
friend,   H. VENN.

TO MISS WHELER.

Huddersfield, Oct. 13, 1767.

——SINCE the moment she left me, I can
compare my sense of her being with the Lord to
nothing but vision ; it is so clear, so constant, so
delightful! At the same time, the Lord gives me to

see His own infinite beauty, and to feel more and
more His preciousness, as a fountain of living waters to those who are bereft of earthly joys. And
well it is that I am so supported! For His own
cause, I cannot but conclude, the Lord does it;
since immediately upon my unspeakable loss, the
opposers cried out, " Ah! now you will see what
will become of his vauntings, of the power of faith,
and the name of Jesus!" They knew our great
happiness; and they said, " You will see your Vicar
just like any one of us in the same situation!"
But my God heard and answered; so that, when
I was mightily helped by Him to preach, the very
Sabbath after her death, and not many hours after
her interment*, their mouths were stopped; and
the little flock of Jesus, who had been praying for me
with all favour and affection, say they have not had
so great a blessing since I have been among them.

Your dear sister, Mrs. Medhurst, was most exceedingly kind in her letter to me; and invited me,
with some of my dear children, to Kippax: but
I am now more closely confined to my home; for, as
there is no one to take care of my children out of
love, I am myself called of God, in this providence,
to be the more attentive to them.

Our church is indeed a Bethel to me! The last
Lord's Day but one I had the sweetest communion
with my blessed wife—I, beholding by faith the Lamb,
before whose throne she was worshipping, seeing

* Mrs. Venn was interred on Saturday night, by torch-light.
Mr. Burnett preached in the church during the service. Mr.
Venn's text, the next morning, was: " Let me die the death of the
righteous; and let my last end be like his!"

Him as He is—I, surrounded with poor sinners like myself; she, with the spirits of the Just made perfect—I, in sure and certain hope of arriving at that inconceivable bliss; she, in the actual fruition of it!—

H. VENN.

TO MRS. MEDHURST.

DEAR MADAM, *Huddersfield, Oct. 20, 1767.*

I am extremely obliged to you for your letter, this day received: and it is scarce possible, I hope, for me ever to doubt your Christian affection towards me, though I should never have the pleasure of a line from you again. I am sorry it was your infirm state of health which prevented your writing; but the heirs of the kingdom must be conformed to their suffering, crucified God. Our own troubles enable us much better to conceive what love burned in that heart, towards our sinful souls, when nailed to the Cross for their salvation. A sword went through my heart, when my blessed wife was lying in the scorching fever; and I then felt what it cost to redeem my soul, more sensibly than ever!

It would give me great pleasure to visit Kippax; and when I may, I shall certainly take the opportunity. But our Leader and Commander fixes our places, in His infinite love; and my post is now, after the best manner He shall enable a poor, ignorant, and helpless man, to supply to my dear babes the want of a most tender mother. A peculiar blessing is vouchsafed to all under this roof, since the dearest person to God in it has been received into glory. My two maids* are, in all appearance, now in earnest seeking the Lord; and our family worship is sweet indeed: so that I can leave my home but very seldom. The hand of the Lord is also much, in mercy, laid upon many in the parish; so that, had I strength, I should be speaking from morning to night to precious souls, who are coming to me and dear Mr. Riland.———

TO MRS. MEDHURST.

Huddersfield, Feb. 21, 1768.

You will easily believe I had much pleasure in the prospect of spending two or three days at Kippax; a place always pleasing to me; but now still more so, as the circumstance of the truly cordial friendship in Christ, with which my beloved wife was always there received, will bring strongly to my mind her past delights in that very scene: and though it may appear strange that I should be pleased with what would be reckoned only to embitter my loss, it is still true; for, feeling such a glorious certainty she is with her Incarnate-God, I take a double pleasure in the places where I have formerly been with her, and seen her soul aspiring to Him; and in the company that still increased those aspirings in her breast. You will believe me, therefore, when I tell you, after I had ridden eight miles on my way

* One of these servants was *Ruth Clark*, who, from this time, became truly pious, and maintained to the last a most exemplary and consistent character. She continued in Mr. Venn's service to his death, and was supported by the family for the remainder of her days. A Memoir of her has been lately published, entitled, "The Single Talent Well Employed; or, The History of Ruth Clark." pp. 23. *Hatchards.*

to you, I was turned back by a consideration which then first darted into my mind. It was this—lest, the weight of the whole duty lying on dear Mr. Riland, it should bring on a relapse of his very alarming attack. Immediately, the uneasiness I felt, and the self-condemnation I should suffer, and the appearance it might have of unkindness in leaving him too soon alone, all crowded into my mind; and I could no way be satisfied, but by being with him. I determined, therefore, (God willing) to postpone my visit to you a little longer; when absence from home, on a Sabbath-day, will in no degree endanger the health of one so justly dear to the parish and to myself, both for indefatigable labour and a most truly-Christian example.

I beg my best respects to Mr. M. and all the family. Sometimes with fervency, though never in that degree I owe it to my dear Christian friends, it is given me to remember them at the Throne of Grace; to make mention of their chief connexions, and the dear parts of themselves, the chief of earthly comforts. It is one of the many striking things in that dark book, the " Serious Call," the wishing to be a righteous man, with this view—to have an interest with our beloved friends at the Throne of Grace.

Since I wrote by dear Mr. B., I have paid a most affecting visit. I saw youth, beauty, good sense, and engaging manners, all hastening to the grave, at nineteen; and my heart has been pained, to speak so very plainly as, in faithfulness to the dear young lady, I am compelled to do. But I trust I shall have my reward. Her conscience seems now to be awakened; and her delight is, to have me visit her. I would beg my believing friends to help me by their prayers, that our words may be given us by the Great Master of the Assemblies, and we may speak thunder till the evil of sin is owned, and then pour balm into the bleeding wound.

I remain, dear Madam, your friend and servant in our Immanuel.   H. VENN.

TO JAMES KERSHAW, ESQ.

DEAR SIR,   *Helmsley, June* 11, 1768.

I took my children to see Harewood House : but how little, how despicable is the superb mansion, and all that pomp can procure, if the Builder of all Things is Himself unknown ! My children were much pleased with the great man's toy ; whilst Mr. Marshall and myself could unfeignedly thank the Lord, who had been pleased to provide so much better things for us. Our Inheritance, and our Mansion, improve in beauty and in value, upon each repeated survey ; and the closer it is made, the more cause we see to prize it.

We all arrived safe at York; and with much prayer, in great concern for my dear child, I carried her to school;—there to hear the language of the world; and to feel, alas! the dreadful passions of her own heart, the passions of her fellows, and to be a witness to the follies of those who live in ignorance of man's true and only felicity.

In this place*, where I now am, the Lord Jesus

* The Rev. Dr. Conyers was at this time Vicar of Helmsley.

L

has a Church; and many souls, who were lost and
dead, have been called, by Sovereign Grace, to partake of eternal life, in the precious Saviour.

With great pleasure, I observed you took time
for sacred retirement, at Park Gate. It has long
appeared to me absolutely needful to appropriate
more time than usual to prayer and meditation,
when we are visiting our friends: by this means
we shall be better enabled to edify them by our
conversation; and they will feel an unction in our
discourse, in proportion as our own hearts are
affected with the things of God. Indeed, this is
one particular, distinguishing a child of God from
others, that, in all his visits, his earnest aim is to
do good, and to receive it; to be careful, that as
each fleeting day carries up its report concerning
us, which is registered in the book of God, it may
be an evidence of the grace of God given to us.

With prayer, my dear friend, self-denial must be
added. It is incredible what advantage I have frequently received from omitting my usual repast, and
occasionally taking an opportunity for a more solemn
pause, and a more clear inspection into my provocations and corruptions, my dangers and enemies, my
mercies and blessings! They wholly mistake the
matter, who suppose we have nothing to do, because
all is done that saves the soul: on the contrary, he
that is born of God is enlisted—enlisted to be a
warrior against himself, as well as Satan. This new
life exercises itself in acts suitable to its own Divine
nature and perfections. And though the 'new lights'
will pronounce it absolute nonsense to affirm, that
the man who knows he shall never perish will take

most pains in subduing his passions, yet the fact is certain, and visible in the children of God. May you and dear Mrs. K. ever prove such riddles to men of the world, and be fools for Christ, in their eyes!

H. VENN.

———

In the autumn of this year (1768), Miss Hudson was married to the Rev. John Riland. The newly-married couple resided with Mr. Venn, in the Vicarage, as Mr. Riland had been accustomed to do before his marriage. By this arrangement, Mr. Venn's young family received the benefit of a most affectionate superintendence, which repaired, as far as possible, their mother's loss: and as Mr. Venn's health, which had become very precarious, required a change of air and scene, he was able to leave home with greater comfort than he could otherwise have done. Accordingly, in March 1769, he paid a visit to London; and, at the request of Mr. Thornton, who was High Sheriff for the county of Surrey, he preached the Assize Sermon at Kingston, which was afterwards published.

The following extracts are taken from letters written to Mrs. Riland during his absence.

———

London, March 7, 1769.

I HAVE been prevented from writing sooner than to-day : but this advantage arises from the inconvenience—I can now desire you, and my dear brother Riland, to return thanks to our kind and gracious Father, for giving us a very prosperous journey to this place. At Rotherham we were received with

Christian love, at Mr. Walker's house. At Olney,
Mr. Cowper, that astonishing instance of grace, and
Mrs. Unwin, as well as Mr. and Mrs. Newton, received us with great kindness. We arrived there
on Saturday evening. But how different the church,
from favoured, dear Huddersfield!—not so many
hearers in the morning as we have at our Sacraments! and at that ordinance how very few! and no
singing with a loud voice. Will not my dear friend
say, I was careful, when she hears I did nothing
till the evening, the third time of assembling on
that day in the House of God? and then I preached
only forty-four minutes. My subject was, 'Looking
on Jesus, and Him pierced:' Zech. xii. 10. There
was a very deep attention; and, towards the close,
I spoke much on the necessity of a triumphant
looking upon Him. It occasioned a good deal of
conversation between Mr. Newton and myself; and
I trust it was made useful.*

* The mention of a visit to Olney will naturally introduce the
following striking tribute to Mr. Venn, from the pen of Cowper;
conveyed in a letter to Mr. Newton, written in 1791.

" I am sorry that Mr. Venn's labours below are so near to a
conclusion. I have seen few men whom I could have loved
more, had opportunity been given me to know him better: so at
least I have thought, as often as I have seen him. But when I
saw him last, which is some years since, he appeared so much
broken, that I could not have imagined he would have lasted half
so long. Were I capable of *envying*, in the strict sense of the
word, a good man, I should envy him and Mr. Berridge and yourself, who have spent, and, while they last, will continue to spend,
your lives in the service of the only Master worth serving;
labouring always for the souls of men, and not to tickle their ears,
as I do. But this I can say—God knows how much rather I would
be the obscure tenant of a lath-and-plaster cottage, with a lively
sense

Cease not to pray for me, my dear friend, that, every day I am absent from my own flock, I may be of signal service to those with whom I converse.

March 21.

THE Lord has answered thus far our prayers. He has given me liberty to preach in His name; and His children have been made to rejoice in His word, preached by a sinful man. My subject at the Lock was, " The Lord loveth and nourisheth the Church, &c." In my sermon, I told them, after my manner, the following story of a widow woman at Olney, with whom I conversed on my journey to town. She thus expressed her desire to die : " I often go into the church-yard, and walk round my Father's house, and cast many a wistful look at it. I see one and another called home ; and I say, ' My dear Father! when shall my turn come ? ' "— The good Lord give us all this faith, and increase it more and more!

Last Friday, after I had preached the preceding day at the Assizes, I took a solemn, but a most pleasing and profitable ride : it was about sixteen miles, all in the neighbourhood of my native village (Barnes). Here I saw and felt that " all flesh is grass, and all the goodliness thereof as the flower of the field." Here I saw one generation after another cut off, and only two or three of my old acquaintances surviving long after their contemporaries. Here,

sense of my interest in a Redeemer, than the most admired object of public notice without it."—*Private Correspondence of William Cowper, Esq., by John Johnson,* LL.D. vol. ii. p. 261.

also, in one part of my ride, I traced the most pleasing walks I took, fourteen years since, and more, with my dear glorified wife: and, what with the extreme richness and beauty of the country, the balmy air, and reviving sunshine, I had a lively idea of that blessed world, of which she has been now an inhabitant for more than eighteen months. In the midst of all my thoughts, you and yours were warmly remembered. Oh, that I could feel a becoming love for you both, and worthily adore that precious Saviour, in whom we are one in heart and mind!

Be sure you thank God in my behalf, for all the tender care He has taken of me, and for all the tokens of love which He shews me. May they be multiplied in me, and in you, and my dear brother! And when I return, may your heart feel that I am made a blessed instrument of God, to build you up in your most holy faith!

March 28.

———THE time of my returning, I long for ; and will do all that lies in my power to hasten it; for I love my home better than any other place, whilst I have such friends there. But I am so much engaged in visiting a condemned man, twelve miles from London, that I fear I shall not be able to leave London before the end of three weeks. I think it long ; but my friends are so kind, and make so much of my company, that I cannot refuse them. The man condemned is a son of godly parents in Ireland, yet a most notorious offender.

He is chained to the floor, whilst I am preaching to him. A sense of his guilt is come upon him ; but he says his heart is hardened, and he cannot pray. I hope the Saviour, who alone can take away the heart of stone, and give the heart of flesh, will have mercy upon him, ere he is called to the bar of Judgment! I am going down to-morrow, to stay two days with him. Oh that *my* hard heart may be softened! Oh, that I may weep for him, and be heard in the very pouring out of my soul for his salvation!——

April 1.

——I HAVE returned from visiting the condemned prisoner; with whom I was a good deal; and preached one evening in the jail to a small company, on those blessed words, "The Son of Man is come to seek and to save that which was lost." The poor man seemed to have a glimpse of that Blessed Redeemer, and His ability and willingness to save them; so that his heart began to feel a hope he never knew before : so certain is it, that the preaching of Christ Crucified is the power of God unto salvation!——

April 8.

——I STILL continue well, and have many pulpits opened to me ; and I believe I could preach charity-sermons every Sunday, were I to stay here this half year. I am frequently delighted with seeing my spiritual children. Last night particularly, after service, I saw the hair-dresser whom I used

to employ seventeen years since. He was then
a country lad; and I used to talk much to him.
He told me, with tears, that, by Sovereign Grace, he
still lived near the Fountain of all life and salvation.
—Immediately after he had done, a lady said to me,
" You, Sir, are my spiritual father." Oh, what an
honour, an unspeakable privilege!—enough to humble me, a sinful man, to the dust!—enough to over-
whelm my soul with never-ceasing astonishment!
—enough to make me flame with the fire of love
and zeal for Christ, to spend and be spent for Him!
Sometimes I feel thus rightly affected; and the
feeling has indeed much of Heaven in it; but corruption and unbelief again work, and all that fine
sensation is gone.——

April 14.

——I HAVE this morning left Mr. Thornton.
Oh, that God would make me, in my sphere, and
my dear friend, and every one of us who dwell
together, such trees of righteousness as he is!
Indeed, his humility can be only equalled by his
bounty, and by his watchfulness and diligent use of
the means of grace.

Thus, by coming at times to be a week or two
with my friends, the cement of friendship is maintained.——

April 18.

——I HAVE more pleasure in writing this letter
than in any one I have sent you since I left home;
because I can now fix the day when, God willing,

I shall leave the life of hurry and noise I am now in, to retreat to my peaceable highly-favoured home, where my two friends will receive me with joy, and gratitude to God for all His mercies to a sinful worm.

I have not been idle. I have been too much pressed to refuse; and, on the whole, I have preached twenty times, during eight weeks, to crowded churches; and, I think, with more boldness, delight, and power, than I have ever done before. The last Sermon, on Sunday, has been made of use to Mrs. ——; so that, though I have often wished to be at home, I have much cause to bless God for my journey. What has most pleased me, is, to find how many spiritual children, of whom I knew nothing, the Lord has given me in this city. One young man, for whom I wrote out a prayer when he was twelve years old, did, he told me, from that time set out in earnest.

Last Sunday morning I preached a charity-sermon in one of the largest churches in London. The curate so hated my name, that he left the church, and there was no one to read the prayers: after making the congregation wait, I was obliged to read them myself. In the congregation I saw two young men from Huddersfield, who had run away from their homes. I took occasion to tell the congregation, that I knew there were present two unhappy people, self-deceivers concerning the doctrine of Grace.——

TO JAMES KERSHAW, ESQ

Huddersfield, July 8, 1769.

I ESTEEM myself much obliged to you, my affectionate friend, for the good news of your safe arrival in London, and the grace of our God manifested to your precious soul, under all the trials you are constantly to meet with from without and from within. The more experience we have of both, the more rational, and indeed necessary, appears to me the glorious doctrine of assurance, founded upon the work and covenant—the one performed, and the other ratified, in God our Saviour.

I was glad you spoke for our dear Almighty Friend, in the coach. To see the boldness of the agents of Satan, and the timidity of the soldiers of Christ, is affecting indeed! Yet how much condemnation have I in my own mind, on that account!—not that prudence is to be discarded in this matter. "Speak not in the ears of a fool, lest he despise the wisdom of thy words," is a necessary caution; yet we are apt oftener to err on the other side. In short, in this case, as well as in others, we stand in continual need of that guidance and unerring direction promised to us: and by daily prayer for the Holy Ghost, He will guide us in that path which, as Mr. Hart expresses it, "the vulture's eye hath not seen." This I have always found—that when I have lifted up my soul to God, to be made useful, wherever I have been going, I seldom or never came away without the answer to my prayer. I had a remarkable instance of this, the other day, in a visit paid to Mrs. Ramsden; whose grief for her loss is, indeed, afflicting to behold! The whole company at dinner was, this Lady, the Marchioness of Rockingham, and her two other daughters. When I came away, I could scarce believe I had near two hours' talk, upon the grand, adorable object.

Oh, pray for me! and I will endeavour to return the favour—that every morning I may rise with an active and steady purpose to be doing something for God, as the miser rises with the design to get more gain each day.

———

In the October of this year, Mr. Venn engaged to preach, for a few Sundays, at the chapel, at Bath, belonging to Lady Huntingdon. At this time, there were only a few chapels under her ladyship's patronage; and they were served by ministers of the Church of England: for it was not generally understood how far the privilege of a Peeress extended. A trial which took place in the Consistorial Court of London, about ten years after this date, respecting Lady Huntingdon's Chapel in Spa Fields, first decided their character, as dissenting places of worship.

The following are extracts from letters written to Mrs. Riland, during his absence.

St. Alban's, Oct. 13, 1769.

FROM Sheffield I rode to Chatsworth, where I slept, and set off the next morning at six o'clock. When I arrived at the top of the hill, I saw a deep valley, full of mist, into which I was to descend— a lively representation of that state in which we lie by nature; and the sun appeared as pale as the moon, and not at all equal in appearance to the mighty work of dispelling so gross a mist : but, in about an hour, the glorious luminary scattered it all, and at once delighted and warmed me by its beams, giving me a very lively idea of the Sun of Righteousness rising with healing in His wings on the sinner's soul; such as you and I, my dear friend, have, through rich and sovereign grace, experienced. Happy day, when Jesus, the light of life, revealed His glory to us!

At Northampton, no Mr. Madan ; so that I fear he is ill. I know what it is to suffer more, long after the blow has been given, than immediately upon feeling it : probably he is now suffering anguish of spirit for his departed Isaac. From Northampton I came hither; and my dear friend Mr. Clarke, of Chesham Boyce, is sitting by me. Had it not been for him, I should certainly have filled my sheet.——

Bath, Oct. 22.

YESTERDAY I was brought in health and safety to my journey's end. Many Christian friends I have met with, all expressing their love for me, a worm, sometimes not able to bear the sight of my own pollutions.   Indeed I feel, under the expressions of kindness I receive, sometimes distressed: and when I compare my reputed with my real self, I seem like a man of supposed large fortune, and living in splendour, who is, in fact, a bankrupt, and nothing worth.

Dear Mr. Clarke I was happy with. He preached, last Sunday morning, a discourse full of good sense, abundant in matter, searching and piercing to the heart, yet truly evangelical. A company of about one hundred hearers have him for their teacher, whose good sense, and knowledge and grace, qualify him for the largest sphere. This is one of the secrets not to be explored by us: it is enough to know that the Head of the Church fixes His ministers as seemeth best to His infinite wisdom.

From Mr. Clarke I went to Reading, and was received with unfeigned love by Mr. and Mrs. Talbot: he rode with me on my way to Bath: we had very much communion of heart. From Mr. Talbot's I rode to Pewsey, and was most cordially received by Mr. Townshend: he is an excellent man, and inquired after Mr. Riland, and all Yorkshire friends, with great affection. From thence I came here yesterday; and found Lady Huntingdon, and my dear son in the Gospel, as he will call himself, Mr. Shirley: we are to share the work between us. I am made very much of, I can assure you! My accommodations are very agreeable; and every thing I could wish for is done to express respect. In fact, I find there is no stronger temptation to vanity, and self-love, than what a travelling popular preacher meets with.

Bath, Nov. 4.

On Sunday evening last there was such a crowded audience, Mr. Shirley told me, as there never was before. The chapel doors were set open; and people stood in the court, as far as the houses. That full description of the way of salvation, and the object of the believer's hope, the condition of His enemies, and the glory of His people, in the concluding verses of Isaiah xlv., was my subject.

Happily, I am much alone! though solicited to spend my time with one family after another all the day. You may judge of this, when I tell you I have read two quarto volumes, with other books, and written near twenty letters, without intermitting my study of the ever-blessed Book. Solitude is a great cherisher of faith : were we more alone, to pray, and look back upon ourselves, and to look into ourselves —not to find any good, but to observe more of the amazing blindness of heart, unbelief, selfishness, and vile idolatry, which so benumb our feelings of the love of Christ—were we to be more alone for these purposes, we should enjoy more of the presence and joy of God. In the exercise of meditation and prayer, I can stand amazed, and be almost lost in astonishment at my misery and sinfulness— misery so great, in not feeling an everlasting admiration, love, and joy, in an Incarnate Jehovah, and in the view of the great things of the Spirit of God which are revealed to me! At the same time that this is my misery, it is my shame and guilt; for every thing ought to be loved according to its intrinsic worth. What a robber am I, and what sacrilege

am I committing, when the affections of my heart
are so cold towards my Lord! Sometimes I have
touches which I would give the world might last;
but in an hour they are gone. Whilst they last,
my heart swells with the vehement desire expressed
in the hymn,

> Nothing in all things may I see,
> Nothing on earth desire but Thee!

In my own experience, perhaps, I am describing
my dear friend's. What, then, can be our hope,
some would say, thus self-condemned? Our hope,
we will boldly answer, is that very precious Lord, to
whom we make such base returns. Our hope is
sure and steadfast. He will have mercy. We are
His. And though now for many years we are thus
poor, yet hereafter, through all eternity, we shall
offer unto Him a perfect heart, a perfect love; and
be lost in Him, the centre and source of our life and
salvation.

TO JAMES KERSHAW, ESQ.

Bath, Nov. 5.

I am favoured with the pleasing sight, and with
the animating example, of a soul inflamed with love
to a Crucified God—that stumbling-block to them
that perish. In Lady Huntingdon I see a star of
the first magnitude in the firmament of the Church.
Blessed be God for free grace, that salvation is to
every one that cometh to Christ! otherwise, when
I compare my life and my spirit with hers, I could
not believe the same heaven was to contain us.

How do works, the works of faith and love, speak and preach Jesus Christ, in that devoted servant of His! No equipage—no livery servants—no house —all these given up, that perishing sinners may hear the life-giving sound, and be enriched with all spiritual blessings. Her prayers are heard, her chapel is crowded, and many sinners amongst the poor are brought into the City of Refuge. Happy is it for us, my friend, that we have been brought into that city—that we know in whom we have believed—that we can say, "Surely in the Lord have I righteousness and strength!"—that we have been happily reduced to the necessity of confessing we have nothing to pay, nothing to plead, but, "Worthy is the Lamb!" This is all our relief, consolation, and triumph; and will be, through all ages. I feel, from Lady Huntingdon's example, an increasing desire, both for myself and you, and all our friends, that we may be active and eminent in the life of grace. Too apt are we to rest in life received, and not to be every day doing something for our Lord; either earnestly engaging in prayer, speaking affectionately to sinners, overcoming our selfish violent passions, or exercising mercy to our needy brethren: but it is by abounding in every good work, that our light shines before men, and we stand confessed the workmanship of God in Christ. I would urge the duty—and may God press it home effectually upon my own heart?—of "opening our mouths wide," to importune Him for the best gifts; and to live, in the sight of all around us, beyond dispute, zealous conscientious worshippers, and dear obedient children.

I have enjoyed in this visit the edifying discourse

and bright example of many of our dear Saviour's family; all of them partakers of one life and one spirit, yet each distinguished by its particular hue and beauteous colour, more predominant than the rest. In one, I have been animated by ardent activity for the glory of Christ, and the salvation of souls. In another, I was pleased and softened by conspicuous meekness and gentleness of spirit. In a third, I was excited to love and good works, by the fervent charity and brotherly kindness I beheld: and in a fourth, I was led to abase myself, and confess the pride of my heart, from the humility and brokenness of spirit which struck me. In the Head alone, all graces, in their lustre, unite.

TO MRS. RILAND.

Bath, Nov. 9.

I HAVE written to———, and told them very plainly and fully my fears and jealousy respecting their spiritual state. Long have I been convinced that it is the only proper way of acting up to our profession, as friends to one another in the Lord, thus faithfully to speak. Much guilt have I contracted, by the neglect of doing so ; but such is the extreme selfishness natural to my heart, that it pains me, beyond expression, to reprove faithfully any particular friend.

I feel desolate sometimes at the thought of my sad bereavement; yet this sensation serves to make the world appear in the light it ought, like a land where I am an unknown passenger, hastening to

M

a rich and immense inheritance in the love and presence of my Lord; whose property each individual
believer is, as much as the angels themselves. In
this confidence I can repose myself on His faithful
arm, to be either full or bereaved, rich or poor, in
pain or ease, as He shall please to appoint. Oh,
mighty force of redeeming love! This, applied by
the Holy Ghost, is an abiding demonstration to us,
that we are dear and precious in the eyes of our
God. From this knowledge proceeds a power to be
willingly subject, without reserve, to His holy will
—an assurance that afflictions and necessities are
appointed for our truest interest.

TO MRS. RILAND.

Sandwell, Dec. 2.

SOME blessed times indeed I have had, since we
parted; and some at the Throne of Grace, whilst
I have been remembering you, and entreating for
your enjoyment, more and more, of the fruits of
the death of Jesus, and of the power of His resurrection. Yet it sometimes occasions a great
trial of our faith, and a painful submission of our
understanding to God, to reconcile the absolute certainty of the promises in Christ Jesus, and the success and prevalence of prayer, with the experience
of the people of God. When I consider the slow
progress I have made, the many, many evil thoughts
and desires, the continual defilement and extreme
weakness and inconstancy of mind I labour under,
I am ready to cry out, " Is there unfaithfulness in
God? Where is his promise?" But, upon maturer

thoughts, all this is quite necessary, to mortify my vanity, to deepen my convictions of sin, to make self abhorred—earth appear a howling wilderness —and a better and a more holy state of existence longed for.

As soon as I came here, the Earl, with as much love as you could wish he had for me, received me; and Lady Dartmouth the same. It often happens to me, that the tender regard of my friends distresses me; as I cannot divide myself, nor spend my time with them as they desire. It is the case at present; Lord and Lady Dartmouth, with an earnestness which makes me blush, and which I cannot withstand, will not let me leave Sandwell till Monday the 11th.

CORRESPONDENCE.

SECTION II.

LETTERS WRITTEN, FROM THE PERIOD OF HIS ACCEPTANCE OF YELLING, TO THE COMMENCEMENT OF HIS CORRESPONDENCE WITH HIS SON.

DURING the early part of the year 1770, Mr. Venn was incapacitated from all exertion by the alarming illness mentioned in the Memoir, which was brought on by excessive labour in the discharge of his ministry. In the autumn of this year, he was recommended to try the effect of a journey to Bath. Whilst at that place, he received the offer of the living of Yelling, Huntingdonshire; and immediately announced the intelligence, in a few lines, to Mrs. Riland; but entered more fully upon the subject in the following letter, written from London, a few days afterwards.

TO MRS. RILAND.

MY DEAR FRIEND,   *London, Nov. 17, 1770.*

I conclude you have, by this time, received my letter dated last Saturday. In that you will find I am Rector of Yelling. I wrote to you of this event the very day I received the account of it from the Lord Commissioner Smythe. I had received some intimation of his design to prefer me, the Saturday before : upon which I immediately wrote to Lady ———, urging her to press for the nomination of my successor at Huddersfield; and saying, in a few words, what I have ever thought of dear Mr. Riland—that he is one of the best creatures living upon earth. If he is not nominated, I hope, for my own sake, his faithful labours will be joined with my feeble efforts, to promote the glory of Emmanuel, in that new place to which I am called evidently by His providence.

Nothing would have prevailed on me to leave Huddersfield, if my lungs had not received an irreparable injury, of which I am more sensible, by several symptoms, than ever.———What I feel in giving up the Huddersfield congregation, and especially your dear sister, and some like her, no words can sufficiently express : instead of being rejoiced at the providence, I barely feel resigned. Looking upon my dissolution as at no great distance, I go to Yelling as a dying man : and if I am to live a few years longer, I look upon this as the appointed means of continuing my life. What new trials and exercises of faith I shall be called to, my Lord only knows : this, I am sure, will be a great alleviation of them, if we all remove together; for never shall I forget how much I owe to you both, and how much you have both shewn to me a truly-affectionate spirit. I beg my best love to Mr. Riland, to your sister and all friends. I am so much hurried, that I have no time to write to any but yourself at Huddersfield.—Adieu, my dear friend !

From yours, &c. H. VENN.

It was not to be expected that the tender and sacred bonds which united Mr. Venn with his flock at Huddersfield could be severed, without exciting deep regret on both sides: but the trial was rendered more severe, in consequence of some of his friends in that place disapproving of his removal. This drew from him the following touching appeals, which equally display his meekness and tenderness of conscience.

TO MRS. RILAND.

MY DEAR FRIEND,   *London, Nov.* 27, 1770.

———— How much I have suffered, these last few days! and what will be my final determination, I am not now able to say: for, though I was *quite* clear, that, from my utter inability to do much in my office, I was not to continue in so large a sphere of action, yet, when you write to me that the dear people suffer so much, and that there is no likelihood of a successor, such as I could wish— when I consider, also, the separation which must take place from two of the very dearest friends I have, and the extreme smallness of the parish I am presented to—I am in great perplexity. I am looking up, with earnest cries, to Him who has Himself most strictly charged us not to turn the blind out of his way; and who, therefore, will surely inform and direct His poor, sinful creatures, who call upon Him. I should be glad if you, my dear friend, would write your whole mind, and tell me whether there are many who seem to feel it would be a great loss to them, were the Gospel to be removed; and whether there is any likelihood that some faithful pastor will be provided. Did I believe it my bounden duty, and the thing most pleasing to God, that I should not remove, I should be happy; and, let what would be the consequence, I would not remove. My mind is ready to say, upon seeing the distance of Yelling from any market-town (which is much farther than I was told), and the thinness of the inhabitants, that I had better speak but a year or two to thousands, and have my work finished. On the contrary, when I consider the pain I have long felt in my mind, to live for years, doing so little, where so much was to be done—when I consider how very soon dear Mr. Riland may leave me —I stagger, on the other hand. Will dear Mr. Riland agree not to leave me, if I stay at Huddersfield? Write to me, without fail, by the return of post, and answer this query. Give my love to dear Mr. Riland. I do not love him the less for his letter, nor believe his affection for myself is diminished. Oh, that I had wings like a dove! I long to be one day at Huddersfield: yet so were the time and circumstances of this presentation ordered, that it was impossible for me, without an absolute refusal, to send for your advice. My love to all friends. I am hurried almost out of my life, and should not wonder if I were taken ill. Adieu! Believe me, in bonds not to be broken,

Your affectionate father,

H. VENN.

TO JAMES KERSHAW, ESQ.

DEAR SIR,   *Brompton Grove, Nov.* 29, 1770.

I was almost afraid of opening your letter. " Strange ! " you will say, when no one's letters are so welcome. The truth is, I knew the contents, before I opened it; and I have suffered so much upon the subject, that my life is bitter to me. The cup was full before; and this made it overflow. The best lights I can give you, you shall have, in order to judge of my conduct.

In the year 1765, I had determined, in my own mind, never to change my situation. I had no sooner done so, than, in the February following the December in which I had made the resolution, the complaint in my chest increased so much, that I was able to do next to nothing for seven months. This complaint, through my own unpardonable length and loudness in speaking, has not mended, but grown worse and worse. Many sensible proofs I have had of it; so much so, as absolutely to refuse an offer which was made, of trying to secure Halifax for me, three years ago; which refusal was grounded on a consciousness that I was too enfeebled for any such charge. I have also found, every succeeding year, that I am more and more hurt by speaking: and therefore, as I am privileged to do, I made my prayer to the God of my life and my salvation, to provide for me, now unequal to the blessed charge entrusted to me. I did this the more constantly, as I saw my beloved assistant begin to stoop under the weight of his work; unable myself to afford any more help.

Without any expectation of such an event, the living falls—the Lord Commissioner thinks of me : uncertain if the power of presenting to it might not be taken away in a few days, he desires my answer. Clearly convinced that this was an answer to prayer, and a very small parish indeed, suited to my lungs, I accepted the offer. Lucrative views were not of force to determine me : and so it will be found ; for, all things considered, the increase of income will not be many pounds, and the increase of trials will be very grievous : for, instead of a large congregation, the glory of the country, I shall have very few—and probably, such is the thinness of the inhabitants, never many ;—instead of yourself and some other dear companions in the way, I shall be very solitary ;—instead of the love wherewith I am loved at Huddersfield, I shall give offence, and be always five or six miles from any conversable people.

Since I have received some accounts from the dear place of my best days, I am greatly perplexed —I am torn asunder—I am sick at heart—I know not what to determine. The leadings of Providence seem to point one way : the care of the dear souls, who have been called under me, another. My love for them makes me wish to live and die with them : the total inability I am under of doing a quarter of the business of the place, seems to say, 'You must retire : your work is over there.' Were I to consult my own ease and peace, I should never stir from Huddersfield. In this sad perplexity of mind, I am, without ceasing, looking to my Lord : I am begging to have my way made quite plain.—

I can appeal to Him, that I would not act from any motive I should blush to have laid open in the sight of men and angels. And must I not trust, and not be afraid, that He will direct me aright? I am sometimes ready to cast the lot for a decision in this matter. Pity me! O my friend, pity me! Pray for me, that I may not be suffered to take a step for which I shall condemn myself at any future season.

Your much indebted and affectionate friend,

H. VENN.

———

On Easter-day, March 30, 1771, Mr. Venn preached his farewell sermon to his flock at Huddersfield. His text was Col. iii. 11 : "Christ is all, and in all." During that week, he finally quitted the place, and spent the next month in visiting different friends. The following letter was written during this journey.

———

TO MRS. RILAND.

Peterborough, April 30, 1771.

THOUGH I could not give, my dear friend, an account beforehand of my stages, I shall make up that deficiency with a recital of the whole afterwards.

I wrote to you on Tuesday last, from Hull. Mr. Jesse met me at Malton, and accompanied me as far as Hull : he is a very excellent man; and seems appointed to evangelize the *Wolds* ; the inhabitants of which are dark almost as the Indians.

At Hull, I was transported by hearing Mr. Milner, on the Wednesday. In my judgment, he is, by much, the ablest minister that I ever heard open his mouth for Christ : indeed, his abilities are of the very first rate. I did not design to force myself upon him ; but it gave me the highest joy when he came up to me, as I was reading the monuments in the church, and, with all the frankness of Mr. Kershaw, invited me to spend the evening with him. This was at the hazard of his character ; for there were persons at church who knew me, and seemed not a little gratified that Mr. Milner gave such a proof of his Methodism. The evening, Mr. Jesse and I spent with him. It answered all I expected from the blessed sermon. I conversed much with him. He had deep impressions of religion when a child ; and rightly observed, " I must go back to my thirteenth year ; when I was waiting upon the Lord, without any reasonings of my own."

I went, on the evening of Thursday, to Wintringham. The dear, blessed man inquired cordially after you. At Wintringham, though desired to preach, I refused ; and have now been four Sabbaths silent. Though I cannot say I am likely to recover, I am better, and feel much less pain in my chest. At Wintringham, I met with a young clergyman, who, some months since, was a careless and worldly character. Dear Mr. Adam talked to him so affectionately, that, through the grace of God, the young man is now beginning to preach the Word of Life. He came with me as far as Lincoln, thirty-four miles, and spent the evening with me. I spoke much to him, and went to prayer at the conclusion. I left him this morning at five, and have ridden fifty-two miles since. It has been a happy day indeed!—happy, in almost perpetual prayer—happy, in being able to present you and yours at the Throne of Grace. What though the way is quite lonely—over a heath of sixteen miles, without a house in sight—the river which maketh glad the city of God flowed round about me : and when I sang one of the songs of Zion, I had you and all my spiritual children with me ; so that I could experience what St. Paul declared, and understood it perfectly : " Though absent," says he, in the flesh, yet am I with you in spirit, joying and beholding your order." I conclude, therefore, this blessed day in the most pleasing manner I can—except in conversing with my dear friend,—in writing to her ; and if I knew more of myself than she will allow, I could venture to say, that if ever this correspondence droops, it will do so on her side. Happy have I been this day : perhaps the next will be a dark and cloudy one. One thing only is unchangeable—the love of God *to* His elect, and the work of Jesus *for* them. To Him I commend you and yours, and remain

Your affectionate father,

H. VENN.

TO JAMES KERSHAW, ESQ.

Brompton Grove, May 10, 1771.

——THOUGH here I meet with abundant favour in the sight of God's children, it does not cause me to grow cool to the affections of my flock. I, in my chiefest joy, think of those whose delight was in the House of the Lord, where His name was proclaimed. I am sorrowful for them; yet always rejoicing. I am ready to wish (though it is folly) that I had not been disabled—that my strength had been preserved. I rejoice in this, that those whom the Good Shepherd found on the mountain of sin, and brought by the power of His grace, with all gladness, into His fold, He will bear up to the last, and bring them to His heavenly kingdom. How exact is His knowledge of them, in their persons, trials, and states! To Him it belongs—and He will do it—to feed them with the knowledge of His covenant, His righteousness, His relation to them, and His love. In the heat of temptation, persecution, or prevalent corruption, it is His office to give them rest in Himself, to exert His providence in their defence, to watch over them, to speak comfortably to them, and, by a frequent glimpse of His eternal glory, to make them patient in tribulation, and joyful through hope. To Him I day by day commend them; and feel, sometimes, I have audience before the Throne of Grace.

My dear friends in London are much afraid my Yorkshire friends should have been severe in censuring me. I tell them, not. I tell them, where a people had loved much, and had profited much, they could not say less. I tell them, I have never suffered one hour's distress, but on their account, because they are grieved;—not from the least doubt whether I have followed the leadings of Providence.

The glorious Gospel prospers. Good news from Oxford—many young men there! "Yet have I set my King upon my holy hill of Zion."—The powerful voice of this King may you hear! His love may you feel! And may your tongue be as the pen of a ready writer, to relate His glory!

After Mr. Venn left Huddersfield, the people who had profited by his preaching were repelled from the parish-church by discourses which formed a marked contrast to those they had lately heard within the same walls; so that they were dispersed in various directions; some to neighbouring churches, some to dissenting chapels. Several of them, at length, determined upon building a chapel, in the hope that they might be united together in one body, under a pastor of their own choice. Mr. Venn gave his sanction and assistance to this plan, and advised the people to attend the chapel after it was built. It was his first hope, that the Liturgy would be used in the new chapel at Huddersfield. Writing to a friend, he says: "You, and all the people, know how I love the Liturgy, and would a thousand times prefer it to any other way of worship." But in this, and in many more important respects, his expectations were disappointed. In a short time, also, another Vicar came to the living; from whose instructions he would never have wished his people to secede: but few, comparatively, returned to the parish-church.

It must not be inferred, from these circumstances, that he was an advocate for Dissent in general, or that his attachment to the Church of England was equivocal: his intimate friends unanimously testify, that he cordially and zealously espoused the interests of the Church, and, especially, that his veneration for the Liturgy was of the most exalted kind. In a letter, written to the Rev. Mr.

Powley, one of his former curates, whom he had presented
to a chapel in the parish of Huddersfield, and who faithfully remonstrated with him upon this occasion, he thus
vindicates his attachment to the Church.

———

How often have I declared my utmost veneration for the Liturgy! How often in your hearing,
how often in the church, declared the superior excellency, in my judgment, of the Liturgy to every
mode of worship, not only amongst the Dissenters,
but that had ever been in the Church of Christ, as
far as I had knowledge! Nay, more than once have
I said, I never was present at any meeting where I
perceived the power of godliness as amongst the
congregations of our Church, where the Gospel is
preached. Now, after all this, I think, in justice,
you ought to have supposed me as much a friend
to the Church of England as yourself.—I have
long, you know, had to combat with the senseless
prejudices against our Form; and see plainly the
advantage Satan makes of these prejudices, and
lament it. But this evil, compared with the sort
of religion taught now by some of the clergy, appears to me but small. One lays waste the grand
fundamental truth; the other only exhibits it in a
less edifying manner.——On Saturday, I dined
with our Bishop. I find he has no objection to a
revisal and alteration of the Liturgy. This change
will one day, I fear, take place; and then the measure of our iniquities will be full, when we have cast
the doctrine of Christ out of the public worship,

avowedly as a nation. May we be the more zealous
and active, according to the utmost of our strength;
encouraging and comforting both each other and
our flocks with the certain success of the Gospel, in
spite of earth and hell!

———

I will here also refer to another circumstance, which is
in some measure connected with this subject. During
Mr. Venn's residence at Yelling, he occasionally preached
in neighbouring parishes, at the houses, and, in some few
instances, in the barns of the farmers; and, in his visits to
London, he officiated at the chapel of the Rev. Rowland
Hill. With respect to this point, I am furnished with the
sentiments of my father, recorded in a detached form,
but with the intention of their being inserted in the Memoir. I introduce them, however, in this place, because
they equally apply, in their general tenor, to the case of
the chapel at Huddersfield; and I gladly avail myself of
the opportunity of expressing my own feelings, with
respect to that transaction, as well as with respect to his
preaching in unconsecrated places, by simply recording
my entire concurrence in the spirit of the remarks which
follow.

———

"Were I to deliver a panegyric agreeable to my
own views of that excellent man, in whom I every day
saw something new to admire and honour, I should
draw a veil over what I am going to relate. But the
faithfulness of an historian compels me to do violence
to the feelings of a son. His mind was naturally
ardent; and he was of a temper to be carried out by

zeal, rather than to listen to the cold calculations of prudence. Influenced by the hope of doing good, my father, in certain instances, preached in unconsecrated places. But having acknowledged this, it becomes my pleasing duty to state, that he was no advocate for irregularity in others; that when he afterwards considered it, in its distant bearings and connexions, he lamented that he had given way to it, and restrained several other persons from such acts by the most cogent arguments; and that he lived long enough to observe the evils of schism so strongly, that they far outweighed in his mind the present apparent good."

In the month of July 1771, Mr. Venn was married to his second wife, Mrs. Smith. The two following letters were written to this lady previous to their union, but after she had accepted his offer of marriage. He was at this time travelling in Yorkshire; but did not visit Huddersfield.

Upper Thorp, near Dewsbury,
June 25, 1771.

PERHAPS my dear friend has written again, though my removals have prevented me from receiving the favour. But I can never want a subject, either for discourse or for a letter, whilst you have a heart to delight in the things of God. I have already sent you some thoughts on that freedom and simplicity with which the faithful in Christ Jesus ought to

N

address the Lord God Almighty—That neither the
sense of our manifold offences, nor the poor stam-
mering tongue with which we can speak, nor the
coldness and deadness of our hearts, ought to discourage us, or beget in us the least doubt of the
Lord's hearing our requests : for, indeed, very small
in His sight must be the difference between the
wisest and the most ignorant—between *this* saint,
who with a peculiar fluency mentions every circumstance, and *that*, who is almost at a loss for words
of any kind. He looketh only to the heart, which
dictates the prayer, and often is full of the *spirit* of
prayer when utterance is greatly wanting.

With respect to the subject-matter of prayer, it
ought to vary with our temptations, feelings, and
various wants : for, as the main design of prayer is
not to inform the Omniscient, but to make us sensible of our own indigence and absolute dependence
upon God for all, this design can never be so well
promoted as by a familiar, and very particular, enu-
meration of those things which concern us. For
instance : I thankfully acknowledge His faithfulness,
in answering according to my petitions, and giving
me, in you, all I could wish, in a friend, in a wife ;—
that when I was going to fix in a solitary place, no
longer able to serve in a large and populous one,
He should indulge me with a companion of peculiar
talents, to entertain and enliven the solitude. It
was a great and pernicious error, which first was set
on foot by formality and superstition, to make men
conceive of Jehovah, not as a loving Father, but a
Great and awful Being only, before whom they were
not thus familiarly to speak.

I have just now received your letter of the 22d. A thousand thanks for it! though it made me much regret my being absent when the good bishop* was with you. I longed before to have seen him: but to have seen him at your table, and talked freely and fully about the grand matter of all, would have been a high gratification. If we live, I shall hope for many such interviews; in which, your being one of the party will enliven me more: and seeing you enjoy the discourse, will make it doubly delightful to myself.

Before this, you will be able to tell all our friends when, by God's leave, I shall be in town. Indeed, I think it long; and I shall stay but one night at Yelling, and there leave the children. Inclosed you receive a letter from my boy. It is his own entirely; for I always choose to have them express themselves in their own way. I dare almost venture to promise that you will have little trouble from him. Pray give my dutiful love to your mother; and tell her, if she loves a warm room, her apartment at Yelling will in that respect please. Remember me to our dear friends in the Grove. I did fully purpose to write to them both, when I set out; but so many are my engagements, that I can find no time to write to any one, but to that person most esteemed and beloved by me, whose I am in the best bonds, and to whom I would ever fervently pray I may approve myself a most affectionate and tender friend and husband.

Adieu, my dear friend! From yours, &c.

H. VENN.

* Dr. Hildesley, Bishop of Sodor and Man.

N 2

TO MRS. SMITH.

MY DEAR FRIEND,   *York, June* 28, 1771.

How glad am I that this is the last letter I hope to write to you for a long time! for when this reaches you, I shall be on my way to Yelling. If I do not see you (God willing) on Friday, it will not be my fault; but I rather fear I shall not, till Saturday. Long was I very backward to think of entering again into the married state, though so blessed in my first connexion : but the gracious God, whom I serve, and whose I am, has provided for me one of His own elect (I doubt not). I have not yet seen Dr. Conyers; but I shall be there this evening; where you will also be present, as much as it is possible for an absent person to be so. You will do what, if present, you would not—engross all the conversation. I begin to feel much more concern than I did at first, lest my children should give you trouble ; for just in the same proportion as I value and love you (and that is just in proportion as I know you) I must feel for every thing that may in any degree affect you. And I say to myself, Oh, how should I be able to bear it, if I was to see my dear wife in tears, or void of that sweet cheerfulness and vivacity of spirit which so distinguishes her, by any of my children, to whom she has so kindly shewn herself a friend indeed! I hope it will not be so ; and if prayer can avail to prevent such a trial from coming upon her, she will never experience any sorrow on my account, or those belonging to me, but by our departure.

You may remember how pleasantly you said Hogarth would describe our courtship.—In what light would the world regard my letters! Strange love-letters indeed! Oh, did they but know how much more blessed are the faithful in Christ, in every relation of life, than themselves, the love of present enjoyment would make them converts to the faith. But all this is hid from their eyes. They cannot understand how a solid acquaintance with a Crucified Saviour diffuses an influence through the whole of life, and renders the husband, the wife, the father, the master, the servant, the child, the friend, a very different creature, and far more excellent than what he would be otherwise.

I beg my love to your mother. Tell her, I pray for her every day, and that I may love her, and study to make her last days as easy and cheerful as possible. John desires, from his heart, to be remembered to you, with the most dutiful affection.

I am yours ever, in the best bonds.

H. Venn.

———

The next letter introduces a new correspondent to our notice—the Rev. James Stillingfleet, who at this time held the Chapel of Bierly, in the parish of Bradford, and shortly after became Rector of Hotham, near Market-Weighton, Yorkshire. He was the descendant of the learned and celebrated bishop of that name; and the intimate friend of Joseph Milner, who composed the greater part of his Church History in his friend's study at Hotham.

TO THE REV. JAMES STILLINGFLEET.

DEAR SIR,   *Yelling, Aug.* 5, 1771.

Your affectionate epistle found me in due time.
Many thanks are due to you for it. It found me
under " great searchings of heart," upon the point
of beginning my ministry in this place. What
a change, from thousands, to a company of one
hundred!—from a people generally enlightened,
and many converted, to one yet sitting in darkness,
and ignorant of the first principles of the Gospel!
—from a house resounding with the voice of thanksgiving, like the noise of many waters, to one where
the solitary singers please themselves with empty
sounds, or gratify their vanity by the imagination of
their own excellence!—from a Bethel to myself and
many more, to a nominal worship of the God of
Christians! A change painful indeed! yet, unavoidable. With a heavy heart, therefore, did I yesterday begin to address my new hearers. I preached
both morning and evening; and never to a more
attentive audience;—in the afternoon, to four times
the number that were ever in the church before.
But what will make you wonder, my dear friend,
I spoke within the hour three minutes, both times
put together! and yet I feel much hurt; and am
ready to conclude I shall not long be able to speak,
even in this whispering church. If I am, it appears,
from the effect to-day, I shall not want hearers.
The will of the Lord, I hope to say cheerfully, be
done! Yet, of all trials I have ever known, this of

having the treasure which is ordained to enrich to all eternity the souls of men, and not strength of voice to declare and to communicate it to our dear fellow-creatures, is one of the most severe. May you understand this, and be wise in time! I am persuaded we do wrong to outdo our strength. As far as it will reach and last, spare not. I would— were it lawful to wish for any thing—wish for lungs of brass and flesh of iron, to rest not, day or night, publishing the glad tidings, saying to sinners, Behold your God!

I was sorry to hear of your disappointment. Tribulation, of one kind or other, is our lot. In vain do we imagine we shall escape it. I sympathize with you in the feeling of a heart desperately wicked. Once I thought some humiliating expressions of the saints of God too low for me—proud, blind wretch as I was! Now I can say, with Edwards, " Infinite upon infinite only reaches to my sinfulness!"

I thank you for your prayers. I often entreat my God to remember me according to the intercession of many of my dear friends and His dear children. Continue to do me this kindness, and to write to me frequently. I answer this the next post but one, to prove my desire of your correspondence. I shall rejoice to hear from you ; and more, to see you. The Lord increase your soul in light, life, strength, and peace!

From yours,

H. VENN.

TO MRS. RILAND.

MY DEAR FRIEND, *Yelling, Aug.* 10, 1771.

I received your last letter on Thursday. Alas! what a distressing account! * It made my very heart sick. Oh! what shall we say to such things as these?—a man in all other respects, ever since he made profession, so very well-behaved. As far as my influence can reach, you may be sure it will concur with yours. Little prospect is there of any success : for how seldom do we see counsel taken! I am wounded to the heart; for I well know with what force the conclusion is drawn against God and His doctrine. Indeed, these are the things which defeat, in a great measure, all our labours of love! Too many professors of religion are, alas! so much like other people, that the world can see no manner of difference, except in a zeal for doctrines, and the use of the means. Well! all we can say is, " The foundation standeth sure : the Lord knoweth them that are His : and, let every one who nameth the name of Christ depart from iniquity ";—unless he would have this naming the name of Christ the greatest aggravation of his guilt.

I came here last night, sadly tired with my ride from Knightsbridge, though I took a chaise one stage. One week more, and, if I have life, I shall be able to say, next week I shall be settled with my whole family in a new place, and in a new situation : consequently, sure to be attended with new crosses : for the righteous decree of Heaven must take effect,

* One of Mr. Venn's late hearers at Huddersfield had acted in a way unbecoming the religious character he had long sustained.

" In sorrow shalt thou eat thy bread, all the days of thy life." You will have heard of my preaching here last Sunday. The people were very attentive. But I have but little pleasure now, in comparison of what I had when I began at dear Huddersfield. Then I concluded the success of the preached Gospel was great indeed: now I see, in an awful light, that very many are called, but few chosen. I see, what we account very extraordinary conversions, turn out to be nothing. May all the evil we feel, and all the evil we see, work in us humility, watchfulness, and a desire, if it please God, to be taken to the land of righteousness!

I came here without a frank; so that you must pay postage for a letter which brings you nothing for your money, but a testimony that I am exceedingly grieved at the misery of man, and the sad occasion of offence given by those who are lifted up to notice by their coming out from the world. My sister and the children desire their love. They are all well, I thank God! May the peace of God dwell in your heart!

From your ever affectionate father in Christ,

H. VENN.

TO MRS. RILAND.

MY DEAR FRIEND,   *Yelling, Aug.* 26, 1771.

I thank you for the accounts from Huddersfield. I have a connexion with many there, which I trust will last through all eternity! I could serve them no longer. The different effect I feel now, from preaching twice a day, is very remarkable. I neither cough, nor am fatigued after the Sabbath is over.

Here I begin to see all that I saw at Huddersfield—amazement, attention, conviction, tears, and a vast increase of hearers, for a country so desert as this is, where a hundred is more than a thousand in your place of habitation. The old clerk, who is as old as James Booth's father, told me we should empty all the churches round about. You and my dear brother, your husband, will be glad to hear how I proceeded. The first Sunday I preached on Rom. x. 1. (as I did at Huddersfield) two discourses. The second on Rev. xx. ' The throne was set, and the books were opened.' The third Sunday, on ' Jesus Christ the same, to receive the vilest, &c.' Yesterday, ' On the sinfulness of sin.' Though the rain was heavy, many were present to hear.—Such honour is Jesus pleased to put upon me, a sinful man, because desirous to preach His glory!—I see two of the parish under evident concern : one of them is my assistant's wife. Oh! that they might, in the great affair, be like you and yours! My assistant is often much affected, when I am preaching. Soon I shall hope to have a conversation with him.

The singers here are very celebrated : one, particularly, sings, amongst the first, at all the Oratorios. I have therefore a difficult point to manage with them. I have, however, obtained thus much —they sing my Collection of Psalms : they give out every line; and a very few voices begin to join them. Last night, the chief singer, who is also

a principal farmer, spent the evening with me, and
was at our family-prayer.

I hope to write by this post to your dear sister :
if not, present my love, and tell her I never think
of her but with thankfulness to God ; and could
wish, were it lawful to wish, that she were a neighbour to Mrs. V.

My love to Mr. R. Remember us on Friday,
when we shall fix in our dwelling.

From your ever affectionate father in Christ,

H. VENN.

It may be worth remarking, that Mr. Venn travelled,
during several successive weeks, from London to Yelling,
and back, to preach on the Sundays, though he had a
resident Curate, in the hope that he might collect a congregation before the winter set in.

TO JAMES KERSHAW, ESQ.

MY VERY DEAR FRIEND, *Yelling, Sept.* 7, 1771.

After five months' perpetual itinerancy, last
Tuesday but one we came to our new residence,
and to a scene of life perfectly new to Mrs. V.
Twenty years ago I was accustomed to solitude; and
I believe no one was ever happier in it. Though I
was then seeking to enter into life, by keeping the
commandments, yet do I still remember the hours
of delightful devotion, the earnest supplications I
was offering up for a heart dead to every thing but
God. I am sometimes wondering how I could be
so blind, and yet so comfortable ; and am myself

a witness, what pains a man may take to go to heaven, and yet be quite in the dark. I have now my lot cast again in the depth of retirement; which I apprehended would be irksome to me, after so long an experience of the sweets of Christian friendship, and the comforts of the nearest and dearest union on earth. My Father and my God foresaw this; and, in His wonted compassion, He provided for me a help-meet, a friend indeed; who, instead of being hurt by the change from Knightsbridge and many dear intimates, to this solitude, is pleased with every thing, and finds out every advantageous circumstance, and dwells upon it. We are likely to be very much alone. How thankful ought I to be!—and I entreat you, my dear friend, to pray that I may be so for such a home.

You will say, "Enough of this subject! How does the grand business, on which you are sent, prosper? Are your hearers increased? Are they affected?"— Adored be the name of our Immanuel! they increase every Sabbath: but my audience is many degrees, in point of education and of condition, below my congregation at Huddersfield; so that I am under a necessity of labouring to be very plain; for even the manufacturers about you are rich and learned, compared with the peasants in this country. I find, therefore, it is very profitable to tell them stories. Indeed, the total inefficacy of the common strain of preaching I ascribe, in part, to its being too studied, and too general; and whilst all the other sciences are flourishing and improving, because all the appeal is to experiments, in Divinity this only sensible method is quite neglected. I have several

shepherds, and shepherd-boys, who attend : they
prick up their ears when I am proving that a
shepherd or his boy, though he cannot read a
word, is not at all further removed from the knowledge and delightful enjoyment of God, than a
scholar or a gentleman : they seem struck with the
glad tidings, when I prove this to them by the instances of the poor shepherds of Bethlehem, the
poor widow in the Gospel, and the slaves mentioned
in 1 Cor. xii. 13. As an instance, however, that the
poor and ignorant can be fully as conceited as the
rich, I met, two days ago, with one of my parishioners, eighty years of age : and upon beginning to
talk with him, he said he had never met with a
man in his life, who could tell him any thing he did
not know. Yours, &c. H. VENN.

TO THE REV. JAMES STILLINGFLEET.

MY DEAR FRIEND, *Yelling, Nov.* 22, 1771.

See the danger of procrastination ! I designed
to have sent you a letter upon your coming to
Bierley from Worcestershire, yet delayed till I received your last. I thank you for it. When I can
pray, I do not forget you ; but I find little of that
lifting up of the soul—that breaking-forth with very
fervent desire—that wrestling with God—which is
the prayer to which such great promises belong.

Your present situation I know perfectly well,
having been in the same. The opposition you experience, I think, is no bad thing. The effect of
preaching Christ may by this means be the longer

before it appears; but the opposition will prove as a wind—a sharp and cutting wind—to drive away many who would be only false professors, which are the mill-stone about the neck of the Gospel—the great means of hardening the despisers of those who are good.

The prejudices against the Gospel you find very strong. This is the case in all places. You would have found it the same at Bierley, if the 'Squire had not built the chapel. Our chief exercise is, to overcome, by meekness, patience, and love, by faith and prayer, this opposition. Were it right with us, our foes and their obstinacy would profit us exceedingly. How much indebted should you and I be to the perverseness, the blindness, and the anger of our opponents, and the opponents of the faith, if it made us resemble Jesus, or his prophet Jeremiah, or his apostle Paul—if we could weep in secret places—if we could pray, though not the whole night through, yet one whole hour through, in heaviness of heart, with strong cries and tears interceding for our condemned, perishing fellow-sinners! You must not look to Pharaoh and his chariots behind, the Red Sea before, the Wilderness on each side; but to the arm of the Lord, the faithfulness of His promise, His zeal for His own honour, His love for the people whom He has chosen. The greatest difficulty, in such a situation as we are both in, is to find out some way to rouse and awaken the attention of our people. This will be done by extraordinary labour, extraordinary attention to our parishioners, and extraordinary liberality. These are facts, which every poor man can judge of: and by these fruits, first a respect, then a regard—a general regard—ensues, and our word comes with more weight.

I am a melancholy instance of overdoing, in point of speaking. I would not therefore have you exceed your strength ; yet certainly you should use it all.

Last Wednesday, Mr. Berridge was here, and gave us a most excellent sermon. He is a blessed man— a true Calvinist; not hot in doctrine, nor wise above what is written, but practical and experimental. Summer differs not more from winter than this dear man from what he was ten years ago : he is now broken in heart, yet fervent in spirit.

I am glad you are likely to be rid of your tenant, in a peaceable way ; for nothing will be a greater bar to usefulness than a notion that you aim at getting money. My children desire their love. Pray for them, poor dear souls ! I hear from Bath, that a young clergyman of some fortune is awakened, and will soon stand forth among the witnesses of Jesus. Remember me ; and believe me

Your affectionate brother in the Gospel,

H. VENN.

TO MRS. RILAND.

Jan. 8, 1772.

——Would it not astonish my dear friend, if I should ever do the whole duty of a Sabbath again ? Yet I am in such a confident expectation of this, that I have given my assistant notice, that I shall want him no longer than till Midsummer : and I should have parted with him three months sooner, if I had not considered his family, and desired to give him time to obtain another curacy. Thus the strength I was praying for, four years before I left Yorkshire, is given me at Yelling. May I return it faithfully to the adorable Giver!

You will scarcely believe me, I conclude, though I assure you that I have now been nearly five months here, and never but one night (to meet Mr. Thornton) out of the village; and though week after week passes, and, except on a Sunday, we see nothing but trees and sheep, and a peasant or two passing over the fields; yet, that I am quite joyous on account of these circumstances; and solitude is, to the full, as delicious as it used to be in the years 1751 and 1752. I suppose you have heard of the controversy between Mr. Fletcher, Shirley, &c. Who would not wish to be in a lonely village, to be free from such disputes?—

———

In a letter to Mr. Kershaw, of the same date, he alludes in a similar way to his health :—

I have not for twenty years known the health I at present enjoy. Pray for me, my beloved friend, that it may be sanctified! When I accepted Yelling, I accepted it as a providential retreat, that I might rest the remainder of my days, like one worn out in the service by much speaking. Little did I expect to speak again three hours on the Sabbath!

TO MRS. RILAND.

MY DEAR FRIEND,   *Yelling, May* 9, 1772.

Though I cannot be indulged with the pleasure of your company, I enjoy the privilege of presenting you before our most merciful and gracious God, as one of His elect—as the purchase of His own blood—and as a member of His body, of His flesh, and of His bones. I think of the approaching hour of your confinement, and of your weakness, and feel for you ; but I am comforted in the covenant engagements of your Saviour, whose power is infinite, and the tenderness of His love equal to that power. He will inspire you with meekness and fortitude. True friendship ever proves itself in the hour of adversity, by rising in its warmth, and exertion of every nerve, in proportion as its aid is wanted. With the Beloved and the Friend of the daughters of Jerusalem, this is ever the case : experience, from the beginning, has confirmed it : the Church of Christ has always had reason to say, and triumphed in the assurance, " I am persuaded that neither death, nor life, &c. shall be able to separate us from the love of God, which is in Christ Jesus our Lord." " Be therefore of good cheer," saith the Lord. Who art thou, that thou shouldest be afraid, when promises, and oaths, and love divine, and angels, and the Holy Trinity, are all engaged, and all united, for thy help, and for thy salvation— all engaged to preserve thee, and make thee an everlasting monument of grace? O my dear friend! how solid, how all-sufficient, how certain the support and consolation, in every time of difficulty or distress, as soon, and in the measure, our Lord sees good for the soul!

The short days are now gone; the bad roads are grown dry; but winter seems still to linger with us, though this is the 9th of May. On Monday, Mrs. V. and my daughter Eling go with me to Cambridge for a few days. This is the first time we have left Yelling. I hope it may please God I may be of some service to the students! I go for no other purpose.

There is a Mr. —— there, who travelled a day with me when I went up to London. This gentleman has a church in Cambridge. I have seen him once, and would hope the Lord is leading him by the hand; but at present he is so very timorous—sees the difficulties, the discouragements, the enemies so many—that he is afraid I should do him a prejudice, by visiting him; and yet says, whatever reproach my acquaintance may bring upon him, he shall be glad to see me. What power has evil shame over us! What unbelief— what mean thoughts, not only of God, but of immortal souls and usefulness to men—have we, till light from above fills our understanding! But when I have been used for so many years to an intimacy with those who have counted the cost, and set at nought both evil and good report, seeking with a single eye the glory of Christ, you cannot think how affecting it appears to me, to hear the censure of the world, and the little persecution we at this time are called to bear, mentioned as a grievous cross.

More wonders from Yelling!—I begin now to

have my people every evening, precisely at seven, at family prayer: by which means I have a little congregation whilst the days are long, and we read a chapter and sing a hymn. But I find it a labour indeed to keep up a spiritual service—to have our meeting solemn—heart-affecting—any measure in it of real prayer or praise. I find particular preparation necessary, and importunate cries, that the God of all grace would look down upon a company of poor sinners, and breathe upon us the breath of life; that our souls may rise a little towards Him, our Father, our Portion, our End, and our All: yet answers to these petitions are not always given. I must be left to know the times and the seasons of Divine Influence are in His power; and that He worketh in us, both to will and to do, of His own good pleasure.

Mrs. Venn and the children all join in most earnest wishes for your safety, and will all rejoice in hearing good tidings. Love to Mr. Riland and my little god-daughter.

From your ever affectionate pastor,

H. VENN.

———

I cannot suffer my readers to pass on, without pointing out to them, that the foregoing letter alludes to the commencement of Mr. Venn's intercourse with the young students at Cambridge, which was so eminently useful to the best interests of many amongst their number.

———

MY VERY DEAR FRIEND,   *Yelling, Sept.* 30, 1772.

I did not forget to inquire about the question you left with me, though I got no satisfaction. As to the terms of admission to the Lord's Table*, I find, by Joseph Scott, that they are settled—and settled in the dissenting way. Poor weak creatures are we! and instead of allowing others to abound in their own judgment of things not determined in the Word of God, we are for binding them up to our own opinions.

This instance, with a thousand more of human corruption, even amongst those who have a heart for God, is to teach us mutual forbearance and patience, and to lay all the stress, where alone it will answer, on our being recovered to enjoy the presence of God, to behold the glory of God, to feel His support, His protection, and victorious arm, stretched out in our behalf; and thus to walk with Him on earth, and endure as seeing Him who is invisible. This is hard work;—at least, I find it so : and this is our daily business, together with that of our particular calling. Against this walk with our God, the company of three armies, as it were—the world, the flesh, and Satan—fight continually. And be not discouraged, or vexed, though humbled, to feel how often you are drawn aside from the path your soul approves and loves to walk in—how often you feel bondage, when you pant for liberty! Darkness, after light in your mind; doubts,

* In the new Chapel at Huddersfield.

after sweet peace; deadness, after life in your soul; and a proneness to murmur, or to be displeased with the appointment of things so contrary to our desire, our convenience—these are the exercises of every individual of the Church, in the race which his merciful and loving God has marked out for him, in the course of Providence, to run. Some of Christ's flock have these exercises in more abundance than others;—some at the beginning, some in the middle, some at the conclusion of their race. But this is our consolation: " The Lord will give strength unto His people; the Lord will bless His people with peace."

Does my dear friend say, " Ah! but here is my doubt: Am I one of His people? You are one by baptism—by education in His family—by repeated dedication of yourself to Him—by His special grace in calling you to the knowledge of Himself— by your desire of His pardoning love and joy, which so revives your fainting soul—by your uneasiness in feeling so much contrariety of will to His, and so much opposition in your heart, corrupt and wicked by nature as it is. Fear not, therefore, nor enter into questioning and disputing about this matter. Only believe; and pray for faith, and faith's increase.

I beg my best respects to Mrs. Whitacre; and my prayers I would offer up for the choicest blessings to descend upon her. Mrs. V., the children, and whole family, send their love. I was much in hopes of being with you this winter; but that cannot be; as I am obliged to go to London early in the spring.

Last Sunday was our feast-day; and the church was full—a sight never seen here before. But we want singers sadly. I think, if we could have some of our Huddersfield voices, these would be ashamed of their manner of singing, and with a loud voice begin to praise our God.

May we meet soon, where all is harmony, love, and holiness, and the voice of the multitude as the voice of many waters!

From your affectionate, obliged,

H. VENN.

TO THE REV. M. POWLEY.

DEAR SIR,   *Yelling, Oct.* 5, 1772.

———I trust you go on well. Be not discouraged at the divisions you see around you, or the attempts that may be invidiously made against you. Even Moses was withstood; and Paul had many enemies in the Church, who strove to make divisions. This was a principal consideration to make me cease to wonder, or even to expect it ever would be otherwise. And when to this consideration I added my own abundant and numberless instances of perverseness and frowardness of spirit against God, I began to grow contented, that things should be as they were. However, there is this great consolation (and a great one it is indeed!) that faithful experimental preaching, which is the fruit of prayer, study, and divine teaching, will always be attended to, will always prosper, and in time will outgrow all opposition, or at least see its efforts become more and more feeble. In every possible situation, trials abound. You have much people; and some of them will be contentious and self-conceited. Where there are shallow conceptions of Christ, slight convictions of sin, no experience of the sweet and solid state of mind which establishment in the faith produces, there will be always, or often, heat and noise, and dispute, and every evil temper. In my situation, I want people; though the church is talked of all over the country, for the largeness of the congregation. I speak not to more than two hundred, sometimes three hundred: there are many of them at the distance of eight or ten miles. The one thing needful is, to be humbly resigned to the good will of the Lord, soberly attentive to our business, and lovingly enduring the frowardness of those who are out of the way. There are some excellent young men at college, who come to me from the University, as I was in hopes they would. Two are just gone out; and three more are going. They have much of the wisdom of the Egyptians; but, like Moses, are all for the service of the God of Israel.

My children join in love to you, and in every good wish for your present and everlasting happiness. From yours affectionately,

H. VENN.

Mr. John Houghton, to whom the next letter is addressed, was an inhabitant of Huddersfield, who had been awakened to a just sense of religion by Mr. Venn's preaching, and ever entertained the most unfeigned regard for his late pastor. The letters to this correspondent will be read with peculiar interest, as exhibiting the

feelings of Mr. Venn towards his late flock. I have
understood there were many letters, of a similar kind,
written to other persons at Huddersfield, which I regret
that I have not been able to recover.

TO MR. JOHN HOUGHTON.

(WRITTEN ON A SUNDAY MORNING.)

DEAR JOHN,   *Yelling, May* 2, 1773.

I never forget, on this holy day, the Church at
Huddersfield. Rising early, I think I get the start,
and am before the Throne of Grace, presenting you
all, for the relief of your various wants, and for the
abundant consolation of your souls in Christ Jesus,
whilst many of you are upon your beds. This day,
I trust, is precious to you. How ought we to prepare for it! How deeply sensible should we be of
our own inability to observe the day according to the
will of God! How foolish and besotted are we, on
this day, if we do not use it to get a clearer knowledge of our manifold corruptions, a quicker sense
of the evil of sin, a more delightful acquaintance
with Christ Jesus, a greater deadness to the world,
and a full assurance of our salvation when we leave
it! Be jealous of yourselves with a godly jealousy,
in those respects: for though we cannot command
the influences of the Holy Ghost, and often labour
and toil in the use of the means, yet receive no
consolation, behold little of the glory of God, and
feel very superficial lamentation for our sins: nevertheless, in this way must we go on, to seek, and
ask, and knock. I hope you press on to become
eminent in holiness, to convince gainsayers, and

the careless and indifferent, by your whole deportment, that a divine change has passed upon your soul—that there is a reality in all the truths which you maintain, and for the sake of which you have joined yourself to the Church of Christ.

Dear Mr. Kershaw, who has been with me one single night, rejoiced my heart by giving such a good account of my dear people. My prayer often is, by myself, in my family, and with the people, that not one of you, who did run well, may be missing in the day when the Lord maketh up His jewels;—that, as we have so often worshipped together before the Throne on earth, we may worship, through all eternity, before the Throne above.

Pray give my love to your father, mother, wife, and brother; to Mrs. Bird, Katherine Goddard, Abraham Littlewood, Mary Haigh, both the Hirsts, and Barbara, and all friends. My book, I trust, will be ready by Midsummer, if it is not the printer's fault. I hope the Lord will give it efficacy, and bless it, to guard you from all fatal mistakes!

The Lord bless your minister! Give my love to him. From your affectionate father in Christ,

H. VENN.

TO THE REV. JAMES STILLINGFLEET.

MY DEAR FRIEND, *Yelling, July* 13, 1773.

Much am I affected, both with the confidence you have in my unfeigned regard for you, and the account you send me of your heavy trials. With respect to the former, be assured I did ever take pleasure in your company, and rejoiced in seeing

the grace of God abundantly manifested in your
ministry and in your conversation. I am not therefore surprised, though I am grieved, for the crosses
you meet with. It must be so. Nothing in this
world shall we have to find contentment in, if we
are Christ's : for whatever it is which fully pleases,
in that we shall take up our rest. Were the children of God what we expect, and they ought to be,
we should fix our attention and our affections upon
them. But they are frail and weak, corrupt and
sinful, as ourselves : they have neither that love to
God, nor to the brethren, they profess : some they
have, without doubt; but, what through precipitate
judgments, misconceptions, and imperceptible bias
towards themselves, they often grieve and vex those
they should comfort.

How much of this has fallen to my share !
Though I never doubted, but for a day or two,
about my removal from Huddersfield, how did, how
does, that dear good man, Mr. ——, judge of me !
—no more corresponding with me, than if I had
turned apostate—no more allowing me to judge for
myself, than if he had been endued with infallibility.
Be not therefore affected, when you find censures
and condemnation of your conduct thrown out. It
is enough that you can appeal to Him whom you
serve, that your eye is single, and your heart cleaves
to Him. It is enough that you are sensible of the
danger to which you stand exposed, so as to cry
unto Him, who delivers from the power of this
present evil world. Be jealous of yourself, and daily
use the means of grace; and you will be brought
through, shouting, " Grace ! grace ! "

You have had a time of growth for some years, without many trials; but this cannot last. If ye are without chastisement, whereof all are partakers, then are ye bastards, and not sons. I am heartily sorry for the stroke that is come so unexpectedly upon you: yet it is admirable, that you are made more than conqueror—that you hear your best Friend, your never-failing one, say, as it were, " It is I! be not afraid, or confounded! What I do, you know not fully now; but you shall know hereafter." Remember that noble saying of Luther: " Prayer, afflictions, and temptations, make a minister of the Gospel." Thus exercised, we learn, from our own experience, the truth we read before in the Bible: our own weakness and frowardness, the supports and consolations of faith, and the many arts of the great enemy, are manifested to us. When we have been tempted long, and in various ways, and to our great distress, we are enabled to speak with a winning tenderness, and know how to have compassion upon the tempted. Thus I look upon you, my beloved friend and brother, as now in the consecrated furnace; as in the Refiner's fire; as weaning from the world—by a demonstration, that the sweetest blessings, which it has to give, are as a dream, when one awaketh. Henceforth, with increasing ardour you will pursue what is substantial; and value it the more, in proportion as you feel all is vanity, beside Jesus, and Him Crucified. Always shall I be glad to hear from you; and should be more glad to see you. I beg of you never to measure my regard by my letters. I have been so busied about my book, that I have scarcely written to any body. I believe I may say, I shall write no more for the public : I am sick of my own performances, though still full of self-love. The Prophecy of Zacharias is the ground-work from whence I bring my proof of the mistakes which are exposed. I am much comforted by the news I receive, from several quarters, of the good the " Duty of Man" is doing. Prayer has been made for this work, that the thoughts, the style, manner, and spirit, might be acceptable, and the unction of the Holy One crown the work.

Mr. Sutcliffe's ill health will not suffer him to attend to his school. John, therefore, has left him, indebted to his care and kindness beyond what I can express. I was at a loss where to find a master ; but have determined, at length, to put him under Mr. Milner, at Hull, for a year. If you go there, I hope you will call upon him. He seems, indeed, to be all I could wish, and still continues fixed in his choice of being a preacher of Christ. Give my love to dear Mr. Adam. I know of no curate whom I could recommend to him, or I should have written to him. The Lord ever bless you!   From yours affectionately,

H. VENN.

TO MISS WHELER.

DEAR MADAM,   *Yelling, Dec .7, 1773.*

At length I shall be able to discharge some part of the debt, which you may long have expected from me ; though your kindness and friendship have laid me under such obligations as can never be returned by me.   My book, which I have taken much pains in composing, is now ready to be sent down into the country; and you and your sister will shortly receive copies.

I look upon you, and dear Mrs. Medhurst, as hastening, with a number of my precious friends, to our better country, where we shall be no more parted.   It is this consideration which fills my heart with joy, in that state of separation I am placed in by my gracious Master, from many much-beloved friends.   Some most sweet hours indeed I find, when, walking in perfect stillness and solitude, I make mention by name of every one of my particular friends and benefactors—benefactors, either by their example, their counsel, their liberality, or their works; thanking God for them, and begging the increase of His grace in their souls, and of usefulness in their lives.   Sometimes, the joy of my soul overflows, in the transporting view of what is reserved for us as our inheritance.   Oh! with what different eyes shall we one day admire Him, of whom we have spoken together, as our God and Saviour!   With what different ears shall we hear His gracious voice! with what different hearts feel our debt to Him—the deliverance from so great a misery, and so total a depravity!

The Swiss have a certain longing, which comes upon them, at times, to see their own country again. I can feel something of this, I assure you, respecting Yorkshire; and as soon as I am at liberty, I shall visit my friends there:—when that will be, I cannot say.   My church is small, and my congregation not larger than that at Kippax, though four times as large as when I came here. Though I have joy over some, I much need your prayers, that I may see "the lighting down of the Lord's arm," the revelation of His glory, and the enjoyment of His love amongst the people.—Dear Mr. Berridge preaches for me every month. Happy am I in having such a loving fervent minister of Christ.— Pray present my best respects to Mrs. Buckley and Mrs. Ingram.

May every spiritual blessing, with temporal ones as far as possible, be yours!

From your obliged friend,

H. VENN.

———

The two last letters allude to the publication of the Essay on the Prophecy of Zacharias. Some of Mr. Venn's correspondents objected to certain passages in that work; which called forth the following letter in vindication of them. The generality of Scripture commentators do not adopt the argument for the Divinity of Our Lord, referred to in the latter part of the letter; but I retain it, in order to shew that Mr. Venn had well considered the critical points involved in his publications, though they contain no display of learning or research.

———

TO THE REV. J. STILLINGFLEET.

MY DEAR FRIEND,   *Yelling, Feb.* 26, 1774.

——— Mr. Thornton had told me that my dear and much-honoured friend, Miss———, was offended at the passage, "If we cannot appeal unto God,

that we watch and pray and keep His commandments, our hearts are *false*":—as if it savoured of a
self-righteous spirit, and as if the expression " keep
His commandments" implied a faultless conformity,
instead of a cordial acceptance of them, value for
them, and subjection to them. I have written to
her, to point out that the Scripture, our unerring
guide, speaks most decisively on the necessity of
faith and obedience. The passages on the one
hand, if not checked by the others, will be most
certainly abused. In adjusting them both, and
allowing them their proper force, consists that understanding in the things of God which He hath
promised to His people. It is grievous to see any
one part of Holy Writ treated with aversion or slight.
Is it not all *equally* precious? Certainly, some would
condemn the Holy Ghost for expressing Himself
no better, if they did not know the words were
His. What think you of these declarations:—" Then
are ye my friends, when ye do *whatsoever* I command you." (Is not that as bad as *keeping* His
commandments?) " If ye keep my commandments,
ye shall abide in my love ; as I have *kept* my Father's
commandments, and abode in His love."? What
offence must be taken at St. Paul's expression,
" Then shall every man have καύχημα εἰς ἑαυτὸν
μόνον "—*boasting* in himself? Gal. vi. 4. Yet these
Scriptures give no encouragement to self-righteous-
ness. In short, it is not to be wondered at that
we are accused of *leaning*, at least, to licentiousness,
if we are not explicit, strong, and emphatical, in
pressing, as much as others, the necessity of righteousness and true holiness. But I have always

been too much on the side of free grace for many
Arminians—too much on the side of experimental
religion for many Calvinists.

Now for the grand mistake, in which my beloved, open-hearted friend, to whom I am writing,
joins quite against me. Observe : my Essay was
not a place for me to advance all the evidence
I have to prove that I am right in my interpretation of *" I am He."* I will now urge some
more proofs. The Hebrew הוא is always translated by the Septuagint, Ἐγώ εἰμι. Why not, then,
so in the New Testament? In two places in the
New Testament it will not bear any other sense
than what I have given it : I mean John viii.
58. and John xiii. 19. You cannot here translate
Ἐγώ εἰμι, " It is I." And allowing it must be so
rendered in some other places, still it suffices, that
wherever the Hebrew word, expressing the self-
existent Deity, הוא is used, Ἐγώ εἰμι is the Greek
rendering of it. And is not this a very noble decisive proof of the grand doctrine ? Not that I would
claim the merit of discovering it. It was urged by
one of the first scholars of his age, and one of the
best of men—Dr. Knight, Vicar of St. Sepulchre's,
the only divine, in London, who rejoiced to see the
Methodists, Mr. Whitfield and Wesley, come out.
In his Sermons on the Trinity, enforced with much
learning, this point is urged. From him I took
the proof, although I have somewhat altered my
manner of urging it : and, being *much* struck and
convinced by it myself, I produced it in the Essay.
And I should be glad to hear what answer you will
make to what I here send you.

Robinson is leaving my neighbourhood, and going to Leicester. I lose much by his removal: much grace is upon him. The good Lord bless, preserve, and keep you! Pray for me, who am,

Yours sincerely,   H. VENN.

The settlement of Mr. Robinson at Leicester, alluded to in the close of the last letter, is several times mentioned about this period: and the following interesting reflection occurs, on the increase of zealous Ministers in the Church.

——WELCOME, thrice welcome, the news of the Gospel thus spreading in large towns! When I set out, twenty-four years ago, I knew but of Truro, and Bradford in Wiltshire. Oh! may this be but the beginning! How reviving to such as I am, now drawing nigh our departure, to behold our prayers in some degree answered by the labourers coming forth into the harvest!——

TO WILLIAM WHITACRE, ESQ.

MY DEAR FRIEND,   *Yelling, Dec.* 20, 1773.

I am much indebted to you for returning me my servant. He has been greatly improved at Longwood House. And now I am happy in having a good hope that all the servants in the family are children of God—happy in prayer; assuredly concluding we are more than two or three who are

P

gathered together in the name of Jesus ; and that we shall have whatsoever we ask, which will be for the glory of God and the good of our souls. I find it affecting to them, as well as to myself, to enlarge upon the *mercies* we have received—upon the great things done for us already, in raising our souls from the death of sin, and making us sometimes feel the pleasure of communion with our God ; and to recount our various wickednesses, comparing them with His superabundant kindness, in our present spiritual enjoyments, and our future infinitely-glorious hopes :—and this I would press my very dear friend to do. We are too apt to dwell on the dark side, when once we are brought to the knowledge of ourselves—on our manifold corruptions, and the treachery of our hearts, the strength of our enemies, and the poverty of our best services, till we almost forget that we are the Lord's—His property by the gift of the Father, by His own purchase through the price of blood—His conquest, through the power of His arm—His New Creation, being born of God, through Him—His espoused wife—the members of His body. O high quality and condition ! sufficient to inspire hope and assurance of victory—to fill us with admiration of His love to us, and love to all who stand in this relation to Him. May my dear friends at Longwood House pray for the knowledge of these great things ! which are freely given them of God, I doubt not.

I suppose, by the time you receive this, you will also receive my book. May the style, spirit, and matter of it be owned of God, to convince, undeceive,

and bring into the way of life, some of my poor mistaken and deluded fellow-sinners! May the approaching festival be a feast to your soul, and the incarnation of God be your delight! Love to all friends.
From your much obliged friend and servant,

H. VENN.

As the last letter will, perhaps, excite the reader's interest in the state of Mr. Venn's family, regarded as a
Christian household, I will here introduce, from a letter
to Mrs. Riland, a pleasing sketch of the domestic arrange-
ments and employments at Yelling Parsonage.

——You tell me you have no idea how we go
on. Take the following sketch. I am up, one of the
first in the house, soon after five o'clock ; and when
prayer and reading the blessed Word is done, my
daughters make their appearance ; and I teach them
till Mrs. Venn comes down, at half-past eight. Then
family-prayer begins ; which is often very sweet; as
my mother's maid, and my own servants, are all,
I believe, born of God. The children begin to sing
prettily ; and our praises, I trust, are heard on high.
—From breakfast, we are all employed, till we ride
out, in fine weather, two hours for health; and after
dinner employed again. At six, I have always one
hour for solemn meditation and *walking** in my

* It was Mr. Venn's habit to engage in devotional exercises of
meditation and prayer during this hour, whilst *walking* alone,
either in a large room of the house, or sometimes in the church.

house, till seven. We have then, sometimes, twenty, sometimes more or less, of the people, to whom I expound the Word of the Blessed God: several appear much affected; and sometimes Jesus stands in the midst, and saith, "Peace be unto you!" Our devotions end at eight: we sup, and go to rest at ten. On Sundays, I am still enabled to speak six hours, at three different times, to my own great surprise. O the goodness of God, in raising me up!

———

The moral beauty and happiness of this domestic picture cannot but forcibly strike every serious mind. In the hope of deepening this impression, I insert two kindred passages from subsequent letters: the first exhibits the true light in which we should regard family connexions: the next will serve to shew us, that such a measure of the Divine blessing upon our households must be expected only in the vigilant and earnest use of the means which God has appointed for the communication of His Grace.

———

——We are all now again under one roof. Important and awful connexion! which I wish and pray may be more and more deeply imprinted in my mind. How contrary is it to our nature, to consider the nearest relations we have in this light; and to say often, solemnly, my father or mother, husband or wife, children or servants, are the very persons, with whom, as I have the most to do, so shall I have the most to answer for! They, even they, will be the witnesses, either to attest my life of faith, or to confront my false, though perhaps confident, pretensions to that precious grace. With what circumspection, with what tenderness of love, with what zeal, should we do good, and edify and comfort one another, were we to think in this manner!——

——The promise you make me of a visit to my house, if you should be recovered, calls for my best thanks; but I fear you give too much credit to Mr. and Mrs. Elton's representation of our way of life. Indeed, I do strive and labour to prevent our family worship degenerating into a form; which I greatly dread, and to which I am sadly prone, so that few can conceive how much pains and prayer it costs me, to avoid such an abuse of devotion. Yet you will be much disappointed, if you should come with any great expectations. I have heard from others of the way in which my Bristol friends speak of our house, and am ashamed : indeed, we are a company of poor, distempered, and defiled creatures, under the healing hand of Jesus! And should we have the honour of your company, I must immediately begin to pray, when the time draws near, that I may not be a prejudice and hindrance to your soul's prosperity, by my falling far beneath the practice I so constantly urge upon my flock.

———

A striking anecdote may be here introduced, from "The History of Ruth Clark," to shew how fully Mr. Venn exemplified the principles which his letters enforce.

" He watched over the morals of his servants, as well as of his children; and felt the misconduct of a servant as a family misfortune, and a matter of general humiliation throughout the household. Hence, on one occasion, when he overheard a violent quarrel, in the kitchen, between Ruth and one of the other servants, he was as much shocked and distressed as if some great loss had befallen him. After speaking to the servants, in the most serious manner, on their sinful conduct, he told them, that family-prayers, while such tempers were allowed, would be a mockery; and that they must all humble themselves before God in private, before he could allow them to meet together for social worship. Accordingly, family-prayers were discontinued for a week; during which time Mr. V.'s deportment bespoke the deepest concern and humiliation; and, during two days of that week, he remained in his study alone, engaged in fasting and prayer. We may easily conceive how deep and solemn an impression must have been made on the minds of all. It was Mr. V.'s constant aim to keep up in his own mind, and in the minds of all connected with him, a strong sense of the evil of sin, and the high necessity there is for every one who nameth the name of Christ to depart from iniquity."—*History of Ruth Clark.*

The next letter commences a correspondence with his nephew, the late Edward Venn, esq., of Camberwell, (son of Dr. Venn of Ipswich,) who was at this time just entering into business in London,

TO MR. EDWARD VENN.

MY DEAR NEPHEW,   *Yelling, March* 8, 1774.

Could you be spared, we should be very glad to
see you. I wish you all blessings in one, when I
wish you the knowledge and love of Christ Jesus
the Lord. May He guide and counsel you! He
can make you (and He alone) possess true peace
and integrity of mind, in the midst of selfishness,
fraud, and the tumult of business. It is too generally thought that business is an excuse for neglecting the salvation of the soul : but this excuse
is pointed out very fully, and very severely condemned, by our Saviour, when He says, John vi. 27 :
" Labour not for the meat which perisheth, but for
that meat which endureth unto everlasting life,
which the Son of Man shall give unto you ; for Him
hath God the Father sealed," or anointed, to this
office.—My dear nephew will easily conceive that
this strong and absolute injunction, to prefer eternal
good to temporary prosperity and opulence, is a
most gracious one ; for it does not prohibit a proper degree of application, but only an immoderate
and infidel pursuit of the things of time. It is only
an affecting call, not to neglect the provision for
endless years. Who, upon 'Change, would not be
laughed to scorn as a fool, if he should risk his all
to be rich for a year, and command the people
under him, but, at the end of that term, was sure to
be a beggar ever after ? Now, our good and merciful God, regarding and consulting the whole of our
welfare through every part of our existence, only

advises and commands us not to sacrifice eternal honours and felicity for the transient gain of a very few years; promising and assuring us, that so far from losing, by this wise choice, any thing really profitable for us here, we shall be the better enabled to succeed, and have the good of this world, as well as of that which is to come. The good esteem and affection I have for you prompts me, without design, to send you these thoughts. Mrs. Venn joins with me in wishing you every blessing; and your two *unseen* cousins desire to be remembered to you, and to all the family.

From your affectionate uncle,

H. Venn.

TO HIS SISTER-IN-LAW, MRS. BISHOP.

DEAR SISTER,   *Yelling, Sept.* 1, 1774.

Your change to your present situation appears much more likely to suit and please you; and as you are easily contented, we hope you will find an agreeable settlement where you are, till God is pleased to point out some other. I have found often much comfort and rest to my soul in that Scripture, " *Run with patience the race that is set before us.*" When men run for the prize, all the ground is measured out for them, which they are to go over. Thus it is with Christians;—the Lord's people, from the womb to the grave, have all their several places, for their childhood, their youth, their riper years, to the hour of their death, as well as the cause and manner of it, appointed, in infinite wisdom and in everlasting love to their souls. And there is a set time, how long their friends shall remain with them; what they shall do in their favour; also, what crosses and disappointments and ill usage they shall meet with, and from what quarter it all shall come. This race, set thus, we are to run with patience; not fretting or murmuring; not desponding or doubting the goodness and love of the Great Ordainer of all our lot; not even presuming to wish there was any alteration in our circumstances, unless God is pleased to bring it to pass. It is a great part of the spiritual worship due to Him, and by which we honour Him, thus to commit without carefulness all our affairs into His hands: and when we do so, He has promised His peace shall rule in our hearts. May my dear sister find and feel this, from day to day! and if you do not, lament and bewail, or pray that you may lament and bewail, the corruption of your heart.

Blessed be God! retirement and perfect solitude, whilst Mrs. Venn is spared and health given, we enjoy even more than much company. It will give you pleasure to hear that —— has returned to all his old affection for me and my family. And thus, one of the best of God's children, after a most unreasonable and unjustifiable resentment of my conduct for three whole years, is delivered from his offence against God and charity. Oh, what are even the best, in the time of trial, unless God uphold! I have lived to see abundant cause for that absolute renunciation of dependence upon the love even of those who are dear to God as well as others. " Put not your trust in princes, nor in *any* child of man."

I hear there are no hopes of ——'s recovery,

though he may linger long as he is. Oh, that sickness, and a gradual visible approach to eternity, may be made a blessing to his soul!

I hope you constantly spend an hour every morning in reading the Word of God, with prayer; and do not trust to Henry's Commentary too much: look up to God for the meaning, and only in some difficulties to the comment. Whilst you continue as you are, it is one very great privilege of your situation to have much time to read the word, and pray. I account it so here: and had rather have hours to pray, than, without them, be with the brightest examples of every grace.

Yours, &c. H. Venn.

TO MRS. RILAND.

Yelling, Nov. 29, 1774.

When I took so large a sheet of paper to write upon, I intended one side of it for my dear friend. But, as I have filled that to your husband, I must fill this to yourself. I have sympathized with you in your illness; and felt for the cause of it—your fatigue. Are the tradesmen in your town to be waited on? Could they not send their goods to be seen; or take orders with sufficient exactness? But this illness was a merciful call to retirement and recollection, after the hurry of your removal, and entrance upon your new situation*. You are already fixed in another habitation. May the eyes of the Lord be over it, by night and by day! May His

* Mr. Riland had removed to Birmingham.

presence be sensible to every heart which dwells in it; and much communion be enjoyed with Him, in secret prayer, reading, and meditating upon His word! Under your favoured roof, may the Lord hearken and hear the conversation of the parlour and the kitchen, and write a book of remembrance concerning it! May all who live in it, live as strangers and pilgrims! and all who die in it, die to the Lord! I now regard you as favoured in a most distinguished manner—happy in your conjugal relation above most—happy in your children, and in the excellent talent Mr. Riland possesses to bring them up in obedience and reverence for their parents— happy in the prospect of a glorious Church, about to be called out of their natural state of ignorance and delusion (cruel delusion, tending to death!)—happy in several excellent and cordial friends, with whom you will soon be cemented in bonds of everlasting love—happy in looking, through all these inferior enjoyments, to the infinitely nobler object of your supreme affection, who gave you His faithful elect minister for your husband; gave you your children; and gave you that manifestation of His glory, which you know how to prize;—and, when all temporal connexions cease, that glory shall be your everlasting felicity. You need not be told—you can well conceive—how sincerely I rejoice in all my dear friend's prosperity and prospects, both for time and eternity; confidently hoping that the period is arriving, when I shall see the vast accumulated felicity which is prepared and secured for her, and all my friends, before the Throne of God.

I have now been here three years and three

months. Take notice!—never absent but eleven, out of one hundred and seventy, Sundays; and sometimes not one single night in a month! Is not this residence?—and never more pleased, than when no visiter came near us; though no one delights more in the company of his friends, and the friends of Jesus. But I find unspeakable joy in the Word of Grace—at the Throne of Grace—in meditation and contemplation—in recalling past marvellous mercies and distinguishing grace—in looking forward to the final scenes of man's eventful history, and my own pilgrimage; whilst the business I have with my family, and my sermons—meeting with a few poor cottagers every evening, who are, I trust, members of Christ—make each passing day glide on apace; and weeks and months and years bring with them abounding evidence of God's faithfulness, and over-flowing goodness and everlasting love to the vilest of the vile—as I sometimes do indeed appear to myself. Oh, that I did always!

My children desire their love; and would exult in joy to see you both, and your dear children. When you can, without fatigue, I shall be very glad to receive, from your own hand, assurance of your perfect recovery: and remember, you are already near four months in debt to me.

The Lord evermore love and bless you!

From your affectionate father,

H. VENN.

TO THE REV. JAMES STILLINGFLEET.

MY DEAR FRIEND,   *Yelling, Jan.* 20, 1775.

Have you not received the long letter I sent to you, near three months since? or have you been ill, and so disabled from writing? or so busy, as to have no time? Many have been my thoughts and conjectures about this long silence of yours. Many my fears, lest you have relapsed into your old disorder. If you are well, let me have, immediately, the joy of knowing you are so. And remember, I expect to hear all particulars, how you go on in your new habitation; which I am very sure is richer than the palace of the greatest monarch; and grander, by the residence of Jehovah, your God, amongst you. Could we move with the agility we shall one day do, how many visits should we both pay to the Rector and Rectoress of Hotham, to be eye-witnesses of the fervent devotion paid by their family to the adorable Redeemer—to behold their affection for their fellow-creatures and fellow-sinners, whose welfare, present and eternal, they are sent to promote—to hear pleasing accounts of conquered sinners, increase of knowledge and grace around you, prejudice against your doctrine and Master's glorious Truth subsiding—and each of you, in your station, filling up your time with good works. Such is the life, through the distinguishing grace of God, of His family here on earth, in different degrees of usefulness.

Since I last wrote to you, I have nothing but mercies to tell of—my health better—my people so many every evening, that the kitchen will but just contain them—several new ones awakened— Mrs. Venn better.   Mr. Daw, who has been six weeks with us, a physician to the bodies of the poor, and glad to feed the hungry and clothe the naked, and supply many who otherwise must pine in want, has left us, two days since.   I mourn his absence.   He has been an example to us all.   I have had also the pleasure of a visit from Mr. Shirley and his dear wife.   He calls himself my son, but quite shames his father.   The last is first, by many degrees.

Pray, can you tell me any thing of my beloved friend, Mr. Adam?   Is he still in his tottering tabernacle?   I hope he will be able to visit you.   His heart will be rejoiced to see one of the young witnesses sent forth, to bear testimony to that grace he has found to be his salvation.

Mrs. Venn joins with me in every kind wish to Mrs. Stillingfleet.   May you inherit all the blessings of the New Testament, here and for ever!   I sent a letter to my son, in the holidays, desiring him to let me know what was really his choice; and reminding him of the importance of the work of the ministry.   He has answered my letter; and assures me, he had rather be a minister of Christ than a prince.   He speaks well!

Pray, O pray for him sometimes, as well as his father—that his eye may be single, and his conscience thoroughly awakened, and then purged by the blood of sprinkling!

Adieu, my beloved friend!

H. VENN.

In the month of February of this year, Mr. Venn was called from home, to attend the funeral of Mrs. Ascough, Mrs. Venn's mother, who was buried at Highworth, Wiltshire. I select, from letters written at the time, the following notices of a visit to Oxford, and of several friends whom he met with during his journey.

——On Tuesday we reached Oxford; where Mr. Stevenson, a *Yorkshire* gentleman, and an honour to your county, came to us : he is full of good sense, faith, zeal, and love. We breakfasted with him and five other young students, all sensible, humble, and zealous, desiring only to be preachers of Christ. There were, they told me, as many more, in the University, like-minded with themselves. It was a most pleasing sight, to behold them listening to every word I uttered, in exhorting and animating them to be bold, and faithful to our Saviour! We concluded with prayer.

——On Sunday, I preached at Highworth, to a large congregation. My text was 1 Sam. ii. 25—a favourite subject with me.

——I staid a day and a half at Wallingford, with Mr. Pentycross. He is in a most useful sphere indeed, and has much favour with the people. I preached for him on Ash-Wednesday. A most attentive congregation were present, to hear ; and, though I preached an hour and a half, not one seemed tired.

——In London, where I was obliged to remain a whole month, I was happy in hearing Mr. De Coetlogon. His discourses are all I would wish to hear—judicious, doctrinal in a proper degree, very experimental, and faithfully applied. In the midst of caresses and admiration, more than any preacher fixed at the Lock ever met with, may he be kept vigilant and humble! I was with him several times. His health is very weak; and by being often dangerously ill, he feels more deeply the emptiness of present things.

Notwithstanding the kindness of many friends, we were heartily tired of the great city, before we left it; and returned to our sweet retirement with a higher relish.

TO MRS. RILAND.

MY DEAR FRIEND,   *Yelling, June* 3, 1775.

I cannot help writing to you now, when I have received from your beloved husband so pleasing an account of the success of his labours, and the good disposition of the people to keep him an assistant. I know not any one to recommend; for curates are like wives—a great comfort, or a great cross. And though I did venture to recommend him one of the latter, and succeeded marvellously, I must not expect to find a curate as able to please and fulfil the duties of his place as a Priscilla. When I received Mr. Riland's letter, I was doubly happy

in this reflection, that we were both greatly encouraged and favoured at the same time. In my
small sphere, there never was so good a prospect as
at present.

I have lately had three delightful cordials, in the
death-bed testimony of Lady Gertrude Hotham, of
Mrs. Nicholson, and Sarah Reeves. The first, my
old friend, was burnt, from her clothes taking fire ;
and after lying fifteen days upon her bed, without
sleep and without food, she departed. The whole
time, she was cheerful—said she wanted nothing—
that she was near her journey's end—a long one—
and she knew she was going to enter into a blessed
eternity. "For this my happiness," said she, to
all around her, "bless the Lord Jesus Christ !"
Mrs. Carteret and Mrs. Cavendish attended her ;
and from them I had this account. Thus, whilst
her infidel brother, Lord Chesterfield, says he was
forced to read till his eyes were almost blind,
lest he should hang himself, his christian sister
can rejoice on a bed of languishing, and edify all
about her.

Mrs. Nicholson was the wife of the assistant
I had for the first year I was at Yelling ; and as
soon as she heard, she obeyed. She became a most
earnest, though a trembling, seeker of her Lord ;
and last Thursday I preached her funeral sermon.
She left a husband and four young children ; and
her last words were sweet indeed : "Trust, oh,
trust," said she, "in Jesus, all of you ! for He has
proved faithful to all His promises, and fulfilled all
my desires."

Sarah Reeves was a farmer's wife at Godman-

chester.   Her youngest son came to Yelling church
the first of the family, out of curiosity.   After him,
the eldest sister; then the second; then the youngest; then the father and mother; and, last of all,
the eldest son, a farmer.   She died of a pleurisy;
and, during the whole time, was a pattern of peace
and patience, and for a sign and wonder in her
village.   Thus is the Lord testifying His grace.

In October, I fully purpose to see you and yours.
I believe I shall come alone, and, for the first time,
leave Mrs. Venn.   My love to your children and
their father.   Adieu, my dear friend!

From yours, &c.   H. VENN.

The following extract furnishes a very instructive sup-
plement to the subject of the last letter.

TO THE REV. JAMES STILLINGFLEET.

Yelling, Aug, 30, 1775.

——You had not before mentioned the death
of the dear female disciple of Christ.   We should
all, I think, do well to keep an account of those
who thus evidently die comforted and triumphant.
You observe, ' a close walk with God is the best preparation for it.'   I believe the same; and that the
knowledge of our acceptance with God is to be constantly urged as one of the greatest motives to
lead a strict life, and to abstain from all appearance
of evil; seeing the Holy Ghost, whose testimony
alone can satisfy the conscience, will never dwell

with the slothful or lukewarm; much less with presumptuous offenders. Scripturally to state, and
firmly to maintain by sound arguments, the knowledge of Salvation, is, I believe, a most useful way
of preaching: guarding against the hypocrites, who
will sometimes speak great swelling words about
this matter, though themselves the servants of corruption, and conscious of the lie they tell in speaking of their joy in the Lord. I judge, one great
reason of the worldliness prevailing amongst the
orthodox Dissenters, is, their teachers not pressing
this point; and, amidst very much error, one great
cause of Mr. Wesley's success, some years ago, was
his urging Christians not to rest without joy in God
from receiving the atonement. Indeed, he erred in
making this knowledge to be justifying faith itself,
instead of the fruit thereof; and also as to the mode
in which the knowledge is acquired:—yet, better
even so, than that uncertainty which leaves believers
and infidels on nearly the same footing respecting
any anticipation of glory ready to be revealed, and
which holds forth no high peculiar blessedness to
excite men to give all diligence to make their calling
and election sure.

————

Many of Mr. Venn's letters, written about this time,
allude to the prospect of his son's leaving school, to reside
at Yelling, and pursue his studies under his father's care,
previously to his going to College. The following extract, as well as the subsequent letters, illustrate his
earnest and pious solicitude for the spiritual welfare of his
son.

Yelling, Sept. 30, 1775.

AT Christmas, my son comes home; and I shall have great need, more than common, of your prayers, that whilst he lives with me, he may see nothing that will hurt his precious soul, and take off the force of those instructions I shall be daily giving him—nothing but what will win his affection, even without the word, to Christ; and make him feel that the knowledge of Him is the way of peace and joy.

TO MRS. RILAND.

Yelling, Feb. 7, 1776.

YOUR *Lilliputian* epistle, my dear friend, was in great danger of being swallowed up in some letter of due size, and never coming to my hands, where it was so welcome; though one part of it, which mentions your poor state of health, alarms me, and makes me entreat Mr. Riland to write me word, instantly, how you do. No other matter, than that you are recovered of your complaint, will make the letter an acceptable messenger to our family.

You very justly suppose that, after receiving the good account of your safe confinement, I should have written sooner, unless I had been much engaged. I most certainly ought, and did purpose it; but I have had my hands exceedingly full. My son has been my pupil since the 16th of December; and my heart perhaps too much intent on his qualifying himself with all learning for the ministry, makes me spend much time with him; for I know that a good understanding, well improved by acquaintance with the best authors, adds great weight and authority to the teacher ; and, as Mr. Berridge (an excellent scholar himself) says, " Learning is a good stone to throw at a dog, to stop his barking."

At present, my son is every thing I could wish— a sweet temper indeed, and very serious, joining with devotion in our meetings in the evening, and intent to please me by studying closely. This, with my two other pupils, the girls, and my own reading the blessed Book, fills my time after I have studied for the pulpit :—this makes me grudge the loss of a day. Another reason of my delay was, a fall I had from my horse, on the 27th of January, that most bitter, freezing, snowy day. I was returning home, from a visit of charity to an afflicted Child of God, when, in the open field, about a mile from home, my mare lost her feet, in a place she could not see, fell upon her head, and threw me violently before her upon the hard ground, and then ran home. Had a limb been broken, I must have been frozen to death, before it was known I had been thrown : or had it continued to snow, as it did ten minutes before I fell, and soon after I got home, I should have struggled in vain against my enemy ; for that very day several were frozen to death. But in mercy to my family, I was preserved marvellously—bruised indeed much on one shoulder, but now able to minister to the people. May the life, thus in tender mercy to my family prolonged, be more earnestly devoted to His service !

I do fully purpose to be with you, to preach your charity sermons, in May. I shall certainly have much pleasure in seeing my dear friend, her husband, children, and the Church of God, in Birmingham—much pleasure in meeting once more those with whom, I trust, I shall spend an eternity in Heaven—and even there remember how by the way we talked of the power and glory and love of our Saviour, and His wonderful dealings with our souls.

Mrs. Venn and my children join in most cordial wishes. I believe there is not that sight or entertainment on earth which would give my children, self, and servants, so much joy as to see you here, and Mr. Riland. You scarcely think how often we talk of you both; and how the children's eyes sparkle, and always remember some instance of your care and tenderness, when they were desolate, and their dear mamma received up into glory. May the Lord Jesus Christ reveal Himself more and more to your soul, and make you a preacher in the parlour to the female circle! for I am sure, if you will speak, you can, most evangelically.

Adieu! From your affectionate,

H. Venn.

TO THE REV. JAMES STILLINGFLEET.

MY VERY DEAR FRIEND,   *Yelling, Aug.* 12, 1766.

When your letter was brought to me this evening in the parlour, I said to Mrs. Venn and the company, "How much I am ashamed, and almost even afraid, to open this letter! I have been *inexcusably* negligent for many months, and deserve not to be considered as a correspondent; and my affectionate friend has still passed over my fault, and favours me with another epistle. I will immediately ask his pardon; fill a whole sheet of paper; and, if there were any credit to be given to resolutions, I would resolve never to offend again."

I will tell you, as you are pleased to interest yourself in my matters, how it has fared with me and mine, since you last heard from me. In December, my son came home. I had the great pleasure to find he had applied himself closely to his studies at school; and still more, that here he was disposed to do the same. But, as I could not teach him to *write* good Latin, and I feared he might be most defective therein, I accepted dear Mr. Robinson's proposal; and he is now at Leicester with him, for two months, in order, I trust, to receive a blessing from that lively, zealous, prudent, and able young minister, as well as to be perfected in the Latin tongue. I have no fear of my son's abilities; they are excellent: and I hope he is indeed drawn by grace to desire the ministry. Nothing can be better than his behaviour here. I pray for him day and night; desiring only one thing, that he may be made an able minister of the New Testament.

Last May, I accepted an invitation from dear Mr. Riland, and went alone to Birmingham. I never left Mrs. Venn before, for so long as three days; and designed only to stay there five nights: but my horse having met with an unfortunate accident, I was detained there during two Sundays. Great was my pleasure to see Mr. Riland evidently filled with care and concern for the success of his ministry.

I preached five times to his people.—What a blessed sphere of usefulness!

There I met with a young gentleman from your neighbourhood, who delights to hear you. He gave me a charming account of your success; and told me your church would not contain the numbers who crowded to hear the Gospel from you.

Mrs. Venn desires her most affectionate respects, with myself and daughters, to you and your dear wife. We remember with regret that we had not her company; and hope, whenever you are called into this part of the world, you will come and *stay* with us. None will rejoice more in the visit.

I still go on here in my poor way. A few more are added, it appears, to the Church; and several of the older disciples seem to prosper. But I have long since found, that if I turn my eyes from Jesus, and expect my comfort from any thing but from Himself, I must be dissappointed. Pray for me, that with a single eye I may labour without ceasing, as far as my strength will go, with all long-suffering and doctrine, till I go hence. This I beg for you, by name; and every Saturday, between six and seven in the evening, I have a pleasing remembrance of you and your flock, hoping I am also remembered by you. I have been nowhere, but to Birmingham —not even to London—this twelve-month. Were I able to bear the expense, I should with exceeding joy come into Yorkshire, and meet once more, before my departure, many souls so dear to me: but we must regard our circumstances, and deny ourselves, when it would be greatly imprudent to gratify our inclinations: yet it does grieve me, when some of my Yorkshire friends are apt to say, that I might, but will not, visit them.

Mr. Berridge is in London : he laboured for three months above his strength : he had the largest congregations that were ever known, for a constancy; and greatly was his word owned of the Lord. He is as affectionate as a father to my son, and gives him many valuable books. He is often telling me that he is sick of all he does, and loathes himself for the inexpressible corruption he feels within : yet is his life a pattern to us all, and an incitement to love and serve the Lord with all our strength. Thus does my affectionate brother resemble that burning and shining light, who cried out, " I have need to be baptized of Thee!" Thus I find it with him. Twenty-five years ago, I was certain I should be able to reconcile the Word of God in all its parts, and be able to pray without distraction. Now, I wait for the light of Eternity, and the perfection of holiness, in order that I may know any thing as I ought to know.

True holiness is quite of another character than we, for a long time, in any degree conceive. It is not serving God without defect, but with deep self-abasement—with astonishment at His infinite condescension and love manifested to sinners—to ungodly enemies, and men who, in their very best estate on earth, are exceedingly vile. It is pleasing to consider how we are all led into this point, however we may differ in others : and were it not for the demon of controversy, and a hurry of employment, which leaves no time for self-knowledge or devout meditation on the Oracles of God, I am persuaded we should every one be so grounded in this matter, that by-standers would no longer reproach us for our divisions.

Adieu, my dear friend! Forgive my faults; pity, and pray for me!

Yours ever, in the best bonds,

H. VENN.

The next correspondent was a relative of Mr. Venn—the late John Brasier, esq., of Camberwell, near London; who had shortly before this time returned from India, and was on the point of marriage.

TO JOHN BRASIER, ESQ.

MY DEAR COUSIN,   *Yelling, Dec.* 2, 1776.

We begin to reckon the days till we shall receive the pleasure of your visit, with your new and nearest relative. What a place for a new-married couple to come to spend their Christmas in!—silence and solitude—winter cold, and miry roads. Yet here I find more of that precious treasure for which martyrs bled, than ever I did in my life. Christ is company in solitude, and joy all the year round. As His beloved name is the cement and the foundation of your connexion, you will be prepared to participate in those enjoyments the world knoweth not of—the view of that Incarnate God, who wedded to him His Church, not seeing in it an excellent spirit and a lovely temper, a fitness for the conjugal relation, a heavenly aim and purpose of life ; — no ; when we were more loathsome than the beggar on the dunghill, and of so degenerate a spirit as to embrace our shame, and glory in our infamy — then was the time of love — then our Redeemer said, " I have betrothed thee to myself in righteousness, and in judgment, and in faithfulness ; I have betrothed thee to myself for ever." Then He determined to take away the filthy garments of our own righteousness, and clothe us with the robe of salvation—to put beauty and comeliness upon our deformed spirits, and give us the same judgment and mind as He has himself ; then He determined to make us meet—by changing us from one degree of holiness to another—to make us ready for the marriage-supper above, and that we should exult at the midnight-cry, with the wise virgins : " Behold, the Bridegroom cometh ! Go ye out to meet him !"

If the day of your nuptials is not past, nor the company invited, I should think you would do well to have none, or as few for your company as may be. It is of admirable use to be much in prayer on that day, that your union may bear a resemblance to that of Christ and His Church. I wish—I pray —I assure myself, it will.

Pray present my Christian love to Miss S. or Mrs. B. Love to Mr. and Mrs. Robinson, and all friends.

From your affectionate cousin,

H. VENN.

CORRESPONDENCE.

SECTION III.

LETTERS WRITTEN TO HIS CHILDREN, AND TO DIFFERENT FRIENDS, FROM THE YEAR 1777, TO THE TIME OF HIS SON'S ORDINATION, 1782.

THE introduction of letters from Mr. Venn to his children will form a new era in the Correspondence. A son and three daughters had now arrived at that critical period of life, in which the character receives its most important touches. The piety and tenderness which these parental letters breathe will give a charm to the wise counsels they convey.

The letters to his son, especially, will be highly valued by those who know the peculiar dangers which beset the entrance into life of a young man of religious education. To these letters, also, an additional interest will be attached; whilst they are regarded as the instructions of a zealous minister of Christ, in training up a son for the service which has long been his own delight and glory; and whilst it is borne in mind, that these instructions were not given in vain, but that the son lived to exemplify the sacred character which the letters themselves so vividly portray.

TO MR. JOHN VENN.

Bath, June 18, 1777.

YOUR letter, my dear son, was very acceptable, on several accounts : it assured us of your safe journey, and contains several Christian reflections. Let our correspondence increase.

Through the Divine mercy, we had a safe journey to Mr. Maxfield's. At Salisbury, your mamma and sister were delighted with the solemn temple. A very noble fabric it is ; and was long accounted, by the votaries of superstition, in a peculiar manner the residence of the Deity. We know, blessed be His name! that *we* are His temple ; for He dwelleth and walketh in us. On our journey, we stopped to see Mr. ——'s seat. One hundred thousand pounds have been expended in laying out the grounds around it! Here is every thing to gratify the eye ; and your mamma and sister were extremely pleased, and particularly with the paintings in the house. Yet the possessor of this fine place is frequently so miserable, his friends fear he will sink into a settled melancholy. Oh, that he knew the Prince of Peace!

After seeing the rich man's possessions, I had great satisfaction in paying a visit to a poor man, aged ninety-six, and his wife eighty-six : the husband blind, yet of strong understanding. I preached to him the Poor Man of Nazareth ; and he cried out, " Oh, Sir! I would crawl on all-fours to hear such talk! But we be all left in the dark : our minister never comes anigh us!"—Who can tell but the word spoken may be as a nail fastened in a sure place! May you and I ever watch for opportunities of doing good, and receiving good!

We came to Bath on Tuesday last, that your mamma might drink the waters. May it please God to bless them to her! They seem, at present, to do her good. My prayer, before we set out, and every day, is, that we may receive good to our souls; and already I have received an answer. In these parts, I see great monuments of the rich and tender love of our ever-blessed Saviour. Captain Scott and his Lady, who set out in the way to glory long, long after me, how they have got beyond me! He said to me the other day, "It was worth while for us to come to Bristol, if it had been only to suffer as we have done under the kind hand of our Lord: for now we can tell of His faithfulness and consolations, which we related before upon hearsay."—His beloved wife was two months at the point of death; and he has been cut for a cancer, the disease which killed his father. Dear Mr. Fletcher, who is sinking under a painful disease, accosted me thus:—"I love his rod! How gentle are the stripes I feel! how heavy those I deserve!" A third witness, a lady, who by excruciating pain has lost one eye, yet still continues in her affliction, told me, that she found, at the foot of the cross, patience and victory over all; though she suffered more than she was able to express.—Everlasting praise be given unto the Lord of all lords for such invaluable supports! Here is the faith and patience of the saints! here the power of Christ!

What an office are you training for, my dear

son!—to publish that Saviour, whose love can thus make bitter sweet, and give songs to our poor afflicted fellow-creatures in the dark night of severest sufferings.

> Oh! for His love, let rocks and hills
> Their lasting silence break,
> And all harmonious human tongues
> The Saviour's praises speak!

To Him, daily, and every hour of the day, almost, I commend you ; begging of Him to direct you in all your studies, and enable you diligently to employ your precious time in acquiring knowledge, for no other purpose than to lay it all at the foot of His cross ,whom even angels adore, casting their crown before Him! and, without self-seeking or self-complacency, be, after the example of His eminent servants, the servant of all—rich in Christ, but less than nothing in your own eyes.

Your dear mamma and sister join with me in love to you.—Excellent is your purpose, to rise early, and study hard. I pray God give you resolution and perseverance!

The Lord Jesus be with your spirit, and give you wisdom and understanding ; the praise of which shall endure for ever!

From your affectionate father,

H. VENN.

———

The following additional particulars respecting Mr. Fletcher occur in a letter to Mr. Stillingfleet.

—I was for six weeks in the house with the extraordinary and very excellent Mr. Fletcher.* Oh, that I might be like him! I do assure you, that I strictly observed him for six weeks, and never heard him speak any thing but what was becoming a pastor of Christ's Church;—not a single unbecoming word of himself or of his antagonists, or of his friends. All his conversation tended to excite to greater love and thankfulness for the benefits of Redemption; whilst his whole deportment breathed humility and love. We had many conversations. I told him, most freely, that I was shocked at many things in his "Checks"; and pointed them out to him. We widely differ about the efficacy of Christ's death, the nature of Justification, and the Perfection of the Saints; but I believe we could live years together, as we did in great love. He heard me twice; and I was chaplain both morning and evening in the family, as his lungs would not suffer him to speak long or loud. He desired his love, by me, to all his Calvinistic brethren; and begged their pardon for the asperity with which he had written. I am persuaded, as I told him, that if he were to live with some of those whom he has been taught to conceive of as Antinomians, and hear them preach, he would be much more reconciled to them.

* At the house of James Ireland, esq., Brislington, near Bristol.

In the October of this year, 1777, Mr. John Venn was entered as a student at Sidney College, Cambridge, under the tuition of Mr. John Hey, a tutor of eminent talents and reputation, and a distinguished Norrisian Professor of Divinity.

TO MR. JOHN VENN.

Yelling, Oct, 30, 1777.

I HAVE now to congratulate my dear son, in his new room, and entrance on his college studies;—a most important period in your life—a seed-time, from which, duly improved, yourself, and many immortal souls, for whom Christ died, will receive everlasting advantage. Now is a price put into your hands—an admirable opportunity of improving your mental faculties—of acquiring a fund of human learning, which will be of great use to you as long as you live—of habituating yourself to study and meditation, and much retirement, the fit preparation for the high and spiritual office for which you are designed.

You have heard so many lessons from me (and, I thank my gracious God! not without effect), that I can only repeat in writing what you have received *vivâ voce.* But, as to write to you on these important snbjects is a pleasure to me, I shall remind you of a few particulars, which we have often talked of already; beginning with what relates to your body, and concluding with some advice respecting your eternal interests.

R

Exert, as you did at Leicester, resolution; and rise early: so will you have opportunity to perform much every day, and with ease give to your studies and your devotions a just proportion of your time. Be ashamed of giving place to sloth and love of sleep. Soon victory will declare for you; and in doing well, you will reap more present pleasure than self-indulgence can give. Be attentive to your health.

Continue, as you have done for nearly these two years, to read the Book of Books : but read it always with prayer : and, before you open it, recollect what excellent things are said in its praise—what good has been received from it by millions now in glory. Beg it may work upon your mind, and be written in your heart. Shun, as poison, all disputes and controversies. Infinite hurt has been done by them; and very little good to any one.

I am very glad that you, with the three friends you mention, intend to meet on Sundays—I suppose, by turns, at each other's room. But I would not have you increase your number, on several accounts. Your knowledge of each other, and confidence of friendship, will enable you to speak without fear, and freely : but more would be a bar to such freedom, and prove a snare, by tempting you to speak for commendation. More would draw upon you the eyes of each College ; and expose you to needless ridicule, and prove an offence, which few young people are able to bear. It would have the appearance of making a party, and lead to several disagreeable consequences. There is no occasion that you should mention your meeting to any one :

and if there should be other serious young men desirous of such improvement on the Sunday, they should make another party ; and so on—three or four making up a company. When you are together, your great temptation will be levity of mind— a sort of merriment very unseasonable—when you should be conversing, with all your attention, upon subjects of infinite moment. But if you are honest, meekly to reprove the first appearance of that spirit, you will succeed ; and the Lord Jesus will, according to His promise, be in the midst of you. Happy shall we be to hear you testify He is so ; and that you find yourselves strengthened, and animated to live, in all sobriety, vigilance, and selfdenial, as becometh Christians. All send their love·

From your affectionate father,

H. VENN.

TO MR. JOHN VENN.

MY VERY DEAR SON,   *Yelling, Nov.* 11, 1777.

Figure to yourself a miser, glorying in his riches ; or the child of ambition, exalted to the pinnacle of worldly honour :—their pleasure cannot exceed what your letter, received this day, gives to me ; and it is neither so pure, nor so well founded. My joy arises from the glorious hope of your immortal happiness, and of your proving the highly-favoured instrument of spreading the knowledge of a Saviour, amongst ignorant, guilty, perishing creatures. My joy arises from the promising appearance, that the prayers offered up for you, from the hour of your birth to this moment, the instructions given to

R 2

you, and the bright examples of Christian piety you
have seen, have made some effectual impression on
your mind.   My joy arises from the delightful consideration, that you, in your early youth, instead of
indulging base appetites, sensual or mental, to fill
you with bitter remembrance of your ways and
doings at college, are desirous to improve a liberal
and learned education, to qualify yourself for the
noblest office entrusted to men—the office of preaching the Gospel, and watching over souls, in love to
them, and to God their Maker.   I immediately,
therefore, take my pen, and comply with your most
acceptable request, in sending you the largest sheet
I have, of advice from the most affectionate heart of
a parent, who has received so much comfort from
you, ever since you were my son.

My first advice is, that you would beware of the
device Satan too successfully practises against novices in religion.   When he perceives they are no
longer to be kept asleep in profaneness or formality—
no longer to be deluded with the pleasures of gross
sin, or the love of fame or of wealth—when he sees
they are determined to come out from the world and
be separate—he alters his method of seeking to destroy them.   " Be more separate," he suggests ; "distinguish yourself ; *immediately* assume the preacher's
office : neglect the peculiar duties of your age and
station, and intrude into what does by no means yet
belong to you : force your sentiments upon others ;
and consider yourself as destined, even in your youth
(without experience, without knowledge, observe !),
to be a reformer, authorised to despise your elders,
to be impatient of submission, to be heady, high-

minded : and then, to complete the whole, abuse learning, and be confident you have an impulse from Heaven, and a Divine call to justify all you do."—Thus I have seen religious young men perverted, and made insufferably disagreeable, by their false ideas of religion, and a stumbling-block in the way of others ; they themselves seldom recovering from their forward, proud spirit. Under the influence of this proud spirit, they are always for overdoing, and for needless, nay, absurd singularities. They will even court persecution ; and then swell with the idea that they are treated, for Christ's sake, as the Prophets and Martyrs were of old. Take knowledge, therefore, of the important boundary between separation from the world, and this offensive self-sufficient excess, in things which our God does not require.

My second advice is, that you would dwell much upon the substantial part of a Christian's life : and be assured, if you are not ashamed of this, the fear of the world is not your master. The substantial part is modesty and chastity, in opposition to pertness and impurity—temperance and sobriety, confronting the surfeit or drunkenness of epicures— humility and meekness, in opposition to natural haughtiness and angry pride—guarded cheerfulness, under a sense both of the Divine presence and the mischief of noisy mirth—love to God and His word, expressed by a stern look when scoffers pour out foolishness ; when a *double entendre*, or an infidel sneer, is uttered—love of diligent study, serious acquaintance, useful conversation—with secret prayer, and meditation on the word of Christ. Conscious

that you are living thus, and that this is your
earnest purpose and your daily prayer, you need
have no fear that you are making a compromise
with the world, or want that zeal for the Lord
which true faith inspires. Whilst thus you lay the
stress upon matters of utmost moment, you will
receive the blessing of the Lord; you will win and
attract both esteem and affection from many; you
will put to silence the ignorance of foolish men, by
well doing. Their idea of your religion is, that it
puffs you up—makes you think yourself better than
all beside; actuating you by a spirit of singularity,
and love to be admired;—that you are a compound
of ignorance, enthusiasm, and spiritual pride. Nothing can convince them of their gross mistake, or
conquer their prejudices, but humility, meekness,
wisdom, and soundness of mind, which those who
are really in Christ possess and manifest: at the
same time, their conscientious attention to their
duty, so striking, gives them no overweening conceit of themselves; abased as they are, from heart-
felt conviction how much the Lord has done and
suffered for them—how much they have received
from His bounty and grace—how infinitely worthy
He is of all adoration and love; a very small part of
which they return to Him, at best.

My third advice is, that you do, without fail,
keep an account of yourself, in a diary, written in
such a character as will be legible to yourself
only. Be bold, and resolute to do this. I know
nothing of greater benefit to youth. You will find
much opposition against this practice, from within;
therefore you must be resolute. A faithful account

of your time, your discourse, your tempers—how pride, and selfishness, and vanity work—will convince you, you are vile—a sinner, exceedingly beyond all you will otherwise believe; needing the help and strength of God, and the atoning blood and salvation of Christ. I began to keep my diary, hoping to find myself in every thing exact, and almost without fault. How was I surprised and ashamed, when innumerable deficiencies, and blots, and corruptions, appeared! How convinced, both of my guilt and depravity!—and so prepared to be truly thankful for the redemption of my soul. This method Mr. Ingham used to practise, and Mr. Hervey; two of the most exemplary men I ever knew.

I will conclude with advising you to study, with much attention and exactness, *their* characters who have obtained the immortal honour, that they pleased God; such as, Enoch, Noah, Abraham, Moses, Joshua, Job, &c. There will be much of entertainment, as well as instruction, in this method. You may be sure, nothing is misrepresented here. You will see what manner of persons the Spirit of God does form. You will perceive, that supreme love to Him, and undaunted valour in His cause, and resignation to His will, fully possesesd them. Then, lifting up your eyes and heart to their God and your God, beg that, under a much more luminous dispensation, and richer helps for spiritual life and godliness, you may be a follower of them, who are set before you for ensamples. There is a great beauty in Scripture characters; which you are always to consider as exemplifications of Scripture doctrines, and animating proofs, how much we, by diligent seeking, may receive from our most gracious and bountiful God.

If you, my dear son, will at any time specify on what particular points you desire my advice, I shall have some guide in writing to you; and shall always do it with pleasure.

I rejoice that your Tutor is pleased with you. " Good understanding," saith the Oracle of God, " giveth favour :" Prov. xiii. 15. Witness Daniel and the Three Children; Ezra, and Nehemiah. You are sensible this is an additional motive to strive to excel.

How do your books suit the shelves? Have you room for them? I hope you mind your posture in reading—making good use of your high desk, and standing full half your time. My respects to Harry Jowett, Farish, and Mr. Smith.

The Lord Jesus be with your spirit!

From your affectionate father,

H. VENN.

———

The following very useful letter to a young man at College, may be introduced with peculiar propriety in this place, though of an earlier date. It was written to Mr. Henry Jowett, then a student, and afterwards Fellow and Tutor of Magdalen College, Cambridge. He succeeded Mr. John Venn in the Rectory of Little Dunham, Norfolk, when Mr. Venn was appointed to the living of Clapham.

TO MR. HENRY JOWETT.

Yelling, Oct. 5, 1776.

You have never, dear Sir, been long out of my thoughts, since you asked me what comment was best on the Bible.   The inquiry indicated a desire to know and please God.   It implied a conviction, which all must feel before they can be saved, that Divine knowledge is infinitely preferable to all human sciences.   In answer to your question, I can, from a happy experience, assure you, there is one certain way (and I conclude but one) of acquiring spiritual understanding.   It is a laborious one, and very contrary to our natural love of ease : you will find it in the 2d chapter of Proverbs, and the first nine verses, compared with the command, Deut. vi. 4—9.   From hence it is plain, that much pains must be taken in pondering on the word of God : we must read it with as much attention as we do a mathematical proposition ; and add to our attention earnest prayer that our understanding may be opened to understand the Scripture.

The parts of Scripture which we must read in this manner, above the rest, are such as describe the majesty of Jehovah ; the Godhead of Christ ; His power, grace, and redemption of sinners ; our natural condition, and the transformation begun and carried on in the souls of the faithful.   These are the material and fundamental articles, called, by the Holy Ghost, " the wonderful things of God's Law." You are to read a little at a time.   What you do not understand, confess before the Lord ; and ask

the explanation, as you would from your own dear
father, of any thing he could make clear to you.
Say, " My Lord! what meaneth this? It is very
dark to my mind. I can receive no benefit from it,
through the ignorance which is in me." Say—
when you read the most glorious account of His
love, His power, His victory, and triumph—" Lord,
I see not these things in a light to charm and cap-
tivate me—not as realities, infinitely interesting to
my soul—not so as to engage me to covet earnestly
a share in them!" When you read the Scriptures
which delineate fallen man, say : " Lord, how little am I humbled under this charge! how little
ashamed of my depravity! how have I flattered
myself, instead of confessing my sin!"

To make more clear this method of reading
Scripture—which alone, I think, honours it as the
word of God—I will give you a specimen upon
Hannah's Song, 1 Sam. ii. 1—10. When I read the
first verse, I look up, and ask, " Oh that my heart
may rejoice in the Lord!"—not in temporal advantages, or creature-good. I say, " O Lord, exalt my
horn or power—enlarge my mouth over my enemy!"
and then I call to mind my peculiar temptations,
my besetting sin, and the dreadful assaults made
upon me. Then I proceed to meditate on the
Lord, Holy, Almighty, unchangeable; endeavouring to recollect the Scripture facts which display
these Divine attributes. In the 3d, 4th, and 5th
verses, I consider the doom and end of the proud
and arrogant opposers of God's government and
truth. In the five next verses, I reflect upon His
absolute dominion over health and strength, life

and death, poverty and wealth—His condescension to the self-condemned, and vile in their own eyes—His love for the faithful, and vengeance against His adversaries. I read and meditate upon these ten verses, till grand ideas of the Lord penetrate my ignorant mind; till I feel His favour is more than words can express, and His displeasure the greatest evil.

By practice and habit, this method of reading becomes delightful: and what knowledge is thus gained, you will never lose. The Bible is a perfect work in itself. Excepting matters of chronology, and the prophetical parts not yet fulfilled, a diligent and devout perusal will be the means of explaining it sufficiently. We often are destitute of the spirit of prayer, and therefore find it irksome to bow our knees; but in this manner of reading the Scriptures I have seldom failed of finding light and love spring up in my heart, and grace to pour out my prayer, as the passage engaging my meditation suggests.

All blessings which can enrich your soul, and make you an able minister of Christ, rest upon you! If I can be of the least service to you, be assured you may always command me.

Yours, &c.

H. Venn.

It was formerly a custom, in several of the Colleges at Cambridge, to allow an annual feast among the young men, at the time of conferring the degree of Bachelor of

Arts; and such occasions too often became scenes of intemperance. The general improvement in the moral habits of the University, of late years, has in a great measure abolished such evils. But, yet, the warning contained in the following letter may not be without its use; for no young man can enter life, either by passing through the University, or by any other avenue, without being occasionally exposed to the temptation of joining in scenes of riot and intemperance.

———

TO MR. JOHN VENN.

Yelling, Jan. 17, 1778.

VERY solicitous, my dear son, for your welfare, I cannot put out of my mind the danger you must be exposed to next week, at the Bachelor's entertainment. I regard the danger as the greater, because you did not seem apprehensive of it; nor to have, as I could wish, a just conception that such meetings are, almost without exception, abused, to intemperance and riot—which I do not think can be prevented: consequently, they should be avoided, if possible. Now, were you to come over for three or four days, I do not see that any objection could be made; and you would be thus out of the way of temptation. But, if you stay, and do go to the meeting, how much need have you to beg earnestly, that you may be kept!—for be assured, that every one, who has been condemned by your exact conduct, will be glad to see you yield; and exert their utmost to overcome you, that you may no more be able to frown on vice. I remember dear Mr. Adam of Wintringham, (observing how little we have to be proud of,) said most truly, that half our virtue was owing to our being out of the way of temptation. The Oracles of God affirm the same thing. The command in them is peremptory : " Go out from the presence of a man as soon as thou perceivest the words of wisdom are not in him." The impression necessarily made by our company is thus strongly expressed : " He that walketh with wise men, shall be wise ; but a companion of fools shall be destroyed." And lest, from some selfish considerations, or overweening conceit of our own prudence and care to resist the evil, we might think we can be with the profane, and remain unhurt, the warning is given in very affecting terms : " Be not deceived : evil communications corrupt good manners." May the Lord, therefore, bring a gracious fear always upon your mind, of entering at all into the place where scoffers sit, and their tongue speaketh against the Most High !

Last week, my affectionate friend, Lady Lowther, entered into her glorious rest. She was indeed an honour to her Christian profession ! What an animating thought, to look up to so many of my intimates, now amongst the spirits of the just made perfect ! It familiarizes the thought of my own departure, as a translation to the society of those who were so dear to me when in the body, and I to them, through the love of our common Saviour.

Your mamma and sisters desire their love ; and wait, with the same anxiety as I do, to hear that you are preserved from disgracing your character, if you must be at the meeting; but if you determine otherwise, let me hear.

From your affectionate father,

H. VENN.

___

After the foregoing letter was written and put into the post, a letter was received from Mr. John Venn, in which he expressed himself so satisfactorily respecting the intended entertainment, that his father immediately wrote a few lines, and sent them by the same post, to say that he should now no longer have any anxiety or fear, even if his son should determine to attend the feast.

___

TO MR. JOHN VENN.

Yelling, Jan. 3, 1777.

How thankful was I, my dear son, that the feast was abolished, and your dangers thus absolutely prevented! What a heathenish way of congratulating each other on taking their degrees, to be intemperate, and exceed all the limits of becoming mirth! How unavoidable the contempt of the Clergy, amongst the gentlemen, who, remembering them at College, even till the time they were ordained, saw nothing in them that would rebuke vice, and lead the mind to fear and love the holy laws of our adorable Maker and Redeemer!

I have just now ventured on an undertaking, out of love to the children of my parish. I have engaged a master to teach them all. How tenderly did our Saviour recommend little children to our regard! Had I my time to begin again, I would give myself more to this work. In these labours

of love, a sweet peace of mind is enjoyed; and
when we teach, we are taught by the Great Master
of the Assemblies. I venerate the name of Dr.
Franck, of Halle in Saxony, who, when a Professor of greatest note, in that University, felt his
bowels yearn over the children of the poor, and
became their teacher, though derided by the University for his heavenly compassion. So differently
did his God regard the good work, that, from a
small beginning, it was soon enlarged to be amongst
the first charitable foundations—embalming his
name for ages to come.

Your dear mother and sisters join with me in
love.

John has been ill.—An excellent servant we
should feel for, as a brother. Adieu!

From your loving father,

H. VENN.

———

The following striking piece of advice occurs in another
letter, written about this time.

———

—— I HOPE, my dear son, you feel how utterly
insufficient you are in yourself to stand before the
trial you are called to, in the way of your intended
profession. Remember Dr. Dodd! I myself heard
him tell his own flock, whom he was lecturing in
his house, that he was obliged to give up that
method of helping their souls, because it exposed
him to so much reproach. He gave it up; and fell
from one compliance to another, with his corrupt
nature;—and under what reproach did he die! Oh!

be afraid of nothing more than the detestable cowardice of a selfish and unbelieving heart! Confess how much power it has in you; and beg, as a man begs for his life, that you may be bold, yet prudent, detesting the pernicious ways of youth left to themselves; and pass through the fire, by the almighty grace of God, without being burnt, or hurt in your precious soul.——

————

TO JOHN BRASIER, ESQ.

Yelling, April 10, 1778.

WHY will my dear cousin call his aversion to writing unconquerable? Surely you write with ease, and as one who possesses a natural talent for it!—and in communicating your own ideas, you will be rewarded; they will be more clear and strong in your mind. Yet I know what it is to find reluctance to take pen in hand. I reckon I have not written less than seventy letters during the last six months; and several of them very long ones, almost as much as a modern sermon. But you, and my other friends, give me encouragement, by saying they are not without their use.

I write now to congratulate you on the birth of your child. A Christian will receive it as a charge of inestimable worth; and, at the same time, as a patient, whose innate depravity must be guarded against, and its cure begun even from very infancy. The child is at first little more than an animal; afterwards, in a small degree, rational; and for some years, in general, is incapable of being treated as spiritual. Wisdom, love, and mercy, call upon us to begin very early with our offspring, to oppose and subdue *self-will*—the plague of man—the disease of fiends—the enemy of God! And early and stedfastly opposed, it is, in most cases, very soon conquered, though not extirpated. No object is more pleasing than a meek, obedient child. It reflects honour upon its parents, for their wise management. It enjoys much ease and pleasure, to the utmost limit of what is fit. It promises excellency and usefulness—to be, when age has matured the human understanding, a willing subject in all things to the government of God. No object, on the contrary, is more shocking than a child under no management! We pity orphans, who have neither father nor mother to care for them. A child indulged, is more to be pitied : it has no parent : it is its own master—peevish, froward, headstrong, blind ;—born to a double portion of trouble and sorrow, above what fallen man is heir to ;—not only miserable itself, but worthless, and a plague to all who in future will be connected with it. What bad sons, husbands, masters, fathers, daughters, wives, and mothers, are the offspring of fond indulgence, shewn to little masters and misses almost from the cradle! Wise discipline gives thought and firmness to the mind ; and makes us useful here, and fit for the world of perfect subordination above.

We all beg our love to Mrs. B ———— .

Yours, &c.

H. Venn.

S

TO JOHN BRASIER, ESQ.

Yelling, April 18, 1778.

It is a great comfort to us, that Christ orders and commands us to bring our children to Him, and dedicate them to the Father, Son, and Holy Ghost— the God whom we adore; that we are commanded to bring them to Him, not by the painful rite of circumcision, which, under the Law, signified the putting away the filth of the flesh, but by the rite of Baptism, pouring water upon them, to signify their natural pollution, and the washing of regeneration and renewing of the Holy Ghost, which all need. Our God declares, that He will be the God of our seed, and own our children. I doubt not, therefore, that you will be particular in observing, as I always did, the christening-day; not as a day of feasting, but of dedication, with two or three friends, who would join in prayer on the solemn occasion, and in singing suitable praises. I am the more particular on this point of Baptism, because I find your servant belongs to the Anabaptists, and has given our servant one of their books; and I know they are a restless set of people, unhinging and disturbing the minds of unlearned persons, by continually stunning them with the sound, "*If thou believest,* thou mayest be baptized." Yet, after much study, for many years, on that particular point, I can assure you, that there is not one single instance, in the word of God, of any person, born of Christian parents, ever being baptized when grown up. All the instances in the Acts of the Apostles are of persons who were Jews or Gentiles. I can also assure you, that there never was any society of Christians that forbade children to be baptized, till fifteen hundred years after Christ : nor is there any mention of the persons by whom infant baptism was first brought in, or when, or of the least dispute about it, in the history of the Church. So that the Anabaptists are injurious to children, without authority from God's word, and in direct contradiction to all the Churches of Christ, for fifteen hundred years. Yet are they so fierce and bigoted, that, in their writings, they deny we are Christians, or have any right to the Lord's Supper; nor would they give it to any of us, any more than to a Pagan.

I would not have said so much, but I very well know the spirit of the Anabaptists, and therefore guard you. And though it is not profitable to read controversy, yet your acquaintance, Mr. Addington, has published so candid, convincing, and short a treatise upon the Divine Rights of Infants to Baptism, that I would recommend it to you. It is sold by Buckland, in Paternoster-row.

Mrs. Venn, and my children, join with me in love to Mrs. Brasier and my sister. If Mrs. Brasier's relations have not yet engaged themselves, and you will accept Mrs. Venn and myself as sponsors to your dear infant, we shall have pleasure in answering by proxy; for we shall not be in town till the last week in May, when I am engaged to preach a sermon in the Mercers' Chapel, on the 29th.

Awful, more than ever, are the signs of wrath gone out from the Lord against us! Should it come, there is a man, " a Friend" indeed " born for adversity," who will be better to us than money, when we have neither silver nor gold; better than a house, when we have no certain habitation; better than national peace and quietness, when the sword drinks up the blood of the slain; better than life itself, when we shall lay down this earthly tabernacle. In Him may we all be found!

From your much obliged cousin,

H. VENN.

——WE have had, amongst our visitors, a serious young man from Cambridge (who was a month with us, two summers ago): he is now quarrelling with our Liturgy and Articles, and going over to the Dissenters. Alas! how subtle are the devices of the enemy! Such instances as these make men of sense and learning dread religion: they say it oversets young minds, who never know where to stop. He has been two days with me; and I have since written him a long letter. The success is such as you would suppose;—for I scarcely ever knew an instance, when young people begin to cavil, and find fault with every thing but sinful courses and a sinful heart, that they ever stop; but get into a spirit of debate and contention, hurtful to themselves and all about them. He is about leaving College: and I trust my son sees his error, and will pray to be kept from it.

TO MR. JOHN VENN
(AT LEICESTER).

Yelling, Aug. 14, 1778.

——On Sunday morning, I was overjoyed with the sight of Joseph Hirst, of Yew Green, near Huddersfield. He came one hundred and fifty miles, on purpose to see me; and stayed till Wednesday afternoon. I really think it would have been well worth all my pains for twelve years, if he alone had been the fruit of them. I could not but admire his great knowledge of the Bible, the strength of his judgment, the wisdom of his words, his great humility, and his active spirit. All his mind is intent to learn and know how to do what is good for others. He saves his money, to lay out in printing useful little books; which he gives and lends to those around him, with much success. He gave me a most pleasing account of John Houghton, and many more; so that when I parted with him, I could not but adore the astonishing goodness of God to me, that I should have been the instrument, by preaching His word faithfully, of forming an immortal spirit to such usefulness and excellency.

Amongst the things which grieved me, relating to many who did set out well, of whom I made inquiry, was poor Mr.——, who now, with his two brothers, lives at——. One brother, the merchant, Joseph Hirst works for: this merchant, like the elder brother, has been awakened; but, alas! the world has gotten the victory! The clergyman has a living, if not two; and resides upon neither. Joseph Hirst says, they are confessedly superior in understanding to all about them ; and value themselves on being able to make the worse appear the better, and conquer in every dispute. Oh, that I could pray for them as I ought ! Oh, that they were wounded in their spirit, till they were ready to despair of mercy ; that they might then be brought to know that Christ is more than all manner of riches. What talents ! and what a perversion of them ! What a curse is a fine understanding, without a humble spirit !

Pray remember me, in love to Mr. Robinson, his wife, Mr. Ludlam, and all friends. I hope you felt your soul on fire at the lecture, to be one day like your dear friend, who spoke to you in the name of the Lord. Oh, study how you may do good to the souls and bodies of men !—This is religion.— The Lord Jesus be with your spirit !

Your mamma, and sisters, and cousin Venn, desire their love.

From your affectionate father,

H. VENN.

TO MR. JOHN HOUGHTON.

MY DEAR FRIEND,   *Yelling, Aug.* 12, 1778.

I received, in due time, your kind present, and your letter : for both I return you my thanks. Joseph Hirst gives me very great pleasure, in assuring me that many of you live like real Christians ; and that you, in particular, are useful and exemplary. I have made very particular inquiry about every one I could think of, and the state of the Church.

I find you are troubled with the Anabaptists.*
———But never, on any account, dispute. Debate is the work of the flesh. No one is ever
found disputing about such external matters, till
sorrow for sin, till love for Christ and communion with Him, till love for souls and desire to be
useful, are departed from the heart entirely, or very
much enfeebled. Little do they watch and pray, and
desire the prosperity of Christ's Church, who can
find time, or have a relish, for any thing but what
edifies, quickens, comforts, and makes us like unto
God in doing good. The best manner of answering disputers, of this contentious cavilling spirit,
is, to ask them, whether they have considered, and
do lament, the mischiefs and evils of separation, of
strife and contention? whether they feel, in their
hearts, a great desire of union and peace, that all
who are in Christ Jesus may together lift up their
voice, and make their attack upon the army of the
ungodly, the worldly, the covetous? Ask such
disputers, what time they spend in visiting the
fatherless and the widows in their affliction? whether they feel joy in supporting the weak, in comforting the feeble-minded, and obey the Scripture
which commands us to "receive the weak in
faith, but not to doubtful disputations?" In the
course of more than twenty-seven years, I never
knew one exemplary Christian a disputer, whether
amongst Dissenters or in our own Church: and it
is a rule with me, to conclude any person who can
be taken up with a desire to make men converts to

* The letter goes on to state the argument in favour of Infant
Baptism; and it was given, in a former letter, to Mr. Brasier.

any notion, and *not to Christ*, or be zealous for any thing more than the life of faith and holiness from knowledge of Christ Crucified, is a sounding empty professor, or, at best, in a very poor, low state. No man in the world more heartily loves our worship than myself, nor has stronger objections against Dissenters ; yet never in my life did I desire to bring one Dissenter to church. If he were indeed alive to God in Christ Jesus, I could praise God for him ; and love him not one whit the less, though he did not worship with me in the same form.

I am going to publish—what will be printed the week after next—a Sermon, for sixpence, proving Popery an enemy to the religion of Christ. A frank will not hold it, or I would send you one. How glad should I be to see you here for a week! —I am not able to come, as I designed, into Yorkshire this year. I hope to be able, once before I die ; for nothing would give me greater pleasure. However, I constantly remember you ; and every Lord's Day, in particular, consider myself as joined with you in one faith, one hope, one baptism, one Lord, one life ; and hastening to one heaven, where brethren will no more vex and grieve one another, and quarrel about any thing, when they should do all that possibly lieth in them to live peaceably together.

The Prince of Peace be with you all, and a lively active spirit to do good unto all, and especially to them who are of the household of Faith!

From your very affectionate father in Christ,

H. VENN

TO MR. JOHN VENN

(AT LEICESTER).

MY DEAR SON, *Yelling, Sept.* 21, 1778.

On Friday, I went over to Cambridge. Finding all our friends had left, I walked to Jesus College; and whilst I was solemnly meditating in the cloisters, and calling to remembrance the days, alas! of vanity and ignorance, Mr. —— came up to me, and invited me to drink tea with him, with the Senior Fellow of Catherine Hall; which I did :—and again had a lamentable proof of the spirit of the University, in the most decent! All our conversation was of books and authors, and our contemporaries— some preferred, some ruined by their own imprudence, and most of them dead. Not a savour of that discourse which honours God, and becomes immortal beings in our uncertain continuance below!

I breakfasted with the very amiable and sensible Mr. Jowett, of Trinity Hall; and afterwards spent three hours with him in interesting conversation. Whilst we were together, Mr. —— came in; and so pressed us to dine with them in their Hall, that I could not refuse. He was alone, at the Fellow's table. In College, only two students; and one of them a Soph, who murdered the fine grace, by gabbling it over so very fast, I could not understand a single sentence, nor half a one. Nothing could be more polite; but, alas! the feast of souls was wanting.

When I came home, I found Mr. and Mrs. Newton, who came here the evening before. He is my brother, and fellow-servant to our adorable Lord. What sweet society! What a different species are

Christians from other men! how greatly exalted above them! Oh, may you be amongst those *few*, whose favourite subject is that which angels and all the company of heaven contemplate with delight; which warms and purifies the hearts of those who hear you, and excites to activity in the service of Christ, and for the glory of God!

Yesterday, Mr. Newton gave us an excellent discourse on the marks of a prosperous soul, from 3d Ep. of St. John, ver. 2. The marks were : 1. A clear well-grounded hope of our acceptance with God, by faith in Christ Crucified. 2. A continued witness of God's Spirit, that our sins are pardoned. 3. A constant exercise to have a conscience void of offence towards God and man. 4. A sweet and calm confidence that all our affairs are under the infallible direction of God, so as to be fully satisfied He will do with us just as seemeth him good; whether we be rich or poor, sick or well, in esteem or despised, living or dying. 5. Life and communion with God, in prayer, public worship, reading the Scripture, and hearing His faithful pastors. 6. An abiding and pleasing conviction upon the mind, that we, and all we have, are the Lord's, that we may serve Him with all our strength.—Thus may your soul and mine prosper! I advise you, by all means, on a Sunday, to set down the principal parts of the sermons you hear. It is of great service. Your mamma and sisters send their love.

On Monday, Oct. 5, I shall send John to meet you at Kettering. You must therefore set out at one o'clock, to ride twenty-three miles. Be sure you are not later in setting out, lest night come on.

And then you may reach home next day by dinner; which will suit better for our horses.—Love to Mr. Robinson and all friends.

From your affectionate father,

H. VENN.

TO MR. JOHN VENN

(AT CAMBRIDGE).

MY DEAR SON,   *Yelling, Dec.* 12, 1778.

I have good news to send you. Mr. Robinson, the active, upright, evangelical Mr. Robinson, is Vicar of St. Mary's, Leicester. He will not now take your cousin, nor any more pupils. I have written to him on the subject, to desire he would consider the vast use he may be of. Children, I think, he should by all means give up :—it is but a poor employment. But students in Divinity, I am sure, ought to be with faithful ministers, and see service, as officers and physicians and lawyers do. Too many clergymen come into their office perfect strangers to the way of leading souls to heaven.

What joy did I receive from one sentence in Mr. Robinson's letter of yesterday! It was this :— *"Your son has been a great blessing* to young Mr. ———." How much better that honour, than the applause of a world! May you adore Him, who is pleased to make you useful; and be more humble, and more desirous of doing good; so that saints, gone before you into heaven, may be your crown; and many travelling on with you towards that world of glory; and many to follow, after your labours of love are ended! O glorious work and wages! How despicable a mitre or a crown, the poet's never-fading laurel, or the renown of the first of philosophers, compared with the gain of winning immortal souls to Christ!

Yours, &c.   H. VENN.

The very striking account which has been given, in the Memoir, of Mr. Venn's behaviour during a thunder-storm, and of the way in which he improved the event to the instruction of his children, will give additional interest to the following extracts.

—— THE new year came in with a violent tempest. It blew out one of the windows of my house, in the garret, and part of the covering of my barn; and roused us up, at two in the morning. Oh, what an astonishing privilege, in such seasons, is it, to be endued with a spirit of prayer—to be able to call upon Him, at whose word the stormy wind both rises and falls! I never was more sensible of it in my life, nor more astonished with the truth, that "the High and Lofty One who inhabiteth Eternity" has made Himself known to His Church under that endearing character — the God that heareth prayer; sitting above the water-floods, and giving strength and the blessing of peace to His Children in the midst of them. How different the brutal insensibility of an infidel heart, which perhaps may not tremble even in such seasons, and the sweet composure of a Christian's mind, fully persuaded that lightning and thunder, storm and tempest, all fulfil His word, and do His pleasure! This is to understand, and feel as angels do.——

Jan. 14, 1779.

——W<small>HAT</small> an awful introduction was there of the new year! To Christians, it preached the necessity of being ready to meet their God: since, had the fury of the tempest increased but a little, their houses would have been their sepulchres. How weak and helpless are whole nations, when the Lord ariseth, either to shake terribly the earth, or smite with the pestilence, or ravage the guilty land with the devouring sword! Yet such is the extreme folly and madness of men, that they put no value on His favour; they have no dread of His displeasure. Oh, may we be wise and happy, separate from the licentious, thoughtless, and proud! May we wait for that hour, when our God shall come, and shall not keep silence—when a mighty tempest shall be stirred up round about Him, and a fire shall devour before Him!—That will be the time of honour and glory unspeakable, and triumph, for the faithful in Christ Jesus.

Think what a sight I enjoyed at Cambridge, the week before Christmas. Eleven young men sat, with great attention, to hear me converse with them about the things of God.—I like them much, because they go on slowly, and most of them study very hard. Religion was never designed to be a cloak for idleness and ignorance.——

TO MR. JOHN VENN.

Yelling, March 9, 1779.

On this your natal day, my beloved son, I address you;—looking back upon the amazing difference between the new-born babe, and the youth of twenty years of age, with great thankfulness to our God and Redeemer!

On this day, when the news was brought, that a son was born to me, I was called up to see you—a mere animal, conscious only of hunger and thirst, pain or ease, warmth or cold, light or darkness; without any power to tell explicitly your wants; and, to me, as every new-born babe always is, a living demonstration of the Fall—a being utterly destitute, and, had not our God implanted the στοργή * in the parent's breast, would be an insupportable burden to the mother who brought you forth.—Then I saw the dawn of your rational nature; and the power of speech, the distinguishing glory of the human race, began to make its appearance. You heard and understood enough to become a very pleasing and entertaining child; but altogether earthly, and sensual, and self-willed; —not one idea yet entered into your mind, of your Maker, and ever bountiful Benefactor. He gave you health, food, raiment, sleep, and affectionate parents; but you only heard His name was God, without perceiving, in the least degree, your debt to His never-ceasing goodness.

Then were you taught to call upon Him for His

* The natural affection of parents for their offspring.

blessing and protection, and reminded of His knowledge and observation of all your actions, words,
and thoughts; that you must never begin the day
without prayer, or lie down to take your rest without imploring His defence, and thanking Him for
His benefits. Taught thus by the precepts of men,
you discovered your zeal to have your God obeyed,
before you were five years old; then choosing to
be a preacher, and determining to compel the disobedient to come in *vi et armis*, if milder methods
would not succeed; for you were determined to
make use, you said, of a good oaken trowel, to
bring them to a sense of their sin, if your discourse
and entreaties should fail. In a few years more, I
saw you gaining fast the meaning of Latin and
Greek words, and, by the help of an excellent
teacher, promising to be a scholar. But I waited,
and your mamma waited, in patience, and in prayer,
longing to see you impressed with a deep sense of
things unseen and eternal. We saw you, with
great pleasure and gratitude to God, an obedient
child, very easily managed, and no complaints of
any thing wrong in your conduct.

After your dear mamma's translation to the spirits of the just made perfect (and you resemble
her in many particulars), I was still waiting for your
conviction, by a Divine power, of what you assented
to through the force of education; for mere restraint from vice and fashionable self-indulgences
is of short continuance; and no dependence can
be placed on this. It was therefore a memorable
era in your life, to me and yourself, when a sense
of your wonderful preservation, in the article of

danger in the stage-coach, going to Hipperholme,
made a deep impression upon you. All the Children of God can record such interpositions ; and by
them very many have been brought to themselves.
In two years after this, you came under my tuition
—not only a son, but a pupil; and much satisfaction I received in your attention and diligence ; in
your deportment, which gained upon every one in
the house; and your steady preference of the best
and holiest office man can take upon him—the office
of a pastor in the Church of Christ.

And now the perilous critical time came on,
when you were to be your own master; when,
leaving your father's house, where you saw no
company but of the Ministers or Children of God ;
heard no corrupt communication ever come out of
any mouth ; no praises, in the warmth of a sensual
heart, of beauty, good eating, jollity, or wealth—
now the time was come, when you must be obliged
to hear and see what evil and madness fill the
hearts of the sons of men ; when horses and hounds,
and plays and players, and courtezans, and their
still more infamous seducers, were to be the subjects dwelt on by those around you ; when self-
gratification in every thing fashionable, and the
lead in acquisition of science, falsely so called, was
to be daily present to your mind.   With what great
thoughts of heart, and repeated pleadings before a
Throne of Grace, was your case recommended !
and with what delight have I seen you preserved
and kept in the midst of the pestilence ; known
and dear to some excellent acquaintance ; and
made an instrument, before you have attained to

the age of twenty, of doing good to the souls of
young men by your conversation! Now is your
once-dark mind enlightened with truth from God :
now the petitions you offered up as a child are
become fervent prayers—a spiritual sacrifice : what
you received with implicit faith from a dear father's
lips, you receive now from the Oracles of God :
you now see the *rationale,* the foundation, in the
nature of fallen man, of the Gospel doctrines; and
fact confirming the Scripture testimony, that there
is no peace to the wicked ; and that it is wise, and
excellent, to be guided, in all our choice and pursuit,
by the wisdom that is from above.

The four succeeding years are the seed-time for
your whole life, respecting human knowledge and
the cultivation of your mental faculties; that, with
every requisite qualification as a scholar, and with
a character unsullied by conformity to the world,
you may, if life is spared, be admitted amongst the
witnesses who testify against the evil doctrine and
evil practice everywhere prevailing, and come forth
engrossed by one grand purpose, from which nothing
shall ever divert you—a purpose, through the grace
of the Lord Jesus Christ, to spend and be spent in
His service—to follow, though with very unequal
steps, yet still with all your might to follow, the
example of the Apostles, in the doctrine you preach,
in the self-denied life you will lead, in the longing
desire of our heart to see the lost saved, and the
slaves of sin and Satan returning to Zion with everlasting joy upon their heads, transformed into the
Divine image, and, with all gratitude, confessing
they heard from your lips what they found the

T

means of their salvation. In this most blessed employment (if it please our adorable Saviour) may you work for many years! and every returning birth-day solemnly present yourself before Him, to be endued with more wisdom, knowledge, and grace; till, in the appointed hour, you are called to give account of your ministry, and find the day of your death infinitely better than the day of your birth! This is the wish, the ardent, constant prayer, of

Your affectionate father,

H. VENN.

TO MR. JOHN VENN.

Yelling, March 19, 1779.

MY design in coming over to Cambridge, my dear son, was entirely to have endeavoured to fortify your mind against your examination, which I concluded would have been at Easter. I must, therefore, speak to you by my pen. Be *anxious for nothing relating to this world,* is the all-wise injunction of our Lord: for anxiety is not only painful, but useless; not only useless, but hurtful—a great hindrance to the exercise of the mind; and productive of envy, as it proceeds from inordinate affection. Yet our Lord, whilst He warns us against anxiety, exhorts and presses us to diligence, labour, and the continual exertion of our faculties; because, by these, the mind gathers strength, acquires useful knowledge, is made more sober and thoughtful, and convinced, if not intoxicated with pride, of the poverty and weakness natural to us; since it costs so much pains and labour to become tolerably acquainted with any one science, or to excel.

But how to value knowledge in human sciences enough to study and labour in a due measure, yet keep free from self-pleasing, self-exalting thoughts, as the grand excitement to close application—how to strive, as one ought, to do our very best in a place appropriated to study, yet not be cast down and vexed at our competitors getting the first place —is a difficulty, to most men, insuperable, but by Divine knowledge, and the victorious aid of the Holy Ghost. I say ' to most men;'—for there are a few, who seem, in a great degree, quite easy whether they are distinguished or not, yet, from a love of knowledge, seek diligently to acquire it. With me, more corrupt, it was quite the reverse. I was exceedingly wretched, for a time, that I was not before Dr. Conyers in honour. But, alas! I then had no higher or better aim than my own glory. It is not so with you, I verily believe : your studies are all subservient to an infinitely-nobler purpose. Be sure always to make your prayer, that you may feel this more forcibly ; and that you may be wise, and learned, and able as a scholar, only to reason about the faith of Christ, and the necessity of temperance and righteousness, and the certainty of a judgment to come; and to place before immortal souls, in the clearest method and the most engaging views, things of infinite moment to every one of your hearers. You know how much the name of ' learned,' and that aptness to teach which knowledge well digested and fluent utterance furnish, contribute, under Divine influence, to success in saving souls. This idea, it is my prayer may rest constantly, and with great power, upon your mind. You cannot impress your mind with it but by prayer; which I trust you make.

Be assured I shall not be wanting, either in our family, or in secret, to implore the Lord Jesus, as Paul did for Timothy, to "be with your spirit";—a great request—the best he could make for his beloved son in the Gospel. For when the Lord is with our spirit, as I well know, there is great recollection and presence of mind; a consciousness of His eye over us, and love for us; a sense of the littleness of every thing which would otherwise agitate us; and a full contentment of mind, from an assurance that all is ordered for our good. May I hear from you, that you enjoy this favour! and I shall greatly rejoice.

Your affectionate father,

H. VENN.

TO MR. JOHN VENN.

MY DEAR SON, *Yelling, June,* 1779.

Now you are to be much with ——, be sure to make it much your prayer, that you may set him a Christian example, in all diligence, seriousness, and profitable conversation—that you may have the comfort of helping him forward in the way everlasting, and proving, before his eyes, the reality, the lovely reality, of true religion. It is with great joy I see you have already been of use to him; and I trust and pray you will be a blessing indeed to his immortal soul. There is nothing, that I know of, worthy a thought, compared with possessing so much grace, that every one who comes near you is enlivened and edified in his own soul. Thus it was with my very dear friends, now high in glory, Mr. Hervey, Mr. Walker, Mr. Grimshaw, Mrs. Lefevre.   Thus it is with Mr. Fletcher, and Mr. Robinson, and Mr. Berridge. What a testimony was that which Bishop Burnet bore to Archbishop Leighton—that he looked upon his acquaintance with him as a talent, for which he must particularly give an account!   So I would have it to be with you, always studying to be of some use to those with whom you have any intimacy. And for this end, it is of great service to be very often entreating the Lord to endue you with the tongue of the learned, and the lips of the righteous, by which many are fed—to enrich you with all utterance and knowledge, that you may come behind in no good gift, waiting for the revelation of the Lord Jesus Christ. Gracious words from a youth are peculiarly striking; and are attended with a deep impression, when spoken modestly and with humility;—and so spoken, I think, your words will be. Too many pour out a torrent of common-place stuff, without feeling. Happy they who speak with recollection, love and humility!

From your affectionate father,

H. VENN

The paternal solicitude which Mr. Venn's letters to his son display, was, it will be readily believed, no less tenderly and strikingly exhibited whenever his daughters were separated from him. I shall therefore next introduce a few letters, written to them when they were from home, on visits to different friends.

TO MISS VENN.

MY DEAR ELING,   *Yelling, Aug.* 26, 1779.

On Sunday last, who should come in, just before eight in the morning, but Mr. Thornton, in his way to Hull. On Monday, I went with him, in his chaise, to Everton, to dinner; and spent the evening with him at Buckden. This interview with one of the saints in Christ Jesus, like that of a few days with the family at Bedford*, would be dejecting —it is so short—but for the glorious hope, that, in due time, we shall be together for ever with the Lord. Often, my dear child! accustom yourself to look upon such as you are now with, as Children of God, educating to stand before His Throne, the dear objects of His eternal love. Some glimpses of such a high distinction may be frequently seen here, in the bowels of mercy and fervent love they have towards all, and in the consolations, and the deep abasement too, they feel and express from knowledge of the Lord and themselves. Whenever I part

* The family of Joseph Foster Barham, esq., a member of the Moravian Church; at whose house Miss Venn was staying, on a visit

with such excellent ones of the earth, I have a solemn pleasing meditation upon their translation to the world of perfect spirits—how they will feel and speak—what they will know—and how rejoice with those who were once in fellowship with them in the body—what a perfect remembrance of all the evil they have escaped ; by what wisdom and power and patience in the Lord their God ; and with what delightful sensibility they will return unto Him, with all melody in their hearts, their praises for ever due ;—and due not in the least degree for the most bitter part of their lot, as it was deemed, for a season, in their short-sighted judgment.

Mrs. Venn joins with me in every affectionate wish to our friends. Mr. and Mrs. Barham have done for you and myself, in the present kindness to you, only what they have been doing, for a course of years, to a thousand besides—every thing that can testify a most loving heart, the very spirit and temper of the choirs above. We shall expect to see the spirit that there reigns transfused into you. The Lord, our compassionate Saviour, keep, teach, comfort, and save you!

From your affectionate father,

H. VENN.

TO MISS VENN.

MY DEAR ELING, *Yelling, Oct.* 28, 1779.

Much were we all excited to thankfulness by the good account we received of your safe and agreeable journey to your excellent friends. I was making my prayer to the Lord our God, and had confidence He would hear and protect you.

Who can enumerate all the advantages of prayer? It is designed, by our most merciful and gracious God, as a relief, adequate to all the miseries we inherit, as the sinful offspring of Adam. By prayer, our sight is recovered ; and though born blind, we have the light of heaven brought into our minds. By prayer, our fears and painful doubts, as to our eternal state, are removed; and peace, and lively hope from the Holy Ghost, given unto us. By prayer the several ordinances of Divine appointment are made effectual, to our great edification and growth in grace, and everlasting benefit. Preaching, through the blessing of secret prayer, teaches, quickens, warms, melts, and overcomes our hearts. Public worship is indeed an entertainment in the banqueting-house of God, where His glory is felt, His presence enjoyed, access to Him as a Father experienced, and the overflowings of a heart, grateful for innumerable blessings, are poured out. By prayer we obtain the witness in ourselves that the Lord God interests Himself in our welfare, secures us in danger, supports us in adversity, and cheers us in the darkest hours ; fights for us against our enemies ; reconciles us to His own will; and is training us up in knowledge, faith, and love, to His own eternal kingdom, prepared for praying souls. Remember, therefore, my dear Eling, that all good is to be obtained by real prayer, and defence from all evil within and without.

A word was dropped, the other day, from your dear mamma, which struck me much. Speaking of some person, she said, " She was always as recollected as Eling, when she came from Bedford."

I instantly thought of the cause. At Bedford, you had your set time for prayer; which, probably, you observed very strictly, amongst those exemplary saints. At Yelling, peradventure, not having a room to yourself, you might be less attentive. I would have you watch, and always examine yourself strictly, about this most important matter. Remember, all, all depends upon this. None are, none can be, exemplary, but praying souls; who can no more live without stated times of drawing near to God than their bodies can live without food.

I write this to you after a slight attack, on Saturday, of an ague or fever—I cannot say which. I am now better; but if it is an ague, probably it may return. I did not know, when it came upon me, what it was sent to do: however, I was exceedingly happy; and though willing, should it please God, to live a few years, for the sake of my poor girls, yet far from unwilling to depart, knowing in whom I have a never-failing, all-sufficient Friend.—Our love to all the family with whom you dwell.

From your affectionate father,

H. VENN.

TO MISS VENN.

MY DEAR ELING, *Yelling, Dec.* 7, 1779.

Probably you are now at ————, or have just returned; and you may have felt your heart too much wedded to the world, when you were in all the affluence it can afford, and were led to imagine your own lot hard;—so obstinately do we conclude the comfort of life arises from fine clothes, fine houses, equipages, and the best meats and drinks. It is from this persuasion, young and old are very fools and madmen. They will neither hear reason, nor the voice of God, nor be convinced by facts, nor by their own experience; for reason is in nothing more clear and indisputable, than that the temper of the mind makes us happy or miserable—not what we possess. Riches always make us think we have a right to indulge; and, bent on self-indulgence, we can never be satisfied: our wants multiply—our appetites enlarge. The voice of God, loudly, in every page of Scripture, assures us the happiness of man is in the knowledge of our pardon—in the kingdom of God within us, and the abounding hope of glory ready to be revealed. Facts attest, none are so passionate, so peevish, so often full of chagrin, as the opulent and great-ones in the world. Even Solomon, with the largest abilities and most intense desire of making out his comfort from things seen, cries out, in bitter disappointment, "Vanity of vanities! all is vanity!" "Fear God, and keep His commandments;"—this, in every station, is the whole happiness of man, now and for ever. Our own experience attests the same truth. The best days we ever know, are those in which we can see something of the glory of God, feel how vile we are, yet so greatly beloved; when we are meek and kind, and full of good-will towards all men. Such divine tempers and sensations leave upon the countenance a heavenly signature—please all beholders, and prove us conquerors over an evil nature and a wicked world.   This was the possession of the Apostles.   This was the glory of the poor Nazarene.   When the Almighty would become a man, he would be no more than a poor day-labourer, to demonstrate that the whole glory of man is righteousness and true holiness.   Happy are they who know and feel this!   Their number is but small; yet all religion, short of this, will fail us in a trying hour—nay, leaves us at present void of true consolation and divine peace.   May God give you to see through all the deceitful appearances which dazzle and destroy so many!

I desire you would perform your promise, and write out for me Mrs. Vaughan's letter, and send it me in your next; and frequently examine yourself very solemnly by it.   We must grow up to that spirit: our life is spared to give us time to do so. I had rather be like Mrs. Vaughan, and be in the lowest station, than be clothed in purple and fare sumptuously, for a hundred years together, without sickness or pain.

The Lord clothe us all with humility, that heavenly dress, which is pleasing to Jehovah Himself! —Your dear mamma and sisters send their love.

From your affectionate father,

H. VENN.

TO MISS VENN.

Yelling, Feb. 5, 1780.

THIS comes to your hands, my dear Eling, on your birth-day; now of age sufficient to understand, and, through the teaching of God's Spirit, both firmly to believe, and be suitably affected with your condition.   You know you are born in a state of exile—at a distance from your God, of whose wondrous name you hear from His own Oracles, but are not yet permitted to see Him as He is. Your life is continued, that you may become attached to Him—be of one judgment with Him—find your felicity in His love, and the lively hope of eternal life in His presence. I wish you a happy year, in considering yourself as none of your own, but the Lord's—*His,* not merely as a creature, made and supported by His hand, but as created again by an act of Almighty Power—rescued from vile bondage—discharged from a debt which you could never have paid—justified from a condemnation that must have sunk you into the depths of hell—raised to the privilege of prayer and praise, of obedience and love to the Lord Most High, and thus already conformed to the very disposition of angels in heaven.

I could wish you to be saying a thousand and a thousand times to yourself, " I am none of my own—I am the Lord's!"—Infinite honour, unequalled grandeur of condition, is included in this relation! May I know how to set a just value upon it!—*I am the Lord's,* to have the benefit of His wisdom and unerring counsel.—*I am the Lord's,* to derive, from His might and power, ability to do those things which by nature we cannot do, and get the mastery of our innate base tempers.—*I am the Lord's,* to be preserved and defended by His tender and ever-watchful care, in this world of pits and snares and seducing objects, and malignant spirits.—*I am the Lord's,* to hear His voice, and treasure up His divine sayings, refusing to listen to the suggestions of my own deceitful heart, the maxims of mankind, and the false promises which sensitive pleasure and gaudy appearances are continually making to prevail over me.—*I am the Lord's*, to do the work He has given me by the allotment of His providence. This I am to be intent on discharging, with all diligence, humility, and cheerfulness; no less so than if I had come down from Him, having received from His own mouth an order, saying, ' Go and employ your time in the body in such a manner as I command you: then shall you glorify me; and, when your work is done, I will confess you as a good and faithful servant, before my Father and His holy angels.' —" *I am the Lord's,*" may you say, not only to live, but to die unto Him! Having finished my education in His school, and been made meet for inheritance with the saints in light, at death I am to enjoy the summit of all my wishes, in perfect knowledge and everlasting love.

Thus may our dear Eling be taught; and thus reckon herself to be alive to God, from the dead, through Jesus Christ our Lord! Then, in all the changing scenes of this mortal life, will you be provided for. In national calamities, you may greatly suffer; yet not without solid consolation, knowing the Lord—whose you are, and whom you serve—sitteth above the water-floods, directs their motion, and decrees their effects. In trouble, He shall speak peace. When hurried away, alas! by some violent assault, or overtaken with a fault, His compassions towards you will not fail: He preserveth those that are His. In pain, you will be

cheerfully resigned, knowing it is the Lord who
chasteneth all whom He loveth, and scourgeth
them. In the loss of earthly friends, however dear
to you, you will have a never-failing friend in Jesus
of Nazareth. This, therefore, is the whole my heart
can wish you. May you, living and dying, *be the
Lord's!*

Your dear mamma is somewhat better; and,
with your sisters, desires her love, and wishes you
all that I do on your birth-day.

Mr. H. P——is now in possession of £12,000 a
year, upon Mr. S——'s death, who left him every
thing. Almost all who hear of this, are lifting up
their hands, and crying out, " Oh! what a glorious
fortune!" Did they believe our Lord, they would
lift up their hearts in prayer, that what with men is
impossible—to have great possessions on earth, and
heaven at last—may, by the Almighty grace of
God, be made possible. Oh, how abject are all
our notions, when £12,000 a year sounds in our
ears as a heaven of delight, affording us ample
means to gratify our selfish nature; and when, at
the same time, peace with God, and likeness to
Him, have no beauty that we should desire them!—
I have been thinking, if matters had been ordered
so that Mr. S—— had died without a will, and by
this means Mr. P—— had gained nothing, yet it
might have been said, " He is dear to God, and an
heir of glory"—how *coldly* would this have been received! " I hope he is so!" they would have said;
" yet it was a terrible misfortune that the young
gentleman should loose such great possessions for
want of a will!" Thus is Mammon exalted above

Jehovah; and the thick clay, which sinks the soul
to earth, above the Holy Ghost, which raises it to
heaven! Our love to your dear friends.

From your affectionate father,

H. VENN.

TO MISS CATHERINE VENN.

MY DEAR KITTY,   *Yelling, June* 27, 1781.

How kind and merciful has our Heavenly Father
been to you, in bringing you in safety to Mr.
Riland's! How much ought we to feel our debt to
Him, and love to His name! I write to you, who
are now in a situation a good deal similar to that
you will be in when you can hear from me no
more. Now, all the advice you have received from
me, and from your dear mamma, you must put in
practice;—and I trust you will!

Rise always by seven. Be sure you do not omit
prayer; and strive to pray in earnest, that you may
be of a meek and humble spirit, which is so pleasing to the Lord, and to every one—so becoming to
us, who are very vile, and deserve nothing good.
Yet are we naturally so proud, as to feel little obli-
gation from our friends, and to be ready to be out of
temper at every thing that thwarts our own will.
The design of religion is to cure us of this vile disposition. Prayer in secret stately, and prayer
frequently in our mind, whatever we are doing, is
appointed to keep us from yielding to our natural
temper, and to bring us to imitate the meek, humble, patient, and loving Jesus, our Saviour, and our
God. This is the work of every Christian;—and

much every Christian has to do, to get the better of self. I assure you, my dear Kitty, the watching, the prayer, the pains, it costs me to get the better of myself, and behave in any degree becoming my profession, are much indeed. But the victory pays for all. It is a glorious end to live for, that we may be like God in our temper, glorify Him for a few years on earth, and then dwell in His presence for ever.

On my return, I spent part of two days at Bedford. There I saw the faith, and patience, and love of dear Mrs. Barham. Nothing can be more dreadful than her disease! It is a cancer; and one of the worst sort. Her pain is sometimes extreme; yet not a word, or a look, discovers this. I prayed at her bed-side; and she is never out of my mind. Mr. Barham, and her daughters, partake of her spirit; and both grieve and rejoice on her account. In this manner doth it please her Lord to try her. But, in all her trials, she can look up to Him, as an infinitely greater sufferer for her sins, that she may be brought to Himself in glory. Oh! how desirable her condition, upon the whole, even in such sufferings as make the heart bleed to think of them!

Your mamma and sisters are all hard at work; and tell me they miss you much. I rejoice to hear them say so; for to be of use and service in the family, is the praise of every female. Now we are absent, we must be particular in remembering each other in prayer. This is the peculiar privilege of Christians; and a great comfort it is, when we cannot see those we dearly love, that we can effectually express, in humble, fervent prayer, the good-will we

bear them, and ask for them the richest blessings.
—All send their love.—The Lord of heaven and
earth teach, keep, and comfort you!

From your affectionate father,

H. VENN.

TO MISS CATHERINE VENN.

Yelling, July 8, 1781.

RISING before any one in the family, on this
blessed day of Sabbath, I write to my dear Kitty,
wishing her not only to refrain from polluting the
Lord's-day by idle talk, but to observe the day, as
Abraham, Isaac, and Jacob, and all the most illustrious persons, have done.

I am at a loss to thank the Lord our God as He
deserves, for this means of holy education, and of
instruction in righteousness, and in the knowledge
of all God's wonderful works—of fixing at once the
attention of thousands of thousands upon the same
object, upon the same adorable Benefactor—of
engaging them all to make a public confession,
both of their own transgressions, and of His un-
wearied goodness—of imploring a larger measure
of His grace, and of representing before Him, by
a general intercession, the wants and necessities
of His poor creatures, and our good-will towards
them — of deriving support and comfort to our
own tried and troubled spirits, whilst we are in
this dark and miserable world, from hearing, in
His own House, His Oracles and promises of everlasting love, and of a Rest for the people of God,
where their sorrows shall cease, and unmixed happiness, such as angels know, shall be their portion!

U

These views should fill every Christian, on the return of each day of the Lord. Be at pains, my dear Kitty, to prepare for this day : pray much and often, that it may be a very high and honourable day in your eyes: lament and complain before God, that your heart is naturally profane, as was Esau's—that you are blind to the excellency of things spiritual, but can feel, with exquisite sensibility, every thing which strikes the eye of sense as showy or pompous.

When I was of your age, I was, alas! a mere pretender to religion. Though I constantly presented myself in the House of the Lord on this holy day, I saw not the glory of the Lord; I understood not His word; I did not hear it when it was read; I asked for nothing; I wanted nothing for my soul; so foolish and ignorant was I! I was glad when the worship was over, and the day was over, that my mouth might pour out foolishness, and that I might return to my sports and amusements. Oh, what a wicked stupidity of soul!—I am astonished how God could bear with me! Had he said, " I swear thou shalt never worship me, never ascend into the hill of the Lord, nor see my face, who findest it such a weariness to be at church, and art so proud and profane in thy spirit! No, dwell for ever with those whom you are like— dwell with the devil and his angels, and all that have departed out of this life enemies to my name and glory!" Oh! had the Lord spoken thus unto me in His displeasure, I had received the just reward of my deeds.—But adore Him for His love to your father! In this state, He opened my eyes, and allured my heart, and gave me to seek Him, and His strength and His face, and join all His saints who keep holy His day—and to be glad to hear them say, "Come, and let us go up to the House of the Lord, and behold His fair beauty, that we may love Him more, and serve Him better!" Nay, more than this, He gave me your blessed mother for a companion, who loved exceedingly the House and day of the Lord;—and repaired to you and to me her loss, by another of His dear children, who sanctifies each Sabbath with delight, and reverences the House of God with her whole heart. Thus, instead of casting me into hell, He has made me the father of one dear saint in glory; and of four more, all of whom, I trust, fear and love the God of their father and of their mother;—all of whom, I have a lively hope, I shall meet in the courts above, in the general assembly of the saints in Christ.

Now my dear Kitty, for your improvement of the Sabbath, and our own, and that you may not want matter to fill a weekly letter, which is often the case with such as yourself, I desire that you will send us the heads, or some of the thoughts, in the sermons you hear, either from dear Mr. Riland or Mr. Sanderson. This will be of great use, to engage your attention more, and to strengthen your memory, and to teach you to write with ease.

We are very thankful that you are well; and still more so that your dear godmother commends you, and that you are well "though in the greatest hurry *imaginable*," so as not to have time to write to your sisters more than the fifth part of a letter. There are many inquiries after you. Your brother is come home. All send their love.

From your affectionate father,

H. VENN.

TO MISS CATHERINE VENN.

To my dear Daughter, C. Venn, on her Birth-Day, August 12, 1781, entering on her seventeenth year.

EARLY in the morning of this anniversary have I been mindful of you, and presented my poor but sincere prayers at the Throne of Grace, in your behalf. It is the pleasure and privilege peculiar to Christians, to make intercession for their children- to be looking up to the Father of Mercies to bestow upon them what is necessary for their *safety*, their *comfort*, and their *usefulness*.

I have, therefore, prayed this day for you, that you might *dwell in safety*. My dear Kitty will not be at a loss to know on what account she need to pray herself, and to desire all that love her soul to do so too, that she may be preserved; for you know, I trust, what enemies are ever working to destroy you:—your corrupt nature is your most powerful enemy. Alas! my beloved child! from your father and mother you derived, as we did from ours, and all from Adam, a self-seeking, self-pleasing spirit— a desire always to have your own way and will; not to walk in Jehovah's way, nor to do His will; a violent love of praise and esteem, when we only deserve shame and contempt—a love for ourselves, making us utterly indifferent how the Lord Jesus

Christ is treated by mankind; and little attentive to the sufferings, distresses, and dangers, of our fellow-creatures. Who shall deliver you from this deep, extensive depravity of your nature? I pray unto Him who is able, who came from heaven, and His high throne of glory there, to seek and to save that which was lost. He *can* and *will*, upon your calling, and lifting up your soul to Him. He will create you again, after His own image—give you wisdom and power to deny yourself, to do the will of God, to love Him in sincerity, and to dwell in love to every one. Then are you indeed *safe*, and recovered from that wickedness of heart which must have kept you out of heaven!

I have prayed, also, that you, my dear Kitty, may spend your days *in comfort*—not in show or dress, or in abundance of the things of this world, but in *solid comfort*; knowing that you are accepted of God, and that heaven is your eternal home. So our ever-blessed Saviour, when about to depart out of this world, told His dearest friends: " I will not leave you comfortless: I will come to you." "My peace I leave with you." " Let not your heart be troubled, neither let it be afraid."— All desire comfort; yet, young and old, rich and poor, despise or neglect Jesus of Nazareth. They cannot believe that the Crucified Man, who died under the hands of his enemies, is the God of peace and hope: hence, none in their natural state have solid comfort. One only can give it! May the Prince of Peace comfort your heart, by teaching you how much he has done and suffered, in order that he might eternally save every poor, helpless, humbled sinner, who turns to him! It is pure, heart-satisfying comfort, to know that you have, in the Lord of all, a companion, a counsellor, and a most familiar friend—who will be ever present with your spirit—who orders all your condition, whether you shall be sick or well, lose or still enjoy the advantage of very dear relations. In a word, this alone is comfort—to have in God a Father, to whom you can apply, and rest satisfied with all His will.

But safety and comfort are not the whole I pray unto the Lord to provide for your soul. *Usefulness* is the very excellency of life. No man, in the real Church of Christ, liveth unto himself. Every true Christian is a tree of righteousness, whose fruits are good and profitable unto men. He is glad to help and to comfort others. He is diligent and industrious. He speaks to edification; dwells in peace, and gentleness, and love. He reproves what is wrong, by an excellent example; and recommends, by his own practice, what is pleasing to God.

My dear Kitty! how have you been distinguished by the Divine goodness—distinguished in the place of your birth, in the land of Gospel light—in your parents being believers—in the examples you have seen—in the instructions you have received, and in the pains taken with you. All these advantages you are to improve, not as a task, but for your own enjoyment—God having inseparably connected our duty and our happiness. I figure you, therefore, to myself, as maintaining a wise, discreet, and godly conversation; satisfied with the portion the Lord divides unto His children; acquainted with spiritual blessings; filling up each passing day, so as to find time too short for all you have to do.

We all join in the same good wishes. We shall be glad to hear you are in health. Your fortnight is gone, and we have received no letter: this has waited two posts; as I expected one from you. I am going to visit Mr. and Mrs. Fletcher, both of them very ill. Several other friends have been lately taken ill. Full of changes is the world we are passing through! Happy they who stand upon their watch-tower, and are not surprised by any thing that comes upon them unprepared! Next month, I hope to see you: but your mamma I cannot prevail upon to stir. She has, indeed, staid so long at home, that she cleaves to it. All send their love.   From your affectionate father,

H. VENN.

TO MISS CATHERINE VENN.

MY DEAR KITTY,   *Yelling, July* 31, 1782.

You have given me much pleasure in writing so full an account of Mr. Riland's sermon: you must have attended closely. Strive to be as attentive under every sermon. Avoid, with all your might, a trifling spirit in the House of God, and in your secret prayer. Great is the gain which is sure to follow from being quite in earnest, and labouring against sloth and laziness. On the contrary, no benefit is received from making many prayers in a spirit of indifference; no benefit from hearing sermons, or reading God's most holy Word. His Spirit is grieved; our hearts are hardened; we bring religion into contempt, and not one evil temper is ever conquered. Be bold, therefore, and of good courage; and press on, and strive to do all you have to do with all your might. Let one improvement lead the way to another. Fix it always in your mind, that you are to answer the end for which you are born in the land of Immanuel;—it is, to follow His example, and be made like Him. Had you seen Jesus from day to day, when He was of your age, you would have seen him very diligent in His work as a carpenter; subject to His parents in all things; losing no time, but always employed in some good work, when He was not taking His necessary rest. You would have seen Him, as He says Himself in the Psalms, at evening, and morning, and noon-day, calling upon His Heavenly Father; and that instantly, or with importunity.

Oh, what an advantage for us, to have the rule of our life and duty all plainly drawn for us in the practice and example of one so dear to us—of one who, whilst He was setting that admirable and sinless example, was labouring for our good—and with this very intention, that, having won our hearts by shedding His blood for us on the cross, we might take pleasure in treading in His steps! For it is surely one of our sweetest pleasures, to copy the manner of those we love, and by whom we are most undeservedly beloved. Keep your eye, therefore, my dear Catherine, fixed upon the Lord Jesus; and pray to Him that He would be your Counsellor, your Guide, and your most familiar Friend.

From your most affectionate Father,

H. VENN.

After these beautiful specimens of parental letters, we now return to the regular chronological order of the Correspondence.

TO MR. EDWARD VENN.

MY DEAR COUSIN,   *Yelling, Dec.* 5, 1779.

This day I heard of your intended nuptials with my cousin Charlotte, on next Tuesday.   From true affection for you both, every one of this family wishes you every blessing that tender union was by Heaven ordained to give. You marry, as all should, filled with mutual esteem, and unfeigned desire to promote each other's comfort and peace every day ;—a desire which must never cease ; as there is no probability that it will.   Yet can there be no security, as facts prove, without the love of God. As His power perpetually upholds the whole creation, so a sense in the heart of His adorable excellencies, producing a steady purpose to please Him, is the only absolute security that we shall not violate our social duties.

Paying the reverence and supreme veneration due from us to our God, every one of His creatures (not the brute part of them excepted) becomes respectable, as His.   A good man is merciful to his beast, because it bears the impress of his great Preserver's hand upon it : how much more to his fellow-creatures—to his servants—to his children—to his wife ! Oh ! it is beautiful to see the whole circle of good qualities kept in continual exercise, and enlivened from a never-failing source— the love of God—a source, the very same with that which angels and saints in heaven drink from, who live in the likeness of their God for ever. So far as this principle prevails, domestic comfort, civil peace, and the blessings of national prosperity, are secured. May you both be in the number of the happy few who possess this invaluable treasure of Love divine! and, as that will prompt you, often pour out for each other the most ardent prayers that you may inherit all spiritual blessings in Christ Jesus! None but those who have made the trial (and I have for more than twenty years, myself) can conceive how this strengthens and enlarges conjugal affection; or with what different eyes husbands and wives look upon each other, when they know their relation to the Lord, and are, in earnest, candidates for the eternal inheritance; from what they must do, when they know no other connexion than the transient one of passing a few years together in this disordered world.

I am much concerned to hear your dear father is so poorly. I have written to him by this post. Should he come to town, and change of air be of use, I shall hope to see him. When you can make an excursion, we shall be glad to see you and our cousin here.— Do you immediately carry your bride to your house in London, or stay for some time at Camberwell? This is a question the females about me ask.—They all desire their most affectionate remembrances to you both. From yours, very sincerely,

H. VENN.

TO MR. HENRY JOWETT.

DEAR SIR, *Yelling, Feb.* 26, 1780.

——The sight of your venerable father, so un-expected, revived and rejoiced my heart. An old disciple, who has always walked uprightly, and been a credit to his profession, is one of the finest sights upon earth. What is beauty, but a snare ? what are parts, but an incentive to pride and self-sufficiency ? what riches, but the poisonous flattery of the mind, making it fancy itself greatly benefited by the sordid dust of this earth ? But a circumspect and exem-plary conduct, a steadiness in principles truly Chris-tian, is a distinguished blessing to mankind—good in all relations. I could not help looking on your dear father as on the verge of a glorious eternity, soon to be admitted to see the Lord as He is, in whom he believed, and whom he loved and obeyed.

I have often thought of the justness and great beauty of that Scripture-image of a fruit-tree, to represent the children of God and the members of Christ. A tree is itself a pleasing figure ; a fruit-tree, laden with its precious produce, still more ; and most of all, when its fruit is fully ripe, and fit for use. Exactly according to the figure, a real Christian is lovely in his outset; more so in his steady progress, unawed by worldly fears and hopes, and uncorrupted by alluring objects of sense ; but most of all, when in old age he bears testimony to the faithfulness of God's promises in Christ Jesus— that He will be as the dew to Israel—and that the path of the just shall be as the shining light, which shineth more and more unto the perfect day. You are in your outset—your beloved father in the close of his time in which he is to remain in the Lord's vineyard on earth, ready to be transplanted, to flourish in the eternal regions. Yet, what a short space of time separates one generation from the succeeding plants!—perhaps not half the age of man, in the greater part.———

From your affectionate friend,

H. VENN.

TO MR. JOHN HOUGHTON.

MY DEAR SIR,   *Yelling, March* 10, 1780.

Your letter and its contents, which I received on Wednesday, much surprised me, and made me feel how unworthy I am of your regard for me, expressed not only in words, but by your present, which I will not in this case give you the pain of refusing; though, large as your family is, I must beg that you will never again put yourself to so much expense.

When I last wrote to you, if I remember, I entreated you not to measure my Christian love for you (and the rest of my people, to whom I was made a messenger of glad tidings) by my writing or not: for the truth has been, all along, that were I to write to all my friends, I should have no time for any thing else; and I was under the necessity of dropping a correspondence so very large. But this I can assure all my Yorkshire friends, that I never forget my connexion with them, nor to pray for

them in secret, and in my family; looking forward
to the day when God shall make up His jewels;
and many from Huddersfield, I trust, shall shine as
the sun, in the beauties of perfect holiness for ever.
It has also been always my desire, though not yet
in my power, to see once more the faces of those
to whom I spoke so comfortably, during the time of
my strength, in the name of the Lord. Whether
that desire will ever be granted, He only can tell.
But cannot you contrive to pay me one visit, as
dear Joseph Hirst has two, and stay as long with
me as your business will permit? I have been
greatly comforted by his account of some of my
dear people, and of yourself in particular; and
greatly edified to see Joseph's wisdom, steadiness,
and sincerity towards God.

What you have heard of my poor state of health,
is true. I have had an ague every third day (with
little interruption) for five months; which has reduced, a good deal, both my strength and flesh, and
has disabled me from doing the little I was busied
in before; so that I cannot any longer speak to my
people in the kitchen, as I was used to do. It may
be, that my work is nearly done. I am able to say,
"Even so, O Lord! if it seemeth good in Thy
sight!" All I desire is, whilst I live, to be of some
use; and, in every step I approach towards my
departure, to behave as a standard-bearer in the
camp of Christ ought—to be not only patient, but
cheerful, thankful, and triumphant; that the for-
malist and profane, with whom I have been waging
war, may hear that I have finished my course with
joy; and my friends in Christ say, "He lived unto

the Lord, and died unto the Lord." It is a matter of great thankfulness, and yet of humiliation, that I receive several accounts of the honour my God is putting upon my labours, poor as they are. My " Duty of Man" is used by Him to open the eyes of many. And I received a letter, only last week, to desire leave to publish a third edition of my Fourteen Sermons, first published in the year I came to dear Huddersfield, 1759.

"O may we ne'er to evil yield,
Defended from above!"

Stand fast, my dear fellow-soldier, in the faith which worketh by love! Take notice, when you read that our Saviour and his Apostles speak much more against the abuses of grace and empty professors, than against open sinners and scoffers. So does man's heart seek his own ease, profit, and indulgence in some sin, that he will be sure to pervert and abuse the doctrines of grace, in order to have his will with the less upbraidings.

My son came of age yesterday. I am greatly blessed in him. He is no great talker; which I approve much: his growth has been slow; which is always a sign things are well weighed and considered. He is much respected for his excellent conduct. So that I hope, nearly as soon as I cease to teach and preach Jesus Christ, my dear son will open his mouth, and declare the glad tidings, and live himself a monument of the power and grace of Christ Jesus our Lord.

From your much obliged friend,

H. VENN.

In another letter to one of his daughters, Mr. Venn
thus describes his way of spending the day on which his
son came of age.

————Last Thursday was a memorable day; the
day your brother came of age.   He and your cousin,
Mr. Hey, Tutor of Magdalen, Mr. Farish, and the
two Messrs. Jowett, came over and spent the day
with us. I commended your dear brother in prayer
to our God and Saviour, after praising Him for the
preserving and restraining grace by which he had
been kept, and for the measure of knowledge and
faith he had received; and then we sang a hymn
proper to the occasion. The day was a pleasant
one indeed to us all, principally in hope of sitting
down together in the Kingdom, when I trust and
pray I shall have the company of my dear children for ever, when they are wrought up to the
fulness of perfection in the presence of God and
the Lamb!

The next letter introduces the name of a new correspondent—the Lady Mary Fitzgerald, a daughter of the
Earl of Bristol, and wife of Edward Fitzgerald, Esq.

TO LADY MARY FITZGERALD.

MADAM, *Yelling, April* 9, 1780.

Two Scriptures I have had, for some weeks, very strongly impressed on my mind, as entirely applicable to your case; and I have not failed to offer them up, both alone, and with Mrs. Venn, not doubting their fulfilment to your precious and immortal soul.

The first (Cant. viii. 5.) is a very affecting representation of the Bride, the Church of Christ, and consequently of every one of the true believers in His holy name. Their present trying condition is represented by their being in a wilderness—in a dry and barren land—a land full of pits and snares— a dreary, gloomy land. Thus, as Israel was led up through this perilous state to Canaan; so we are to be exercised, and brought into circumstances which call for Divine support to bear them well. *Who is this that cometh up from the wilderness?* The question is asked by the members of the Church, with a tender sympathy for an afflicted sufferer, and also with comfort and assurance for the grace exercised in this case. *Leaning upon her Beloved,* not trusting to her own vain reasonings, in matters which are much above our understanding; not attempting, by a philosophic spirit, to calm her mind, or, from a consciousness of strength in herself, labouring to make her way through surrounding difficulties. These are not the weapons of our warfare. The Church has a Friend and a Beloved. Abandoning all hope of relief from herself, she not only looks to Him, but finds Him very nigh, offering His all-sufficient arm, with a look of more than parental love; on which He invites her to take hold, that in His strength she may be carried through, and over all, with advantage, and even matter of thanksgiving, in the end.—A *beloved* Friend, known and tried, of tender feelings, and able to enter into all that most affects us; to whom we need not even use a word to manifest what we would have, because He perfectly conceives every desire formed within. A *beloved* Friend, who esteems himself the more honoured the more we lean upon Him, expecting no degree of help from the creature; and who, at the same time that He upholds us by His arm, will speak to us by the way, and tell us of His own sorrows and trials, and fears, and cries, and agony, during the whole of His humiliation; pointing these out as proofs how fully bent He is to keep us and pre-serve us, so that none shall be able to pluck us out of His hand.

Such a Friend, and such a *beloved* Friend, have you, Madam, found, through the adorable and spe-cial grace of the Lord towards you. And whilst you are walking in the dreary path, He is with you, infusing unconquerable strength, and sweet acqui-escence, under the stroke of His holy hand, re-peated several times in a short space. But what are our sharpest sufferings, compared with the honour of such a friendship! Thus, in considering your Ladyship as exactly in the case above de-scribed, coming up out of the wilderness, leaning on your Beloved, I have received comfort and assur-ance you are and must be blessed, even under your afflictions.

x

The other striking Scripture which, in my mind, has been connected with your case, is the command given to the children of Christ: Isaiah xxvi. " Trust ye in the Lord for ever! for in the Lord Jehovah is everlasting strength . . . Thou wilt keep him in perfect peace, whose mind is staid upon Thee ; because he trusteth in Thee." Such a positive declaration, from such a mouth, what authority and power does it carry with it! What a full proof, that very particular care is taken, from the Divine foresight, of the several calamities and distresses his children are to feel! And full provision is surely made for their long-suffering, when everlasting strength is to be their place of refuge; when Divine veracity is engaged to keep the mind (as a city is kept by a brave garrison, which strikes terror into the enemy), however besieged with outward troubles, in peace. Not that this peace extinguishes the most pungent feelings of anguish. It did not in the Captain of our Salvation. He poured out prayer and tears ; and though His trust was unshaken, His soul was full of trouble. Though this is a paradox to the world, the children of God understand it, and know it to be true ; just as they can suffer torturing pain of body, yet the peace of God rules over all that is evil.

I am praying now—as I am sure I should be the basest of men did I not—that my approaching interview with my London friends may be of some use ; —that they who are so attentive to my welfare may receive something for the comfort and growth of their souls, under the word I may be able to preach. For though, adored be the grace of God!

I always do wish to profit my hearers, yet I cannot but wish especially to speak some good to those to whom I am exceedingly indebted.

I was, a few days since, greatly encouraged by a young farmer, who was educated for a higher form of life at the University, and came to settle, three years ago, in my parish, a perfect infidel. He is now going to be a steward in Ireland; and said, in company, lately: "Though I have lost more than £.200 by my farm here, I shall never repent my coming. I have gained at the church what is worth more than the world."—Yet was my wretched, unbelieving heart vexed at his coming, and the removal of the farmer he succeeded. I have had several conversations with him; and trust, though he will neither hear nor see many Christians where he is going, the Lord Jesus will be his Prophet, Priest, and King, for ever!

To that adorable Lord I commend you; and remain your very much indebted friend,

H. VENN.

TO LADY MARY FITZGERALD.

MADAM, *Yelling, July*, 1780.

I received your Ladyship's letter in due time; and write now to give you, I am very sure, a pleasure in perusing the epistle I am going to transcribe, after I have acquainted you with some circumstances relating to the writer of it. She is a Lady of Family; and, when about nineteen years old, was dressing, in the bloom of youth, for the county assembly, when instantly all the gay ideas which

x 2

filled her mind, and all her flattering prospects, were changed into painful terrors of death and judgment, by the accident of swallowing a pin. Fearing that the consequences might be fatal, she looked upon herself as called upon to prepare for death, and began to do so. It was not long before she had an opportunity of hearing the Gospel, which came upon her mind as the showers that water the earth. The love of Christ Crucified constrained her; and for near thirty years she has been a shining light, laying herself out, in every way in her power, for the benefit and salvation of her fellow-sinners. I am not myself so happy as to know the Lady, though intimate with some of her very near relations. Hearing this letter read, I desired a copy; and, as I think it very excellent indeed, I transmit it to you. It is as follows:—

"When we come with our whole heart to stand before the Saviour, we shall see our own corruption so great, that we shall think every one better than ourselves; and therefore we shall be such poor worms in our own eyes, as to bear to be pushed about on all sides, and bow and bend to every thing. We shall take whatever befalls us patiently, and be in a state of submission to every body. Our own deficiency will so fill our eyes, that we shall not be able to see that of other people. We shall love every creature for His sake who made them; and shall have the mind which was in Christ—a desire of ministering to others, rather than of being ministered to ourselves. We shall wish to serve all the world; but shall desire no service from the world; knowing we deserve none. We shall wonder

at the kindness and love shewn to us, feeling ourselves unworthy of it: much more shall we be
sometimes in astonishment, to consider that our
Saviour should love and suffer so much for us.
We shall look at Him on His cross, and weep. We
shall look at our own hearts as the cause, and then
weep again; and our whole attention will be to
Him and His service. Thus viewing Him, the
world lessens in our eyes more and more. We feel
our time too important to be taken up with any
thing in it. We have nothing to do here, but to
serve Him in love, and watch against the sad re-
mainders of our corruption, which so frequently
remind us of our sinful condition. This is the proper state of a soul entirely attached to Jesus; the
sweetest name that ever was heard!"

I know, Madam, how much these are your
own feelings and views. How exceeding great
the power which can implant, and cause them
to increase, in hearts so opposite to them as ours
are! What a marvellous transformation of character was effected by the swallowing of a pin,
which became to her a loud call to prepare to
die! But for this, dress, equipage, visits, cards,
pleasures, as they are called, in quick succession,
would have engrossed her immortal mind! Instead
of wisdom flowing from her lips, a continual effu-
sion of idle talk;—instead of an example of meekness and heavenly affections, haughtiness and love
of pre-eminence would have reigned in her;—
instead of many won by her life, and relieved in
soul by her instruction, and comforted by her
bounty, there would have been many confirmed

in folly and delusions deadly to the soul, by her conformity to their practice and the fashion. Here is the truth and reality of Redemption, seen and felt in its incomparable fruits!—an anticipation, in some measure, of that state we are training up for, when we shall be perpetually dead to all that is selfish, and be filled with all the fulness of God.

I am very happy that you are much acquainted with my honoured friend and patron, Lady Smythe; and how should I be transported, if the day of her deliverance from the spirit of fear, which has pain in it, were come! It is indeed hard work to hold on in the narrow way, in opposition to the world, without the light of God's countenance, and the pleasures of His holy service.

I see, by the papers, Dr. Knowles has written upon the Passion of our Saviour. I hope he has found his life in those tears, and groans, and wounds, and agony, and death. It is rare for a Doctor in Divinity to exercise his thoughts upon such a subject. How is the remembrance of that adorable Redeemer gone out of this land! May we consider ourselves as witnesses for His despised truth and salvation! We shall soon, from being amongst the few, stand with the vast multitude, whom no man can number, before the Throne of God and the Lamb.—Mrs. Venn begs her best respects.

From your much-indebted servant, for Christ's sake, H. VENN.

———

In a life of such even tenor as that which this Memoir records, an event now occurred of great comparative

interest. Mr. Venn had long desired to revisit Huddersfield ; ten years having nearly elapsed since he had left
it ; but various hindrances prevented the accomplishment
of his wish. The next letters describe the circumstances
of the visit, and some striking occurrences connected
with it.

———

TO MR. EDWARD VENN.

MY DEAR NEPHEW, *Yelling, Sept.* 14, 1780.

Though I have lost my ague since the 9th of
July, yet I have but little strength. I am therefore
advised to try riding by short journeys, and change
of air ; for which purpose I intend setting out next
week for Yorkshire, and shall be absent two or
three months. Mrs. Venn is afraid of the journey ;
and chooses rather to stay with my daughters. If
this journey does not help me much, I am to try
Bath waters.

Thus I am taking a great deal of trouble, at much
expense, to recover the health of a body impaired
and old, and which, after all, can stand but a few,
a very few years. But what do we not owe to our
Immanuel, who opens a transforming prospect
before us, when our body is decayed? He is present with us, to cheer the mind, and prevent the
gloom which would otherwise oppress it ; and to
assure us, that we shall immediately, by death,
join the vast society of spirits perfectly free from
all error and all sin—all living in the light which
will not admit of disagreement—knowing the truth,
and beholding each other's hearts full of boundless

love to God, and to every angel and saint around them—active, without fatigue, like the Great Father of the family—and appointed to the most noble exercise of immortal faculties, without the least corruption or abuse of them; all being incessantly employed according to the will of their adorable Author; when, instead of seeing human nature, in ten thousand instances, so depraved as to make us blush we are of the human race, we shall see it exalted and honoured, without spot or wrinkle upon it.

Such, my dear nephew, are my prospects.— Though I love my family, and have from each of them much satisfaction, and would do all to make them comfortable, yet neither wife nor child can fill me with regret, should I pass into eternity before we have lived much longer together.

I write this to you in the openness of my heart, that you may see godliness is indeed great gain. Oh! it is worth a thousand worlds, to be ready to depart, and to finish our course with joy.

From your affectionate father,

H. VENN.

TO MISS JANE VENN.

Halifax, Oct. 11, 1780.

TELL your beloved mamma, my dear Jane, that the account of her cheerfulness and good health has made me rejoice; and without any alloy, save such as absence from her must cause. I now take pleasure in the wonderful scene passing before my eyes. By this expression, I mean the very great degree of affection so many are expressing for me; and the delightful account I hear of so many souls walking in the light, and living in the love of Christ. Would it not bring tears into your eyes, to hear one after another, with a countenance full of love, declare they have reason to bless God for ever, that they had heard my voice?

Last Sunday, I preached at Huddersfield twice. Fifty minutes was the length of the first sermon: fifty-three, of the second. No vociferation at all, in the first: in the second, *very little.* The church was more than filled in the morning: in the afternoon, several hundreds were in the church-yard, and hundreds went away. The gallery was so loaded, as to crack and give way during the Prayers; but was, by bringing a strong prop immediately, kept from falling. This vast congregation was silent, and still as possible. After sermon in the afternoon, I was less fatigued than I could have supposed possible, considering how very hot the church was. The hymn was admirable; and every creature joined. It was a picture of heaven!

You can hardly conceive the care they all express for me; and desire I may not preach more than will agree with me. When, from the pulpit, I beheld so vast a multitude in and out of the church, I was very awfully struck with this idea—what dreadful consequences must follow, should the man they make so much of, fall into wickedness! How would the ungodly triumph, the weak be stumbled, and the Christians mourn in secret! Pray for your father, my dear child! that God, for His own truth's sake, may give me to persevere in His good ways. Terrible is the falling away of any who make profession, and act quite contrary to convictions!

A lady here, Mrs. ——, thus relates her own sad case : "Madam, once Mr. —— and I were both in the right path. I drew him into the world again. I am now the most miserable of beings! When I lie down, I fear I shall awake in hell. When I go out, full-dressed, and seem to have all the world can give me, I am ready to sink under the terrors of my own mind. What greatly increases my misery, is the remembrance of the dying speech of my own sister; who told me she had stifled convictions, and obstinately fought against light, to enjoy the company of the world. 'Sister,' said she, 'I die without hope. Beware this be not your own case!' —But, indeed," said Mrs. —— to the lady, "I fear it will!" Pray, my dear children, for singleness of heart, and for such a revelation of the excellency of Christ Jesus as will leave no place for halting or dividing your affections. May they all centre in Him!

You will like to know what my subjects were at dear Huddersfield. The morning was, Psalm xix. 12—14: the afternoon, 1 Cor. iii. last verse. I am to preach, if well, next Sunday, at Dewsbury.— I parted, this morning, with Mr. Richardson of Howarth, who asked very kindly after you all; and with Mr. Wilson, of Slaighthwait, who gave your brother an excellent character, for his behaviour at Hull.—Let me know if Mr. Jowett can serve Yelling longer than the four next Sundays. You must order in a fresh supply of coals. Oh! what fires have we here! You are a Yorkshire lass: you need not be ashamed of your county. My best love to your mamma, your brother, and sisters.

The Lord be with you all, and, if it please Him, give us a joyful meeting!

From your affectionate father,

H. VENN.

TO THE REV. JAMES STILLINGFLEET.

MY VERY DEAR FRIEND,   *Yelling, Jan.* 24, 1781.

Yours of the 3d instant was a most acceptable letter. I was afraid, when compelled to refuse your kind invitation, and deny myself a very great pleasure, you might be *uneasy* at it; for where there is love, even Christian love, there will sometimes be a little stirring of jealousy: yet I assured myself that you knew well there is scarcely a man in the world with whom I have so much intimate communion as with yourself; consequently, I should with exceeding joy have visited you in your own habitation, and at the head of your flock—with your very excellent partner, to see her keeping in good order all the matters in her own province. Glad indeed should I have been, to have confirmed the word of your testimony, and proved to your people how exactly we agree in our manner of preaching Christ Crucified! To all these pleasures I should have added the sight of some of your excellent fellow-labourers, and of my old, venerable, and much-loved friend, Mr. Adam. But if you had heard how peremptorily the doctor forbade my travelling so late in the year; and considered what pain Mrs. Venn and my family would have felt, if all my absence from home, and expense, had been frustrated by imprudence at last; you would conclude I had acted wisely.

But since, in Providence, I was disappointed of my visit to you, you shall read a good deal of what I should have told you in your own house.—It had long been my wish once more to see the people who were called, by the grace of God, under my poor ministry. For this I had offered up many prayers; but I little thought my long ague, and the wasting of my strength, was to be the immediate cause of obtaining my wish. The second day after I left home, the excellent Pastor of St. Mary's, at Leicester, met me; and we had sweet conversation together: indeed, he is always doing good—wise, learned, zealous, yet very judicious — sound in moderate Calvinism, yet truly practical and experimental. His enemies have their mouths stopped; their revilings having lost all their impression. I could see him, when I was walking with him through the streets, revered by young and old, and in many countenances a joy at the sight of his person. Oh! there is a divine influence very perceptible in every one whose whole heart is intent upon exalting God, and bringing the poor sinners to His own Son for life! From him I went to Mr. Walker's at Rotherham, an old disciple, living, with his wife and some of his children, in a spacious mansion, surrounded by a large village filled with his own manufacturers, and built by him for their use. He has a love unfeigned for our God and Saviour. There I staid two nights: and the next day I dined at Thornhill with our friends; and saw our dear Powley. The day after, which was Friday, I reached Shaw Hill; and, passing through Elland, engaged to preach there the Sunday following. This was presently known in that populous country; and I met with a great number from Huddersfield, in the House of the Lord. After Service, we saluted each other; and our meeting was exceedingly tender and affecting. They were cast down, to see me so thin and weak, compared to what I was when I left them. But the Yorkshire air, and constant riding, soon gave me a good appetite and good sleep, through the Divine blessing. I had strength to speak thirty times in the nine weeks, without hurting myself. Nothing can exceed the kindness and love all my friends shewed—and the joy they expressed at my visit—and the *good*, many persons said, they received. I could not but bless God for dear Mr. Olerinshaw. I heard an excellent sermon from him in the Chapel of Bierley; which gave me the more pleasure, because of the loss your people sustained upon your removal. From Halifax I travelled to Birmingham; and saw our honest and highly-favoured brother, in his unintermitted attention to the work of his ministry. I had an opportunity of speaking five times, in eight days, to his very numerous congregation. I left him on the Monday, December 10; and arrived safe at home the Friday following, laden with mercies, to see my family in peace. Oh, that my health restored, and life prolonged, may be more useful than ever! I have again my people in an evening—a third of the village—to hear the Word of God, twice or three times a week, not without comfort and a blessing.

I am persuaded, if our strength will bear it, we must work in the week-days. Pray remember me most affectionately to Mr. Adam. Now my health seems restored and my life a little prolonged, pray for me, that both may be of some use to my family, friends, and the Church of God!

Mrs. Venn, my son and daughters, with myself, send love to you both. May you be wiser—stronger in body and mind—more useful—full of peace and joy in believing—all athirst for Christ, and for a rich participation of His salvation! How truly happy shall we soon be in Him, when we go hence!

From your own affectionate friend,

H. Venn.

P. S. What a length of writing! Some men would sooner ride from Hotham to Yelling than write at all!

———

The following letter was written, during his journey home, to one of his Huddersfield friends; and records a pleasing testimony of the affection and gratitude they still cherished for their late revered Pastor.

———

TO MR. JOHN HOUGHTON.

MY DEAR FRIEND,   *Birmingham, Dec.* 9, 1780.

Our bodies are again far distant from each other. Not so our souls :—they are, I trust, bound up in the bundle of life, with the Lord our God; and are nourished by the same heavenly food, taught by the same unerring Spirit, made glad through the same joyful tidings, and intent on the same work— to serve and please the Lord. Faith realizes these

things; and gives us all to look to the gathering
together of the saints in Christ, when Pastors and
Teachers, with their people who received the word,
shall all know as they are known.

So many were the mercies, and so great the kindnesses of my dear Yorkshire friends, that I shall not
be able, whilst on my journey, to take a due survey
of them.   When I am at home—which, God willing,
I purpose being on Friday next—I shall be quite lost
in wonder, that such a one, as I know myself to be,
should ever be so highly esteemed.   Indeed, it was
much my desire and prayer that I might, once
before I died, bear afresh a testimony in favour of
the practical and experimental knowledge of Christ,
and Him Crucified, by which all the good that is
done upon earth is done by the Lord.   I have had
many precious opportunities of so doing; and verily
believe it will be found, in the Last Day, that my
visit was not in vain in the Lord.   How much do I
owe to the esteem and love of my friends, that they
have taken such ample care that all the charges of
my journey should be defrayed, and much more;—
not that I desired, with much truth I can say, any
gift, but fruit—the fruit of more grace, faith, and
love, abounding in your souls.

Pray give my love to your dear mother and
wife.   Happy was I to see you all so united, and
living in the fear of the Lord, and in the comfort
of the Holy Ghost!   Remember me to Joseph Hirst
and Barbara, William Scholefield, and all friends.—
The Lord Jesus be with your Spirit!

From your friend and pastor in Christ,

H. VENN.

In January 1781, Mr. John Venn took the degree of
Bachelor of Arts. The event is thus noticed:—

——My son has taken his degree. He was very
much embarrassed and agitated in mind, through
excessive fear—a terrible hindrance to him in expressing himself, when examined. He has not,
consequently, obtained so much honour as he
would otherwise have done. The Examiners assure
my friends he deserved a much higher place. My
design is, that he shall stay one year at College, till
he is ordained, to employ his time wholly in proper
study and much prayer, as I have reason to think
he will.

TO MR. JOHN VENN.

MY DEAR SON,   *Yelling, March* 18, 1781.

——Yesterday I had a melancholy ride to ——,
to visit Mr.——, dangerously ill in his bed. He
sent for me. Oh, how has he smarted, and been in
terrible fear, for having loved the company of the
ungodly, and given into their evil ways! He was
very weak; and some of his relations were with
him; which prevented my speaking so closely and
particularly as I should otherwise have done. I
had a little enlargement of heart in prayer; and a
good deal of comfort in comforting his poor afflicted
wife, who has long been serving the Lord. Nothing

is more pleasant than such employment as this; and it is always followed with the cheering influence of the Holy Ghost in the soul.

My ride home was very different from my ride thither, in the frame of my mind. *"He went about doing good":*—this is the pattern for every Christian. He is a counterfeit one, who does not strive to imitate it. The strength, the alacrity, the joy of the soul, is connected with this imitation. Religious people are heavy and moping, and cast down, principally because they are idle and selfish. The active, benevolent spirit of watching for opportunities to do essential service to our fellow-creatures, they often feel no more than the profane. What then avail notions and doctrines, believed to no good purpose? More especially, I look upon it as the great sin and reproach of *scholars*, that they almost universally neglect their fellow-creatures. They are lamentably selfish : they make no use of their learning, and the influence it gives them, and their ability to teach, as they should do every day, in setting forth the great things of God's Law, and pleading the glorious cause of God against the world and all the deluded votaries of pleasure.

Were it lawful to wish, I should wish for strength to work and labour more; for I am not yet able to preach in the week-days. Remember me to all friends. The Lord Jesus be with your spirit!

From your affectionate father,

H. VENN.

Y

TO MRS. BRASIER
(ON THE DEATH OF AN INFANT).

DEAR MADAM,   *Yelling, March* 27, 1781.

Be pleased to thank my Cousin for his letter.—
In reading of your loss, I felt for you both; but more
especially, as there appeared something of a doubt,
whether you could say, with full assurance, the child
is blessed. I have known several Christians troubled
with doubts on this head; and few things have appeared to me more strange ;—for we may say, with
truth, What could God have done, more than He
has done, to prove His love for the infants of the
human race ? They were always admitted to be
members of His Church. A regard for them, he
mentions as a reason why Nineveh, in which there
were so many thousand infants, should not, as Jonah
desired, be destroyed. The Saviour himself embraced and blessed them. Again: not a soul is
destroyed for ever, but for wicked works ; they are
hypocrites, they are unbelievers, they are impenitent to the last, after warnings, admonitions, and
calls, &c., who perish. But what works have infants
done, that are evil ? Some are ready to say, for
Adam's offence they perish. The Scripture says,
they die a natural death on that account; expressly
mentioning, that they have not sinned after the
similitude of Adam's transgression, but never that
they suffer the pains of Hell. Now, can such a
thought be reconciled with the character of God,
drawn by Himself; as, " slow to anger, and of great
kindness ;" as swearing, He hath no pleasure in the
death of a sinner ?—It is His strange act to punish.

Nothing but a contention against His government to the last, an impious denial of His Gospel, or a base, hypocritical assent to it, draws down His vengeance. Be assured, from such evidence, our dear children, taken away almost as soon as we see them, are safe in the hands of their merciful Creator and Redeemer.

My sister gives us a good account of your health, and Mr. Brasier's; and of your little John. Be jealous of yourself with regard to him. He will be much as you fashion him. Dread nothing so much as self-will. Do not tire and burden him with religion, of which he can bear but a very little: but ready submission and obedience, and temperance in eating and drinking, without which the body and mind must suffer, he can very well know and observe.

Mrs. Venn and my family, who are in good health, desire their love. In three weeks I may probably just catch a sight of you; but, as I can be only one Sunday from home, it will not be in my power to do more than call. My health is very much restored; yet I am forced, I think, to pay dear for it. I am obliged to be on horseback every day, and cannot study and apply as my heart delights to do. I began to make trial of preaching four times one week; but I smarted for it for more than a fortnight; so that I must be content with doing very little indeed in my old age. Oh that I may enjoy more meditation and prayer, and communion with God, till I am with Him, whose Name is most glorious in my eyes, and His service the highest honour!

My sister Patty desires her best respects to you both.   I tell her she looks very old: but that word *old* she cannot yet endure:—yet to be old in the faith, is to be near, and on the very borders of, joy eternal.   Oh for an overcoming faith, to possess the inheritance of the saints in light, by hope, before we are translated to it!

From yours very affectionately,

H. Venn.

<hr>

TO LADY MARY FITZGERALD.

MADAM,   *Yelling*, 1782.

I waited a long time, for several reasons, before I would write.   The shock you felt required time for recollection.   Human advice, or exhortation, is of little value, when sorrow must have its vent.   I wanted also to be informed of the full extent of your affliction: yet, though I deferred addressing you so long, I did not sin against Christian affection, so as to forget your fiery trial, or cease to join the many supplicants to God for your afflicted soul. You have been always in my mind, both when with my wife and with my family, as well as in secret prayer: and, in numberless ejaculations, your case has been spread before the God of hope, whose mercy and help go far beyond the utmost sufferings of His children.   Once in particular, when my dear Mr. Berridge was a visiter, and bowing his knees with us, I indeed cried unto the Lord to give you strength and consolation in the furnace.

I must add, what will certainly give you pleasure

and cheer your soul, if it does not also surprise you. Your heart loves to do good; and fears, as we ought, nothing more than being of little or no use in the world. You would say, 'Welcome sorrow, and every kind of tribulation, if by this means I may be of service to any soul!' Be assured, from your distress, I have learnt more than I ever knew before. I knew before, how salutary and blessed to the *sufferers themselves* all corrections are made, at last, by that heart of love which ordains them; but I did not know how much good a Christian is doing *to the Church,* even at the time when her grief and anguish of spirit are the greatest. Yet then it is that her Christian friends are stirred up, as the Prophet was by Hezekiah's representation of his extreme distress, to lift up their prayer with importunity. Then it is we feel more abundantly the sweet affection of soul—a sympathy most real; so strongly described by the Apostle, when he says, " If one member suffer, all the members suffer with it." Then it is we are led more deeply to consider the use, the necessity, the certainty also of a happy end of all our trials, when those who are most dear to the Lord are so deeply exercised. How many of your friends have now seen you taking refuge in the sure mercies of David, and been edified by the filial fear of your heart, lest you should be found impatient and untractable under the rod! How many have been led to consider and believe the friendship of Jesus to be, of all things in the world, the most desirable, from the fruits you have enjoyed from it! Thus, as the faithful, when they suffered bonds and imprisonment, and gained the crown of martyrdom, became much more the objects of notice to the Church—had the benefit of its prayers—quickened, convinced, converted, established many more than they would have done by their holy life; so it is now, when a member of Christ is brought into great tribulation: our attention is arrested and fixed; our friendship is much interested; we receive, with peculiar advantage, instruction from their sufferings; we listen to the sayings which drop from their lips; and are animated afresh, with the hope of being gainers ourselves, when we shall, in our turn, be tried in the fire.

The concluding months of the last year are memorable in my life. Not only was your Ladyship in great affliction, but several of my friends. I went from one house of mourning to another; and was seldom two days at home for several weeks, but riding from one place to another. The Scripture was fulfilled: "The house of mourning is better than the house of feasting." I was eye-witness to our Lord's love, and unsearchable riches of grace.

One intimate friend—called under Mr. Berridge twenty-two years since, but chiefly attending my ministry, because so much nearer—died honourably indeed! He left his beloved wife, and four young children, without reluctance. "I have more than peace," said he; "I have joy! Sing with me a hymn!" The hymn was this:—

> How happy is the Christian's state!
> His sins are all forgiven;
> A cheering ray confirms his hope,
> And lifts his soul to heaven.

Though in the rugged path of life,
 He heaves a mournful sigh,
He trusts in his Redeemer's name,
 And finds deliverance nigh.

If, to correct his wandering steps,
 He feels the chast'ning rod,
The gentle stroke shall bring him back
 To his forgiving God.

And when the welcome summons comes,
 To call his soul away,
His soul in rapture shall ascend
 To everlasting day.

Thus have I seen a Christian depart!—' O world! produce a good like this!' we may boldly say; and then it shall have our best affections. Till then, may we be only for the Lord!

Another most encouraging reward I received two months since, in the comfortable and joyful departure of a farmer's wife—Mrs. Papworth, of Elsworth. When she first came to Yelling, four years ago, I observed her deeply attentive, as one who was hearing for her life. She came five or six times after; but every relation being much against it, she could not come oftener. When she was upon her death-bed, the fear of death and sense of sin exceedingly distressed her; on which account she desired her husband would ask me to visit her. I did so; and pointed out the cause and cure of the fear of death, which had full possession of her mind. Then a short prayer was offered up; three declarations, from the mouth of the Lord, of His willingness and ability to save all who call upon

Him, were repeated; and then a short prayer for the application of them, which (oh! never enough to be admired condescension!) were made effectual.   Her doubts were all gone; her soul rejoiced; she spoke with a new tongue; she preached to her husband, her sister, her relations.   She told them they were all wrong—that Jesus Christ was all.   She said: "You see the change!   What do I feel!   I would not come off this bed for all the world!   Mr. Venn told me the Lord would put a new song into my mouth.   He hath done it already; and I shall sing it for ever."   Then, laying her hand upon her breast, she repeatedly said, "Blessed Jesus! Blessed Jesus! Thou wilt receive me!"   Tears and astonishment in her husband followed.   The scoffers were struck dumb; and her husband desired I would preach a funeral sermon on the occasion.   The text was (Acts xiii. 38): "Be it known unto you, men and brethren, that through this man is preached unto you the forgiveness of sins;" and the two following verses.   Many came out of curiosity, which the Lord always overrules for good to some souls.   How small are dignities, estates, crowns, to this privilege of seeing men brought to enjoy heaven on earth, and testifying it with their dying breath!   What manner of persons ought we to be, who partake of this wondrous love?   Let not your heart be troubled; neither let it be afraid.   Thy truth, Most Mighty Lord! is on every side.   How shall the courts above ring with the praise of the salvation of our God!

Your ladyship, I hear, is now released from your attendance on the Princess: but in the courts of the King of kings you will always stand, and wait and admire, and enjoy His beatific smile.   Let me entreat you not to think yourself at all obliged to answer this letter.   I could wish you were in health to do it; but it would give me pain you should write one line, so poorly as you are.   The dear sisters will let me know, from time to time, how you are in health; and I shall be assured the Lord, whom you serve, is always with you.

The week after next, I purpose setting out for Birmingham, to bring home a daughter, who has been there eight months, to see what change of air would do; and our good God has recovered her. I shall speak to thousands before I return, of the Name of Jesus.   Oh, pray for me, that my testimony may be clear, bold, and effectual, through His own power!

Pray remember me to your two noble sisters. Hope to the end, for all your relations.   It is an enemy only who opposes this hope.   "The last shall be first."   It is worth all the pain we can ever feel, to have it removed by a smile of our Saviour— and all tears wiped from our eyes, *by His hand,* whom angels adore.   That will soon be your glory! To Him I earnestly commend your soul.

Your ever indebted,

H. Venn.

TO JOHN BRASIER, ESQ.

MY DEAR FRIEND,   *Yelling, April* 13, 1782.

If it will be convenient, we purpose to bring my daughter Jane to your hospitable house, on the last day of this month—in the evening.   We shall be ourselves at my brother Gambier's. We have been in alarm since I last wrote to you. My son was ill of a fever at College—as bad a place as a jail, to be sick in. Most happy was I to get him home, upon the first leave from his physician! Under the anxiety I felt for him, when ill, he told me I ought to have no will of my own—he was perfectly resigned to live or die; for he had given himself up to the Lord, to be His for ever: either life or death, therefore, were equally welcome to him. He stayed at home a fortnight; and the bark being blessed, and no relapse, on Monday he returned to College. It was a great comfort to me to see the respect paid to him, when ill, by the Master, Fellows, and all his companions in College. A good report from them that are without, is one of the requisites in a candidate for the ministry.

We are now praying, that the visit we are soon to make to our kind friends and relations may be profitable to our souls, like the visit of Mary the Mother of our Lord to her Cousin Elizabeth—that the Incarnate Saviour may be the chief subject of our discourse—that we may encourage and warm each other's hearts, to live less to ourselves, and more to Him who died for us and rose again; and be speaking so one to another, that even the Lord Himself may hearken and hear us, His elect children, talk with a new tongue, and edify each other. Parents have peculiar delight in viewing the accomplishments of their sons and daughters, in listening to their excellent and wise observations, and in seeing the expense of their education well repaid in their improvement: our Heavenly Father represents

Himself no less pleased with the tongue of the wise, by which knowledge is spread; and by the lips of the righteous, by which many souls are fed. I particularly am concerned, in gratitude, to pray that those who have so undeserved a love for me, and give so many proofs of it, may reap some spiritual advantage from my ministry. My time must be short here. I am feeling the decay of my strength, so that I cannot labour as I once did, and speak with much less force. A Christian would have his lot as the Lord is pleased to appoint it. It is right and fit the children should suffer in some measure, as their Saviour. How did He feel bodily weakness and pain, before He tasted death! May we ever sing,

"Ours the cross, the grave, the skies," &c.!

From your affectionate friend and pastor in Christ.

H. VENN.

TO MISS RILAND.

MY DEAR MISS RILAND,   *Yelling, Nov.* 14, 1782.

Accept my congratulations on your return to your dear parents from school, after so good an improvement of the time you spent there. Hence we are naturally led, with pleasure, to conclude your attention, to all that is peculiarly becoming and excellent in your early years, will increase.

You have received from the Blessed God, an active mind; and reading, I am assured, is an entertainment to you. I beg, therefore, your acceptance, as a *keepsake*, of a very celebrated work,

entitled, "Nature Displayed." This author will bring
you acquainted with a thousand wonders, which
surround us on every side. He will prove to demonstration the adorable power, wisdom, and goodness
of our God, in the preserving, framing, and pro-
viding for all animals; and point out the way of
beholding God, with great delight, in every thing
which contributes to our safety, health, and comfort. In reading this author, you cannot help
admiring the strength of his piety : and what we admire, we soon, in a measure, contract. " Nature
Displayed" was written by a French divine.

The Meditations and Contemplations which I
send you are the fruit of Mr. Hervey's pen—the
most extraordinary man I ever saw in my life! as
much beyond most of the excellent, as the swan,
for whiteness and a stately figure, is beyond the
common fowl. These thoughts deserve your most
serious regard. You may look upon them as you
would upon Aaron's rod, by which such wonders
were wrought : for these thoughts have been made
the means of giving sight to the blind ; life to souls
dead in trespasses and sin ; and winning the young,
the gay, the rich, to see greater charms in a Crucified
Saviour, as your own dear parents do, than in all
that glitters and dazzles vain minds. How happy
shall I be to hear Miss Riland say, " How tender,
affecting, and irresistible, are the pleadings of Mr.
Hervey, for his adored Immanuel ! "

The Moral Lessons which I have sent you are
much admired. They are written by a physician,
still living at St. Alban's. His name is Cotton. You
will fine many sensible lines, and beautiful repre-

sentations of virtue and benevolent tempers, in his work : yet there is a lamentable defect !—his virtue and benevolence are of the Heathen stamp; they have no relation to our God and Saviour.

You will receive with these, also, our famous English Dictionary.

Such books as these are entertaining and profitable, in qualifying us for conversation with each other; and afford a very pleasing amusement. There is one book already in your study, which an old writer addresses thus :—" Thrice blessed volume! Thou art the great deposit, once delivered to the saints ! Thou art the mean by which Jesus Christ keeps intercourse with His Bride on earth ! Thou art the Charter of all the Church's mercies, and of our hope through eternity !"—You will immediately say, " This is *my Bible*." It is ! Glory be to God for this Book ! Yet is it full of dark sayings ; consequently, dull, and even irksome to read :—this must be allowed. But there is a Divine Teacher, given to all, who, before they read this Book from heaven, ask Him of God.—May you every day desire this Teacher ! and say, " Open Thou mine eyes, that I may see the wonders of Thy Law !"—So I began. So your honoured father and mother began, many years ago ; and the Book that was dark, and of little use, is now our delight, sweeter than the honeycomb—more than all manner of riches. *You* will find the same success, by reading, with prayer, a small portion of the blessed word of God : and when you once understand and believe it, you will have an evidence, in your own mind, that you are a daughter of the Lord God Almighty, an heir of glory, in a state of education for the happiness of heaven. And when the appointed time comes, that your dear parents must leave you, to go to their God whom they have loved and served, you will still remain most nearly related to them in Christ, and live with them for ever in His presence.

That this may be your portion, is the earnest prayer of your sincere friend and godfather!

H. Venn.

CORRESPONDENCE.

SECTION IV.

On the 22d of September 1782, Mr. John Venn was ordained Deacon, by the Bishop of Lincoln, on the title of his father's curacy.

To this event the father had been looking forward, for many years, with ardent hope and ceaseless prayer. But the son, during the same interval, was frequently suffering distress, under a deep sense of his own unworthiness for the sacred office; and had at one time even abandoned the thought of undertaking it. It is no uncommon circumstance for young men of religious sensibility to suffer in the same manner. They more particularly, who have been habituated to the contemplation of a high standard of ministerial excellence, are apt to despair at the contrast suggested by their own inferior pretensions. Yet that very humility, which at first oppresses them with fear, may be the germ of future eminence in piety and usefulness. The case before us was an instance of this. Many of my readers may therefore be interested, and some may be comforted, by the introduction of a letter written by Mr. John Venn to his father two years before he was of age to take orders, in which the misgivings of a tender conscience and self-diffident spirit are affectingly exhibited. The letter was sent to Mr. Venn whilst he was paying the visit to Huddersfield which has been already mentioned.

The father's answer is also added.

FROM MR. JOHN VENN.

MY VERY DEAR FATHER,   *Yelling, Oct.* 18, 1780.

The natural reservedness of my temper, and the fear I had of giving you pain in your bad state of health, prevented me from opening my whole mind to you at Yelling; especially as the subject was of the last importance, and required all the time and attention I was able to bestow upon it.   But, since you have always treated me with a peculiar and undeserved tenderness; since I know how much you are interested in whatever concerns me, far above the common feelings of a parent; and since you have kindly desired me to look upon you rather in the light of a friend than a father; I think it is my duty, without reserve, to disclose to you the whole state of my mind;—which I now do, as in the presence of Almighty God, divesting myself, as much as lies in my power, of all reserve, of all disguise, and of all undue bias of the mind whatever.

For some time past, but especially since February last, has my own unworthiness for the blessed office of the ministry appeared in a forcible and convincing view.—My poor abilities, and small share of faith and grace, may, perhaps, through the infinite clemency of God, enable me to glorify

Him in the humble walk of a private Christian ; but the weighty and important charge of the souls of others is what I dare not presume to undertake. I speak as in the presence of Almighty God, who sees the depths of my heart, and who will be my Judge hereafter.

The office of the ministry I esteem as far more honourable than any employment relating to temporal concerns can be ; but, at the same time, the danger is proportionably great, and the importance of it tremendous. Ever since I had a thought of it, my prayer to God has been, that he would take the matter into His hands. I begged, for His Name's sake, that if He, who alone could see into futurity, and who alone knows the temper and disposition of men, judged me improper for the work, I might never be suffered to profane it. I begged, that if this reluctance was from Him, He would increase and confirm it : but should it be a temptation, as you seemed to judge, or should it proceed from the deceitfulness of the heart, I entreated, for the glory of God, and the sake of the prayers of many of His saints, that it might never be suffered to prevail. I can call God to witness, that, as far as human imperfection allows, I have been sincere, and faithfully waited on God, to know His will ;—and surely, He would never suffer so many prayers to be in vain, and in such an important matter too, who hath so repeatedly said, ' Ask, and ye shall have ' ?

Much, for seven months, have I suffered, bewildered in my mind with suspense, and harassed with the prospect of surrounding distress ; but all that I have felt, or thought, tends only to confirm me in

z

the opinion of my own insufficiency. At present, indeed, I enjoy a calm in my mind; which, I trust, is the effect of prayer, and a resignation to God, by reflecting that the matter is in His hands : but still I see more fully and more strongly than ever my own incapacity. I well know I am not to look to myself, but to God, for assistance. I well know that God is merciful to our errors; but I dare not therefore presume upon that mercy, in matters where I am before warned by a foresight of these errors ; especially since the weakness of a minister, unlike that of other individuals, has effects dreadfully general. Your partiality and tenderness for me may cover a multitude of faults, which, to the eye of an all-just God, appear in their proper colours ; but I see my temper and disposition such, and my infirmities and weakness so great, that, as I would answer it at the bar of the judgment-seat of Christ, I cannot undertake this holy employment. Next to the awful concerns of eternal things, nothing could have given me more joy than the fulfilment of that pleasure which you had always promised yourself, in seeing me a fellow-labourer in the ministry. The prospect of your disappointment has, indeed, filled me with a sorrow I cannot express ; and, were it not a matter which will affect my soul far beyond the narrow bounds of time, I would be content to suffer misery in this world, that you might be made happy. But filial affection ought not to sway in matters of conscience ; and I am persuaded you would suffer more from seeing me discharge improperly that sacred office, than, from a due sense of my own unfitness, decline it.

It is true, I see much distress in every line of life. I see misery, and grief, and bitterness, unavoidable, and such as makes my soul shrink back with horror; but I dare not bestow a thought upon that, as an inducement to comply with what my conscience disallows. My great support is, that I can, in the most solemn manner, appeal to God, the searcher of my heart, that I have not, knowingly, had any sinister end in view—that I have laid the whole matter upon God, sincerely begging the guidance of His Spirit, and to do His will—that I have reason to believe the present determination to be His will—and that my conscience has not aught to accuse me of, in this affair: and then, if it please God that I must endure much distress and sorrow through the rest of my life—He knows best, and is merciful—His will be done!

You, my dear father, have prayed for me incessantly, from the hour of my birth. You now see a necessity, stronger than ever, of the most fervent prayers in my behalf: and may God give you an abundant spirit of prayer suited to the occasion!— I have not an unfeeling heart: and I anticipate with exquisite keenness the shock you must feel from this declaration. Judge, then, the distress of mind I have long endured.—Once more I beg you to pray for me earnestly!

I am your ever dutiful son,

JOHN VENN.

P.S. I have had this letter some time by me; but it required much time for consideration. I shall stay at Yelling till I hear from you, in answer.

z 2

TO MR. JOHN VENN.

MY DEAR SON,   *Huddersfield, 4th Nov.* 1780.

Your letter has never been out of my mind since I
received it : and after much attention to its contents,
I, upon the whole, cannot but be thankful—not for
your trouble and smart, but for many other reasons.

Those whom God peculiarly loves, to them he
discovers their guilt and vileness—their miserable,
depraved, and helpless condition: consequently,
they must feel their own insufficiency, and, at
first, often in a very afflicting degree. Would to
God every young man intended for the ministry
were penetrated, as you are, with abiding convictions
of his own weakness and ignorance, and manifold
corruptions, so as to tremble at the thought of being
employed in the very high and holy office of a
Preacher of Christ, and a Pastor to his sheep! Yet
when, in peculiar mercy, this just estimate of ourselves, and of the ministry, is given, are we to ascribe
it to nature or to Grace ?—to Satan or God ?—to
pride or humility ?—as a *necessary* qualification to
enter into the office, or a prohibition ? It is granted
that all you allege on this head is true : but if
of force in your case, it holds equally against every
one who would enter into the office, or is already
in it ; because every one is insufficient, is extremely
vile, offends in many things, and can never say,
' There is nothing wrong to be seen in me.'

But, whilst you look upon yourself in the true
light, as a miserable sinner, you forget the very
merciful intention of the Redeemer, in which He

secures to Himself the glory.   It is, we are taught, that the excellence of the power may be seen to be of God, that such worms of the earth are entrusted with the dispensation of the truth in Christ.

You have also lost sight of the compassion and faithfulness of the Redeemer; and continuing to do so, you can never have strength or comfort in any employment. You must sink in despondency, whilst you have any regard to yourself, and wait to see your abilities or faith sufficient.   Now this is your case, though by yourself unperceived: for you write thus: —" My poor abilities, and small share of faith and grace may, perhaps, through the infinite clemency of God, enable me to glorify Him in the humbler walk of a private Christian; but the weighty and important charge of the souls of others is what I dare not presume to undertake." Here, it is plain to me, you have some trust in those abilities and that faith; and were both greater, you might then, without presumption, undertake to preach and teach Christ:— on the contrary, no sort of confidence is, to be placed in any thing we have; but all, in the power, grace, and faithfulness of the Lord, to them who call on His Name.

You also, unperceived to yourself, limit the Holy One of Israel;—for you say: " I begged, that if this reluctance was from God, He would increase and confirm it; but should it be a temptation, as you seemed to judge, I entreated it might never be suffered to prevail. And surely, He would never suffer so many prayers to be in vain, and in such an important matter too, who hath so repeatedly said, ' Ask, and ye shall have '."

But hath God anywhere promised to grant any of our requests in that way and manner we may choose to prescribe ? Certainly *He will not ;* when the mode we fix on would lessen our dependence on His own blessed word, were our request granted : for His word alone is given to be our director in matters of duty.   But you do not ask the Lord, my dear son, to direct you into what is duty, *by His own word,* but by some impression made on your mind. Supposing, now, your great reluctance to the ministry, on account of your great insufficiency, were removed ; then you would be well satisfied God called you to it.   But how very fallacious is this, and very wrong ! For do not the best find very great reluctance against doing what is plainly required of them ? and are they from hence to conclude they must not act till the reluctance is taken away ?   The word of God loudly condemns this aversion to a good work (which, it tells us, the office of a Bishop is).   His word calls upon every man to be filled with love to God, and ardent zeal for His glory and the salvation of sinners.   This is equally and indispensably necessary in every private Christian, and in every minister : only, ministers are employed in a public manner to do this, which private Christians are not.

But, besides this, Providence, in a very remarkable manner, has done every thing to prove you are destined to be a preacher of Christ, by His own will ; —for did not God give me, and your dear mother (now a saint in heaven), desires, the hour you were born, to set you apart to His service, with never-ceasing prayer ?   Has He not ordered your educa-

tion for that end ; and inclined you to make choice
of it, six years since ? Has He not, in the judgment
of all, endued you with very sufficient abilities ; and
even given you grace to live soberly, righteously,
and godly, in the midst of the most daring impiety
and open lewdness ? Has He not even made you
useful, young as you are, to your serious acquaintance ? Has He not brought you into such circumstances, that you can follow no other profession,
nor engage in trade, nor surely join the navy or
army ? Has He not evidently thus directed your
circumstances, which all call upon you, as a matter
of bounden duty, to be what you have been destined
and brought up for ?

You are afraid, lest, through you, one soul should
perish. But do you think the salvation of immortal
souls is left to such a hazard ? or that a young man,
who has such a *fear* upon his mind, is ever likely,
by his principles or practice, to be a stumbling-block
of iniquity in the way of any ? Will not this fear
stimulate and keep the soul attentive to duty ? The
vicious and proud and idle are charged with the
blood of souls—not those who have any knowledge
of their worth, and love for them.

Further ; supposing (which the good Lord forbid should be the case !) you do not enter the
ministry ; have you no fear of the much greater
snares and temptations to which you must be exposed in every other way of life ? For there is no
situation so advantageous to a man, who desires to
please God, as the ministry ; because here all his
business *coincides* with his Christian calling : in any
other situation, it has a strong tendency to make

and keep him earthly. Here he is regarded as a witness for the Truth, and a maintainer of God's cause. It is expected he should rebuke vice, and speak with wisdom and piety. His very profession keeps him out of the company of ungodly men, and connects him with the saints of God, who will help him by their prayers and by their conversation.— Much cause, indeed, have you to fear, should you reject the evident design of Providence in your whole education—lest, like Jonah, you run away from the commandment of God, desponding of success, without cause; or looking upon Him as an austere man, and therefore desire to be excused serving at His altar!

When you have followed your present gloomy and most unreasonable resolution, will you be able to clear yourself from such a heavy charge as follows?—You were, in the judgment of men wiser and older than yourself, well qualified for the work —you were made deeply sensible of its vast importance, the necessary preparation to discharge it aright, and to make you cry for help, day and night —you knew Christ the Way, and might have called many to Him for their salvation—you saw sinners dying around you, for want of faithful preachers; and had even resolution enough to plunge yourself into the most perplexing circumstances, to the unspeakable distress of your whole family, sooner than do what you suppose to be wrong;—yet, after all this evidence of God's designation of you to, and fitness for, the work, you would refuse, merely because you thought you never should have grace given you sufficient to discharge the pastoral office!

How can you reconcile this with your duty? What is presumption, if such a conduct is not? With what reason can you expect the blessing of God, when acting so directly opposite to the manifestation of His will concerning you, in His own providential appointment?

"Much, for seven months," you say, "have I suffered, bewildered in my mind with suspense, and harassed with the prospect of surrounding distress; but all that I have felt, or thought, tends only to confirm me in the opinion of my own insufficiency." —Upon this I remark, that would you open your mind more to those who are certainly able to direct you, and had you written to Mr. Berridge, or Mr. Robinson, or myself, you would have used the proper means, and probably it might have pleased God to have blessed them for your relief: for, as too much reservedness is contrary to the social and affectionate spirit so pleasing to our Maker, it is no wonder it should always bring with it its own punishment; neither is it any wonder that you, raising, much higher than the Scripture does, the sanctity and the abilities necessary for a due discharge of the pastoral office, should be more and more convinced you are not sufficient. Young men are naturally prone to carry their ideas, in every thing they are engaged in, beyond the truth. But, granting you do not, in this matter—all you have thought and felt is no more than both Scripture and the history of God's most eminent and faithful ministers teach us they have known. How very backward were Moses and Gideon! How did Jeremiah see his own insufficiency, when he cried out, "I am a

child! I cannot speak!" How did he, even after
years spent in the office of a Prophet, express his
reluctance, to our great surprise : "Thou hast deceived me; and I was deceived;" *i.e.* I had never
been a Prophet, hadst Thou not hid from me what
I was to go through, in being one. I scarcely
know one who has been remarkably successful in
winning souls, and in a holy life, but he has felt
what St. Paul did—weakness, and fear, and much
trembling, in view of the difficulties and dangers.
But be not afraid! you are not to go the warfare at
your own charges. The Great Head of the Church
is to be your Counsellor. He is to hold you, as a
star, in His right hand. Though not sufficient of
yourself to think a good thought of yourself, your
sufficiency is to be of God.

But this qualification for the ministry, more necessary almost than any other—I mean, a deep sense
of your own insufficiency—necessary to make you
speak with consciousness of your poverty, ignorance, &c.—necessary to teach you how to speak a
word to the weary and tempted soul—necessary to
make you take pains, and give yourself wholly to
these things, that your profiting may appear—this
very blessed qualification you turn against yourself,
contrary to the Divine intention in it. Faith in
Christ is always, at first, a venture, in opposition to
doubts and fears :—but who ever ventured, and was
disappointed? When the Lord is more fully revealed to your soul, you will see and find in Him
more than all you can need, for acceptance, strength,
comfort, and usefulness. And what delight will
you then experience, in holding Him forth, to poor

guilty sinners, as all *their* salvation and yours—all their desire and yours.

You write: "I am persuaded you would suffer more from seeing me discharge improperly that sacred office, than, from a due sense of my own unfitness, decline it." Here again, your gloomy thoughts represent the matter to your mind in the falsest colours. Do you apprehend I should (if life be spared so long) make no allowance for youth? Do you imagine I should expect more from you than I see in all serious young men who have a single eye to the glory of God? or that young men are to be compared with pastors well improved by years in the service of Christ?—I am apprehensive you may compare yourself with such; and, concluding you are very short of them indeed, therefore decline the office; or, because you may suppose so much is expected from you, pride, without your discovering it, may work much against your soul, and create much reluctance in you to come forth. What must I think, when your intimates, Wilson, Garwood, Jowett, &c., have so good a testimony of their attention to the ministry, and do so well, that you, no less serious and exemplary than they, should turn your back upon the blessed employment? Had I, or your dear mother now in glory, any other motive to have you a minister than the very best? Indebted, beyond expression, to His grace and love, we longed to have them published abroad; and for that only purpose, and the salvation of your own soul, did we wish it might please God to give you abilities and disposition of heart, such as He has evidently bestowed.

I have written thus, to shew you how much I ponder upon your present condition, so distressful! I have nothing more to add, but a few requests, which I do most earnestly beg you would grant me. The first is, to think of nothing so much, next to your walk before God, as the matters which you are to be busied about, till you take your degree. 2dly, That you would not *reason* with yourself;—only pray that you may not do any thing rashly. 3dly, That, as a very young and inexperienced man, you would remember it is a plain duty to pay a due regard to the Elders of the Church; and to persuade yourself you can never be so proper a judge in your own case as very excellent and godly, and wise and aged men in the ministry can be for you. Lastly, Remember, though you are at present distressed and full of unbelieving fears, when the Lord comes to you, as I have no doubt He will, then darkness will become light before you, and crooked things straight, and rough places plain.

To His tender mercies and guidance I fervently commend you, and remain your affectionate father,

H. VENN.

The tone of this letter may seem to want, in some degree, the usual tenderness which characterizes Mr. Venn's parental letters. The fact was, that he regarded his son's state of mind as too much influenced by a morbid sensibility; which it was necessary to conteract, by the exercise of parental firmness and authority.

The considerations urged in this letter, and in many

subsequent conversations, tended gradually to remove the fears and scruples of his son; so that at length he was enabled to devote himself to the service of the sanctuary, with a cheerful confidence in the gracious acceptance of his labours by the Great Head of the Church. I need not remind my readers how abundantly those labours were afterwards owned and blessed, in the very important sphere in which he was placed.

In the letters written about this time, I find the first mention of the much-honoured name of Charles Simeon. His entrance into holy orders preceded, by a few months, that of Mr. John Venn.

TO THE REV. JAMES STILLINGFLEET.

MY VERY DEAR FRIEND, *Yelling, Oct. 9, 1782.*

Your goodness, in inquiring so affectionately about us all, has spirited me up immediately to take my pen. Often have I remembered you; and been thankful for your mercies, in dear Mrs. Stillingfleet's health, and in your own and son's health. He is a great trust committed to you both; but with joy I can believe his parents will not be blinded with fondness, and cruel enough to cherish in him the plague of a fallen spirit—self-will. I have no doubt he will be educated under a mild, steady authority. Happy lot for the child! Happy for the parents! Much have I seen to lament, in many who make a profession! Their children are lawless, or miserable under an iron rod. My poor pains and constant attention to this matter, how graciously hath the Lord rewarded! My children are now my companions and friends, obedient, affectionate, and, amongst earthly things, my chiefest treasures;—if *they* are to be accounted amongst earthly things, who are immortal spirits, and joined in fellowship with the Church, and with whom I hope to spend an eternity in the presence of Immanuel. Till that period, we must be companions in patience and in sorrows; one or other of us frequently sick, or in pain, or taking leave, and parting from each other.

On the 22d of last month, my son was ordained; and the Sunday before last preached his first sermon to my people, on the feast-day. His text was, " Who is able to save unto the uttermost, &c." It was extraordinary, for a young man's first attempt —(I will not call it Essay); for it was very Scriptural, and full of Christ. He stayed one week : and now, by the advice of our Hippocrates (Dr. Rait), is gone to visit his relations and friends in town. And if he does not recover his health, he is to try Yorkshire air; and the very idea of being with you makes him smile.

He has had much to try him. Nothing could have been a greater disappointment to him than not being chosen Fellow of his College; after the Master made an apology for not choosing him last year, even before a senior; and after two of the Fellows told me he was a sure man. Yet, from circumstances with which my son was only indirectly connected, his prospect of success was reversed ; and whether he will now ever be chosen, is very doubtful. By this trial, he is taught to know more of the heart of those who are in trouble; and to speak to them, not by hearsay, and awkwardly, as I did for some years.

My small parish is very much altered for the worse, within these few years. Three farmers, in whose families there were some hopeful hearers, are removed; and a fourth is upon the point of removing. They have been succeeded by men of a very profane spirit: scarcely will they ever come to church. To this add the departure of a few, in the faith of Christ, I trust. I preach therefore, now, to a handful of people indeed! However, I have cause to bless and adore God, that I can and do cry unto Him, to awake, and glorify His word; and wait in hope He will, before it is long, come down and work mightily, for His own Name's sake. Much I am encouraged to do so, by an account I have lately had from good hands, of the wonderful success Mr. Maddock has had in his ministry at Creaton, a village in Northamptonshire. Hundreds, I am told, in his neighbourhood, now love the Lord Jesus in sincerity. Whilst I continue, therefore, to plead His own promise, and feel compassion and bowels of mercies for my poor people ready to perish, I have hope.

Miss Hervey pleased me much with the account of your congregation. Glory be to God! If you find the building or repairing a house a sad damp upon your soul, it ought to teach us how to pity the multitude who labour or trade for their bread. I am sadly defective in that blessed temper!

On Trinity Sunday was ordained Mr. Simeon, Fellow of King's College. Before that day, he never was in company with an earnest Christian.

Soon after, he was visited by Mr. H. Jowett, and my son, and two or three more. In less than seventeen Sundays, by preaching for Mr. Atkinson, in a church at Cambridge, he filled it with hearers—a thing unknown there for near a century. He has been over to see me six times within the last three months : he is calculated for great usefulness, and is full of faith and love. My soul is always the better for his visits. Oh, to flame, as he does, with zeal, and yet be beautified with meekness! The day he was a substitute for Mr. Atkinson, he began to visit the parishioners from house to house. Full of philanthropy was his address :—" I am come to inquire after your welfare. Are you happy?" His evident regard for their good disarmed them of their bitterness; and it is amazing what success he has met with! Let us hear soon from you, and some good news of souls converted from darkness to light, in dear Yorkshire. A letter from Hotham is a joyful sound to all my family. When you see your brother, pray remember me to him. Love to Mrs. Stillingfleet, yourself, and son, from all here.

Yours &c.

H. VENN.

TO THE REV. JAMES STILLINGFLEET.

MY DEAR FRIEND,   *24th Dec.* 1782.

    I mourn at the relation you send me of your own village : yet be not discouraged. Many years since, I was much struck with that passage of St. Paul, " If, by any means, I may *save some.*" ' *Some,*' said

I to myself; 'why not all? why not many?' Long experience now has taught me, that a *few* only do, in fact, believe to the saving of their souls; even where the Gospel is faithfully delivered by a man of God, whose life and example add weight to all he teaches. How lamentable this view of the Church visible! Still, to be in any measure a mourner, and an earnest supplicant for those who are destroying themselves—to be grieved for the injurious treatment our God and Saviour every day receives from His reasonable creatures, who are baptized into His Church—affords a solid satisfaction. In this temper, we are conformable to the Prophets, Apostles, and the Son of God. The world rejoiced, and were gay and thoughtless, in all their provocations and dangers; but these retired, and wept in secret for their pride and their delusion. I am apt to think, that till we are deeply affected for the multitude who are profane, or evidently dissemble with God, we shall never be able to look with desire for our dismission. When Elijah wished to die, it was from a survey of the wide-spreading idolatry in the children of Judah.

Six weeks ago, an unexpected opening at St. Neot's tempted me to undertake, with the help of my son, the supply of that church; from whence the curate had been suddenly called away. The offer, on my part, of doing it gratis, was, to my surprise, readily accepted; but so long has the church been deserted, and all worship of God given up, that even curiosity will not bring them to hear; and, in a morning, not one hundred, out of sixteen hundred, are to be seen at church! In less than

an age, things proceeding in the present train, our
churches will be like those now at Jamaica. A lady,
who was for some time there, assured a friend of
mine, that they were not used in the country. The
doors were opened, and the bells rung ; but neither
the people nor priest attended. So doth atheism
advance, with horrid strides !

My son's health is still far from established.
You are very kind and partial to him. I learn
from him, with grief, that there is a spirit of debate got up amongst the ministers in the West
Riding, about the Arminian and Calvinistic doctrines.
The enemy certainly doth thus gain much advantage ; and no good can debate ever produce. Living
and working for God, and to save souls, is the only
way of knowing more and more of His truth and
His salvation.

W—— came last month to College, and immediately began disputing. My son told him how greatly
he had longed to see him, that he might receive a
blessing from his company ; " But you," said he,
"entirely disappoint me : and I will ask you only one
question : Do you love the Lord Jesus Christ more,
and pray more, and feel more life and comfort in
your own soul, since you have begun to dispute
about these points ?" To this he made no reply.

Last Wednesday, Mr. Berridge preached to my
people. How gladly could I have wished for you!
Mr. Waltham came over from Royston, where he
is doing very well. Mr. Berridge preached from
Ps. lxii. 1—3. Just such a Calvinist as he is, I wish
all ministers of Christ to be. I think his voice grows
weaker. He is sixty-eight in February—a great age

for one who has laboured so much! Dr. Conyers, Mr. Madan, Mr. Newton, and myself, are all fifty-eight in March. How soon shall we be dismissed from our work! Oh! to be found even the least and last amongst the pastors after His own heart! The Lord grant us to meet each other in that number!

From your ever affectionate friend,

H. VENN.

TO MR. EDWARD VENN.

MY DEAR NEPHEW,   *Yelling, Jan.* 7, 1783.

I heartily return thanks to the Giver of all our earthly and our heavenly comforts, for the preservation of your beloved Charlotte, who has, in all appearance, been so near her departure. You will now receive her as given back to you and your children, doubly endeared by her apprehended loss. Now you have had a fresh instance brought home, of the absolute uncertainty in which we stand respecting our condition, when it is pleasing and prosperous—how suddenly the stormy wind ariseth, which may sweep away all in this world which is dearest to us.

Accept our salutations; for we all join in them to you and our niece. May this year prove a happy year! May you grow, both of you, very rich indeed—much more so than in any preceding year—rich in durable riches and righteousness, in communion with God, in the high pleasures of a spiritual mind, in the abounding hope that all things are yours, whether life or death, things present or things to come!

The new year has begun in a manner very

afflicting to me. Mr. and Mrs. —— so suddenly involved in distresses. My dear friend Mrs. Kershaw at the point of death. Oh, what troubles and adversities, my dear nephew, are the lot of man! How much need is there that we prepare for what may so soon be our burden!

You will be pleased to hear your cousin, my son, has gained the favour of all the inhabitants of St. Neot's. His father is not to be named with him! I thought my voice, old as I am, was not worse than his; but they give that also to him.

——Pray let us hear how Charlotte recovers; and the little tender branch, how it thrives. I wished for your presence with us on New-Year's day. Princes have no such fare to feast on! Mr. Robinson, from Leicester, was in the pulpit in the evening; and in a manner masterly, solemn, and affectionate to the last degree, he exhorted young men and maidens, old men and children, believers and unbelievers, to awake out of sleep, for it was high time! Many attended, and great was the seriousness of one and all. Mr. Simeon and Mr. Farish, from Cambridge, were here; and we all set out for Everton the next morning. The venerable father, Mr. Berridge, received us, though unlooked for, with open arms; and his prayer, and Mr. Robinson's, were again most edifying and animating. We parted in fervent love, looking upward and forward, till we shall meet to dwell together in love for ever. Such is our present honour, to be with the excellent of the earth, educating together for glory in the highest heavens. Accept from us all our best wishes for the new year. May peace national, peace domestic, peace internal, and peace everlasting, be with you, and all our fellow citizens!

Pray remember us to our sister and niece at Ipswich.   From your affectionate uncle,

H. VENN.

———

The Churchwardens of St. Neot's sent a petition to the Vicar, who was non-resident, signed by all the principal inhabitants of the place, to request that Mr. John Venn might be appointed their Curate. At the conclusion of their services at St. Neot's, Mr. Venn thus speaks:—

—— Next Sunday is the last of ten that my son and myself have served St. Neot's. It is surprising how their strong prejudices are removed, and how much civility we receive! They, in general, wish to have the Gospel preached. But we long to hear of more than approbation—of conviction of sin, and their receiving Christ with gladness and singleness of heart.——

———

At the close of January 1783, Mr. John Venn was presented to the living of Little Dunham, near Swaffham, Norfolk, by the late Edward Parry, Esq., a Director of the East-India Company, who was then residing at the Lodge, in that parish. In announcing this event, in letters to different friends, Mr. Venn writes thus:

—— The patron, who lives in the parish, and his wife, are both young, and extremely in earnest to please God, and to have the Name of Jesus magnified. He is one of the most agreeable men I ever saw. My acquaintance with him has been for little more than two years, and but slight.

—— The clear value of the living is 135*l.*: it has come entirely unexpected and unsought, as the appointment of our Great Lord and Master, who sendeth his servants whithersoever He pleaseth. The place is fifty-three miles from me. So soon comes our separation! I shall suffer much from the absence of such a son ; but my consolation is, to look forward to the time when we shall meet to part no more—when all the faithful pastors of Christ shall, at the head of their respective flocks, receive the crown of glory which fadeth not away. Till then, we must both be about our Master's work, in different parts of the vineyard ;—I, in my old age and decline ;—he, if it please God to give him health, strong to labour, and to do more and more for the good of souls.

—— A more pleasing son no man could wish. On all sides, I am congratulated on his account ; and not without reason. I only wish my disposition, and temper, and self-abasement, and conscientious regard to duty, were equal to his. I could have wished you had been with us, in family prayer, the morning after he received the letter containing the offer of the living. It was very affecting to hear with what self-abasement and earnestness he besought the Lord to bestow upon him abilities and grace for the work of the ministry.

—— We shall not cease to pray that Mr. Parry's hopes may be fully answered—that the poor may have the Gospel preached to them—and that his own soul, and his dear wife's, may be fed in the House of God.——

Yelling, Feb. 28, 1783.

—— SEVERAL days I lately spent at Cambridge with four young clergymen—Mr. Atkinson, Fellow and Tutor of Trinity Hall, *full brother* to Miles of Leeds, Mr. Simeon, Dr. Jowett, and Mr. Farish: all our discourse was to the purpose. I prayed with them twice a day. Their affection for me was expressed in the most obliging manner. They have, since I left them, been over with me. The Lord has touched their hearts to love the Truth;— for this is the footing on which our acquaintance is built. He who knoweth all hearts, knoweth I long to be doing something for Him!

—— Mr. Simeon's ministry is likely to be blessed. We may indeed say, " A great door is opened!" Many gownsmen hear him. What follows, is as true—"there are many adversaries." He comes over, to advise with me on every occasion; but the wonderful Counsellor is with him.

TO THE REV. JAMES STILLINGFLEET.

MY VERY DEAR BROTHER, *Yelling, April* 26, 1783.

This morning I received your letter, in which you express a consciousness of *my accusing* you for your silence. I know you too well, and I love you too much, to admit even a thought to your disadvantage. But I should be without excuse, if I did not instantly write to you, as I would talk with you had I the pleasure of being in your presence.

I perceive you are too much affected with the base return of some of your people. A base return, indeed, for all your pastoral care, and truly Christian kindness! Had your spirit been less lowered, you certainly would have paid no regard to what, perhaps, a *single* ungrateful person, hating the Truth and your faithfulness, rashly uttered; and this was then multiplied into the saying of many. Be not discouraged. Our dear Lord felt, and foresaw, what you have met with, when He said, *" Do good, and lend, hoping for nothing again."*—What! no gratitude, no cordial thanks, no esteem and praise!— *No! nothing!*—And why should we be so much cut to the heart, to find our kindness and benefits received with as little regard as we ourselves have received all the mercies, the temporal mercies, of our God?—There is much use in these things. Were the gratitude of those we help (perhaps feed and clothe) to be such as we naturally expect, we should be pleased, and tempted to think well of our bounty, and be led to do good from impure motives. As it is ordered, we can have no motive, but love, to persevere in doing good to those, who even take the lead in abusing and slandering us;—none, but bowels of mercies, which all the elect of God put on.

Thanks be to God, that you are now recovering, and able again to minister! I congratulate you, also, and dear Mrs. Stillingfleet, on the recovery of your dear son. Had he been taken away, though from the evil to come, you would both have been greatly distressed. But our God spareth us, and in all respects treateth us with tenderness, when the sharpest sufferings are not needful.—I heard not one syllable of your distress, till last Sunday sevennight. May power and might be given you from above! Study the usage which all the Prophets and Apostles received, for speaking in the Name of the Lord. Are *we* to be exempted? Are we wiser, and better, than they? Do we hope to live with them for ever, and yet to escape the persecution which, in so large a measure, was their cross and trial?

The last week I returned to my family; having left them for near seven weeks; which I spent in London, with more than usual comfort, on several accounts. I had a more lively sense of the presence and loving-kindness of my Lord, and more of the spirit of prayer. I had much pleasure in seeing the prosperity of the souls of several dear and aged friends. Like fruits quite ripe, and beautiful to look on, they appear ready to be gathered;—some under sanctified affliction of a meek and humble spirit, blessing and praising God;—others still more distinguished by grace, able to manage wealth, and making to themselves everlasting friends of the mammon of unrighteousness. With the evangelists and pastors I was also much pleased;—with the wisdom and knowledge, and truly amiable temper, of the Rector of St. Mary Woolnoth—with the simplicity and watchfulness, and unblameable life and labours, of Mr. Foster—with the admirable talents and eloquent evangelical preaching of Dr. Peckwell—with the apostolical spirit, and abilities, and great grace of Mr. Cecil—with my old friend and fellow-labourer, and a wonder of a man, who seems now drawing toward the end of his highly-honoured labours, Mr. Romaine—with the ingenious and very useful Mr. De Coetlogon, and Mr. Herbert Jones.

It gave me great satisfaction to think, that when we, who are aged (I mean not to apply this epithet to yourself), Messrs. Romaine, Berridge, Newton, and myself, are called home, there are raised up so many messengers and preachers of the same glorious Gospel of the Blessed God. The Rector of Dunham, I trust, will more than supply his poor father's place in the Church. He has begun to teach and preach the Adorable Saviour to them. They are a people sitting in darkness; no less without God, without Christ, without hope in the world, than the inhabitants of Japan! His first sermon was on that blessed word, " He is able to save unto the uttermost all who come unto God by Him." One of his people, with whom he conversed afterwards, assured him they were good Christians, and not incarnate devils, as he seemed to think.— Help him with your prayers! 'He needs them much.

—— I am now returned to my own station. My prayer, day and night, is for success; yet I find but little. My church is fuller than it was some time since; but I have still to lament that the Holy Ghost is not sent down from heaven. Last Sunday, the number of hearers was large, and they were attentive; but they were not pricked to the heart;— however, our business is to work, and to wait. We shall know hereafter, though now we know not, why there is given from above a vehement desire to do good to souls, and glorify the Name of Jesus, yet the preachers who feel it do no more good. I know not how I should bear up, if I did not find this same trial appointed to all who labour in the word and doctrine.

Let me hear from you soon; but never think I can entertain one surmise that you want affection for me, whether you write or are silent.

From your affectionate brother in Christ,
                                   H. VENN.

TO THE REV. JOHN VENN
(AT LITTLE DUNHAM).

MY DEAR SON,   *Yelling, April* 29, 1783.

Yesterday, our eager expectation of a letter was gratified. And we are thankful to the Father of all our mercies, that you got safe to Dunham; as I did, also, to my family, on Wednesday; after experiencing, most undeservedly, the friendship and love of many excellent people,.for the sake and name of Jesus, whom we serve.

I am not pleased that you begin with two sermons. Stay till you are quite strong.

You are now to consider yourself as a Missionary, sent to teach and preach Jesus Christ. Savages are not more ignorant of His glory and His love, or their need of His arm to save their souls, than nominal Christians. Look upon your people as prisoners under condemnation; for whose pardon and recovery you ought to feel, as a tender mother does for the child at her breast. Lament an unfeeling heart in *yourself*, as well as in them. Beg earnestly that you may long after their salvation in the bowels of the Lord Jesus Christ. Be sure, speak not against the clergy around you : on the contrary, be an intercessor for them too, before the Throne of Grace.

I would have you preach upon the Commandments. God always blesses that preaching. But when you have explained how much more the commandment requires than men suppose, then shew how reasonable, how necessary it is, that such a commandment should be given; and that the design of it is, not to destroy men, but to constrain them to come to Christ for life. You might take for your text, either that in Romans iii. : " Now, what the Law saith, it saith to them, &c.;"— or that in Gal. iii. : " Now the Scripture has concluded (shut up, as in a prison) all under sin, that the promise, which is by faith of Jesus Christ, might be given to all them that believe."

Be not discouraged, if you see the people little affected for a time. I was here nine months before one person of this village came, of his own accord, to speak to me about his spiritual concerns. Christ's ministers must bear the contradiction of sinners against themselves, and wait with all long-suffering, as He did : and with respect to the most, they may say, at last, " I have stretched forth my hands, all the day long, to a disobedient and gainsaying people."

Endeavour to speak within the compass of your voice; or you will strain it, and lay yourself aside. Remember me! How have I suffered! I should never have been but in a sphere larger beyond comparison than this, but for that violent over-doing, which was not necessary.

We all should wish (if wishing were not the "hectic of a fool"), to have you with us, or near us. But He ordereth all things well, who is King for ever and ever. To Him I heartily commend you, body and soul! From your affectionate father,

H. VENN.

The present will be an appropriate occasion for intro-ducing Mr. Venn's judgment on the question of written or extempore sermons. It was given in a letter to a young clergyman, who consulted him upon the point.

——You desire my judgment on the important subject of preaching written or extempore sermons. I believe most men, who have thought on the subject, are agreed, that young men should write for some years—perhaps five, or seven; and afterwards, when they speak, they certainly should have a plan, and the great outlines of their sermon, before them. They should speak, not extempore, but after preme-ditation, study, and self-abasing prayer. When these rules are constantly observed, no written sermons will, in general, be more connected, more full of matter; nor can they ever be delivered with so great advantage: for, after such due preparation, a pastor comes up into the pulpit, weak and ignorant in his

own eyes, yet full of affiance in his Great Master;
so, that he will be jealous of his glory, and pity
the people.   He will have *His* presence; and find
his understanding enlightened, even while he speaks;
and feel His word has authority and power over
the congregation.   When he has done, he will feel
ashamed of himself; and be filled with wonder that
the Lord God should make use of him.   In this
manner, joined to constant reading the word of God,
and constant cries to be formed and fashioned as a
vessel of honour to bear witness of Christ, an able
minister of the New Testament is formed.   Those
ministers, whether young or old, who dare to be
idle, to venture into the pulpit without looking up
and sighing—without feeling their total inequality to
the subjects they are to prove, explain, or enforce—
are in a terrible state; and some severe correction
will be sent, to bring them to themselves; or they
will proceed from bad to worse.   It is too true,
I fear, that many times we all offend, in neglecting
to prepare : but when a strict watch is kept on this
head, and we beg of our Lord, that, with all reverence and godly fear, with all carefulness and understanding, we may fulfil the ministry we have
received, we shall, in the tenour of our ministry, be
found faithful, and blessed in our work.—Mr. De
Coetlogon is a charming proof that you may speak
with clearness, strong reason, fulness, and pathos,
by taking pains.   Dr. Peckwell I have heard no
less excellent; and Mr. Whitfield, with others of
my own particular intimates.   I have known them,
sometimes—that is, by due preparation—do justice
to their subject—instruct, convince, exhort, persuade,

to the feasting of the soul. At others, through sloth, love of company, self-confidence, and little love to souls, I have heard them lean, incoherent, defective, and sadly ludicrous. I have been myself greatly guilty, through the causes above named ; and suffered and smarted for it, long after ! But when I had prepared myself, and sought the Lord fully, I do not know that I have been left to wander or to utter small talk, and any thing that came uppermost, above five or six times. Upon the whole, I much prefer speaking to writing ; but upon this condition, that the speaker read much, write much, think and pray much. As for those speakers who know not their subject till the Bible is opened in the pulpit, their preaching must be deplorable.

———

It will be interesting, as well as instructive, to add to this statement an account of the way in which Mr. Venn himself commenced the practice of extempore preaching ; especially as it has been stated, in print, that he was the first London minister who revived the practice ; preceding Mr. Romaine in this respect.

From his first entrance into the ministry, he devoted much time and thought to the composition of his sermons, and frequently transcribed them afresh. He wrote out his first sermon ten times before he delivered it in public. In the year 1754, after having been nearly seven years in the ministry, and twenty-nine years of age, he first attempted extempore preaching. He made the trial at the Wednesday Morning Lecture at St. Antholin's, taking up into the pulpit with him a sermon which he had before delivered : upon which I find, after the notice of its delivery at two other places, the following remark :—

" Preached at St. Antholin's, March 20, 1754.—This morning is much to be remembered by me ; for, after many doubts in my mind, whether I should endeavour to preach only by premeditation—and recommending the matter to my God in prayer, beseeching Him, if it were most for the edification of hearers and the furtherance of His Gospel, to assist me mightily, and to put strength and confidence into my feeble timorous spirit — I have found an assistance, which I have reason never to forget."

Far however from bestowing, after this time, less pains upon the work of preaching, he continued, for above four years, to write out, with equal care, the whole of the sermons which were to be delivered before his more important congregations ; so that he composed, after he had commenced extempore preaching, above twice the number of sermons he had made before.

It was also his custom to write at the head of all his sermons, even of the slightest sketches of his extempore discourses, the Greek words—

Δόξα τῷ Θεῷ· μοὶ ἁμαρτωλῷ ἔλεος.
Glory to God ! Mercy to me a sinner !

How strikingly did this practice indicate the spirit and frame of mind in which he composed and delivered his sermons !

TO MR. THOMAS ATKINSON.

MY DEAR FRIEND, *Yelling, June* 16, 1783.

We all rejoiced at the receipt of your letter of the 23d of May, for your safe arrival at your home, after seeing your daughter well.—I remark, in your letter, with much sympathy, what you say of your visit to Yelling. No family, I believe, enjoys the company of yourself and Mrs. Atkinson more than we do. It was mortifying enough, therefore, that we had no more than a glimpse of you: however, we must have no will of our own in any thing. Yet it was not selfishness which made me wish for more of your company : it was, to have more discourse with you about the most interesting matters.

If I mistake not, you are apt to be *cast down*, in the view of our extreme depravity ; whereas, you should not, in the least degree, be less confident of your eternal salvation for such humbling views. Flesh and blood never produce them ; nor our enemy the wicked-one. Conviction of our evil nature is from on high, and cometh down from above. It is peculiar to the saints in Christ Jesus ; and works in them humility, and love, and adoration, and a most thankful acceptance of Christ. Before the veil is taken from our hearts, it is only from report we prize Him, and for what we hope one day to get from Him. But when we feel the corruption of our nature—envy and pride, and impurity and unbelief, and hardness of heart, and brutish stupidity in secret prayer and in public, then we can sigh and groan,

B B

being burdened; and then we know that we are as
vile and wicked, to the full, as the word of God
declares us to be. Many and great are the spiritual
advantages attending this very humiliating sight of
our condition : it stops our mouths from railing and
evil speaking: it inclines us to take the lowest place:
it makes us poor, and of a contrite spirit; and to
tremble at God's word, if He were to enter into
judgment with us. Now, this is the very disposition
and temper He declares to be well-pleasing in His
sight. It is well for us He doth so : for if I may
judge of others by myself, after thirty-six years'
attention and care, and earnest seeking after God, I
have more reason than ever to say, "In me, that
is, in my flesh, there dwelleth no good thing." I
sometimes pour out my complaint in the Hymn,
which I now transcribe ;—because you will not find
it in any of the Hymn-books ;—and I think it will
admirably suit you, when you are bemoaning your
corruptions before God.

> Thy miracles of love, no joy to me impart ;
> In me no tender passions move, O my unfeeling heart !
>
> When, Lord, to Thee I turn, nail'd to th' accursed tree,
> With no transporting love I burn, although Thou diedst for me !
>
> When I my sins recall, to pass before my eye,
> Scarce one bewailing tear will fall; I scarce can heave one sigh!
>
> Thy promises I lay close to my pained breast;
> Fain would I hope :—hope flees away; and still I find no rest !
>
> Thus dark must I walk on, in fear and misery ;
> And never shall my bosom glow with fervent love to Thee ?
>
> Unclose, unclose these eyes ! pour in the longed-for day !
> Before me bid Thy glory rise ! my darkness chase away !

Last week, my son came over, to stay only one day and a half. It is good to bear the yoke in one's youth; and he has many more trials than if he had been Fellow of a College and a Curate. But our place and station in the world are not left to our choice. God forbid! His infinite wisdom appoints them; and to all who call upon His name, it shall work for the best. Mr. and Mrs. Riland, and my daughter and my son, all left us the same day; and my heart rather sunk at parting from my son, so far as we are separated, and so seldom as we are to meet. How merciful the command!—and how precious the grace which enables us to conform to it!— " Seek those things which are above"! On them set your affections. They are always present with us; and never disappoint our utmost expectations.

Within these nine days, I have had two long and very warm letters, full of heavy charges against me. To the first I returned an answer without the least resentment; only telling my correspondent we could be no more acquainted. To the last I shall return none; for nothing hurts the mind more than debate and controversy. The writer challenges Mr. Newton and myself to join forces, and answer his book: however, I shall not cease to pray for him, nor to wish we may meet at last in the kingdom of our Saviour above.

We have had a most gracious rain, just before the plants were beginning to wither. Oh that the pouring out of the Spirit might be vouchsafed, to make the inhabitants of our land know their Maker, and engage in His service; lest it should be said, " Yea, I have cursed their blessings"!

I had like to have forgotten a circumstance of much comfort to us here—the happy and joyful departure of as poor a creature, to the eye of flesh, as can be conceived; but she was all-glorious within. I preached her funeral sermon, in a large company, last Sunday.   Oh, may we be comforted in the trying hour!

From your indebted friend,

H. VENN.

TO THE REV. JOHN VENN.

MY DEAR SON,   *Yelling, Sept.* 2, 1783.

You have no cause to be discouraged, that you yet see no fruit.   How little, in comparison, have the ablest, brightest ministers ever seen—in comparison, I say, of what they might expect!   Hear what the Good Shepherd, and the only infallible Preacher, saith: " All the day long have I stretched forth my hands to a gainsaying and disobedient people." When He opened the eyes of the blind in vast numbers, a very small part, even of them, *beheld His glory !*   When He cleansed at once ten lepers, *one only* gave God thanks!   When He made the lame, by thousands, to walk, scarcely any of them would follow Him!   Shall, then, the servant wonder his word is treated as was his Lord's? "Yet," saith He, " though Israel be not gathered, I shall be glorious." So each of His pastors may say; 'Though, after many prayers and tears, and much crying unto God, and setting plainly before the people the *Way* of life in Christ Crucified, I find scarcely any one that will receive my testimony—whilst I, in my own *example*, do honour the Gospel—shall I conclude I am not sent of the

Lord? shall I be disquieted and miserable?' By
no means! The purposes of God will be surely answered: and not the minister who has most success
in his preaching shall stand highest in the day of the
Lord; but the minister whose eye has been single;
whose prayers have been fervent; whose bowels of
mercies have been yearning over the ignorant, and
those who are out of the way; and who has most
readily sacrificed his own will and temporal interest.
Such are conformable to Christ; and upon such He
will put the greatest honour.

Further, we are not proper judges of the good
that is done by us. Very often we are not to know
it: it would puff us up. Even here, at Yelling,
where many think there is little good done, I hear
from one and another of glad tidings. This last
week I have visited Mr. Heading, of Little Paxton,
who is dying in the peace of God, and inquires most
affectionately after you;—Mrs. Brichard, of whose
life also there is no hope; and Mrs. Ivitt, who is at
the point to die;—each of them looking unto Jesus.
You have been only six months in October—and
what are six months? Only read, and pray, and
watch; and take no denial. If you see no success,
you are not to be cast down; but, with more vehemence plead, and claim the promises made to those
who speak His word faithfully. Think how Mr.
Joseph Allen, of Taunton, waited from year to year
for those who set at nought the word; yet, at length,
he was the instrument, in the hand of Christ, of
bringing them to heaven.

I cannot but approve your taking pupils; but this
must not be lightly determined upon. You must

have well considered and digested your plans, that you may do full justice to them in their education. I think it will be no hindrance to the discharge of your ministry. But ask counsel, in all this matter, of the Lord; beseeching Him to direct you, and to set aside every intention of your own, if it will not be right in His eyes.—All send their love.

From your affectionate father,

H. VENN.

———

At the close of this year (1783), Mr. and Mrs. Venn visited several friends in Warwickshire and Shropshire. The next letter was written at the end of the first day's journey, to his two daughters, who were left at home.

———

TO MISSES JANE AND CATHERINE VENN.

MY DEAR JANE AND KITTY,   *Thrapston, Oct.* 21, 1783.

Blest be the dear uniting love
Which will not let us part!
In body we may far remove,
But we are one in heart;—

one in faith, in life, in hope, in pursuit, in the chief object of our happiness, and shall be (I make no doubt) one for ever and ever.—I feel too much in parting from you. I should sit more loose to all creature comforts than I do: and so should my dear daughters. You should love your parents, and dearest friends, with a limited affection, and let your whole soul flow out in love to the adorable Immanuel. See Him on His throne, ordering all things well, in love, for all who call on His name, and put their trust in His mercy;—as I am very sure you both do.

It is with unspeakable satisfaction that I think

you are both, my dear children, able to be alone, without *ennui*—that you are able to be alone, without feeling any want of any creature, It is a noble independency of spirit, which even the princes and monarchs of the world want.

Nothing will satisfy me, but your living with me, with all the spirits of the just made perfect! Be assured, that you ought to resist all those fears which cast you down. God is love to all His praying people, who allow themselves in no evil way. He is love to you—and only love—and love for evermore. Have you any doubt that I should give you heaven, and eternal glory, if I had it in my gift? " Oh no!" you both immediately reply.— If I then, being evil, know how to give good things unto my children, how much more shall God, your Heavenly Father (repeat the sweet name!) give unto you that eternal inheritance! Watch therefore, and pray against hard thoughts of God; as if He were austere, and waiting for our frailties, to punish them; whereas He is a God delighting to pardon. He hath loved you with an everlasting love; and therefore with loving-kindness hath He withdrawn your hearts from all the idols which young persons worship, till they are divinely changed.

To descend now from things of highest import and excellence to ourselves :—God has given us a safe journey hither—your dear mamma not at all fatigued. We are just setting off to see our friends. I shall be more glad when we are here, on our way back, to see you both.

From your most affectionate father,

H. VENN.

From letters written during this journey, I extract the following notices of several friends whom he saw on this excursion.

My soul has been much refreshed and quickened by the company and example of several excellent Christians, who indeed walk before God to all well-pleasing.

Mr. Riland, in labours of love, in visiting the sick, in giving largely to the needy, in love to the Saviour, and in humility, has no superior. I suppose he walks five or six miles every day, in visiting his people. He has just begun catechizing the young people, on Tuesday evenings: the young men one week, and the young women another. This is the luxury of life! I looked upon him with the most pleasing and full assurance of seeing him among the most faithful, in whom God shall be glorified, when I shall be many ranks below him in our common Father's kingdom. He, and Mr. Burnett of Elland, have a steadiness in them, surprising. They are men who "abhor that which is evil," and "cleave to that which is good."

Mr. Fletcher, a genius, and a man of fire—all on the stretch to do good—to lose not a day, not an hour. He is married to a lady worthy of him—Miss Bosanquet—a lady with whom I was acquainted twenty-nine years ago. She was then sixteen, and bred up in all the pride of life; her father being one of the chief merchants in London. By the grace of

God, she at that time renounced the world, from her heart, and gave up herself to the Lord. Since then she has bred up seventy-four destitute young girls for service, and seen them placed out to her satisfaction; and, instead of dressing, visiting, and conforming to all the vain and expensive customs of the world, she has been wholly employed in doing good. I left this happy house—as Cecil, Secretary to Queen Elizabeth, left Bernard Gilpin's —saying, " There dwells as much happiness as can be known on earth."——

From thence I went to Mr. Jonathan Scott's. He was once an officer in the army, amongst the gayest of the gay : now he is a bright example of every Christian grace, and spends all his strength in preaching to crowded congregations.——

I visited also Mr. Robinson, at Leicester. For learning, wisdom, grace, and humility, he resembles Daniel. Though without wealth, he has done more for the town of Leicester than the rich : he has raised a charity-school for boys, where there was none before, and instructs them occasionally himself : preaches twice a week at the Infirmary, and three times in his own church. When you are with him, his whole air, and manner of conversation, affect, and please, and profit. Such honour does the Lord put upon his saints ! It is a great privilege to be with them.—All my deiight is in thy saints, O Lord, and in such as excel in virtue ! How shall I triumph, to be found in the same world with them.——

TO LADY SMYTHE.

MADAM,   *Yelling, Jan.* 9, 1784.

On the first day of each new year, I am particularly called upon to remember, with gratitude and
Christian love, the several kind friends to whom I
am so much indebted; and, above all, my patron;
while my situation is so suited to a disabled man,
past labouring in a larger sphere. I remember
your ladyship, as *faint*, yet *pursuing*—as waiting for
the revelation of the glory of Christ, and His unsearchable riches And, as the most suitable subject I can write upon, I have chosen this—the capital points in which consists the difference between a
weak and strong faith in Christ; earnestly wishing
you may be enabled to perceive you are a believer,
though a weak one, and desiring and praying to
grow strong in faith, and to triumph in Christ Jesus.

Weak faith seeks salvation only in Christ, and
yields subjection to Him, and brings the soul to His
feet, though without assurance of being as yet saved
by Him.   There is not one duty a weak believer
slights. Weak faith is attended with sorrow and
humiliation; as in his case, who spoke with tears,
" Lord, I believe! help thou my unbelief!" It
produces new desires and affections, new principles
and purposes, and a new practice, though not in
such strength and vigour as is found in old established believers. It produces an attachment to
our Saviour, invincible. Ask the weakest and most
disconsolate believer, whether he would forsake and
give up his hope in Christ: he will eagerly reply—

" Not for the whole world !" There is no reason, therefore, why weak believers should conclude against themselves ; for weak faith unites as really with Christ as strong faith—as the least bud in the vine is drawing sap and life from the root, no less than the strongest branch. Weak believers, therefore, have abundant cause to be thankful; and while they reach after growth in grace, ought not to overlook what they have already received.

The evidence of a strong faith is a clear apprehension of salvation already obtained in Christ Jesus. " We have known and believed the love that God hath to us. God is love ! " We have wisdom for direction, pardon for sin, grace to keep and preserve us. " All things are ours ; for we are Christ's, and Christ is God's." Strong believers can say, ' God is ours ' ; though they want the present sense of His love, or the comfortable frames they have rejoiced in formerly. And they see the affection of a Father, though clouds and darkness encompass them. This is exemplified in all the saints ; and remarkably in the case of Job :—" Though He slay me, yet will I trust in Him ! " A man weak in faith would have said : " I am cast out of the sight of his eyes ; and He will no more have mercy upon me." Strong faith will trust in the Lord Jesus Christ, when the means of help in the time of difficulty do not appear, when all means fail, and all props are taken away. When the word of the Lord is tried to the uttermost, and in the lowest strait to which His children can be reduced, its faithfulness and truth shine the brightest. Thus Moses trusted in God, when the Red Sea was before him, the Egyptians behind, and the mountains on each side. Thus David, when the people were going to stone him at Ziglag, comforted himself in the Lord his God. Thus Daniel and the three children. Oh, glorious persuasion! which can keep the mind in perfect peace, even in the extremest difficulties! Strong faith can overcome those doubts and objections which distress and perplex weak believers. In particular seasons, there are doubts in the most established believers: even they are sometimes afraid lest they should perish, or be found hypocrites at last: but, after prayer and cries, and sore conflicts, the sun again shines bright, and all their doubts are dispelled. Strong faith is pursuing, and can wait long; when weak faith is discouraged, and faints under the delay of the help and mercy it craves. Strong faith can even take denials well; not only respecting temporal things, but respecting spiritual enjoyments; saying, " Not my will, but Thine, be done!" And strong faith, in its highest actings, enables us to rejoice in necessity, in distresses, in circumstances most dismaying to the nature of man.

From hence it appears what a race Christians have to run, and to what growth in grace they may attain. Watchfulness, prayer, and self-denial, and a heart quite in earnest, looking unto Jesus, will bring us to it. Let us not think it too much for us to receive. " Open thy mouth wide, and I will fill it,' is the command of our God.

From your much-indebted servant,

H. VENN.

TO LADY MARY FITZGERALD.

MADAM, *Yelling, January* 19, 1784.

It is high time for me to write, and send you my best wishes, that your ladyship may enjoy a *happy* new-year. *"Happy"* is a proud word! much too high for a sinful creature! Granted;—but not too much for God our Saviour to bestow. " My peace (saith He, in the largeness of His affection) I leave with you. My peace I give unto you." And again: " These things have I spoken unto you, that my joy might remain in you, and that your joy might be full." Thus may you be blessed in the midst of trials and manifold corruptions of heart!

Many fears I had, lest your journey should be more than you could bear; and lest you might be very ill upon the road, far from every friend but one. Most pleasing, therefore, was the news I received from our two friends in St. James's Place, of your better state of health. Oh, sing unto the Lord! for He is good, our Guard, our Guide, our Shepherd; and we His sheep! We go out, we come in, feeble and faint, in the midst of dangers and enemies, inflamed with rage and malice against us; but our hairs are numbered, and no evil befalls us. How superior your pleasures! far above what the grand world can conceive; while you have seen so many of the family of Christ—in some, one feature of his own likeness more predominant; in some, another; but none complete and without defect. One reason may probably be, to prevent our admiring too much the living image, and setting our affections on it, to the hurt of our souls, and neglect of the Great Original, in whom alone is perfect beauty.

It gave me joy to see Mr. and Mrs. Elton much c oncerned for the good of the poor people of West Bromwich. It is grace, indeed, to condescend, from love, to men of low estate! What a privileged station have Christians! We have enjoyed it exceedingly this last month : though shut up in our house, without a visiter, in the midst of snow, so as neither to walk nor ride, our happy life sweetly glides away. We say one to another, How short is our time! We wish those who find it a burden could give us some portion of it. When we were in Warwickshire, my two youngest daughters were six weeks alone, literally ; but so far from being gloomy, they read, and worked and enjoyed their time exceedingly. Oh, what a noble independent spirit is produced by the power of godliness! How mistaken and wretched are the multitude, who eagerly and greedily indulge their low earthly appetites as the way of true pleasure; whereas, *that* is found in the wise and holy use of the highest faculties of the soul, on the things unseen and eternal.

I have good news to send you from Cambridge. —Mr. Simeon is made for great usefulness. There are near twenty promising young students. Several of them come over, at times, to me ; and make me happy, in the opportunity of commending to them the best Master—the best service that men or angels can be called to work in. Pleasing is the hope, that many shall, by them, be made rich in peace and love divine, and meet for heaven! They listen to my instructions with great simplicity : and I inculcate much moderation, obedience to superiors, and no breaking out to be teachers, when they are mere novices. Hard lesson to young men! Yet they observe it, and bring credit upon their seriousness.

In my own parish, I have small encouragement. Several who were called, are removed, either by death, or fixing in other places. However, I look off from every discouragement, to the Lord, whom I serve. My trust is in His promise: my aim is, to make Him known and loved supremely. He hears me pray—Be Thou exalted! Be thou extolled!— And in my want of success respecting many, I must submit; saying, " Even so, Father! for so it seemeth good in thy sight."

Mrs. Venn and my daughters desire their best respects. I beg to be remembered to the Ladies at Brighton.

From your much-indebted servant,

H. VENN.

TO THE REV. JOHN VENN.

MY DEAR SON,   *Yelling, April* 19, 1784.

Very pleasant indeed to us all was your visit, and caused many thanksgivings for the favour God has been pleased to shew you. My prayers are heard —my desires concerning you are fulfilled. You are a pastor in the Church of Christ; and in you, an earthly vessel, is put the inestimable treasure of the light of the knowledge of the glory of God in the face of Jesus Christ. Instead of doubting, therefore, you have the greatest cause imaginable for rejoicing that you are in Christ, and He in you. Remember, no command in the New Testament is oftener repeated, than, "Rejoice in the Lord!" Nothing more becomes us, than assurance (in the full view of our unworthiness and corruptions, and the purity of our God) grounded on the purchase paid for us—on the promise and oath of God. Nothing more honours him, or commends His cause. Nothing more discourages and damps the hearts of men, than to hear those who are acknowledged to be walking circumspectly, and with a single eye, speak in terms of suspicion and fear. This is the device of the enemy, to perplex and vex those who are faithful, by endless fears and the spirit of bondage. "Ask, and ye shall have," &c.—this is enough to make us confident.

On Thursday, in the last week, I learnt from Mr. Simeon that the condemned malefactor, at Cambridge, had been amongst my hearers at Huddersfield. I went, in a post-chaise, with Mr. Simeon, to Cambridge, on Friday. The man knew me; though twenty years had passed since he had seen me. He was much affected; and fell on my neck. I was with him near two hours; but I am not able to say whether he hath received of the Lord the gift of faith. Now his life is spared by Mr. Pitt (who was on Saturday chosen member for the University), it will be seen whether he returns to his old courses, or is a new man. Very, very few are real converts from jails!

Yesterday I was at Everton. The pastor was well, and most affectionate in inquiries after you.

I would not that my declining health should be any matter of grief to you! It is my prayer to be taken to my Father's home, before I am useless in the Church. What have I to expect, but days in which "I can have no pleasure," through infirmities, if life be prolonged. I am exceedingly thankful to see your very tender regard for your sisters. Were I to give way (which I do not for a moment) to any wish, it would be for them, that they might be kept from those crosses to which my removal might expose them.—But who am I, to take upon me to say what is best for them? Thy will, dear Lord, be done! All I desire is, that they may, from the heart, say the same. I am daily praying for myself, that I may die well—I mean, in much peace, and hope, and cheerfulness; for the comfort of my family, and the honour of the doctrine I have preached ;— and that whenever I depart, my dear wife and children may say, with consolation the world knoweth not of—

> Why should we mourn departed friends,
>   Or shake at death's alarms?
> 'Tis but the voice, which Jesus sends,
>   To call them to His arms.

I verily believe we are united in Christ; and shall soon meet in his kingdom, and be found numbered amongst the Children for whom He died. The Lord Jesus be with your Spirit!

From your affectionate father,

H. VENN.

TO THE REV. JOHN VENN.

MY DEAR SON,   *Yelling, April* 21, 1784.

"He hath chosen me in affliction," you may truly say! He hath called you to follow Him, bearing

c c

your cross.   I should be *uneasy*, did I not know that
the merciful and gracious Lord does much afflict and
scourge His elect;—did I not know, from His infallible words, from my own experience, and the case
of many of my friends, that all things work together
for good to them that are in Christ.   But I am not
uneasy in any improper way.   Parental feeling for
a beloved son will work; and I am, by the same
afflictions which are laid upon you, called to humiliation and prayer for you, and for us all.   And
since I received your letter on Monday, I can truly
say, " As the eyes of servants (corrected for their
faults) look unto the hand of their masters, and as
the eyes of a maiden unto the hand of her mistress,
so are my eyes unto the Lord, until He is pleased to
have mercy"* on you, and restore you to health and
strength.   Blessed be the name of our God ! I have
found such solemn seasons of heavy trial, as you
have too, very profitable.—The uncertainty how you
do, and the suspense, is a great part of the trial.   But
so much have we to be thankful for, on your account—so joined are we in the light, love, and
liberty, and hope we have in our dear Lord Jesus
Christ—so fully assured am I that He is purging
you, as a fruit-bearing branch, that you may bring
forth more fruit—and that all your grief and
pain is measured out with tender and everlasting

* The application of this text (Psalm cxxiii. 2.) is different
from that usually adopted.   Commentators generally regard the
Psalmist as looking up to the Hand of God for defence and direction under the oppression of others : according to Mr. Venn's
interpretation, the Psalmist refers his afflictions immediately to the
hand of God.

compassion—that I am greatly cheered in these thoughts; and am able to say, " Lord ! I cheerfully leave my son in Thy hands. After he hath suffered awhile, perfect, stablish, strengthen, settle him !"

If you are not able to write a line, cannot you get Mr. Raven to let me know how you do ? You should also have a good nurse. Do not, my dear son, when you are ill, be afraid of expense. I will most gladly defray it. Yesterday, dear Simeon came, and brought your letter. I had but just time to give him a hint not to speak of your illness, that your sisters might not be uneasy. I want much to come, but I am confined. As you cannot serve your church, I wish some means could be devised for the supply of it; so that you might be with your sisters while we are in town, where we intend to be on the 5th of May.

Dear Mr. Adam finished his course at Wintringham, three weeks ago, after being fifty-nine years rector of that parish, Exceedingly small was his success amongst his people, after preaching the Gospel thirty years !

Mr. Waltham was here ; and gave us, on Monday and Tuesday in Easter-week, two excellent sermons, in our kitchen. He is much alive, and is comforted with some success.

Do not be discouraged at the present state of your people, and all around you. Take for an example of suffering affliction, on this account, the Prophets : how small was their success ! Our business is, only " to declare the whole counsel of God" —to live the life of a minister—and not to cease praying. Our reward is sure—our record is on high.

We must not expect to be happier in our work than the most distinguished of the servants of God. Some fruit you will have;—and to be among the least and lowest of those who turn sinners to God, is an unspeakable honour. How am I tried!—thirteen years I have spoken to, and prayed for, R——— A———, &c. &c. ; and they remain just what they were. Dear Simeon feels for you; and we pray to gether for you.

The Lord comfort your heart, and give you to abound in hope. By and by, we shall enjoy immortal health together in our Beloved!

Your affectionate father,

H. VENN.

TO MISS JANE C. VENN.

MY DEAR JANE, *Yelling, July* 14, 1784.

Yesterday, your welcome letter arrived; and we all, as you conclude, unite in praising our God, who hears our prayers, and is richly deserving our love, for His benefits bestowed upon us in this world, even of a temporal nature. The natural man loses the sweetest part of enjoyment, even of the *only things* he can enjoy. He eats and drinks, and feasts upon the creature, as a brute, not knowing from whence it comes. If his pleasure and comfort are in a tender and beloved wife, an amiable child, or affectionate friend—the wife, or child, or friend, is all. A true Christian, on the contrary, enjoys the gift more richly, as a gift from his bountiful God. " This excellent woman, so beloved by me," he says, " the Lord found out and bestowed upon me.—This pleasant child, who gives me growing delight, is a plant of His planting. Care, in education, would have been fruitless, had not His grace crowned it with success."

I am rejoiced to see you are led to be thankful; and to receive, with thanksgiving to our blessed God, His tender protection. By returning praise for the daily favours we receive, we shall acquire a habit of thankfulness, which is pleasing and honourable to God, comfort to the mind, and health to the body, in most cases; for a cheerful heart doeth good, like a medicine.

Such improvement my beloved daughter is enabled, glory be to God! to make of temporal blessings. Yet these only lead the way to, and prepare the mind to be the more affected with, the spiritual blessings we enjoy. What cause have all those to break out in holy joy, who have a heart given them to seek after God, to desire restoration to the proper state of an immortal creature—a state of love to his Maker, of entire dependence upon Him, of union of will with Him, of delight in His name, of an abiding supreme desire to please Him in our place and station! What cause to sing with joy, that the certain possession of these tempers is gained by the knowledge of God manifest in the flesh!—for *there*, love, beyond every thing seen or known by men or angels, is displayed! "My God," the believer says, "who hast lived, and laboured, and fought, and been wounded, and slain, in getting life and salvation for me—how shall I thank Thee with becoming ardour! how shall I love thee as I ought!—I am thine! Oh, save me from ever grieving Thee, by forgetting my immense debt to Thee!"

Such aspirations as these, souls which are born from above, at times, feel; though the best are often dull, and stupid, and cold, to astonishment, in this matter. When you find your precious soul in this unbecoming frame towards your God and Saviour, be not discouraged; much less call in question your faith; but confess, frankly, your corruption, and enlarge upon it; and then humbly beg: "Quicken me, O Lord, according to Thy word—according to Thy loving-kindness! I should never have had one thought of gratitude and love, hadst Thou not excited it in me! Hast Thou begun to restore my soul, and wilt Thou not carry on the work? That be far from Thee!"—Such humble expostulations are pleasing to the Lord, and not without success.

The very same thunder-storm you were in, reached, in great violence, to Orlingbury. It is good to be above fear that "hath torment," in such awful weather. Christians should labour much not to fear, as men without God have cause to do. And if fear of death makes us dismayed at the storm, we ought to examine whence that fear arises; and not rest, till we can say, 'Death is ours.' It is but a bad return for all His precious promises—and love stronger than death which Christ has had for us— to tremble and quake, in case He should take us to Himself. I grant that our nerves are soon shaken; but our God has access to our spirits; and can strengthen us, and give us firmness;—and will, when we pray to Him; that, for the credit of our faith in His Name, we may not fear for the body, but sanctify the Lord God in our hearts, and let Him be our fear, and let Him be our dread. Wishing you much of His presence, much more knowledge and faith, and love, and every divine temper—and often, every day, thinking of you—with kind love from your dear mamma, I remain your affectionate father,

H. VENN.

P.S.—What is this? All this a Postscript! Why, it is almost as long as the long letter!— So it is. And all this Postscript is, to inform you, and your dear fellow-travellers, how it fared with me after we parted, and of several other particulars, in the way of conversation.—Charming was the summer's breeze; and nothing, in my way to Kettering, to interrupt my most serious thoughts on the constitution of things here—plainly concurring, with the word of God, to prove that "*this* is not our rest." Friends, who are most happy in each other, and tender relations, are not long together : their interviews are soon at an end. How is the mind relieved by particular prayer for them, and lively hope of their safety, being interested in the great salvation of God!—With thoughts of this kind, and prayer, and singing, I reached my destination.—No sooner was I come to Orlingbury, than Mr. and Mrs. Scott from Olney (who were visiting in the parish) came in; and very glad we were to meet. He is a man of right spirit, always about his Master's business; and has a tongue given him, which is " a well of life," always ministering grace to the hearers. One hour was all the time we could spend together; and then he engaged me to make an exchange on the last Sunday in August, God willing.

Kitty sets out well. James M. sent for medicine for his wife, who has a fever. Kitty desired immediately, she might walk over to see the patient ; for she could not otherwise tell what to prescribe.— I am very glad to see her tread in your steps. Oh, may we all love the poor more, and study to help them, and not fear the fulfilment of the promise! —I paid J. Peters her eight shillings ; and she gets into her little house this day. She went away from the parsonage, rejoicing.—A parsonage should be a place of refuge—a house of mercy. The very sight of it should be pleasing to the poor and deso-late. Prayer, to be helped, and enabled to help the poor, will be answered ;—and such aid, so ob-tained, is matter of great thankfulness.

TO MISS RILAND.

MY DEAR PRISCILLA,   *Yelling, Aug.* 5, 1784.

Next to your honoured and truly affectionate parents, no one, I trust, is more interested in your welfare than myself. You are the child of two beloved friends, who have been fellow-travellers with myself, for a great many years, to the same heavenly country ; and fellow-soldiers, under the same ever-blessed Captain of our salvation. You have been included amongst the offspring of the faithful, in all the prayers offered up for them, since you were born. You were in your earliest infancy baptized in the Name of the Father, Son, and Holy Ghost, as a public mark that you were born in the family of God ; and at that time I became a sponsor for you. To these calls upon me, tenderly to regard your best interests, others are added—your very amiable deportment, when a visiter under my roof, and the pleasure you

expressed in being one of our family. All these
considerations unite in engaging me to enter most
cheerfully into a correspondence with you; in which
you are to regard *me* as your godfather, who is very
soon to go hence, and is extremely desirous of helping you to guide your judgment and your affections,
to choose and delight in the best things. The more
confidence you can place in me, the more pleasure
I shall receive : and be assured, the correspondence
shall be entirely between *ourselves,* and divulged
to no one, without your leave.

I am chiefly excited to wish for this correspondence, on account of the many difficulties and discouragements which occur to young people who in
earnest set out to serve and please God—difficulties
and discouragements which afflict and distress for
a much longer space of time than they would do, if
the wisdom and experience of Christians, much older
than themselves, were consulted. I recollect how
many objections rose in my mind against several
grand truths of the Bible; what hard thoughts
I often had of the ways of God; how foolishly I
judged many Divine prohibitions irksome and unnecessary, which are the counsels of mercy and love.
I recollect on how many occasions I should have
gone on in the good ways of the Lord, with alert-
ness and assurance of being right, had some kind
counsellor been at hand ; whereas I was a long time
in uncertainty, and turned often to the wrong path.
Many passages of Holy Scripture, which I wished to
understand, were very dark ; and I wanted an interpreter.—Concluding that young people in general
are in the same perplexities as I was myself, I should

be glad to point out the way, and be the means of delivering them the sooner from their embarrassment.

Our correspondence shall begin with a few thoughts upon a very interesting subject—the love of God toward the children of men, expressed in the tender language of a Father, and calling upon each of us in these words, " *Give me thy heart !*— Love me *supremely ;* and every thing you may and ought to love, in a subordinate measure !"—But can the high, and lofty, and eternal God, indeed make this demand ? The distance between the worm and the first Emperor in the world is not discernible, compared with the distance between man and his adorable Creator. Why, then, does He make this demand ? Our righteousness cannot profit Him. But a paternal affection for us, a desire of our felicity—only to be obtained in giving him our poor, corrupted, wicked heart—moved Him to call for it. Other objects are deceitful : they promise much, and perform little : they give pleasures which do not satisfy : and they soon fail. Other objects communicate nothing excellent : they make no one the better or the wiser, or the more seviceable to their fellow-creatures. Other objects debase the spirit of man, formed for eternal things; and make it meanly dependent upon what is most uncertain in its nature ; and will pierce it through with many sorrows. Other objects will not bear the solemn thought of the hour of death and the Day of Judgment, though both are absolutely unavoidable. How superior, then, is the understanding, and how highly favoured the mind, that answers to this most condescending demand of our God, "Give me thy heart"!—Take my poor heart, just as it is! set up therein Thy throne! Oh, may I love thee above all, and live for Thee alone!

Now, to engage our affections (which a mere demand of them will by no means do, nor the natural perfections of Jehovah), He took upon Himself our nature; and calls Himself the Bridegroom, the Husband, of His Church and people; who set His love upon them with such an ardour, that He gave Himself (after a life of labour and sorrow) for Her, that, freed from condemnation and defilement, she might appear a glorious Church for ever in heaven.—If you can ponder on this, and believe its reality, there will spring up in your heart, my dear Priscilla, the temper and affections of an angel, and a pure delight in this divine love, and a steadfast desire to please God, and an ardent spirit of prayer, saying, "Speak, Lord! for thy servant heareth." And this will be followed with living communications of more faith, and love, and peace, and hope. And this is the earnest wish of my heart, who am

Your sincere friend, for Christ's sake,

H. VENN.

"Jane! Jane! what shall I do?—The letter I was afraid of, is come.—I almost wish you had stayed at Yelling!—Now, I must write an answer: and what can I say?—Well, you must write for me; and tell your papa, that to be sure I have a very great respect for him, and love him as if he was a relation; but how to begin a single letter, much more a correspondence, it is what I never shall be able to attempt." Jane replies: "Only make the trial:

mountains in appearance are no more than clouds to the traveller, which, in his journey, he passeth through with ease. Besides, there is no time fixed for the answer; and I am sure my father will wait till you can freely and gladly take up your pen."

Mrs. V. and Kitty send their love.

TO THE REV. JOHN VENN.

MY DEAR SON, *Yelling, Aug.* 12, 1784.

We have been every day thinking how busy you are, in finding out the fittest places for all your furniture; and then, with what surprise and thankfulness you survey the plenty of good things you so early in life have about you. And then, if it please the good Lord to give you life and health, I shall hope to hear what I much long for—that you study hard, and carefully write your sermons, and pay attention to your style; otherwise, you will get into a careless and slovenly way of doing your work. Remember, and lay to heart, that the grand temptation, by which thousands are vanquished, who set out well, is, indolence and lukewarmness. In every situation there is some peculiar snare, to which we are exposed; and all the art and malice of the wicked-one is used to take us in that snare. When our hearers are few, and those of low degree, without continual watchfulness and prayer we shall certainly grow very remiss, and find no heart to take pains for so few. We may judge of the force of this temptation, when we see so few are able to overcome it. But I pray daily for you, my son, that you may be a hard student in the Bible, and in the best Commentators—(they are but *few*)—who have written upon it. I would have you a hard student; because it is profitable to be so, on every account. Your understanding will be thus much enlightened, and your mind enriched; so that your conversation and discourse will be edifying, and your preaching be full, and much to the purpose; and the people will be fed, and your ability to instruct them be acknowledged; and God will give the blessing. You will by study be kept out of temptation, and be an example to your flock. The life of a pastor in the Church ought to be a life of holy meditation, study, and doing good; and only so much exercise taken, as health requires! I hope also to hear that you *finish* your sermons, and take much pains to correct them; and that you apply, if health be restored, to your Hebrew Bible, till you can read a chapter with pleasure. Your people and your servants will observe how you spend your time. It is not enough we are sober, temperate, or kind : we must be exemplary all through, unblameable, and unreproveable, before men.

It is one valuable privilege in our profession, that we can read and be instructed by the excellent and most eminent ministers ever employed in the church, whose writings are still in our hands.—I can speak feelingly on this subject! This last week has been very gloomy, cold, misty weather : we have not had one visiter; but I have enjoyed a feast, in reading M. Dailée on the Colossians. What a judicious writer! What a masterly expositor! The truth, the fulness of Christ, are so set forth by him, as to make my heart glow; and I am the better for what I read.

The Lord love, comfort, and save you!

From your affectionate father,

H. VENN.

TO MISS VENN.

MY DEAR ELING,   *Yelling*, *Oct.* 2, 1784.

With what pleasure did I hear from your friend at Bedford, yesterday, that your health was perfectly recovered! How different is your situation, and dear Miss Barham's! How beautiful does the grace of our Lord Jesus Christ make both! To see a young lady, in the very prime of youth, gradually losing her strength and flesh and appetite, and visibly hastening to the grave; yet placid and meek, and well satisfied to be weak and to be sickly, and to be just what her Lord appoints; is a striking object, not to be viewed by a considerate mind without much profit! But a young woman in health and spirits, surrounded with friends, and much beloved by them, still using these comforts with moderation and caution—and holding them in due subordination to her beloved Lord and Saviour —teaches and preaches by her example, powerfully, as the sick and dying saint. Indeed, every branch, vitally united to the True Vine, brings forth fruit, and does not cease. I please myself, therefore, in the thought, that you, led by the Spirit of Christ, make rich improvement of your present lot. Often be looking up, and speaking with an humble cordial confidence in our Incarnate God: " Make me like

Thyself, in my manner of life ; as thou wert in private life, before Thou didst appear a preacher in Judea! May I be diligent and useful, watching opportunities to instruct, and speak a word in love to perishing souls !"—If nothing will satisfy, as nothing ought, but usefulness, be not afraid, there will not be wanting opportunities, more or less. Awkward you may and will feel it at first, as we all have : for every thing we have to learn is done with difficulty, till practice makes us ready at it.- Be not therefore discouraged. Venture !—you will never repent—in speaking to the poor women, and to your brother's maids.* Express your desires, that they may be happy. Few but feel any instance of love we shew towards them. If, at first, they take it not as they ought, our good advice may not be lost. The great depravity of man is, indifference to his fellow-creatures : this is nearly as bad as want of love to God. Yet how seldom do books or sermons, or serious people, urge with earnestness this point! How many thousand prayers did I put up, that I might love God, and be delivered from the curse, and from the power of sin! How few, that I might love my fellow-sinners—not only to have pity for their sufferings, but compassion for their souls!

All the blessings which flow from Jesus be with you and Johannes !

From your affectionate Father,

H. VENN.

* Miss Venn was at this time staying with her brother, at Little Dunham.

Yelling, Oct. 2, 1784.

———I HAVE just returned, this day, from Creaton, a small village in Northamptonshire, where our God has been pleased, in a very remarkable manner, to make use of Mr. Maddock. Much had been told me, by Mr. Scott of Olney, Mr. Newton, and Mr. Robinson, of this work. I had a desire, therefore, to go and see my old acquaintance, Mr. Maddock. Accordingly, last Thursday was the day appointed; when I preached twice, to near three hundred people; as many as could be crowded together in so small a church; some few also standing without. The eager attention of all, their sweet and heavenly looks, and the lively singing of the whole congregation, was equal to any thing I ever saw. All these have been gathered, with twice as many more, by the preaching of Mr. Maddock. He began life as an attorney in London —was ordained when forty-five years old—was Curate at Kettering, and at two other places; but had little success till he came to Creaton, at the age of sixty-one. Now he is seventy-two; and will soon enter into rest. There is a beautiful simplicity, and much love and kindness, among his people; and no disputings, or laying any stress upon matters of doubtful disputation. My nephew was there, and an attorney of chief practice from Kettering, who has left the tent of Socinus and Priestley, to follow Christ, and adore the Crucified Saviour. Dear Mr. Robinson also, from Leicester, twenty-three miles distant, gave me the meeting, and Mr. Scott of Olney.———

TO THE REV. JOHN VENN.

MY DEAR SON,   *Yelling, Oct.* 16, 1784.

The melancholy account you send me, of a Dissenting preacher coming amongst your people, is certainly a very heavy trial: yet be not discouraged! This is a trial all the pastors of Christ meet with. Your conduct is to be the same as theirs has been—to warn your people against this device of Satan; to tell them that points of doubtful disputation are never of any service, and only work to the hurt of the soul; and in your society,* to desire them to mark how much is spoken of the necessity of union—the mischiefs of disputing and dividing: and shew them the solemn charges given to all, who receive benefit from their ministers, to esteem, to obey them, and follow their instructions, enforced by the Scripture. When we have done this, we have done all, as far as teaching and exhortation can go. To this we must add our constant prayer and intercession; and take up our cross, after the example of all the Prophets, who mourn over the obstinacy of the people in rejecting their word.

In such corners, and amongst so few as you and I speak to, our want of success is more sensible, but not greater, than in numerous congregations. I feel much on this account: but, by the help of God, I will persevere, till my last breath; knowing the Lord saith to him who is received into His joy,

* This alludes to a meeting of a few of the more serious persons in his congregation, at his house, on the Sunday evenings, and one other evening in the week.

not " Well done" *successful*, but " good and faithful, servant." The former epithet has not been applicable to many of his dearest ministers : the two latter, to all. Be then of good cheer, and watch and pray ; and believe the hand of the Lord will work in some degree. Happy the servant that is found watching !

When Mr. C—— was here, a fortnight since, he read a letter from Mr. ——, the Travelling Fellow, now at Frescati in Italy, relating his great distress of soul, under great weakness of body, after a relapse into a fever ; and expressing his deep compunction for having acted against light; and desiring now to seek for happiness, where alone it can be found, in the knowledge and love of Jesus Christ, and obedience to His will. These last are his own words.—I thought it would excite you to pray for him.

I have now gone through Daillée on the Colossians, and never was more instructed and entertained. But Daillée complains sorely, that Protestants, who would die sooner than be at mass or worship an idol, would, alas! worship gold, and love the world, and be dissemblers with God. I was particularly struck with his beautiful and just remarks on the case of Onesimus ; once, a slave, a thief, a fugitive ;—by the grace of God blessing Paul's word, afterward a faithful brother and pastor in the Church, and an eminent light. Here was the triumph of free and sovereign grace. *Nil desperandum, Christo duce, et auspice Christo!*

I am just going to visit J. G., in a fever. He, I trust, is one of the sheep who shall never perish.–

The Lord Jesus be with your spirit! Let us daily remember each other!

    From your affectionate father,

                    H. VENN.

P.S.—I have been to see J. G.—One such is worth the labour of years!—humble, well-informed, patient, and thankful. Yet his wife, who has been under concern, seems to have lost it all, and is not affected by the inward supports and sweet consolations given to her husband. The reason of her receiving no good, and her loss of the convictions she had, is owing to her neglect of prayer.—If we pray, our souls shall prosper: if we trifle, and are idle, and take no pains in the use of means, we must perish. Prayer is like our food. The *natural* life is weak, and ready to faint, if we eat little, and without appetite;—the *spiritual* life declines, when we have no hearty desire to pray, and are not affected with this decay. I know she would say, " I cannot give myself a heart to pray." No, nor can you do any thing that is right!—But what an answer! God tells us, He will fulfil the desires of them that call on Him—that every thing shall be given to a praying soul; and men reply, " We cannot pray." They should speak out, and say, " We care not for His blessings! Let those seek them who need them : we do not!" This is shockingly impious, but no more than the truth : and the consequence is certain, in the nature of things—The proud must be sent empty away, while the hungry are filled with good things. Oh, for hunger and thirst after righte- ousness—a constant intense desire, which shall be satisfied!

I lately preached at ———. The audience was very large ; but such inattention to the prayers and worship, that it quite damped me. What miserable delusion, to think sermons will profit awakened and enlightened people, when they have no heart to call upon God, and worship Him in spirit and in truth! Often call upon your people, to pray with importunity. Nothing short of this will do.—— H. V.

I add an extract from another letter, in which the same point is urged which occurs in the last paragraph. Indeed, no one ever entertained a higher sense of the importance of prayer and praise in public worship, or laboured more earnestly to keep up a devout and attentive spirit in the congregation.—The following extract was written after Mr. Venn had been preaching for several weeks to crowded congregations in London.

———Oh, that power from on high might be vouchsafed in answer to prayer! Full congregations are but poor things, if the arrows which are very sharp do not pierce to the heart the king's enemies. This, alas! is seldom the case to what it used to be in former times. Prayer is much wanted here. I see the people greatly inattentive to the worship, and yet hearing with seeming earnestness. This will never do! Worship in spirit and in truth must mellow the heart, and dispose it to hear with humility, and desire to profit; otherwise God's Spirit is grieved, and withdraws. The preacher may be praised, but the soul will not be profited.

TO MISS JANE C. VENN.

MY DEAR JANE, *Yelling, October* 19, 1784.

Yesterday we received yours of the 14th. We can readily believe you are in too great a hurry to write much; and I would excuse you the trouble, only we want to hear of your health, and of the dear friends you are with. The very short time allotted for Yorkshire must be a great alloy to your pleasure. We shall hope one week more may be gained.

I thought your mind would be affected, as you describe, with the sight of Huddersfield, and the comparison of its present state, and your connexion with it in your childhood. Such scenes impress on us the awful truth, that we, in a transient world, are poor, and soon to lose the little we have here, in the smiles and loving care of those who are dearest to us. Such reflections are distressing to men who have not a more enduring substance in the heavenly world. I have felt many times as you have now at Huddersfield; and found relief in the hope of immortality, where all the family of Christ shall love each other with perfect love, and know no more separation by death or absence.

The old house was a melancholy object to me, four years ago. In that dwelling, how many of the excellent of the earth have been received! Within those walls, how many precious sayings, from the lips of the sons and daughters of God, have I heard! How many prayers and praises offered up by your dear mamma!—now a saint, with the spirits of the just made perfect. Within those walls, line upon line, precept upon precept, were given, with great delight, by your father, to instruct and sanctify your hearts unto the Lord; which His own Spirit—adored be His Name!—has made effectual. So, that could you have seen and conversed with your beloved mother, what mutual joy would you have had! for your hope, and light, and love, your mind and affections, are all one with hers. When a few years have taken their rapid flight, you will, I doubt not, speak, and think, and feel, as she does now. This will be a change not many degrees greater than you have experienced, my dear daughter, in your soul, during the space of seventeen years, since she left me.

Now for Yelling news!—Mr. Simeon and Mr. Coulthurst have been here together. The latter improves every time I see him. Betty Field is dying —I trust, in a very good state—with great comfort, and a full view, she says, of Christ. John Gatehouse is ill, but happy—a truly meek and humble follower of his Lord. Miss M. of Gravely, also, is not expected to live. I heard, with joy, from her own lips, that the Saviour is precious to her, under all her pain and burning heat. How does sickness, and a dying bed, demonstrate the wisdom of her choice, in joining herself to the Lord, as soon as she heard of Him! Let us remember poor Miss ——! she is amiable indeed, and very sensible. I have spoken to her, with fourteen young people who were confirmed last Thursday at St. Neot's:—our servant was among them. I spoke to them three evenings; but I could not see any impression on any one, excepting young John Alsop. I gave Miss ——,

Doddridge's Rise and Progress ; and particularly desired her to consider the prayers, which are very affecting. However, I do not despair. The command to us all, who know the Lord, is—" Sow thy seed in the morning ; and in the evening, slack not thy hand ; for thou canst not tell which shall prosper—this, or that."

We expect Joseph Scott here, to take home his wife, who is something better for our air ;—though, at best, she enjoys poor health. Her soul prospers ; though she laments that her children keep her affections too much below. " A sad difference," she one day said, " between my state and St. Paul's ! He desired to be gone ; and I wish to stay." How few of us ever get to that most blessed state—wishing to be gone ! Here we have abundant cause to cry out, Lord, help our unbelief ! Lord, increase our faith !

I direct this to you at Thornhill. Pray give my kindest love to them. Tell them I shall never forget the many pleasant hours I have spent with them, nor the true and cordial friendship we had in times past. I often remember them, when I am praying for my friends and fellow-citizens in Christ ; and often anticipate the day, when we shall fall at the feet of the Lamb, adoring the grace in which we share, and by which we shall be saved. Remember me to Mr. Powley, Mr. Burnet, and at Mold Green. Were I to allow myself to choose, I would wish to be near my Yorkshire friends. But, choosing for ourselves is not less ridiculous in men and women, than it would be in a child of three or four years old : our understanding and wisdom are no more proportioned to judge what is best for us.

We are in the hands of a Heavenly Father—dear name! implying all we can need, as a ground for cordial confidence that He will certainly order all for the best.

Mark it well, my dear daughter, that we have to do with a *Father*, whose love is as great as His other perfections, towards all His children! Our Saviour always proposes Him, to His people, in that character. He does not say, God Almighty knows that you have need of all these things, but, " your Heavenly Father." " It is your Father's good plea- sure to give you the kingdom." " When you pray, say, Our Father, which art in heaven." " How much more shall your Heavenly Father give the Holy Ghost"—"give good things to them that ask Him!" The Spirit of His Son is sent into the hearts of His people, that they may cry, Abba, Father.—May you, my dear Jane, be more and more acquainted with God, as your Father, loving you, and delighting to do you good in Christ Jesus. Beg of Him a cordial confidence in His mercy, such as shall be a healing balm for all your wounds, and lead you to recline your weary head, in peace, in all sickness, pain, and grief.—" My Father, God! how sweet the name!" This will support, when all below turns its back upon us;—when either friends are taken away, or with unavailing pity behold us in sore conflicts.

Tell me, in your next, how you have been af- fected with the strong and high mountains of Derby- shire. Though barren, the idea of grandeur they suggest pleases the mind. We are made for gran- deur. We are to behold it in all its majesty. Oh, may future scenes—in the course of our existence, which is here in its infancy—be ever before our eyes! —and an abounding hope of glory, ready to be revealed, animate our drooping spirits!

From your affectionate father,

H. VENN.

TO MRS. RILAND.

MY DEAR FRIEND, *Yelling, Jan.* 4, 1785.

Many uses are to be made of times and seasons. Our dearest friends have then a more particular remembrance in our prayers. When the first day of a new year dawns, I am called upon to commend them, who are very precious to me, to the loving protection of my God, at the same time as I give Him thanks for all His loving-kindness towards them in the years that are past.

Thus have I been remembering my dear friend, and blessing and praising God for your knowledge, faith, and love of Him, which began so many years ago. I have been calling to mind our Christmas fare, at Huddersfield; when the name of Jesus made the feast, and our souls delighted themselves in fatness;—when the wonders of His grace, and the blessings He communicates, were new and surprising to your precious soul; and a joy, spiritual and heavenly, began to be known by you. Happy times! the fruit of which we shall enjoy, together with dear Mr. Riland, in the world of glory.

What will you think, when I tell you, that last Christmas-day, in my cold church, and my few sheep around me, I had a most delightful season; and think I was never more helped in preaching in my life, and the people all listening, while "God manifest in the flesh" was my subject. This great mystery is the centre of all the truths; and itself a fountain of light, like the sun. Concerning this article it is, that we may well cry out, "Blessed is the people that know the joyful sound!" This is precisely the sound: "Unto us a Child is born; unto us a Son is given; who is Christ the Lord!"

How is your health?—When am I to see your hand-writing? It seems an age since your last letter! —I have been out nowhere, but to see a few sick people, this month: not once on horseback. Yet, blessed be God! I have my health well; and twice a week our kitchen is full of the people. I am now upon the point of expounding to them the 119th Psalm, which I never did go through: yet I know not any part of Scripture much more profitable. In that Psalm, the whole inner man is delineated; and the several changing frames of our poor hearts, and the several blessed motions and inspirations of the Holy Spirit, are touched in a very affecting manner. This is the Psalm I have often had recourse to, when I could find no spirit of prayer in my own heart;—and at length the fire has kindled, and I could pray. What has been your experience regarding this extraordinary Psalm? I know you do not read the Scripture idly, and without self-application. Have you not found it pleasant and nourishing to your soul, and fastening upon your mind? —All love, and all peace, to you and yours! A happy new year!

From your affectionate pastor,

H. VENN.

TO MISS JANE C. VENN.

Yelling, March 19, 1785.

I KNOW my dear Jane and her friends will be glad to hear from Yelling: and having to write to Mr. Thornton, I take the opportunity of getting the letter franked.

Last Sunday I finished a course of threescore years: and I had much to humble me to the dust—that I had sinned in childhood, youth, and riper years, against the glorious God;—much to excite wonder, and love to His name, who never ceased to do me good, to deal bountifully with me, and even to bless me with special mercies. Mr. and Mrs. Atkinson, with their daughter, were with us.

My subject was, that striking character of Christians, " *We look not at the things which are seen;*" which are the natural, constant objects of pursuit, and deemed the means of happiness; " *but at the things which are not seen*"—God and his Christ, the redemption He hath obtained, the spiritual blessings He bestows, and the " house not made with hands, eternal in the heavens."

The things seen are low and poor, only to sustain the body and natural life;—can never raise, exalt, and enlarge the mind, or make it wiser and better. *The things unseen* are high and noble; such as angels, and the whole company of heaven, contemplate: they enlarge and purify the mind—they inspire purposes and intentions grand and pleasing to God, transforming our minds from earthly to heavenly—are rich, and full: all, possessed of them, say so. By the knowledge of things unseen, the conscience is purified, the mind at rest, the heart rejoiced ;—so full the contentment, that our Saviour, commending the choice of Christians, saith, " He that drinketh of the water that I shall give him, shall never thirst "—after any thing beneath holiness and heaven !

The things seen are uncertain.—No one can tell how long a man and his possessions shall stay together; or whether he shall be taken from all he holds, or lose them. The first, and chief, in our towns and cities, often sink down to poverty ; and, in the course of a few years, the same person is the general envy and the object of compassion. There needs nothing more than a tempest at sea, a dreadful fire, or a great bankruptcy, to overturn the pile and fabric of wealth and opulence. Gold, houses, lands, we see continually changing their masters ; and even the lawful objects of a *subordinate* affection and love, from whence a great share of comfort is enjoyed, are no less uncertain. A pleasant child, an affectionate endearing wife, or husband—a friend, steadfast and warm, as Jonathan to David—all these things are but like beauteous flowers in the garden ; they soon fade, they wither, and " are not."

Things not seen—if once your own, are so for ever. They are above this world's whirling sphere, in the hand of God, and, like Him, unchangeable. These are His gifts, which He preserves—they are secured by oaths, and promises, and blood. Whether we are caressed in the circle of our friends, or despised, and slandered by our foes—whether we bloom in health, or languish and decay—whether we abound, or are in want, this treasure is the same. All temporal advantages add not the weight of a grain to it; and the fiercest attacks on our character or substance, or even on our bodies, cannot diminish it.

Things seen, are temporal.—The revolution of a few years exhausts them. All here soon ends. *But the things not seen, are eternal.* Eternity of knowledge, love, and holiness! Eternity, added to every thing we enjoy! this swallows up all thought, and can only be understood when we enter into our " house not made with hands."

Such was the substance of a birth-day discourse of one who, forty years ago, was, alas! as ignorant and blind to all things not seen, as " the horse or mule, which have no understanding." Mr. Atkinson said he had a happy day: it brought old times to remembrance. From his hand I received the following account from Mr. John Houghton :—" I do not find a spirit of murmuring or dissatisfaction at the stroke of Divine Providence, in bereaving me of one of the most promising and affectionate children—a daughter, in her sixteenth year. No: I have ever had cause to bless the abounding grace and mercy, towards her and myself, in that dispensation. The Lord heard my petitions, and answered them to the full: yea, He abundantly exceeded all my expectations, in opening her heart, in giving her to lament over the vanity of her mind, and her neglect in not improving the means of grace ; and then to rest her eternal concerns on the salvation that is in Christ, in such a manner as gave her a calm composure in the prospect of death. Several passages of Scripture were a stay to her mind; especially that, ' Come unto me, all ye that labour and are heavy laden! and I will give you rest.' She repeated it a few hours before she died: and to such a departure I was never witness. She longed to be with Christ. She took leave of us, with many thanks for all our attention to her, and with prayer for the presence of the Lord with us; and having repeated the word ' salvation,' she fell asleep."

What a most honourable office is that of a minister, who is an instrument, by preaching Christ, of producing such fruit! Such a happy change, Christ Crucified, known, and believed in, will surely effect! —A fortnight since, I had a most pleasing encouragement in Mr. Bennet. Extremely afflicted with illness, and unable to attend his business, tortured all the night for weeks—I found him not only quite patient and resigned, but thankful for the chastisement—full of peace and Divine knowledge. He told me he had a fear of offending God even at six years old, and always was preserved from presumptuous offences. " But grossly ignorant, and dark, was I," said he, " and knew nothing of Christ, till I had heard you for more than a year. About my children, I am perfectly easy. I only beg for them the grace of God."

Could I afford it, I should give you a peep at Birmingham; for I am engaged to preach at Leicester the Sunday after Easter: but I am obliged to be as frugal as possible. Nevertheless, do not *you* want any thing necessary. Make your dear friend your banker: I will repay it. I have received my appointment to preach the Visitation Sermon, on the 12th of May.—Your mamma, and Kitty, send their love. We all want to see you.—The Lord love you!

From your affectionate father,

H. VENN.

Yelling, May 14, 1785.

—— I HAVE had comfort in the answer of my prayer for usefulness. God generally stirs up a desire for the blessing, before He gives it; that it may be the more noticed, and with true thankfulness. Within these five months, my church is fuller— scarcely one in it drowsy. And I have more young students who visit me from Cambridge, and seem to be going on well. How they may *stand fire*, when their maintenance is at stake, or preferment—that bewitching thing!—must be sacrificed in appearance, who can say? However, the young tree is beautiful in blossom, though the blossom never come to proper fruit. I have one, now in the house, who has stood his ground well; and though confessedly one of the first Tutors in the University, he is humble as a child, and comes to hear, from an aged servant, some good of our dear Lord. The Master of his College is not only a confirmed, but a most active and daring, Socinian. I feared much he would destroy my dear friend by his subtlety; but there is no cause now to fear.

On Thursday, I preached a Visitation Sermon at Huntingdon—to a very numerous audience, for that town. I am going to print the sermon, at the desire of some of the clergy, intitled, " Plain Proofs of the Scripture Character of Christ ; and of the great practical benefits of believing in Him, as described in Scripture ; and of the pernicious consequences which unavoidably follow from controverting and denying his Deity."——

H. V.

—— Much was said, *pro* and *con.*, about my Visitation Sermon ; and the whole town was divided—a few on my side, and the many against me ;—a few glad to hear so peremptory a condemnation of the adversaries of our Lord—more offended at my bigotry and uncharitable zeal, in passing sentence on good men, who *only* deny the virtue of Christ's blood and intercession ! However, I am much indebted to my Lord and my God, that I was quite free from all restraint, and spoke to the clergy, with the same consciousness of the certainty of the doctrine, as I do to my own poor people.——

—— I preached one hour and eight minutes ; but no one seemed tired. Several came from Cambridge ; and a Master of one of the Colleges.——

TO MRS. RILAND.

Yelling, Aug. 1, 1785.

YESTERDAY, my dear friend, your letter, which came to Caxton, was brought to my daughter. Immediately, many tender feelings for you were strongly excited in all our hearts : we entered into your sorrows, fears, and distress ; and into your thankfulness and joy for the preservation of your dear Priscilla. Give our kindest love to her ; and tell her we shall all be glad to pay every attention to her. Our air, we trust, will be balmy and restorative ; and as young people very soon recover after illness, it will be the best physic, to change air, and come by gentle stages hither. *You* will want air and quietness, no less than dear Priscilla and John : we therefore promise ourselves the pleasure of hearing very soon that you have fixed the time for your journey.

How very uncertain are all our enjoyments here! Last month I was delighted with the prospect of preaching often in several different places, as I so well bore the fatigue of preaching in town; and last week I was to have begun. A few days before, one of my legs swelled, from relaxation—by over-exertion, as my surgeon thinks. I am confined therefore to my couch, and am told I must not expect a cure before many weeks are passed. My lot is wonderfully gracious! I feel but little pain; and have the most tender attention, from a dear wife, children, and servants. And when you come, all my comforts will be increased; and you may be sure of my company.

Kitty is with our friends in London; and Dr. L. has prescribed for her the most pleasant prescription;—which is, to take all the pleasure she can; to speak to twenty-five people every day; and trouble herself about nothing.—" Is he not the cleverest of all physicians?" Kitty asks.

What a new face the earth wears! Abundant showers have swelled the grain, and produced much grass and fodder for the cattle; and removed the melancholy fears of many, too apt to prophesy evil. —Mr. and Mrs. Saunderson left us, after spending one week. We were much pleased with them.— I am sorry to learn, from Jane, that any of the people are to have a vote in choosing your curate. This will introduce confusion, and make the curate conclude himself not dependent on Mr. Riland. Much trouble I foresee arising from this mode.

We all send our love to Mr. Riland, yourself, and

E E

all your branches. I am perfectly cheerful, and reckon myself as a preacher, twice every day ;—for the Lord I serve, taketh the will for the deed ; and my will, He knoweth, is to do as much.

From your affectionate father,

H. VENN.

————

In a letter written to another friend, he describes his situation in the following terms.

————

I am as happy as I could wish ; because I have not one single desire to have my complaint less, or shorter, than it pleases my God. Many advantages I enjoy from being laid aside. I have much time to think of my dear friends, and remember them more fully before the Throne of Grace ; and to dwell on the delightful, never-fading joys we shall share, when light and knowledge and love shall all be perfected—when every cause of separation and division shall utterly cease, and self be swallowed up in a perfect union with our God.

TO LADY MARY FITZGERALD.

MADAM,   *Yelling, Sept.* 26, 1785.

Two days since, after searching in vain for a copy of Mrs. Lefevre's, my dear Christian friend's, letters, I was going to tell you of my disappointment ; but yesterday I was so happy as to find one, which shall be sent, in a week or two, to your house. There is a most fervent strain of divine love in her letters : all is genuine, as I can well attest : yet I must caution my much honoured and esteemed friend against the mistake in them that is sometimes very apparent ; namely, the idea that we can arrive at perfection below, and be without fault, and out of the *hospital*, before we are out of the flesh. The dying saint, you must remember, in the last letter but one she ever wrote—(it was to myself)—wrote thus :

" I, all sin and misery—the Saviour, all tenderness and mercy—no sting remaining—no clog upon my chariot-wheels." See Mrs. Lefevre's Letters, p. 74, four lines from the bottom.

Oh, may the Teacher infallible, by His own word and Spirit, keep us from extremes ! And may we know when we are right, and give God the glory, by exhibiting a constancy and steadfastness in a truly Christian life—which will yet ever be an imperfect one ! Some better thing than we can know below is reserved for us above. Upwards may we ever tend, and be more and more spiritual and useful; but we must wait, and tarry, God's leisure. How slow is the growth of the babe, to be a man of service to his fellow-creatures ! how limited and scanty his services, at the best ! It is the same in the Church : and though we know not now, we shall know hereafter, why the longings of the new creature in Christ Jesus to be without fault are so strong, yet not to be satisfied till mortality is swallowed up of life.

I had the honour of a visit from your full sister in the Lord—Lady Glenorchy. She spent a Sabbath with me, and slept under my roof ;—and—shall

I tell you ?—to my surprise, like yourself, is not a little troubled with fear, lest she should prove but as counterfeit at last :—at the same time, her body, soul, and spirit, are consecrated, with all she hath, to the Lord. She grudges whatever she spends upon herself; and many hundred souls, who were ready to perish, have been saved by the preachers she has sent to them. I spoke in nearly the same terms to her as I did to your Ladyship. Oh that you may both walk in the light of God's countenance, and daily rejoice in His name! May the voice from Heaven speak to your inmost soul, and say, "Fear not! I will save you!"

These lines, I suppose, will find your Ladyship at the Wells, or at Bath. May the one inseparable and all-sufficient Friend be with your spirit! and then the pastors He sends will be more profitable ; or, if none are sent to you, your soul will still prosper and be in health.

From your Ladyship's much indebted servant,

H. VENN.

About this time, Mr. Richard Venn, having retired from business in London, came to reside with his brother at Yelling. The event is thus noticed in a letter to Mr. John Venn.

Yelling, Oct. 15, 1785.

———Your uncle is now come to take up his abode with us, for the short remainder of his days. We meet now, eleven, at family prayer. Oh that the Spirit of grace and supplication may be poured out upon us! I am more and more convinced, that all the difference between those who bring forth no fruit, and those who do, depends upon the different manner in which they hear, and read, and pray. What violence must we do to ourselves, in order to be earnest, steadfast, and persevering, in fighting against our enemies! Pray for me, as I do for you, that we may be able to pray fervently in secret, in the company of the faithful, and in the congregation.———

TO THE REV. M. POWLEY.

MY DEAR FRIEND,   *Yelling*, *Oct.* 26, 1785.

I was glad to see your hand-writing; and return you hearty thanks for your kind inquiry after me, and concern for my complaint. It is, beyond expectation, abated; yet I have not strength to work according to my desire; nor have I any prospect of being ever able to do more than the Sunday duty in my own little church. However, the Lord knoweth our hearts; and where there is a willing mind, He accepteth the will for the deed.

Report always enlarges matters. I cannot say I was *so much* favoured in my trial as to be longing and panting to be gone; but I was kept in perfect peace, and without any will of my own, or any desire but this—that I might not dishonour the cause, nor shew, by a peevish expression or a look of impatience, an ignorance of my own demerit, or a forgetfulness of the dying love of my God and Saviour: for shall such as we are, who speak continually in the congregation such great things of our God and our Rock, not rejoice in suffering His will? When friends and enemies, too, will be sure to inquire whether we practise what we preach, shall the one be cast down, and the other be hardened, by our behaviour in the time of peculiar trial?

It rejoiced me much to hear how greatly you are enabled to bear your heavy cross, in your dear wife's very ill health. What abundant cause have we to say, " Who is a God like ours, doing wonders for the children of men!" Continue to remember me, my dear friend, now I am old and grey-headed. My faculties and my affections were never lively, as they ought to be, in matters of a spiritual nature; but, chilled by age, I feel them already less so than before. I can neither think, nor preach, nor pray, as I have done in time past. Blessed be God! my trust is in the blood and righteousness of Christ, in His promises and covenant; and all is well! Now, in a very few years, we shall meet in the world " where the Lamb receives the honour due unto His name," and where all agree and conspire to help each other to love and praise.

My son goes on well; and is so strict a resident, that I have not had his company for more than a fortnight, this year and four months. I expect him to visit us next week. Dear Mr. Riland, and his wife and son, left us only one hour ago. What a man of God is he! How high in glory shall we soon see him!—His visit has done me good.

From your indebted and affectionate friend,

H. VENN.

TO MR. EDWARD VENN.

Yelling, Nov. 14, 1785.

—— Our house has been, for eight weeks past, full of guests—Mrs. Riland and two children, three daughters of my own, and my brother Richard; and added to these, some visiters;—so that our solitude gives place to society. Cheerfulness, with sweet discourse on things which are the honour of man, and the chief token of God's love to him, make our time pass very swiftly. Presently the scene will change.

The Sunday before last, Mrs. V. and my three daughters received, from the hands of myself and my son, at the Lord's table, the memorial of His precious death. It was a solemn time—probably never to return. There, I trust, we were united in one faith, one hope, and one Lord; and afresh surrendered ourselves to His service, without reserve— chose Him as our portion, and committed into His hands our immortal souls.—Who ever repented of doing so? Would not the language sound prodigious and horrid, if any man, at any time or place, in any situation whatever, should have said, " What a fool have I been for serving Christ so much—for governing myself so much by His commands—for taking so much pains to save my soul!" This simple evidence, then, is decisive and complete in favour of the true Christian's choice: for if the wisdom of his choice were not founded in the unalterable nature of things, it could not fail but some or other, amidst the millions who have made that choice, must have repented, and expressed their disappointment or mistake. Let us therefore, my dear nephew, be more and more earnest in the service of our God— doing all with singleness of eye to please Him; and feel more and more how slight and transient is our connexion with the objects of sense—how strong and permanent our connexion with spiritual things!

We often talk of you and yours, and should enjoy your company with us. It has pleased God now to remove my complaint; but I find an inward weakness when I preach, which indicates the tabernacle of clay has not long to stand. Would to God I could always feel as a dying creature should, and be on the wing for heaven!

The Lord bless you and yours!

I remain yours, in the best bonds,

H. Venn.

On the 20th December, 1785, Mr. Venn's eldest daughter was united in marriage to Mr. Elliott. Miss Jane Venn was staying with Mr. and Mrs. Elliott, on a visit, when the following letter was written to her.

TO MISS JANE C. VENN.

MY DEAR DAUGHTER, *Yelling, Dec.* 27, 1785.

—— An infinite preference of what God delights in, and creates in His own children, is the mark of a sound mind, the source of pure satisfaction, and of pleasure never fading. A great part of our warfare is, to overcome our natural propensity—of seeking happiness in meats and drinks, in dress and show; which only nourish our disease, and keep us from communion with God, as our chief good. More than thirty-seven years since, He was pleased, in His adorable mercy, to give me a demonstration that all was vanity and vexation of spirit, but Himself. From that hour, (such is the energy of Divine teaching!) rising up and lying down, going out and coming in, I felt this truth. I begun and continued to seek the Lord and His strength, and His face evermore. I then was led to know how the poverty and empti- ness of all terrestrial good could be well supplied from the fulness of our adorable Jesus. And, oh! how unspeakably blessed am I, that I see my child- ren impressed with the same precious and invalu- able feelings! and that I hope (though a very few years will finish my life on earth), upon the best grounds, that we shall enjoy an eternity together in glory!—when you shall know your father—not the poor, polluted, *hasty*, sinful creature he now is—but holy, " without spot, or wrinkle, or any such thing;" and when I shall know my dear children, not as emerging from a sea of corruption, and struggling against the law in their members warring against the law in their minds, and needing such frequent intimations to do what is right ; but when, naturally and constantly, all within and without will be per- fectly holy. Oh, what a meeting will that be, when all my prayers for your precious souls, ever since you were born—when all my poor, yet well-meant instructions and lessons from the Word of God, and all your own petitions, shall be fully answered ; and we shall dwell in a perfect union together, inconceivable on earth, in the love of God for ever and ever! Such sensations I enjoy, in these views, as give me a foretaste of heaven—such sensations as compel me to break forth in fervent prayer—

> Oh that all may seek and find
> Every good in Jesus join'd!
> Him may all our souls adore,
> Love Him, praise Him, evermore!

Let this spiritual good be what you seek after, more and more. By no means rest satisfied with the communications with which you have been favoured; but plead them—as I do, after no less an example than that of Moses—for much greater. He prayed, " Lord! thou hast begun to shew me thy greatness and thy glory;" and then desired brighter discoveries.

We all send our most cordial love to our son and daughter. Tell my son, I shall hope to hear from him, before it is long. I daily remember him; begging of the Lord, that, after all his employments are over, he may be enabled to come into the presence of the Lord, and bow before the Throne of Grace, with a contrite spirit, and a soul longing after God, and the salvation of his wife, his mother, his children, and all his near relations.

To God our Saviour I commend you all!

H. Venn.

TO MR. CHARLES ELLIOTT.

MY DEAR SON,   *Yelling, Jan.* 24, 1786.

Many thanks for your long letter! We all join in congratulating you that the ceremonious visits are done, and your purgatory and penance are over. Strange and absurd is the way of men, to consume so much time with people who care not for them; and not to select a few, whose spirit, taste, and pursuits, being quite congenial with their own, the intimacy would be pleasing and profitable: but for serious Christians to fall into this practice, is lamentable inconsistency with their great business. *Their* time is wanted (all they can spare from necessary secular employment) to gain more knowledge of the glory of the Lord, and the excellency of their God—more bright evidences of their union with Him, and more likeness to Him; which cannot be, if time is not well husbanded, and companions well chosen.

We feel wishes, as you do, were it lawful to give them place, that we might pass our time together here; but, in wisdom and mercy, our Lord and Saviour will have it otherwise. Probably we should be less in prayer, and less fervent, were we not separate. Occasional visits, being short, have a tendency to raise our desires intensely to that better country where all the endearments of Christian love, between husband and wife, parents and children, brothers and sisters, flourish in perfection; and, contrasted with the transient interviews below, the permanent eternal abode together in the regions of bliss will be inconceivably sweeter: for I am fully persuaded, from Scriptural warrant, that all the persons we are particularly interested in, while in the body, and closely connected with—all who have been the constant witnesses of our example, and either edified or infected by it—all such will be eternal witnesses to us, and we to them, that we are adjudged according to our works. The full tide of love, for ever flowing and circulating through all the company of heaven, is founded, maintained, and increased, first, in and by the love of God to them all; then, by the recollection of offices of love which were done on earth, which will be repeated in heaven with all alacrity. The angels, who minister to the heirs of salvation, have all their desires fulfilled respecting them, when they have brought them into Abraham's bosom: and those heirs love them for their services. Evangelists and pastors love the sheep called by their preaching; and those chosen souls behold with rapture in heaven the men of God to whom they owe themselves. And this ground of mutual love increases from the life in heaven; which certainly is inconceivably active and useful, while gratitude, and every generous sensibility which perfect souls possess, reign there. With steadfast expectation of *our* eternal abode there, I at large remember yourself and my daughter, day by day. I am never out of your company. " Faith, the evidence of things not seen," makes you and Eling, and all my children, present with me. We are travelling on to God; looking out for the coming of the Lord.

We all unite in love to dear E.— Mrs. V. holds up charmingly.—I have begun again to have the people one night in the week : near fifty come. Oh that Jesus our Lord would win their hearts !

The best blessings rest upon you !

From your affectionate father, and servant in Christ,

H. VENN.

MY DEAR FRIEND,   *Yelling, Jan.* 25, 1786.

I thank you heartily for your kind wishes respecting my daughter, who took the name of Elliott the 10th of last month. I am filled with admiration at the good and gracious providence. Such are her husband's profitable conversation, amiable manners, and fervent prayers, that, instead of losing an instructor or pattern of good works, in going from her father's house, her change is much for the better, respecting both.

I am glad you are going to the press, in your own name. May our Lord give you the desire of your heart! And where you cannot come to speak, and when you are dead, may you speak to the purpose, in your Catechism!

God be gracious (I can say from my heart) to your precious little branch! May you be taught of God to bring him up wisely. The great danger is, from surfeiting a child with religious doctrines, or over-much talk. Doctrines they are too young to understand; and too frequent talking to them is wearisome to them. Too many parents greatly err, in expecting the religion of a child should be nearly the same as their own. Much have I thought on the subject; and much pains, indeed, have I taken with my children; and, God knoweth, desiring this one thing—that He would give them the knowledge and love of His ever-blessed name. But I did not give them formal instructions till they were eight years old; and then, chiefly set before

them the striking facts in the Old Testament, or
the miracles in the New; and laboured much to
set before them the *goodness* of our God, in things
they could understand—in inclining my heart
to love them—in all the comforts we enjoyed
together.   And, watching providential occurrences,
I made use of them, to give a body and substance to
spiritual truth.   One method, I remember, used to
affect them much, which I was careful to improve—
carrying them to see an afflicted Child of God,
rejoicing in tribulation, and speaking of His love.
To this day, they tell me of one and another whom
they saw happy, though poor and in pain.

My son has been blessed in his work, and is very
much favoured in his situation.   Mr. and Mrs. Parry,
who brought him there, treat him as a brother; and
keeping very little company in the country, they
are much together: this, as he is quite alone, we
are very thankful for.

Last month I preached in Cambridge, after an
interval of thirty-seven years.   I exchanged with
my friend Simeon.   Many gownsmen, and some
Masters of Arts, were present.   I read my sermon,
on 1 Sam. ii. 25.

I also went over to hear Mr. Isaac Milner keep
his Divinity Act.   His subject was, 'Justification
by faith only:'—his Thesis admirable: taken in
substance from Jonathan Edwards.   He did well.
The Schools were crowded, more than ever was
seen of late years; and, no doubt, good will come
from men of the first-rate abilities holding out to
notice Divine Truth.   May he preach and live as a
minister of Christ!—You will say, Amen!

Mrs. Venn joins me in best respects to Mrs. Stillingfleet.—Pray for an aged minister.

Yours, in Christian love,

H. VENN.

TO MRS. ELLIOTT.

Yelling, Feb. 22, 1786.

NEVER, my dear daughter, did I remember, with more solemnity, a 7th of February, than I did the last. Before the day dawned, I lifted up my soul to God; and then, in the family, we implored Him to guard, guide, and bless you and yours. Your birth-day led me to serious meditation on the present state of your existence, compared with that you will, I trust, enjoy in eternity. An inspired writer states the difference in four remarkable particulars; which I shall choose for my subject, in addressing you on your birth-day.

You made your appearance in this world, clothed in a body sown in *corruption*, composed of so many frail and perishable parts, that no care or medicine can prevent its continual tendency to decay, and, after a few years, its total dissolution, when not one part shall remain joined to another. This your body shall be raised again in *incorruption*, firmer than the strong mountains, more durable than the sun: millions of ages shall pass without making the least impression, to impair it.

The body, which is now your appointed tabernacle, is sown in *dishonour;* brought forth, not with smiles, with joy and gladness, in comfort to mother and child, but in pain and sorrow, in tears, and under various marks of the righteous penalty inflicted for the great offence : the child is, of necessity, subject to pains and diseases, which disfigure and emaciate its form. By and by it waxes old and deformed, as a moth-eaten garment; stoops, and totters ; till it becomes, at last, ghastly to the view, and, like a thing most dishonourable, must be sunk in the earth. The same body you are to receive, raised in *glory*, fashioned exactly after the pattern of the Saviour on Mount Tabor, when His face shone as the sun in his strength—every limb more radiant than the brightest gem in a monarch's crown. The glory of your body shall excite and command admiration of so noble a work of God, from all saints and angels, evermore.

The body you now have is sown in *weakness :* it must be watched and tended, continually, to be safe ;—in weakness, not only during infancy, but always exposed to falls, and bruises, and broken limbs ;—in weakness, so as to tire with employment, and, unless its springs, like those of a clock, be wound up every night by sleep, good for nothing ;— in weakness, soon reduced, by disease, to lie upon a bed, not able to help itself; and then placed in the tomb, where it soon becomes the prey of worms. This, your body, shall be raised in *power*, strong and mighty ; never subject to weariness ; swift to move, as with eagle's wings ; in no more need of dull sleep, the image of death, to recruit its strength;—in power, to persevere, without intermission, in the great services to which it shall be appointed ; and able to bear " an exceeding and eternal weight of glory," a very small part of which would sink the body of flesh into a swoon and fear, great as was seen in the beloved disciple, who fell as dead at the feet of Jesus.

Your body was sown a *natural* body—at your birth, to be sustained, like all other animals, by the fruits of the earth, and by the elements; fashioned to relish nothing higher than what can be seen by the eye of flesh, and handled with the hands; so that its joys and griefs, fears and hopes, and all its sensations, are low, and like the brutes. But it shall be raised up a *spiritual body*, i. e. one every way accomplished to see, admire, and delight in spiritual objects and exercises;—no more a hindrance and clog to the glorified soul; but an aid and help, sinless in all its tendencies—all eye, all ear, all sense, respecting the visible works of God: and an excellent medium of conveying still greater bliss to the soul than it would know without the body; otherwise it would not be re-united to its former inmate.

The inhabitants of such an incorruptible glorious body, mighty and spiritual, I hope to see my sons and daughters; and, in such infinite dignity, dwell with the Lord our God, who hath formed us for Himself, for ever. May this our future eternal existence be ever before our eyes, realized to our minds, and the desire of our hearts! Amen! and Amen!

Accept love from us all, to yourself, and my son and Jane. My plan is, to come alone, on April 20th or 21st, to you; your mamma and uncle to follow. I believe (as my son is so very kind as to offer me a stable) I shall come on horseback, as riding is of so much service. I am going with this to Caxton, where I expect a letter from you. K. is very poorly, and grows much thinner. I feel much, and pray for her. Were she well, I should have no cross, but the plague of my own heart. Such a state we must not expect here. What thankfulness should fill our hearts for such an open winter! The cattle must have perished, if deep snow and hard frost had continued. I did not mention what a good Sacrament our last was—forty-six communicants! and the time solemn. Mrs. J—— told me she never desired so much to live, as she does now to die. " Oh," she said, " Sir, I would not part with my portion in Christ for a king's ransom! I tell my husband I shall presently leave him; and that if he do not cleave to the Lord, he will soon be a poor creature."—An evident simplicity, and godly sincerity, give weight to her words, and comfort to my heart. Poor Mr. —— looks guilty and miserable: alas! he is ruining his wife and family, and his own soul, by the company he keeps. It grieved me to see him and his wife here! She, poor woman! I hope will be upheld. The Lord Jesus be with your spirit; and unite us both, and all of us, with you, in life for evermore!

From your affectionate father,

H. VENN.

During the months of May and June, 1786, Mr. Venn visited London for a few weeks, and preached each Sunday at Surrey Chapel. The following extracts refer to this visit:—

—— I have crowded audiences. Many of the clergy are generally present. The Sub-dean of the Chapel Royal was there last Sunday, and came into the vestry to speak to me. Mr. Cecil says I do very wrong to come for so short a time. He would persuade me to undertake for half the year. Vain would be the attempt, unless I kept a curate. Mr. Wilberforce has been at the chapel, and attends the preaching constantly. Much he has to give up! And what will be the issue, who can say ? ——

—— How religion prospers in this great capital, I cannot say. The hearers are very numerous ; but success in the sound conversion of the soul is but rarely found. This is matter of great grief, everywhere. My son tells me he has preached to large congregations, for some months, at Sporle, two miles from Dunham; but he is much cast down, because none have come to him, inquiring what they must do to be saved. However, we must go on, with all long-suffering and doctrine. And much shall we need the Spirit of God, to quicken and comfort us, that we faint not.

—— If I mistake not, Mr. R. knows Mr. ——. Alas ! the poor man is sadly deluded, and is doing mischief daily. He is a vehement maintainer of the heresy of Universal Salvation. Twice I have been in his company ; and both times he was full of debate. In short, he will soon think, if he does not already, that his error is the only gospel.——

F F 2

TO JAMES KERSHAW, ESQ.

Yelling, Aug. 1, 1786.

—— How did your description of your Sabbath-day's journey to Huddersfield bring to my mind some of the sweetest hours of my life ! With thankfulness to the Head of the Church, I bless God you were welcome at the vicarage ; and from thence could go up to the House of the Lord, and hear His Gospel from His faithful servants. The worship of His Name, in self-abasement, and in the Holy Ghost, is both an imitation of the work above, and a foretaste of the bliss there enjoyed. And when both the preacher and the hearers come prepared to meet in the House of God, as soldiers do for a review before the king, or as musicians for a jubilee, how far beyond all that gives the senses delight are the pleasures of God's House! To be morning-preacher at Huddersfield, for some Sundays, would revive me, even in my old age. But our lot is not ordered according to our will, but in unerring wisdom and love. I have a dear brother confined to the house, and an affectionate wife too infirm for journeys.

P. R. has been with us on a visit. She is what her father, in his prayers and singleness of heart, has always desired she might be. You will think so too, when I tell you it will be a great grief to her heart to leave my house, where there is very little company, and no amusement or entertainment of any sort which the world takes pleasure in. Our comfort and delight (for we have both in a high degree) is what *they* enjoyed, who wandered about in sheep-skins and goat-skins, and had no lodging better than the dens and caves of the earth.

You will ask, how I bore my work in London?—Thanks be to God! very well.—I took care not to walk, as I did the last year. I had very large and very attentive audiences—not one sleeper, that I could see. My last discourse (when there were many who could not get in) was on 'the sinfulness of sin.' This, and what this subject prepares for (as you sweetly remark in your letter), the glory of Christ, are the whole of my preaching, and, I am persuaded, were the whole of Paul's. Happy is the man who at once beholds the cause of all the misery in earth and hell, in time and in eternity—*sin!*—and the cause of all peace with God and love, of His name, here and in heaven—*Christ,* and His cross!——

H. VENN.

TO LADY MARY FITZGERALD.

MADAM, *Yelling, Aug.* 17, 1786.

A fortnight ago, I received the affecting news of the removal of your loving and beloved sister in Christ, Lady Glenorchy. Very soon after, my daughter, coming from London, informed me you were on the road, and near her house, in order to spend some time with her. This circumstance affected me much. See how uncertain are even the best and most-allowed pleasures we can receive from the creatures of God! Well! I consoled myself that you have made all your happiness in Jesus, and Him Crucified. And though the sudden and unexpected translation of your friend to glory, and

to her exceeding great reward, must, at first, deeply
affect you, you would be soon led to many soothing
and sweet reflections upon your spiritual union with
this departed saint—would rise, in sweet meditations, to the world where your name is enrolled with
hers, as one for whom a mansion is prepared, even
in your Father's house—where all His children meet
together, favoured with His unclouded smile—where
His whole will is done without weariness or defect—
where all His excellency, and all His love, are ever
present to the mind; and the whole family, in love
and perfect harmony, contribute to each other's fulness of felicity, without fear of diminution, or possibility of a change.

My dear fellow-pilgrim and fellow-soldier! yet
a few more conflicts, and yours too shall be the
victory and the triumph!   From all the consecrated
chastisements you have so well endured, to the credit
of your profession, to the undoubted proof of your
heart's whole attachment to your Saviour—being
here partaker with Him in sufferings, and made
conformable to His death—you shall enjoy " a far
more exceeding and eternal weight of glory." Then
will you say, with an accent not to be conceived
below, " Oh, what great troubles and adversities hast
Thou shewn me, and yet broughtest me from the
depth of the earth again!"

Oh that your God may make you strong in that
faith which realizes to His saints their inheritance,
the end of their high calling of God in Christ Jesus!
—that not a doubt of His eternal love to your precious soul may lodge within—that you may reckon
yourself appointed as a pillar, to stand for ever in

heaven, a monument of grace reigning in your salvation.   Scarcely a day passes that I do not remember you at the Mercy-seat; and, sometimes, with
those sweet sensations which Christian love, height-
ened by a great debt of gratitude, excites, when
entreating *Him* to recompense our friends—friends
most kind and condescending—whom we cannot.

A single line, to know how you do, I shall much
prize; but shall be grieved you should write more,
so poorly as, I fear, you are in health.—The comforts of the Father's love, the consolation of Christ,
and the fellowship of the Holy Ghost, ever refresh,
support, and fill your soul!

From your most indebted servant in the Gospel,

H. VENN.

Lady Mary Fitzgerald's answer to this letter has, happily, been preserved.   I take the liberty, therefore, of
inserting it in this correspondence, as it presents an interesting view of her state of mind; and will also serve to
explain the first part of the letter of Mr. Venn, which will
follow it.

FROM LADY MARY FITZGERALD.

MY DEAR FRIEND,   *Quorn, Aug.* 1786.
Your kind and very precious letter really distresses me.   I cannot bear my fellow-creatures
should see me in so different a light from what my
God does.

Dear Lady Glenorchy's departure, which was the
occasion of your writing, was a most blessed change
for her, but a sad providence for the Church below.

—But, oh! I dare not think of myself as a sister to that blessed spirit, who am the meanest, and most unworthy, of all our dear Lord's servants: but true it is, if I do not deceive myself, "I had rather be a door-keeper in the house of God," &c. She was, indeed, a dear and highly-favoured Child of God!

Her removal made me give up all thoughts of going to Matlock. Bath would not agree with my present state (unless it were absolutely necessary for my health); therefore I persuaded my kind and attentive friend, Mrs. Mendis, to stay with me till next week: and having earnestly prayed our dear and compassionate Lord to open or shut any door which shall be to the profit of my soul, I have written to Mr. Robinson, begging the favour of him to look out for a quiet airy lodging for me at Leicester, for a few weeks. I passed a Sabbath there, in my way here, and found his preaching very profitable; but I desire to be divested of self-will. The air is remarkably good and clear there, which made me think of it.

I felt, with gratitude, your delicacy in not mentioning my heavy affliction*—yet taking occasion, from dear Lady Glenorchy's safe landing in the spiritual Canaan, to inquire of my health. My nerves are much shattered, as you may imagine; and my health indifferent, though greatly better than I could have hoped, after so dreadful a shock, at the end of long and painful anxiety. I needed to be severely chastised and humbled. Gracious is the Lord, in all His dealings towards His creatures!

* The death of an eldest son, under very distressing circumstances.

His long forbearance and patience with us astonish me. He is not only just, but merciful, even in judgment. Glory be to His adorable name! He put a song into my heart, that I might glorify him in the furnace. I can truly say, that, instead of daring to murmur any one moment during this afflictive dispensation, I have been constrained to admire the patience of our adorable God and Saviour.—But I must have done: the subject is too much for my feelings.

I am much concerned to hear that useful and valuable minister, Dr. Conyers, is probably by this time removed from this world to a better. This sounds cruel to him, for whom I had a most sincere regard; but, self apart, I think him so great a loss to the Church militant, that I should rejoice the Lord had seen it expedient he had waited some time longer for his crown. This, you will say, is a bad return for the comfort he has often been made to me by his conversation: but I am a poor selfish wretch—I condemn myself for it. Our Lord certainly knows best what is good, both for His church and people. However, I comfort myself that I may be thankful for my dear friends who are spared; and earnestly hope and pray you, my dear Sir, may long be of that number! Forgive me! but I do most sincerely hope and trust our Lord has much more work for you on earth.

I return you many thanks for your precious letter, though it is truly painful to me to be so mistaken by my friends; and find it hurtful to be looked upon as something, though I am really worse than nothing. It seems to me as if it brought judgments on me, to bring me down again to the dust, where I ought ever to lie in the deepest self-abasement. Believe me, I need much pulling down, or our gracious Lord would not inflict so much. Yet, oh! how tenderly does He deal with such a wretch, in "the midst of judgment remembering mercy," and inclining the hearts of His dear children to be so kind, attentive, and tender towards me!

I have disobeyed your kind command of writing but three lines.

Believe me, with most sincere respect and regard, your unworthy, truly affectionate friend and servant,

MARY FITZGERALD.

TO LADY MARY FITZGERALD.

MADAM,   *Birmingham, Sept.* 14, 1786.

I hope, when you leave Leicester, you will try Yelling air; and if much fervent prayer, to make your visit of use and comfort to your soul, may prevail, it will not be wanting.—By Mr. Simeon, I received your Ladyship's letter.

When we speak of the grace of God which our Christian friends have received, it is not to be concluded that we forget they are still polluted exceedingly, and in many things offend;—it is not that they should cherish one thought of self-complacency. We know it is contrary to their best feelings. But do those of a sorrowful spirit, who are in the midst of severest conflicts, and, withal, too apt to write bitter things against themselves, want no word of encouragement? Ought they not to give God thanks that they are enabled to walk before the

Church uprightly — when their fellow Christians assure them they do? I labour to copy, as nearly as I can, from the unerring word. Now, in that book, I find St. Paul and St. John, especially St. Paul, speak in terms of high commendation of the Christians of Philippi and Thessalonica; and telling even them of Corinth, that they were "the Epistle of Christ, known and read of all men;" and were an honour to him, as His epistle. He well understood this would animate them afresh, and invigorate their minds more zealously to serve the Lord. Indeed, where there is a spark of ingenuity, commendation does good: I have seen it work gratitude and self-abasement. How does St. Paul commend his beloved Timothy! How does St. John extol his beloved Gaius, declaring he could "wish him nothing better than that his body should be healed and prosper, even as his soul prospered"! I did therefore, and do still, think it is very fit and right for me, when my highly-esteemed friends in Christ are sorely afflicted, and under storms and great distresses, to put them in remembrance that the Lord "hath done great things" for them; and, with the consecrated cross, has assured them the crown of life, and given them the pledge of it, in changing them into His own likeness, in lowliness, patience, and submission.— I will write no more on this point, hoping, as I do with great satisfaction, that I shall have an opportunity, at Yelling, of conversing largely on this matter.— I enjoy my friends much more at home than in London. I have them to myself, without interruption.

Glory be to God for his love to us! The night

of darkness and woe, of the miseries and corruptions we groan under, is far spent : the day, the mild, sweet, joyous, triumphant day, is at hand.

> When, in th'eternal world unknown,
> I'm call'd to appear before Thy throne,
> O Rock of Ages! cleft for me,
> Then will I hide myself in Thee.

To that dear Saviour I do not forget, frequently, and sometimes (I can say) fervently, to commend you.———

I know not when I shall see my beloved friends again in London ; but soon I shall meet them all on Mount Zion, and drink with them there of the river which flows from the throne of God and of the Lamb. Within this last year I have had more knowledge, and more meditation, of the state of those who die in the Lord, when they are with Him, than in all the years I have lived before.

I am so much enfeebled, that at three several sittings I have been employed to finish this letter. I trust I shall never be weary, while I breathe, of praying for my friends ; but the work of writing is a burden.

Though our heavenly inheritance is not in its value fluctuating, yet the state of the Church militant, varying much, makes it more desirable at some times than at others. *Now*, then, when Atheism, and a bitter enmity against God and man, rages, and spreads wider and wider, how sweet is the thought of entering into rest! May it please God we may soon enter!

From your much-indebted friend,

H. VENN.

TO MRS. RILAND.

Yelling, Oct. 25, 1786.

My dear friend is, by this time, we suppose, returned from the excursion.   Dear Mr. Riland, we
hope, is better of his complaint, and glorifying God
by his suffering with cheerfulness what the flesh
would resent—confinement, or cutting off in point
of active usefulness.   You must be sure to mention
how you all go on—particularly yourself.

We have been disappointed of our friends' intended visit.   Master Parry was not well enough to
be left.—Now we are on the point to be quite
solitary—three old people, decaying evidently ; but
not cast down.   The hope set before us is an exhi-
larating cordial.

I awaked the other night with a very pleasing
sensation of the joy of being with " the spirits of
the just made perfect."   The several ingredients
which undoubtedly constitute their exalted felicity
at once occurred ; full light, and zeal, and love,
and holiness—full conviction, never ceasing, from
whence we were taken, by what means, how preserved, how distinguished, how rich to all eternity !
—" They thought not of that pleasant land," was
the reproach laid to Israel of old, and which I am
sensible belongs to me also.   Seldom have I dwelt
and pondered on the inheritance reserved in heaven
for all that belong to Christ.   But nothing less than
close habitual attention to the felicity of God's
chosen will give it due weight.   On this pleasing
subject let our contemplations dwell, and our

thoughts unite, till we know perfectly, above, what is "the hope of God's calling, and what the riches of the glory of his inheritance in the saints."——

The Child that was born, and the Son that was given to us, be your Counsellor, your God, your Father, and your peace! In Him may we live, here and in eternity!

From your affectionate father,

H. Venn.

TO MISS JANE C. VENN.

MY DEAR JANE,   *Yelling, Oct.* 28, 1786.

In expectation of your letter, I sent this morning to Caxton. We were not disappointed. To Him that heareth prayer be all praise returned, for His goodness to us—for His preservation of mother and child!

—— By the same post I received a letter from dear Mr. Thornton, saying that he, the last Sunday, introduced Mr. Samuel Johnson to two hundred and fifty of his future congregation, aboard the Hulk at Woolwich. Through the influence of Mr. Wilberforce with Mr. Pitt, he is appointed Chaplain to Botany Bay, with a salary of 180*l.* per annum. I trust he will prove a blessing to these lost creatures! Those that stole, will there steal no more; for having no receivers of stolen goods, no alehouses, &c., they will be under no temptation to steal. With what pleasure may we consider this plan of peopling that far-distant region, and other opening connexions with the Heathen, as a foundation for the Gospel of our God and Saviour to be preached unto them;—when "a vast multitude, whom no man can number," shall "call upon His Name;"—when "the wilderness shall become a fruitful field," and all the savageness of the Heathen shall be put off, and all the graces of the Spirit shall be put on. Though neither I, nor you, who are yet in youth, (much less I, who am stricken in years) shall be living on earth when this fact comes to pass, yet we shall be well informed of it above. All heaven will break forth in that song of praise, "Allelujah! for the Lord God Omnipotent reigneth!"— See what honour God putteth upon them who love Him in sincerity! To be the means of sending the Gospel to the other side of the globe—what a favour! Mr. Thornton says the Archbishop of Canterbury and Sir Charles Middleton seem much to approve the sending of Mr. Johnson.

We shall expect to hear from you once a week.— We suppose you are much taken up with the little stranger, and give it many kisses. May we all now feel afresh the force of that holy exclamation—"Oh that men would praise the Lord for His goodness, and declare the wonders that He doeth for the children of men!"

From your affectionate father,

H. VENN.

TO JAMES KERSHAW, ESQ.

MY DEAR FRIEND, *Yelling, Nov.* 25, 1786.

What a cause for thankfulness, that you can use the Buxton waters; and use them as the preparation of your Heavenly Father, and in the spirit of the lame man at the pool;—and, when you are relieved, can ascribe your help to Him, of whom cometh your salvation, and the medicine to heal the sickness of your soul!

As I shall not be able, as soon as I could wish, to come and preach to you myself, I will send a friend, whom you used much to esteem, in my stead. There is no fear but you will give him a kind reception. His name is Adam, "who being dead, yet speaketh." I forward you a copy of his Private Thoughts. Much have I been profited by them. Though the writer was an Arminian, I read his works as if his words came fresh from his lips, sitting by my side. Among many beautiful and striking passages, I will mention one, which I instantly turned into a prayer for myself, and you, and all my Christian friends; and hope often to do so, till I pass hence. The passage is, that we may have a distinct consciousness of the infinite superiority of the heavenly state, above the present—strong desires after it—a meetness for it in Christ—so that, when the summons comes, we may rush into it with joy and transport. May you enjoy this blessed preparation for a glorious eternity! —Give my love to all your branches; and tell Henry, my namesake, he can now get the start of me, as I did six years ago of him, in running. I am a grandpapa; and appear with a pair of spectacles, reading the papers.

The first week in September, we went to my son's—the thing he had perfectly longed for. We staid three nights at his house. Eight of us went on the Monday, and returned on the Saturday. His name is up in the country. He lectures on Tuesdays and Thursdays, in his house—generally to more than fifty, sometimes seventy, hearers.—

" A wise son maketh a glad father." Help me to be thankful!

Every one who knows our good friend —————— is struck, as you are, at his wildness. A man of fifty, in a most useful sphere, greatly honoured by his ministry, after laying the stress on things essential and vital, to turn aside to contentions—oh, lamentable! We met, eleven in number, to receive his Paper of Objections*; not one of which is new, or has not been debated over and over again. We all gave him our judgment, which was unanimous. Instead of aiming all his blows against sin, Satan, and the world, as heretofore, they must now be levelled against the Church of England.   Indeed, it is a step which will have sad consequences, respecting many serious souls who were serving God in quietness and comfort, and adorning their profession, having no objections to make.   Now they will be tossed to and fro, while many will conclude religion itself is nothing substantial.   The good Lord be our guide!——   H. VENN.

TO THE REV. JAMES STILLINGFLEET.

MY DEAR FRIEND,   *Yelling, March* 7, 1787.

Your letter was very acceptable to me, as some months had passed since I had heard from you. " We know not what a day would bring forth," and

---

* The Objections were against the discipline of the Church of England.   The person alluded to did not leave the Church.   He was dissuaded from that step, chiefly by the advice of a Dissenting Minister ; who frankly laid before him the disadvantages he would have to encounter ; and assured him, that if he were himself in the Church, he should thank God for it, and remain in it.

how it may fare with our friends; and are, on that account, glad to hear of them frequently.

I sympathize with you in your troubles from the corruption of nature; feeling myself harassed with hardness of heart, coldness of affection towards God and man, and by slightly performing secret duties, when I so well know God is " a rewarder (only) of them who diligently seek Him." How totally does the estimate I made of myself, thirty-five years since, differ from what I know now to be my real condition! I then confidently expected to be holy *very soon*, even as St. Paul was; and that there would be no other difference here between me and angels, than that I, by watching, fasting, and prayer, without ceasing, had conquered and eradicated sin, which they had never known. *Now*, I compare myself with the Great Apostle, and can scarcely perceive a diminutive feature or two of what shines so prominently in that noble saint.

Nay, in reading the life of a minister many degrees inferior to St. Paul, I see so much grace abounding in him, as to make my own poverty very conspicuous—I mean the life of dear Mr. Fletcher. —What a shining example! What a proof that zeal, and constant application, and self-denial, can work wonders! What a proof, that communications of the Spirit of Christ, though not for merit of any thing in us, yet are always in proportion to the pains we take in setting apart solemn times for humiliation, and for seeking after God, that we may have much counsel, direction, and blessing from Him, in our work, and in our own souls. Without the aid obtained from Heaven, in this way (yet still holding the Head, and depending on Christ alone for righteousness and strength), our conversation will never be convincing and striking as becomes our office; nor will there be a fulness, a solidity, an unction, and nourishment for souls in our ministrations: we shall see little fruit of our labours.

I have been long kept back from practising what I did for seven years, with much profit—*fasting*. My wife and daughter have exclaimed, I should ruin my health, &c. I have at last come to a composition; which is, that on Fridays I shall not breakfast, nor be with them till dinner. By this means I have some time for solemn recollection, and more attention to the things of God. And the advantage even of this little sequestration is evident: I find more of a spiritual mind—am more sensible of the Divine Presence—more watchful that no foolish conversation proceedeth out of my mouth—and I am more helped in preaching. Indeed, ministers of Christ must be a good deal in retirement, to gird up the loins of the mind; or we shall be in a great strait at last.——

Yours, &c.

H. VENN.

TO MRS. RILAND.

Yelling, March 21, 1787.

WE reckon, week after week, my beloved friend, upon receiving tidings from you; but are disappointed. This comes to quicken your pen: or if, as we fear, you are not well enough to write, tell my pupil we hope she will take up her ready pen; for a ready one it is, whenever she pleases to use it.

Since you heard from us last, we have been afflicted with much sickness in our family. I brought on my illness by my own folly ;—for, being at Cambridge the last Sunday in January, I preached there three times the same day ; and for five nights sat up talking, with great delight, and conversing, with Dr. Jowett, his brother, Mr. Coulthurst, Mr. Simeon, and Mr. Farish, till past twelve—a very late hour for me! Our whole conversation was concerning the glory of our Lord, His infinite love, and the happiness of all who know and serve Him. The joyful inexhaustible theme gave me spirits during the time ; but when I came home, I suffered for it.

Upon my return home, I received a letter from my son, saying, that Mr. and Mrs. Parry were much afflicted by the loss of their youngest daughter, and the dangerous sickness of the son. I determined to pay them a visit ; and set out on Monday, the 4th of February, on horseback, by seven in the morning, in a very cold, frosty east wind. Before I had ridden four miles, I was so overcome and oppressed with the cold, that I was forced to turn back, and was taken ill, and have been confined nearly three weeks. One Sunday, the post to Cambridge failing, Mr. Simeon could not come, as had been given out ; and the bells had called the people together. I desired that they might come to my house. The kitchen and scullery were full ; and several stood outside. I spoke on that glorious declaration of Paul, " I have learned, in whatsoever state I am, therewith to be content." Many shed tears, and deep was the attention : in short, I think they were much more impressed with my discourse, in such circumstances, than if I had been, as usual, in the pulpit. Shall I tell you what a tax I paid for my preaching?—It did me much good, and almost removed at once my ailments! But Ruth was sure I should kill myself: Kitty looked as if she believed as much : Mrs. Venn was as much out of temper as she can be: but Jane, the wise, the discreet Jane, was, alas! quite angry to see me so very imprudent. I could only meekly reply, " It is good, sometimes, to venture." Within this last fortnight I am much stronger; and, what is better than strength, my congregation is increased, and I have some of the hearers in a hopeful way.

———— Were it lawful, how should I give way to wishes that I were in the neighbourhood of my dear friends and dear children! but that is, to a Christian, forbidden. Too much pleasure, in our situation here, might damp our desire after a better. It surely would.—My dear friend, since we can spend so few hours on earth in sweet society as Christians and pilgrims, let us be the more earnest to get into the world where all is solid and permanent, and we shall be ever with the Lord.

Tell my dear pupil, I know I am in her debt, and I shall hope to pay before I go to London. I think of her with pleasure ; and hope to hail her arrival one day on the heavenly coast, where all that is sweet and amiable in her disposition shall be brought to perfection ; and what is so pleasing to behold now only in the bud and the blossom, shall be unfolded, and shine in beauty, surpassing far all that is admired in the Church below. Tell her, Nanny Marchill died last week—one of the meekest

on earth—whom God has now, I doubt not, beautified with his salvation. I preached her funeral sermon with great comfort, on Rev. xiv. 13.

We all join in love to Mr. R., yourself, and the
branches. The Lord preserve you evermore from
all evil—preserve your souls and bodies, your going
out and coming in, henceforth and for evermore!

Your affectionate friend,

H. VENN.

TO MR. ELLIOTT.

MY DEAR SON, *Yelling, April* 3, 1787.

Scarcely a single day has passed since your
letter was received by me, which mentioned your
desire that I would send you some directions how
you might be heavenly-minded, that the request has
been forgotten; though I could give no answer till
now. There are no other rules and directions to
be trusted in, than those which the inspired writings
contain.

As soon as a Christian desires to be of a heavenly
mind, he has already begun to be so. The light
from above has shined into his heart. He is a child
of the light and of the day. His walk, consequently,
will be governed by this light; which will increase
by his frequent aspirations after his God, in such
language as this : " Whom have I in heaven but
Thee ?" and, " Thou, O God, art the thing which I
long for!" Sweetly drawn by the beauty and love
of your heavenly Bridegroom, you will be jealous of
His rival, which is, in all of us—self-love.

I can only relate to you how I have hitherto (and

I am nearly at the end of my warfare) been preserved. I never had such a weight and variety of affairs to manage, as a man engaged in so much business as yourself: but I had a large young family, very dear to me, and not enough for their maintenance from year to year; and, in case of my death, they were to be destitute. I was, however, wonderfully free and cheerful in my heart. I think I should not have been more so, if I had been without a child. My preservative was wholly this: " He that hath the Son, hath life ; and he that hath not the Son, hath not life." A full and powerful conviction of this truth was necessarily attended with constant prayer for them and myself, that we might have this one thing needful;—which grew, by this means, in price and value ; and nothing was suffered to come for a moment in competition with it. I used often to think, and say to myself, " Was Christ enough for peace, comfort, and joy, to the first Christians ; and is He not now the same ?—enough to the poor, destitute, afflicted members of His body, with whom I hope to live for ever ; and will He not be enough for me and my children ?" So (with great thankfulness to God for it!) I conclude you do; that when you have prosperity, and your gain increases, you immediately lift up your soul, and say, " Let not money, but Thyself, be my exceeding joy! I thank thee for the success! O let it not corrupt and poison my mind, by increasing worldly lusts!" In like manner, when you suffer loss, and are unjustly treated, or basely deceived, your spiritual mind will feel disposed to accept the matter as a fresh proof that all below is vanity and vexation. Thus will you grow more and more spiritually-minded.

But, above all, be sure that, together with the knowledge of Christ Crucified, you take the certain method advised by Him—that is, of giving liberally. " Give alms of such things as ye have." The more you receive in prosperity, the more give. They nobly serve God, adorn their profession, and ensure a blessing upon themselves and family, who are afraid of withholding more than is due—who are afraid of pleading a large family as a reason for not being merciful and liberal. This truly Christian spirit will bring down plenteously the dew of grace upon your souls, make your faces shine, your family comfortable, and your departure full of peace. Ministering to the saints, is a grace which accompanies salvation.

I am much exercised by the sickness of half my family. Yet all is from a Father's and a Saviour's hand. To Him we always commend you; and with all our love, I remain

Your affectionate father,
H. Venn.

TO MR. ELLIOTT.

MY DEAR SON,   *Yelling, Dec.* 7, 1787.

I can easily conceive your want of time to write; and willingly shall we dispense with your letter of thanks.

Our minds are united, and our hearts are one in the union spiritual and eternal. If we communicated any pleasure to you both, we received full as much. We only regretted we could have no more

of your company, and that your health was so indifferent. We are always either talking of, or
thinking of, or praying for you. Moses' prayer in
the mount, while the host of Israel engaged hand
to hand with the enemy, is a striking lesson to the
ministers of God. So ought they to lift up holy
hands, when so many of God's dear children are
in the multiplicity of business, and ready to be
swallowed up by its cares—cares unavoidable. In
my poor way, I follow the example of Moses. Often
I remember you and yours at large, and enjoy a
delicious hour in secret.

What do I not owe to that Almighty grace and infinite love, which has wrought in me such a change!
When I look back forty years of my life, I remember I was perpetually in company, full of animal
spirits, thoughtless, self-pleasing; and solitude would
then have been the heaviest burden to my mind.
Now, to be alone, to be looking on my bed as
probably the spot on which I am to fight the last
battle, before I win Christ, and see Him as He is—
to consider, with the closest attention, the origin,
and the nature, and the consequences of death, to
the friends of Christ—this work invigorates my
mind, and nourishes my soul. I accept the privilege and power of doing thus, and the great opportunity I have for this exercise, with joyful gratitude; saying, " The lot is fallen unto me in a good
ground; yea, I have a goodly heritage."

Not that the men of business, and those exposed
to much greater trials than mine, have cause to
envy such a lot. They who are Christians carry
the good savour into many places; while we are

fixed to a spot. They shew that godliness is
practicable in the most active sphere; they shew
the invincible power of patience, under great provocations; of probity, under strong temptations to
be dishonest; and of mercy and of pity, notwithstanding all incitements to love money, and with-
hold more than is due. I expect with delight to
see yourself, Mr. Evans, Mr. Neal, and many more,
in the Great Day, when admiring and rejoicing
angels and saints, and elders of the Church triumphant, shall say, " Lo! these are the men who
trusted not in riches, but in the Lord; and He was
their hope, their love, their all! "

My wife is much better than she was a fortnight
since. I feel not the least hurt from my late
accident. We enjoy so much, that we often agree
nothing earthly could make an addition to our comfort, but (what we must not wish for one moment)
that we could all of us be much oftener together.

Yours in all love,

H. VENN.

CORRESPONDENCE.

SECTION V.

WE are now arrived at that period in Mr. Venn's life,
when the decay of his bodily strength, and the symptoms
of approaching old age, became more and more apparent·
Hence, his letters may, perhaps, from this time, manifest
an abatement in vigour and comprehension of thought;
but they acquire an additional value, as containing the matured reflections of a mind furnished with long and extensive experience in religion; and also as exhibiting both
the peace and resignation of an aged Christian, during
the last stage of his earthly pilgrimage, and his full assurance of faith in the glory ready to be revealed.

TO THE REV. JOHN VENN.

MY DEAR SON,   *Yelling, June* 19, 1788.

Yours, dated the 12th, came safe, and gave us all
much cause to be thankful. What do we all owe
to the grace of our God, for withholding us from
evil—for delivering from the dominion of our corrup-

tion! Very few are free from sloth and idleness. Averseness to all labour, and all cultivation of the mind, is a considerable part of the universal depravity. With pleasure I read of your progress in human learning : for you will know how to improve it, and use it well for the glory of the Giver of every talent. Our ministry is hindered, because so very few preachers of Christ are pains-taking men, to read much, and to think much, in order to be full men in the pulpit; which, joined with prayer, gives a relish in the people's mind, when they hear us; whereas it is very different, when either reading or thinking is neglected.

Through the goodness of my God, I left London well, and had several very profitable seasons. I am persuaded we are very negligent in respect of our texts. Some of the most weighty and striking are never brought before the people ; yet these are the texts which speak for themselves. You no sooner repeat them, than you appear in your high and holy character, as a messenger of the Lord of Hosts. Within these few weeks, I have found it so. In London, I preached on—"Thus saith the Lord: Cursed be the man that trusteth in man, and maketh flesh his arm, and whose heart departeth from the Lord. For he shall be like the heath in the desert, and shall not see when good cometh ; but shall inhabit the parched places in the wilderness, in a salt land, and not inhabited. Blessed is the man that trusteth in the Lord, and whose hope the Lord is. For he shall be as a tree planted by the waters, and that spreadeth out her roots by the river ; and shall not see when heat cometh, but her leaf shall be green ;

and shall not be careful in the year of drought,
neither shall cease from yielding fruit:" Jer. xvii.
5—8. I contrasted the character described in the
first verse, with the Child of God in the latter.
The very reading of my text fixed the attention,
and raised, as I could see, the expectation of
the hearers ;—and much affected they seemed to
be.   Last Sunday, I saw the same impression,
from—" And the Lord descended in the cloud, and
stood with him there, and proclaimed the name of
the Lord.   And the Lord passed by before him,
and proclaimed, The Lord, the Lord God, merciful
and gracious, long-suffering, and abundant in goodness and truth :" Exod. xxxiv. 5, 6 ;—on which I am
to preach again, God willing, next Lord's-day.   I
feel the good of selecting these passages, to my own
soul.   I have to lament and bewail my ignorance
and great defects for so many years; one thousandth
part of which I do not yet perceive.   I wish you may
attend to this point; and be led to make the chief
and vital parts, as they may be called, of Scripture,
your subjects of discourse.

God be praised for His help, that you have been
able to speak so faithfully to Dr. P. !   Indeed, it is a
rare thing to tell our friends what we see is likely
to hurt them and destroy them.   While I write,
I suppose you are at ———.   May our Lord and
Saviour be with you both, and hear your prayers,
and knit your hearts together in the love of His
name !

I have heard, since I came home, of the death of
old Mrs. Houghton of Huddersfield, and of Mrs.
Kershaw.   Both of them departed in much peace,

enjoying the salvation of God, which I felt with some thankfulness.

I dined yesterday at ——. Mr. B. and Mr. D. met me there :—not a syllable, from either, to edification ! Oh, how suspicious does it appear, when a minister never speaks of his Master, or of all the good things He bestows, except in the pulpit !

The Sunday before last, I preached in the afternoon at Everton: my brother Berridge in the morning. Four years have passed since we heard each other. We both perceived how our voices were weakened; but had a sweet interview, while we talked together of the pity and tender love of our adorable Master towards all His aged ministers, when they are almost past the service of their office. He told me he could pray little out of his own mind ; but the method he used was, to read his Bible, and, as he read, to turn the word into prayer for himself.

Mr. Samuel Knight* lately visited us, from College. He is very visibly increased in knowledge, and his ministerial abilities are very considerable ; and, what is best of all, he seems not at all to know what gifts he has. Adieu, my dear son !

From your affectionate father,

H. Venn.

In another letter, Mr. Venn again alludes to the importance of preaching upon striking texts.

----

* The late Vicar of Halifax.

———— I PREACHED lately upon a subject I never did at Huddersfield—to my shame be it spoken!—nor any where else : Jeremiah xvii. 5—7. It is very humbling to see, at more than threescore years of age, that I have never set before my hearers very many of the most striking and the most instructive parts of God's word. It is a comfort to me, that I am preserved to prevent other pastors doing so poorly as I have done. My friends at Cambridge often ask me for a text, which they make use of. I have advised Simeon, and Coulthurst, and H. Jowett, to mark, as I have done, the capital parts, all through the Bible. Blessed be God, the night is far spent, the day is at hand, when we shall no more, with labour, and study, and prayer, get a little knowledge of the Lord; but a flood of light at once shall break in upon our mind, and we shall know even as we are known!

TO MRS. ELLIOTT.

MY DEAR ELING,   *Yelling, June* 23, 1788.

Were my children enjoying health and prosperity, I believe it would be the worse for them and for myself. The earth would then appear free from the condemnation and curse which it, and its inhabitants, are under. I should forget, that I, the father, and you my dear branches springing from me, are both corrupt, and doomed to feel for a moment, compared to our future state, what we derive from the first Adam, as our natural father—that we may know what we owe for our recovery and salvation to the second, the Lord from heaven. When I think of my dear

children, as I do continually, I find much cause of
thankfulness, that they have all been preserved—all
kept from doing any thing contrary to their Christian profession. What affection I see in them for
their aged father! What hope I entertain, that we
have one Lord, one hope, one pursuit, and one heart
and mind, in preferring Christ to all that dazzles
and leads captive poor mankind!

What, it may be said, can you wish for more?
As a Christian, I answer, Nothing. As a man and
a parent, I am ready to say, The comfort of children
in health and strength. But presently I correct
myself, and pray for my sons and daughters—with
simplicity, only for the comfort of the help of God
—that each of us may see in His light—that from
our birth, to the moment of our death, every step
is a part of the race set (or measured out) before
us, for the trial of our faith, our love, and our patience. So that we never ought to reckon upon the
enjoyment, my dear Eling, even of our most lawful
comforts;—not of a beloved husband or wife—not
of a pleasant child, whose presence exhilarates, and
whose excellency amply recompenses all the watchful care and indefatigable attention we have paid to
form and fashion it for usefulness.

Now is the time of our warfare: we are to fight
under Christ's banner;—not once, or twice, but to
our life's end;—not against a single foe, or a feeble
one, but against the world, the flesh, and the devil.
Though these words, by being familiar to our ears
from our very infancy, make a very slight impression;
yet each enemy, considered apart, is very formi-
dable, and, combined in their aim and attempt to

destroy, invincible, by all human efforts. The Lord
God Omnipotent alone can defeat and trample them
under his feet. To him day by day—I might say,
hour by hour—I am looking for aid and for victory.

On Friday, I received, with a ring, the following
lines from dear Mr. Kershaw :—" To her, whose
name the ring bears, you were very dear. Often,
and especially of late, we recounted our Huddersfield days. They were our golden days;—for to
them, under your instrumentality, we owed ourselves. She walked in the same faith, in humility,
and love, and full dependence, as a sinner, on the
Saviour. As she lived, so she died. Six weeks she
struggled with extreme pain, in fixed composure and
amazing patience : the fear of death was removed,
and his sting drawn : till, on the night of the 16th
of May, she fell asleep, without a struggle, sigh, or
groan ; the very night fifty-two weeks on which my
ever-lamented son fell away on the same arm—the
arm of the Father, and the Husband : and both
were interred on the 20th of May."——

—— May the Lord bring us to drink of the rivers
of pleasure at His right hand, for evermore !

From your affectionate father,

H. VENN.

TO MR. ELLIOTT

(ON THE DEATH OF HIS MOTHER).

MY DEAR SON,   *Yelling, October* 7, 1788.

I join with you in thankfulness to our dear Lord,
for giving your beloved parent so easy a deliverance
from this evil world ; and a happy improvement of

H H

the Gospel, which you were the instrument of bringing to her ears.

When we see the remains of those so dear to us deposited in the grave, how unavoidable are many affecting questions of this sort! Where are they now? How does it fare with them? The answer from our own minds, when we think upon the subject, apart from the written word, is mere conjecture. He alone who made us, and placed us here, and in his own appointed time removes us, can resolve our inquiries. And how full and consolatory is the voice from heaven, which says, " From henceforth," immediately after the spirit returns to God who gave it, " blessed are the dead, which die in the Lord !"— Oh what a cluster of blessings instantly are in their possession! Neither pain, nor grief, sin, or corruption, shall they feel any more ! No more shall the spirituality of their affections be cramped and fettered—no uneasy tempers rise for a single moment —no darkness of the understanding—the vision of God, and the presence of Christ, fill the vast capacities of the immortal spirit!

I have often, and still do, wonder, and have cause to lament, that death is not with great eagerness expected by me. Thanks be to God! I am day by day thinking how near it must be in the course of nature, if not much nearer in the counsel of God! But I want to rush into the joy of my Lord, as men who are going, in the full force of curiosity, and at great expense, to visit the grandest spectacle on earth, hasten to see it. I think of the young Grecian, who, after hearing in the evening a lecture, in Plato's school, "On the soul's immortality," drowned himself the next morning in the river, to take possession of it.

May the Lord of all Lords bless you, and keep you in His good ways, till we meet on Mount Sion! From your affectionate father,

H. VENN.

TO MR. JOHN HOUGHTON.

MY DEAR FRIEND,   *Yelling, Jan.* 25, 1789.

I have not often felt a more pleasing sensation than I did the last week, upon receiving the kind token of your remembrance and love to me, manifested in the piece of cloth and the stuff you sent for my poor neighbours.

I rejoice much that your love for children continues, and your endeavours to instruct them. Nothing, I am persuaded, turns to greater profit, or is more necessary, than beginning early, and being beforehand with the evil world; though it is not possible for us to be beforehand with the flesh. Some sense of good and evil before God is thus excited, and a rebuker within will then be often heard. I have a Sunday-school here, but in a poor way: the children cannot, any of them, yet read, though it has been set up two years. The master, the best I can procure, is not sufficient: and on Sundays, having scarcely strength for my business in the Church, I can give them no help. Nevertheless, the Lord's-day is not, as it used to be, the day for play and mischief; and the children constantly attend church.

I have a strong wish that you and Joseph would

pay me a visit for three or four days ; which, I trust,
may be spared.   I want to see you, before I depart.
Much cause of thankfulness you have given me, for
many years ; and I want to tell you how fully persuaded I am that the doctrine you have heard and
believed, and the manner in which it has been proposed, is according to the Oracles of God.   My
endeavours here are but in a small degree effectual
to the good of souls ; yet some, I verily believe, are
joined to the Lord : and the numbers who attend,
surprise my friends in the ministry who come
to preach for me : and sometimes the singing is
lively ; so that Ruth says, " Sir ! the singing was
like Huddersfield."   Pray give my love to dear
Joseph Hirst, and to every one of the children of
the Most High.

Last October, Mr. and Mrs. Riland, with two of
their daughters, paid us a visit of three weeks.   He
preached in the afternoon, and I in the morning ;
as we used to do.   It was a blessed visit ! Both he
and Mrs. R—— had a great desire to hear my son
preach, whom they knew an infant.   He came
over, and preached on those affecting words : " He
shall see of the travail of His soul, and shall be
satisfied."   Mr. Riland's eyes sparkled with joy all
the time.   He gave my son his hand, saying, " I
glorify God in you!   This is preaching indeed !"

I am much blessed in my wife, in my children,
in my friends at Cambridge ; and with gentle decay,
and a pleasant prospect, I am going to the mansion
prepared for me.   My strength is much wasted, and
my appetite more ; yet I speak and expound still,
and my Sabbaths are sweet to my soul.   The

Lord bless you and your dear wife; and give you to see more and more into the depth of iniquity within, and into the immense love of God in Christ Jesus the Lord! Remember me to young Mr. Bradley. I am heartily glad to hear he continues in earnest, seeking the Lord.

From your affectionate servant in Christ,

H. VENN.

TO THE REV. JOHN VENN.

MY DEAR SON,   *Yelling, March* 4, 1789.

I shall be heartily glad to see you and Mr. M——, whenever you can come—next Monday, or any day. You are ever in my heart, to live and die with you. I have but a small part of the span of man's little day to go through. Through grace, which will be ever adored, not only by myself, but all who shall hear of my salvation, I look for the time when the Lord shall come and take me to Himself. And I have much comfort, that, after having experienced, alas! so deeply the corruption of my nature, and the vanity of the world, and the sad defects in the best duties I have performed, there is a day approaching when I shall be free from sin, as an angel of God.

The 19th of April is the first Sunday I have fixed to be in London. I do it with much doubt, not knowing whether I shall have strength of body. Your mother prompts me much to go, and, in a great measure, is the preponderating cause. Pray fervently, that, if I do go, my preaching may not be in vain!

I am very thankful your Visitation Sermon is

talked of so long after it was preached. If you would be persuaded by me, you would carefully revise and correct it, and then print it. I am sure it would do good. It shall be no expense to you. Young ministers, who have ability, and are fixed in villages, should publish. Each fresh publication opens a new channel for the Truth to flow.

I know you have Kennicott's Two Dissertations. I have just gone through them a third time. I regard them as most masterly—never to be refuted. The fundamentals of Christ's religion are there so clearly proved, that one does not know which most to admire—the author's strong intellect, Hebrew learning, extent of reading, forcible conclusions, or his youth and great modesty—not twenty-four when he published, and was immediately ranked with the first-rate writers! I have a plan to publish a new edition. It is incredible how few have read them, of late!

We are as warm for Mr. Pitt here as any of the nation; and all in rapture on the recovery of our beloved King.

Your affectionate father,

H. VENN.

About this time, the nation was filled with joy by the unexpected recovery of the King from the temporary derangement of his mind; a day of public thanksgiving was appointed; and the King and Royal Family went in procession to St. Paul's Cathedral, to return thanks to Almighty God. These circumstances are thus alluded to, in different letters.

We have just heard our dear King is better. " God save the King! Long live the King!" is the prayer of thousands and thousands of thousands, more fervently than ever;—and when he is gone hence, may he live for evermore, through Jesus Christ his Saviour!

Even in our small village, and alone as we were, we joined with glee in the national acknowledgment of God's great mercy. Though we had no lights, no transparencies to strike the eye of sense, we could, and I hope did, instead of external signs of festival joy, put on the armour of light, trim our lamps, and express strongly our gratitude, because the Lord was ready to save.

TO MISS CATHERINE VENN.

MY DEAR KITTY,   *Yelling, April* 8, 1789.

Very great is the comfort we enjoy, from the pleasing account our very dear friends give of you, and from your own letters. Only exert yourself, and believe you are capable of gaining the esteem of all your friends by good behaviour, you will find the thing not only practicable, but easy.

Thanks be to God, that you have access to Him, as His child! Oh trust in His goodness and love! Hear Him proclaim His glory, in answer to that earnest petition of Moses, who had seen such displays of His omnipotence in the plagues poured out on Egypt, and in dividing the Red Sea!—" And the Lord passed by before him, and proclaimed,

The Lord, the LORD God, merciful and gracious, long-suffering, and abundant in goodness and truth, keeping mercy for thousands, forgiving iniquity and transgression and sin, and that will by no means clear the guilty;" *i.e.* obstinate rebels, and sinners hard-hearted and impenitent.   What a glorious God of love!—Hear the same character in Jeremiah ix. 23, 24: " Thus saith the Lord, Let not the wise man glory in his wisdom, neither let the mighty man glory in his might; let not the rich man glory in his riches: but let him that glorieth, glory in this, that he understandeth and knoweth me, that I am the Lord which exercise loving-kindness, judgment, and righteousness in the earth : for in these things I delight, saith the Lord."—Get by heart, and ponder on, these two Scriptures.   Often confess your ignorance of Him, your false conceptions, and hard thoughts of Him, as if an earthly parent had more bowels of mercy towards his children than the Lord Almighty;—when, indeed, as is His Majesty incomprehensible, so is His pity toward them that fear Him.   He is much dishonoured and injured in our thoughts, by our doubtings and fears; and they do us no good, nor work in us any amendment, but vex and make us weary of His service, cloud the soul, darken faith, and keep off those strong beams of divine love, which warm and exhilarate, and set the heart at liberty to run the way of God's commandments.   Now, just in proportion as our trust in the Lord, as our God, increases, so much the more shall we mortify our vile affections, be patient in adversity, and thankful in every condition!

Your dear brother left us last Friday, after a

second short visit. I wished you had been present, one morning, when he prayed! Oh it was indeed drawing nigh to God!—such real self-abasement, such holy pleadings for more grace and entire devotedness to God, such dependence upon the Saviour, that it refreshed and profited us all!

Next Thursday I purpose setting out for London. I am to preach eight Sundays. It is a great work, to stand up and speak for God and His Truth, before so great a multitude! Pray for your father, that he may have a deep sense of his own utter insufficiency; and be thoroughly furnished for the service, so as to speak, with wisdom and understanding, sound doctrine which cannot be condemned. I have fixed on my subject for the first Sunday—the Judgment of the Great Day. My intention is, to shew how the King's procession to St. Paul's may be of use to direct our thoughts to some of the grand particulars when the King of Kings shall come. The parallel is striking—the mass of people immense—all pervaded with the same feelings—all exalting and extolling the same person, in whom all have a supreme interest. This spectacle, though but a poor little momentary thing compared with the Great Day, may yet serve to carry forward our thoughts to it. Then the Heavenly King shall come, with all His angels and saints, more than ten large capitals can comprehend—all of one heart and mind —all singing songs of sweetest melody, in love most fervent—all seeing the Saviour as He is! Oh! for " faith, the substance of things hoped for—the evidence of things not seen!"

I am not sorry you have heard Mr. Wesley—

a very extraordinary man, but not to be believed in
his assertions about perfection. It is an error,
built upon false interpretation of some Scripture
passages, in flat contradiction to others which
cannot be mistaken. It is an error, the Church of
Christ has always condemned. It is an error, that
matter of fact confronts. So far from being perfect, alas! Christians fret, and quarrel, and fall out,
and have so many faults, that if God, as Job speaks
of himself, should contend with us, we could not, no
not the best upon earth, answer Him, one of a
thousand. "Behold! I am vile!" belongs to all in
the Church.—I hope you were not shaken in your
mind. Never give absolute credit to what you hear
from the pulpit, which is not proved by plain Scripture. How much more good would Mr. Wesley have
done, had he not drunk in this error! as there are,
doubtless, many very excellent Christians amongst
his people ;—but the best are sadly harassed by this
false doctrine.

Mr. Thornton sends me word, that Mr. Bentley has
had a stroke of the palsy, and is very poorly. The
God whom he serves will support and comfort him
and his; though the shock is great, at first, no doubt.
The Lord God, good and gracious, and of great
mercy to all who call upon Him, bless, preserve
and keep you!

From your affectionate father,

H. VENN.

In September 1789, another member was added to Mr.
Venn's family, by the marriage of his son, Mr. John Venn,

to Miss King, daughter of William King, Esq., of Hull, and sister to the late Rev. George King, Prebendary of Ely. This lady had enjoyed the benefit of the friendship and ministry of Joseph Milner; and so congenial were her sentiments with those of her future husband, that Mr. Venn's letters contain many expressions of gratitude to the Giver of all good, for a connexion which, in every respect, promised a large accession of happiness. I subjoin a few extracts, in reference to this event.

———

Yelling, Aug. 31, 1789.

—— We had the pleasure of hearing from my son, on Friday, that Miss King had agreed to crown his wishes and take his name. No marriage can promise fairer. They both have one intention, one pursuit, one judgment of what is man's chief happiness; and both are equally free from any sordid motives. How pleasing to reflect, that my son will be settled just before his aged parents finish their course! Mr. Thornton, who has been applied to, by the mother, for my son's character, writes to me of the lady in these words: " Now all is sure, I congratulate you and your whole family in having Miss King one of you. She is indeed a treasure ; and will be an example to every one."——

—— Mr. Milner said, the other day, to my son : " Many ministers of the Gospel are sadly hindered by their wives, who are afraid their husbands should do too much, and cry, ' Oh! spare yourself!' You, Sir, have not this to fear : Miss King will be glad to see you wholly given up to your work, and full of zeal for God and for the salvation of sinners."———

TO MRS. ELLIOTT.

MY DEAR DAUGHTER,   *Yelling, Oct.* 14, 1789.

I remembered you affectionately on the Lord's-day, as a confined Christian, debarred from worshipping the Lord with His Church. Your confinement arose from a temporary complaint;—your dear mother's, from infirmity, never to cease, but to grow more and more, till the fleshly fabric drops. My comfort respecting you both was, that you hear Him that speaketh from heaven—speaketh to the heart, and manifests Himself to all who love Him, by His own Spirit working mightily within. By this means He is more precious to His afflicted people than to those who enjoy, in an ample manner, creature comforts. Wherefore much more of spiritual benefit is very often gained by being cut off from the use of public ordinances, than from a constant attendance on them; because our communion with God is increased. In heaviness, weakness, and pain, Christians think upon Him; and His comforts revive their hearts. They feel a living proof that His loving-kindness is better than life itself.—These were my thoughts on Sunday, respecting you and your dear mother.

Tell dear Charles, we all thank him for his purpose to give the bride and bridegroom a meeting, and bring you with him. This will be a great heightening of our pleasure; and I am daily looking up for a blessing to crown the whole, by preserving us from lightness of mind, and from all the evil which is wont to mix in our conversation, and often sadly hurt us. Oh that a sweet cheerfulness may prevail—the cheerfulness of sober-minded Christians, thankful for all that we have enjoyed from the Divine bounty ; and, most of all, for spiritual blessings —for our new birth—our adoption into the family of Christ—our well-grounded hope of living in the perfection of holiness, and in the fervour of Divine love, when all selfishness shall be done away !— I am expecting every day a letter from Hull, fixing the time when we are to see them.

On Monday, F—— left us. I was glad to hear Kitty say she was not without a sense of her soul's worth. She told her she should never forget, she hoped, the instructions she had heard.—So it should be in every Christian family, and eminently so in every Christian minister's. Whoever sojourns but a day with the members of Christ should perceive that to love and fear God is their joy.

To morrow I go to Cambridge, to meet Mr. Burnett and his wife, who return with me on Saturday ; and I conclude we shall have their company till Thursday following. Delightful friendship ! of more than thirty years' standing—steady and unalterable—not to be reflected on without gratitude to God, who giveth us to say, " All our delight is in the saints that are on the earth, and such as fear the Lord ! "

From your affectionate father,

H. VENN.

Nov. 6, 1789.

——THE bride and bridegroom have been with us one week, and will not leave us till after the next. I see a circle of my children around me, all smiling, and affectionate—all united with their aged parents in nearer and better ties than those of natural relation—all of one heart and mind, respecting good and evil, the way of life, the character of Jehovah, and of the people He hath chosen for His inheritance. Short is our interview, and probably the last : for so it pleaseth our Heavenly Father to appoint, that after our children, the children of many prayers, are grown up, they are removed to a distance; lest we should settle upon our lees, and give too much of our affections to the children— defrauding Him who claims the whole heart for Himself.

TO MRS. KING

(MOTHER OF MRS. JOHN VENN).

Yelling, November, 1789.

I WILL address myself to you, dear Madam, with all the freedom which love of the same adorable object, and the same supreme desire in us both, suggest. It would be most contrary to our Christian profession, and to all gratitude, if we forgot your present trial, occasioned by the very acquisition which we so much wished—the union of your daughter with our family. The more we see of her, the more we are persuaded the high character given of her by all her friends is just ; and the prospect is very favourable indeed, that the bride and bridegroom will be of one heart and of one mind; will be imitators of the primitive believers, " eating their meat with gladness and singleness of heart;" and praising God, most of all, for the gift of His Son—all the hope and peace of fallen man! Such a cement of their affections will continue, like the cause producing it, firm to the end, and be both a comfort and a defence in all the vicissitudes of life.

I am, like yourself, ready to wish the situation of our beloved children was near to us: and now the pleasant plants nurtured by us, and bringing forth fruit from the grace of Christ, would fill our hearts with joy on their account, it is a matter of regret that we shall see so little of them. But this regret must cease, when we consider it is the wise constitution of our condition in this present world, that dearest relations should not dwell together, lest they should be entangled by inordinate affection, and take up their rest in each other, instead of in God. And I have found my heart more drawn out in presenting my absent children, than in remembering those with me, before the Throne of Grace. Thus our love for them is more spiritual; and with greater pleasure we anticipate the day when we shall be with the Lord for ever.

I have to add, I consider your state of widowhood. It is a state to which God has shewn very peculiar respect. He has chosen to describe Himself by the endearing name, " The Father of the fatherless, and the God of the widow." The prayers of the Church are constantly ascending up for them : and He regards widows indeed, who trust in Him, as needing His presence and comfort : while the Great Intercessor is "touched with a feeling of their infirmities;" remembering well the hour, when He beheld His own beloved mother, a widow, at the foot of His cross—her heart pierced, as with a sword, by the death of her son. Be assured you are by us all commended unto God's gracious care, in our family worship, daily.

Your daughter will write to you to-morrow. She and her husband desire to be affectionately remembered to you.

From your very humble servant,

H. VENN.

TO MR. ELLIOTT.

MY DEAR SON, *Yelling, Jan.* 8, 1790.

We wait to hear how you and Eling go on, in point of health. We shall have much joy, and give thanks, on your return to London, if it please our Lord and Heavenly Father. My brother, Dr. Alvey thinks, is not likely ever to recover the use of his limbs*. However, he is very cheerful, and speaks, more than ever I heard him, on the great subject of Christ Crucified; and believes he shall be in heaven, when he is called hence. It is a great blessing, my wife is much better, and in charming spirits.

On Monday, my affectionate friend Simeon walked over, and slept here. Oh! how refreshing were his prayers! how profitable his conversation! We were all revived : he left a blessing behind him. How shameful is our depravity, and how exceeding great,

* Mr. Richard Venn had been visited, a short time before, with a stroke of the palsy.

when we can be content to live without doing
good to the souls of men—call ourselves Christians,
and constantly be in the House of our God, and
not desire to instruct, to edify, to animate those
with whom we converse! They are the truly excellent of the earth, its salt, who, wherever they go,
reach the heart and conscience, and excite the devout wish, ' Oh, that I may follow Christ, like these
true-hearted disciples!' He preaches twice a week,
in a large room. My new daughter attended there,
when I preached ; and his people are indeed of an
excellent spirit—merciful, loving, and righteous.
My servant Thomas was much affected, when he
was amongst them. They spoke to him in such a
spirit, that he wished to live amongst them; and
thought he should then grow in grace, fast.

We all send love to you both ; and wish you to
flourish in the courts of the Lord's House, and
answerably to all the advantages the Church of
Christ enjoys, in point of knowledge and revelation
of the grace of the Lord Jesus Christ.

If you are prevented paying us a visit, which we
hope will not be the case, then we shall be obliged
to you to send the parcel for my brother.

Now to Him, who is "as rivers of waters in a dry
place," I commend you. May he be exceedingly
precious to you both! May you love one another
in Him, and for His sake ; and dwell in love, till we
all meet before Him in the world of love, without
end!

From your affectionate father,

H. VENN.

TO MRS. ELLIOTT.

MY DEAR DAUGHTER,   *Yelling, Jan.* 28, 1790.

Whether it be in reality, or only in appearance, a longer time than usual since you wrote, I am not certain; but we feel it the more, and therefore it seems longer, on account of our affliction. Indeed, we are tried; and I trust shall not be forsaken, so far as to lose that evenness and composure of spirit which is justly expected from all who love God, whatever be their sufferings.

My dear brother is, in the general state of his health, as well as ever, but quite helpless. Your mother has been confined to her room, but now comes down. Jane has been ill, but is better. Kitty and Ruth very poorly. We were for a little time afraid Jane was going to have a fever, and then began to feel exceedingly; but this cross was not sent. I have gone from one chamber to another, visiting my sick; and have not had more than two in family worship; and some Sundays, only one out of the house at church. Yet the Lord is good to us: we do not faint. He is a strong-hold in this time of our trouble. He suggests to our minds those truths, which assuage the pain, and fortify the soul to bear up against the pressure of evil; namely, what we deserve—what our brethren and sisters in Christ are suffering—the end for which the rod is appointed—the benefit it brings to the afflicted in due time—and, above all, the deep sorrows of our God and Saviour.

To these topics our thoughts are turned: and

when, in family prayer, we can feel though but a little measure of self-abasement, our spirits are revived. I look with tender pity on my two children, and feel much for them. However, the promise is theirs: "It is good for a man to bear the yoke in his youth." In appearance, all is very dismal for them; but admirable is the fruit, when they sink down in silence and humiliation before the Lord; waiting upon Him as just and good, wounding and healing. Knowledge of His name, obtained in this conflict, is never lost: it is mighty in operation, effectually sobers the mind, and keeps us, as soldiers under arms, prepared for the assault of our restless foes.

To my great surprise, I this moment hear my brother is got into your mamma's room, by the help of Thomas. He thinks he shall yet come down again. Amazingly strong is our love of life—even of the very dregs of life!

Your most affectionate father,

H. VENN.

TO LADY MARY FITZGERALD.

MADAM, *Yelling, March* 22, 1790,

It was exceedingly kind in you to write so fully respecting my dear friend, and her love, most undeserved, to me and my children.* It is some relief to a mind burdened with her liberality, that, with more gratitude than my heart can feel here, I shall

* Lady Smythe, who bequeathed pecuniary legacies to Mr. Venn, and to each of his children; and the Advowson of Bidborough, Kent, to Mr. John Venn.

know, and love, my benefactors in the Promised
Land. There, all the glorified saints not only do
love one another as they love themselves; but know
they do, beyond the possibility of doubt.

Your letter bathed my eyes in tears, to think
of the several merciful circumstances in our dear
sister's departure. How often I have heard her
express her apprehensions of the awful hour of her
dissolution, and tremble as she approached the
verge of eternity! But our good and gracious Lord
pities and indulges us in things not necessary to our
salvation, only for our consolation and ease. In my
last visit, I congratulated her on her good appearance; observing, the Gospel preached at Bidborough
was a medicine which gave her strength and spirits.
And I thought I should rejoice in her company
more than before, from her cheerfulness of spirit,
when I came to London. I do rejoice, while I
grieve. In her present existence I rejoice; in which
she possesses the vast recompence of her warfare,
in the love of her Great Leader, the Author and
Finisher of her salvation. When I read your letter,
I had all my children, but Mrs. Elliott, round me,
who were melted also into tears. Her regard for
me, during thirty-three years, was from a firm belief
I was in earnest serving the Lord. Oh, that it may
be found so! Nothing can be conceived so dreadful, as a hypocrite in the garb of a pastor and
teacher! Well may we cry to all who love us, and
our Master, " Brethren, pray for us!"

Be so kind as to return my best thanks to Miss
Lambert, for her good-will to me. I will make the
only return in my power—recommend her at the

Throne of Grace. I have already, very particularly. I truly sympathize with her ; and remember how often I have seen her departed friend, with close attention, listen to her Christian discourse.

I shall see you, and the little circle, in a few days —not without emotion. Soon our meetings will be transferred to the heavenly mansions; but there remembered as elementary institutions, in which the same Name that fills heaven with adoration and bliss was the name we were always seeking to know.—I beg my best respects to the two sisters : and, wishing you a fulness of peace, I remain,

Your much and long-indebted servant,

H. Venn.

In May 1790, Mr. Venn went up to London, to preach for a few Sundays at Surrey Chapel. In the prospect of this work, he writes (April 9, 1790):

Next week I go to town, on that arduous and glorious business of preaching the Name of Jesus to thousands of immortal souls. Oh! who is sufficient for these things ?

In a subsequent Letter (June 22, 1790) he writes .

On the 13th, I took my final leave of the Chapel, addressing myself to a great multitude, from Heb. x. 23 : " Let us hold fast the profession of our faith without wavering: for He is faithful, that promised." —My work is nearly ended ; for my mental faculties are very dull, and my bodily strength greatly reduced.

TO MRS. JOHN VENN.

MY BELOVED DAUGHTER,   *London, May* 20, 1790.

Before you set out on your short voyage,* I take my pen, to wish, as I pray, that it may be for your health and your husband's—that the wind may be favourable. And may the Holy ever-blessed Spirit breathe upon you both, and help you to see your Father and your God in the canopy of heaven and the vast ocean; and in sweet meditation may your hearts anticipate the glorious scene which death shall unveil to your admiring eyes, when you come " to the haven you would be"!

I am much obliged to my son for his invitation to Dunham. Nothing would give me more pleasure than to pay a visit there: and, if circumstances will permit, I shall do it;—but this is very doubtful. I lose my strength; and am overdone by what I did last year without much fatigue.

This morning dear Mr. Parry breakfasted with us, and satisfied many inquiries we made concerning his family and yourselves. What a distinguishing blessing, that, in these licentious and infidel times, you and my son should have two such friends for your friends—your friends in the love of Jesus, an unchangeable Friend, and our life for evermore.

Pray say for me every thing that is most kind and affectionate to your dear parent. I could indeed rejoice to sail with you, destined to the port of Hull, where so many dwell who are my very dear and

* From Lynn to Hull.

near relations.—Remember me to Miss Howard, whom I salute in the Lord, and never remember without lifting up my heart for her best interests.

On Wednesday, I hurried down to Clapham, to see Mr. Thornton, who has been suffering greatly from an accident which caused a great loss of blood. However, he is now in good spirits, and has had two good nights. Still he may feel serious consequences, and his life, seemingly so important to us, be brought to an end. I write by the post, sooner than send by dear Mr. Parry; as I am uncertain whether you may not set sail next week. We shall hope for a letter, a post or two after you are in Hull. Direct for me in London. Charles and Eling desire to be remembered. I have received my son's sermon, and shall take all care of it. My love to him.

The Lord Omnipresent bless and preserve you, and establish us all in Christ, and give us to press forwards without weariness!

From your affectionate father,

H. VENN.

TO MR. ELLIOTT.

MY DEAR SON, *Yelling, Aug.* 5, 1790.

If you have received the two letters I have written to Eling, since I left town, I shall stand clear of the charge of neglecting you. Letter-writing is indeed now become burdensome : you will therefore conclude I shall write less frequently. What a felicity, that prayer for each other is never intermitted! What a rich and abundant provision is made for us, by allowing, encouraging, nay, commanding us to commit all near and dear to us, and in whose preservation and welfare we are so deeply concerned, into our Heavenly Father's hands! By this constant prayer, not only our faith grows, and our experience of God's love for us, but the love of our family, and confidence of Divine mercy towards them. When I call to mind the way in which I have been led for more than thirty years, I stand amazed at the peace and quietness of mind I enjoyed whilst my children were so young, and there was no visible place of refuge for them, had I been called away! The Lord was pleased to give me a single eye. His favour only I asked for them and myself: His wrath revealed against sin I deprecated—petitions which he never refuses, because His own Spirit suggests them. What anxieties are in this way avoided! What is our part, we do cheerfully ; and thankfully receive His kindnesses.

Tell dear Eling I was delighted to hear how she was supported, and the rising impatience of her mind soon sweetly subdued. It was a memorable time of love. She is blessed, glory to God! with a spiritual husband, whose value is most sensibly felt in time of trouble, as an intercessor for his dear wife, when discomposed and ready to faint. Oh! the dear affection such prayers beget and increase!

I was low and uneasy about —— yesterday. Mr. Simeon did me " good, like a medicine ;" and his prayer with me took off the weight which lay heavy upon me. He calls me his father: he pours out his prayer for me, as an instrument from whose counsel he has profited; and was as fervent and

importunate with God for me, as my son or yourself. Oh! what am I, that I should be so distinguished? Love to you and your Eliza.

From your affectionate father,

H. VENN.

———

In the month of November, 1790, occurred the death
of John Thornton, Esq. To this event there are many
allusions in the Letters written about this same time.

———

—— I HAVE very sensibly felt the loss of my old
affectionate friend, John Thornton, after an intimacy of thirty-six years, from his first receiving
Christ, till he took his departure with a convoy of
angels, to see Him who so long had been all his
salvation and all his desire. Few of the followers of
the Lamb, it may be very truly said, have ever done
more to feed the hungry, clothe the naked, and
help all that suffer adversity, and to spread the
savour of the knowledge of Christ Crucified!——

TO THE REV. JOHN VENN.

MY DEAR SON,   *Yelling, Nov.* 28, 1790.

I staid till the post came in this day, hoping to
receive another letter;—but there is none. However, this may be owing to the neglect of the post.
Oh! what a Christian is your dear wife! and how
truly does she deserve all that has been said of

her! Never was I more affected—never more thankful to God our Saviour.*

To-morrow I go to London. My sister Gambier is likely soon to depart; and her husband would not ask me, at this time of the year, to come up; but took a very affecting method, by sending, in a letter, the measure of her arm above her wrist—a sufficient proof of her poor emaciated frame. I go entirely to pay her a farewell visit. Oh! that I could feel a strong concern for her; and be qualified, by the Spirit of God, to be a comforter to her heart, and an instrument of helping an affectionate sister, just passing over Jordan!

The post brought me to-day a letter from Mr. S. Thornton; in which he says, in reference to the death of his father, " I earnestly pray that his children may follow him in his faith and practice; and may their latter end be like *his*—which was indeed glorious, through the power of Him who hath conquered death and the grave. My dear father has left you a legacy of 50*l*. He had named you a trustee for his church patronage, in a former will; but the change was made for your son, as a younger life." A ring also was inclosed in the letter. I shall eye it often with a mournful pleasure. No such memorial was needful to remind me of my oldest friend on earth, but one. My parlour, my study, yourself, and his liberal donations to me for many years, are memorials never to be effaced.

Our love to your dear Kitty; and to her beloved mother, for whom I have felt much. How do we

* Mrs. J. Venn had suffered very severely during her confinement; but exhibited a remarkable degree of Christian patience.

long to hear it has pleased God to restore some strength to her, and to the little stranger! Love to Mr. and Mrs. Parry. Was ever a more pure and Christian affection! What a proof of that truth has my dear daughter felt!—I take pleasure in distresses, that the power of Christ may rest upon me. It was, as she supposed, at evening, morning, and noon-day, I was ever remembering you and her.

You are now, my dear son, called into greater notice. It is a high honour the glorified saint has put upon you.* Watch and pray for more wisdom and grace; which you will need, in making your choice, if any vacancy happens. It is a hard matter, indeed, to act with a disinterested spirit.

Let us know how the Lord is pleased to deal with you. May He be with your spirit; and do as much for us all as He has done for your Kitty— swallow up our self-will, in a love that His will should be done in us, by us, and upon us! All send their love.

From your affectionate father,

H. VENN.

TO MISS JANE C. VENN.

MY DEAR JANE,   *London, Dec.* 3, 1790.

On Wednesday I went to Camberwell; and found my poor sister better than I supposed she was, from

* Mr. Thornton left the patronage of several livings to the disposal of three Clergymen, as Trustees, of whom Mr. John Venn was one, in order to secure the appointment of proper Incumbents. He also named other Clergymen, who were to succeed, in a certain order, to the trust, upon the death of the respective Trustees. The patronage was eventually to revert to Mr. Thornton's heirs.

my brother's letter; so that there was no absolute necessity for my journey on her account.

However, I rejoice I am come, to see the children of my dear departed friend, John Thornton, and to hear of his life, acts of love, and death; many particulars of which I could not have heard at home. Some of these I send you now, which I received from the nurse who attended him. She said: " To see the sons, the day before he died, weeping tears of grief and love, and to hear the dying saint affectionately exhort and press each to hold fast the faith, and to lead the life of a Christian, was to the last degree affecting. They asked him whether he was now happy: 'Yes,' said he, 'happy in Jesus: all things are as well as they can be!' And the last words he was able to articulate were, ' Precious, precious....!' *Jesus* would have been added, but his breath failed."—Lady Balgonie did not see him for three days before he died. She was herself seized with a scarlet fever, of a very infectious sort: her children and her servants all were ill of it, nearly at the same time.

Last Sunday but one, dear Mr. Foster preached at Camberwell his funeral sermon, on that text, " Blessed are the dead which die in the Lord!" Mr. Newton also preached at his own church; and told his hearers Mr. Thornton had given away, in acts of love and mercy, 100,000*l*. But the fact is, 150,000*l*. would be nearer the truth, or an estate of 6000*l*. a year. He has died worth no more than 150,000*l*.

At Mr. Henry Thornton's request, I spend, God willing, the next Lord's-day with him, and speak at the old house:—" Not," says Mr. Wilberforce,

" to a mourning family; but a family who has abundant cause to rejoice and sing!"

I have again altered my plan, and shall not come down till Friday.   The Lord bless, preserve, and keep you! and, if it be His good will, may we meet again with stronger desires to love and glorify our Saviour more than ever !

From your affectionate father,

H. Venn.

TO MRS. JOHN VENN.

MY DEAR DAUGHTER,   *Yelling, Jan.* 29, 1791.

Dearer and dearer still you are to every one of our family, as well as to myself: and though I have not for months past done myself the pleasure of writing to you, you have been constantly in my mind, with a strong sympathy with you in all your trials and supports, your conflicts and victory. Had not my own illness prevented, I should three weeks sooner have written, to let you know how much we all reckon upon your visit, with your beloved mother. It will be a right Christian visit, I trust; a union of hearts engaged in the noblest service, desiring all the same thing—to love and to serve our Redeemer better all the days of our life.

My indisposition was an alarming one—a paralytic affection, with which I was taken in the pulpit, on the Sunday before Christmas-day. I am now called to a state of passive obedience. I cannot speak nor pray, nor do any thing as I used to do. I am come to the days of darkness; but not of dejection ;—for why should not Christians be afraid of dejection, as they are of murmuring and complaining? Surely we may comfort ourselves, that our health and sickness, not less than our life and death, are all in the disposal of the Lord over All, rich in mercy to all who call on Him. If these things were left to us, how would fond relations ever know when it was time to let us go? Behold the tender partiality of a husband and wife for each other, or of both for a beloved child, or of a friend that is nearer than a brother! However needful a fit of sickness might be in such cases, it would never come; much less, should death separate. The sovereign power, therefore, is lodged in better hands.

In my late attack, I was much comforted to see my beloved wife, daughter, and brother, possess such a calmness and composure of mind. I was apprehensive they would have been overwhelmed with fear; but, on the contrary, they behaved like Christians—they were cheerful. It was the will of God, and they acquiesced. This made me hope, that, should it be the adorable will of Heaven to take me from them, they will find Christ Jesus the Lord their light, and the strength of their life. We attribute this illness to my frequent exertions in London. —I am yet to learn a little of Pythagoras's discipline. Silent I cannot be!—but, I observe, Pythagoras had not Redemption to talk of.

When in town, it was pleasing to hear only of one subject, in all the serious circles—the Beloved Gaius,* and all his goodness: and the grace, from whence it all flowed, was in every one's mouth.

* The late John Thornton, Esq.

All join with me in love to yourself, your dear mother, and husband. The Righteous Branch reign over you! May you know you are saved, and dwell safely! From your affectionate father,

H. VENN.

TO THE REV. JOHN VENN.

MY DEAR SON, *Yelling, March* 4, 1791.

Pray return your dear Kitty many thanks for her last letter; the best—for the same reason Cicero pronounces one of Demosthenes' Orations to be so —because the longest I have ever received from her.

We have the very same feelings here that you have—desiring much to have your company ; and I hope it will be so contrived that my necessary visit to London, in the latter end of April, will not interfere with your design. Sooner than have your visit put off, I would make mine in London as short as possible : as it is, I design only to be absent three Sundays.

Your observations, on the declining state of health of so many of your relations, I like much ; and the conclusion you draw is truly Christian-like. I waked the other morning in a most pleasing contemplation—of which my mind was full—on that promised felicity, " We shall know even as we are known." Then, thought I, we shall know, fully and completely, what was our ruin—the means and method of our recovery, the Author of it all—our utter unworthiness—and the vast treasures of felicity we are put in possession of, never to be lost, as Adam's noble heritage was.

My dear wife evidently grows weaker. Your uncle is worse. I am quite well myself: my chief trial is, to check the activity of my spirit, which far exceeds my strength. I know not how to pass an hour sitting still; but the flesh, weighed down with years, will not bear work as in former time. The author of the excellent Sermon on Mr. Thornton's Death, is Mr. Scott of the Lock.—Pray, when you write to Mr. Grant, tell him I hope he received my Memoir of Sir John Barnard. I sent him a copy in December.

I thank you, my dear son, for Mr. Adam's work: it is a fine copy, and some excellent things there are in it: but they formerly knew not how to digest their matter; and the mixture continually of Latin, and often Greek, is unpleasant: however, the sermons upon the Church I esteem excellent.

My sister Bishop's joy in death, when she was remarkably destitute of consolations all her life through, was very delightful to hear; and I trust it will please our Lord to lift up the light of His countenance upon your dear mother, before He takes her to Himself!

Ruth is quite well; and doubly attached to us, after her long absence. She is indeed as a daughter: no creature living can be more thankful on account of the favour shewn her. Oh! what comfort and mutual satisfaction do masters and servants lose, when there is no Christian love, no union in the Reedemer!

Our best love to your mother and Kitty, and Mr. and Mrs. Parry. Tell the Squire I hope yet to strike a blow or two more upon the head of the Antinomians

in London, though I have not voice enough to fill
Surrey Chapel again.

Dear Simeon (now Mr. Vice-Provost) paid us a
visit, and slept here last Wednesday but one. He
gives a charming account of Mr. Newton; who made
me quite ashamed of my little scrawl to him upon
his wife's death, by writing, in return, a very long,
excellent, and most affectionate letter to me. How
am I distinguished, by a wife, children, relations, and
friends! I may truly say, " the lot is fallen to me
in a fair ground; yea, I have a goodly heritage."
Only pray I may not be utterly ungrateful.

From your affectionate father,

H. VENN.

TO MRS. RILAND.

Yelling, July 12, 1791.

IT is, I think, a long time, my dear friend, since
I heard from Sutton. I wrote to dear P—— the
19th of May; which letter, I trust, reached her in
time, before her natal day. I will yield to none but
those in her own house, in degree of love and prayer
for every good thing which the God of her father
and her mother hath promised to them that love
Him.

I write now, to give you my diary since my last.
Admire, my beloved friend, my unshaken resolution!
Never, during the long space of forty years, did I
ever visit the great city, before last May, and for
weeks, and yet not once appear in a pulpit; but,
withdrawing from the sacred office of pastor and
teacher, retired into the ranks of a hearer during four
Sundays ;—and much edified and comforted I was.

K K

I returned last Friday three weeks, and was very far from continuing my good resolution. On Sunday fortnight, I preached, as if I had been quite strong, very much indeed at liberty, an hour and ten minutes. And again, on the Tuesday following, I preached at Cambridge for dear Simeon ; whither I went to meet Mr. Newton, and invite him over to visit us ; which he did most kindly, the week following : and in the mean time, on the Saturday and on the Sunday following, I lost my speech ; and, to satisfy my wife and daughter, I sent over for the physician. Thanks be to my God, the attack was gentle and transitory ! On Sunday last, I preached with comfort and liberty on a text (shame be to me !) I never spoke from before. It is one of those texts which hath great complaints against Gospel ministers, for neglecting it wholly. You will find it in Eccles. ii. 26.*

In London, I met with great affection amongst my friends and relations. I have half a curate now, and soon shall have one entirely. I am doing what I can to get one ; but we have no convenience for lodging any gentleman. I am past my labour ; and frequently feel so dull in my faculties, and so unable to speak for want of strength in my chest, that I think I offer, in the church, " the torn, and the lame, and the sick :" and I have long been of another judgment decidedly—that it is proper to retire, if we live till we come to the dregs of life.

* " For God giveth to a man that is good in his sight, wisdom, and knowledge, and joy : but to the sinner he giveth travail, to gather and to heap up, that he may give to him that is good before God. This also is vanity and vexation of spirit."

My dear wife is extremely feeble, and my brother requires two men to get him up; but both are beautified with meekness, and are patterns in the furnace.   We are dealt with bountifully!

Yours, &c.

H. VENN.

TO MRS. ELLIOTT.

Yelling, Sept. 27, 1791.

It is my Dear Eling's turn to have a letter; and I know the dregs of my pen are welcome to you.

My dear brother is exceedingly reduced; and from day to day we expect his dissolution.   He cannot speak.   The doctor thinks it most probable he will fall asleep; and not know when the messenger comes to bring him the joyful tidings, that all his sorrows and sufferings are ended.   There is not the least probability that he will be with us when you receive this.   Thus his earnest prayer is heard; which was, to go before me: and your mother believes that it was owing to my illness that his was increased.   It is a solemn season; and I find it good to be alone, in a dark chamber, presenting my dying brother to my God and Saviour, " who hath tasted death for all believers, and hath opened to them the kingdom of heaven."   Compared with such solemn thoughtfulness, amusements and pleasures of sense are poor things indeed!   There is no greater delusion than that which the multitude embrace, when they are confident that the happy men and women are those only who figure in the circles of the gay and brilliant, and go on without restraint in a career of selfindulgence.   So far is this from the truth, that

K K 2

solemn meditation on things unseen and eternal, and sweet peace, and lively hope, amidst our dear dying relations in Christ, afford the most solid satisfaction.

I am glad that dear Jane is not with us. She will know how to be thankful that her affectionate uncle never wanted the most tender care and attention to his infirmities. I hope ever to be mindful of my servant Thomas's kind treatment of him.

God has been very gracious to me in the curate.* He has provided for my people. On Sunday he preached twice: his first sermon on Isa. lv. 1.; his second, on John iii. 36. He is modest and humble, and bears an excellent character. The people are much taken with him.

From your affectionate father,

H. VENN.

P. S. This minute my brother has breathed his last. He had no pangs in his death. Thanks be to God!

In several Letters written about this date, Mr. Venn alludes to a visit which he paid to Mr. Berridge, " the venerable pastor of Everton." In one of them, he thus describes the interview.

I LATELY visited my dear brother Berridge. His sight is very dim, his ears can scarcely hear, and his

----

* The Rev. Maurice Evans; who remained curate of Yelling till Mr. Venn's death; and then undertook the neighbouring curacy of Eltisley; from whence he removed into Wales.

faculties are fast decaying; so that, if he continues any time, he may outlive the use of them. But, in this ruin of his earthly tabernacle, it is surprising to see the joy in his countenance, and the lively hope with which he looks for the day of his dissolution. In his prayer with me and my children (for two of them accompanied me), we were much affected by his commending himself to the Lord, as quite alone, not able to read, or hear, or do any thing ;—" but if I have, Lord," said he, " Thy presence and love, *that* sufficeth !"

TO MR. THOMAS ATKINSON.

MY DEAR FRIEND,   *Yelling, Jan.* 3, 1792.

Yesterday, with great pleasure, we received your very generous relief for my poor neighbours; and I now write to return you grateful thanks, in my own name, as well as in that of the people.

This festival-week we are rejoiced with the prospect ;—coals, clothing, and meat, are distributed. To the Parsonage, as to a house of mercy, the poor should resort in their distresses : and though we see them little more disposed to receive the Gospel by acts of kindness and love to them, yet their opposition to it dies away ; and some are reformed, and restrained from setting the evil example they did. At all events, the merciful do receive mercy, and their own souls are made fat. How often, when my heart has been cold and dead—when I could not pray or meditate for days together—have I been quickened, by the loving-kindness of the Lord, upon doing something kind and loving for a fellow

creature, and more especially for a fellow-Christian !
This is highly necessary to be noted, and frequently
dwelt upon in Christian conversation, because of
the gross selfishness that is interwoven in our fallen
souls. We are very prone to turn the doctrines of
grace into poison ; not only predestination, and
election, final perseverance, and particular redemption, but, no less, justification by faith only, and the
pardon of all our sins by the blood of the Lamb. It
is therefore a great comfort when I see and hear
of my Christian friends, that they are glad to dis-
tribute, and willing to communicate. Were there
but one thousand loving Christians of great opulence, in Britain, like-minded with John Thornton,
lately gone to heaven, the nation would be judged
and convinced of the good operation of the Gospel.
Indeed, I sometimes indulge the joyful hope, that
the Philadelphian state is approaching, when Christians shall be as much distinguished by their bowels
of compassion, and active love, as by their creed.

Will you crown your kindness to me by a visit ?
I am weak and withering away, but content and
cheerful.   I can read but little—write less ; and my
intellectual faculties are benumbed.   I seldom stir
out.   Oh what a change will perfect health, immortal
vigour, and spotless purity, be to my poor soul !

Mrs. Venn and Jane send love to you and all
friends ; as I do.

Yours,

H. VENN.

TO THE REV. JOHN VENN.

Yelling, Jan. 7, 1792.

——The placing ministers is one of the chief prerogatives of our Lord and Head.   His thoughts and ways in this matter are totally different from ours. Hence we see several of His pastors and teachers in spheres very unfit for them, as it appears ;—men of abilities, zeal, and application, preaching to a handful of peasants ;—others, without talents, in places of great resort, amongst men of education.   But every mouth must be stopped ; and no inquiry is allowed, why He doeth so or so.   Our business is indisputably plain—"Work while it is day."   Be zealous and pure from the blood of all men, whether you speak to one hundred or some thousands.   None more glorify God than patient satisfied pastors, who never admit the thought of choosing for themselves.   You write the very truth, when you write, " I rejoice now particularly that I am not my own, nor, in respect of my situation in life, am left to my own choice."——

———

About this time, Mr. John Venn began the formation of a Clerical Society, amongst a few zealous but distantly-situated Ministers, who were to meet twice a year at Little Dunham, for the purpose of mutual consultation and encouragement.   The prosecution of this scheme called forth his activity and zeal, and opened a prospect of more extensive usefulness than the situation of Little Dunham had hitherto promised.   The following Letter was written in allusion to this circumstance.

TO THE REV. JOHN VENN.

MY DEAR SON,   *Yelling, Jan.* 20, 1792.

I have just finished your precious letter. How am I called upon to cry out, " What am I, that I should ever live to see my prayers for a beloved child, a son, a Gospel minister, now more than ever answered !" *Usefulness is all, in Christians.*

I am now at the age of sixty-seven, lamenting how very little I have done for God and man, compared with what I might have done, had I been active in doing good, as I ought. I could not help clapping my hands, and singing, " Hallelujah ! hallelujah !" with a most joyful heart, when I had read your letter.

Your visit here, as circumstances are, I would by no means have the joy of receiving ; for it is not in the order of Providence. I am not at all solicitous for your removal from your present situation ; now you are endued, like the disciples at Jerusalem, with power from on high. Your proposal of meeting twice a year is from above. Your usefulness is indeed enlarging.

With fervent wishes for your growth in grace,

I am yours, &c.

H. VENN.

In a subsequent Letter, written to Mr. John Venn, I find the following animated address to the Members of the Clerical Society, upon their first meeting together.

—— Though pressed for time, I cannot but send you, and your dear fellow-labourers in Christ's great Cause, the wishes of my heart respecting you all; as I cannot make one of your meeting. I hope the letter will come before you part.

I wish you may covet earnestly the best gifts, and all the fruits of the Spirit; knowing you are to be examples of the truth of God's promises, and of the power of His grace to all your people. I wish you to be ever diligently employing yourselves in some good work, either respecting the bodies or the souls of men, that the slothful and lukewarm may be convinced and quickened by your example. I wish you to consider yourselves as the friends, the fathers, of the poor and needy; not only appointed to instruct, and preach unto them words whereby they may be saved, but to be at much pains to supply their wants. This, I am persuaded, gives the greatest weight to sound doctrine; and exhibits, in a strong light, the good-will to men which should abound in the ministers of Christ. I wish you to value time and retirement: these are necessary, in order to gain, by much reading and prayer, more clear and enlarged views of God and His salvation, and a fulness of matter in preaching which cannot otherwise be attained. I wish you wisdom and skill to be cheerful, without levity; and, without affectation, to give a profitable turn to conversation; evidently shewing, that " out of the abundance of the heart your mouth speaketh."—I shall be with you in Spirit.

In the month of February 1792, Mrs. Venn's health began to decline rapidly. The following extract and letters will furnish an affecting picture of her state of mind, and of the last scenes of her sufferings.

TO THE REV. JOHN VENN.

Yelling, March 16, 1792.

——THERE is no material change in your dear mother, though Mr. Simeon thinks she is much altered.—We are called to pray without ceasing. I find a rich blessing in this affliction. I feel more deeply my poverty and my dependence upon the Lord; and the spirit of prayer is increased. And while the Lord is pleased to keep from me the uttermost distress I should be in, if dear Jane should be ill, I can be cheerful. One of the exceeding great and precious promises, which I had overlooked before, is now opened to my mind, and pleaded by me before the Throne of Grace, with great expectation. It is in a very favourite Psalm of mine, the 37th, which you have heard me expound many times; and runs in these words, verses 18, 19 : " The upright shall not be ashamed in the evil time"—of suffering, from confinement, sickness, and pain (as Lazarus was said to have received " *evil*" things when he was afflicted in his body); "and in the days of famine "—that is, when no creature-comfort can be enjoyed—" they shall be satisfied,"

from the knowledge of God, and fellowship with
Him.   So I abundantly find it, in my present state.
I see my dear companion, my other self, dying
daily ; and am perfectly resigned.———

TO THE REV. JAMES STILLINGFLEET.

Yelling, March 29, 1792.

MY DEAR BROTHER AND SISTER,

I have some of the best news to impart.   One
beloved by you both, and who delighted in you, has
accomplished her warfare, has received an answer to
all her prayers, and everlasting joy rests upon her
head.   My dear wife, the source of my best earthly
comfort for twenty years, departed on Tuesday.

Our prayers and hers were heard at large ; and
many circumstances of tender mercy and loving-
kindness have been vouchsafed.   We were much
afraid, from what the physicians said, that she would
suffer extreme pain ; but this trial was spared us.
She was confined to her chamber eight weeks, and
to her bed only six days, yet without a murmuring
word.   Sorely distressed in her soul for her sins,
yet nevertheless all submission and acquiescence,
humbling herself, and praying continually ; she
could hardly believe that she had saving faith,
because she loved Christ no more, and served Him
no better, and was not more zealous of good works.
It rejoiced therefore our hearts, to hear her say, two
days before she left us : " I hope I do not deceive
myself : I hope I am not too sanguine : I shall now
go to Christ : He is now with my spirit.—It is not
possible for me to tell you (she proceeded) what

distress I have gone through, from a sense of my own vileness." The change of her frame of mind was painted in her pale, emaciated countenance: and while Jane, Ruth, and myself, stood around her, she literally fell asleep, without our perceiving when she drew her last breath. Verily, God hath heard our prayer, and hath not turned His mercy from us!

I have lost as excellent a wife as I can figure to myself; and with her, a considerable part of my income : yet I am light and glad of heart, in full assurance of her salvation, and that I shall certainly soon follow her. Jane is much affected, having lost so tender a mother, and so wise a counsellor. She bears her cross nobly, without a brother, sister or companion, but her aged infirm father. Though quite alone, we are not desolate.—We both beg you will accept our warmest wishes for your best welfare.

Your affectionate and much indebted,

H. VENN.

———

In April, 1792, the Rectory of Clapham in Surrey became vacant, which was one of the livings in the patronage of the Trustees under Mr. Thornton's will. There was a specific direction respecting this living—that the Rev. Henry Foster should have the first offer of it, upon vacancy occurring ; and that, if he declined it, Mr. John Venn should have the next offer.

Mr. Foster now declined the presentation, in a manner which displayed extraordinary humility, and a noble superiority to all worldly considerations.

The option of the presentation next devolved upon

Mr. John Venn; who accepted it, and was instituted in the following month.   The next extracts allude to these circumstances.

May, 2, 1792.

——My brother Gambier sent me the first notice respecting Clapham.   What an honour and lustre is thrown upon Mr. Foster's character!   To what a difficult and dangerous post is my son called!   He is in great weakness, fear, and trembling.   Now is the time of temptation.   Now, more than ever, prayer should be made, that he may glorify God.——

TO THE REV. JOHN VENN.

——Children, the old adage says, are careful comforts.—I find the truth of this now particularly respecting you.   I was careful to see you called out to usefulness; and, now providentially a great door is opened, I am in daily concern lest you should be hurt, and suffer loss in your new station.—— You must beware of company.   You must be much in secret and retirement.   Visiting friends, and being seldom in a solemn spirit before the Throne of Grace, ruin most of those who perish among professors of godliness.

In the summer of 1792, Mr. Venn was obliged, through increasing infirmities, wholly to relinquish the public discharge of his ministry.   Upon the earnest solicitation of his children and friends, he took a journey to Bath; but experienced no material benefit from the waters at that place. He next went to Mr. Riland's, at Birmingham; and, accompanied by his daughter, and part of Mr. Riland's family, visited Buxton. By the use of Buxton waters, his health and vigour were, for a time, remarkably restored. He was absent from Yelling for more than a year.

TO THE REV. JOHN VENN.

MY DEAR SON,   *Buxton, Aug.* 27, 1792.

I this day received your very affectionate letter. It added in no small degree to my comforts, which were abundant before. Indeed, I am not able to reckon up the mercies which are multiplied upon me. Unfeigned esteem, for my poor work's sake, because of the Master I have served, I meet with in every place; and your very affectionate manner of taking care of me excites me, with peculiar emphasis, to cry out, " How am I compassed with mercy on every side ! "

We came here on Saturday. I hear great things are done by the waters. One thing I know—it will prove no disappointment to me, if I receive no good; for I expect none. I make the trial, in order that my children may see I use the means, which, if it please God, may prolong my days a little, and lighten my sufferings. But I cannot think my sufferings are worthy to be named, while my faith and hope continue ; and my desire is earnest after a better country, secured by oath, and promises,

and blood.   Indeed, I am very much indulged with
the comforts of love, the consolations of Christ, and
the spirit of prayer.

My continual prayer for you will be, " Ἐν ἀληθείᾳ
καὶ παρρησίᾳ—may he speak and preach ! " And if
you will take no denial, it shall " be unto thee even
as thou wilt." For, oh! marvellous!—and, without grace given to believe, undoubtedly incredible !
—the Holy Lord God maketh Himself tributary to
poor sinners; saying, " Open thy mouth wide, and
I will fill it."

Three weeks is the time we purpose to stay,
if the waters agree; and then return by Sutton.
Inclose your letter to me, under cover, to Sir
Richard Hill, my old friend, who is trying the
waters here. We meet every day. We dine at a
long table—twenty-five guests; and we have variety; so that my appetite is well consulted : but a
sad famine respecting spiritual things! However,
I trust we shall get good.

A clergyman was yesterday giving me an account,
truly affecting, of the great afflictions of Bishop
Lowth, which I hope never to forget. After many
years of honour, and the fulness of prosperity, his
days of darkness began with the loss of his beloved
daughter Maria, the sweetest flower conceivable.
The blow rent his heart. This was soon followed
by the death of his son, at twenty, who was every
thing he could wish. Soon after, another daughter
died suddenly, when at dinner with him. He then
became deranged in his mind for three years; and
afterwards was attacked by a severe complaint,
which filled him with excruciating pains; till, worn

out with distress, he breathed his last.—Oh, what a spectacle! what a lesson!

Present my best respects to my friends. Assure them I pray for them every day, and hope to dwell with them above for ever.

From your affectionate father,

H. VENN.

TO MRS. ELLIOTT.

MY DEAR ELING, *Buxton, Sept.* 6, 1792.

I write now, what you will be much pleased to read.—The waters have done my health great good, and I am much stronger. Dear Charles and you will pray earnestly for me, that I may have wisdom from above, to make the most of life, and be blessed with a triumphant end. The people here teach us from what a state of death we are saved. We feel and enjoy that inestimable blessing. We are led " beside the still waters, in green pastures ;" while persons of rank and distinction, in the world, are in one continual hurry, and immersed in dissipation.

Dr. Hulme of Halifax, Mr. Kershaw, and Sir Richard Hill, are here; and their company is very enlivening. Mr. Thomas Atkinson, John Houghton, with his wife, and several others of my old flock at Huddersfield, are coming over, to pay a visit once more to the man who first called upon them to behold the Lamb of God—in whom they have enjoyed light, life, and joy, for many years. I have seen Joseph Hirst—an example and ornament of his religion. He tells me that the people in general about Huddersfield are flourishing in righteousness.

Since I began this letter, Mr. Powley is come to see me ; and tears filled his eyes on seeing me so much reduced. We have had sweet conversation to-gether.

You may see, by my writing, how much more strength I have gained ; but observe, I do not sup-pose this change in my health will last. Adored be the superabundant grace of God!—I do not desire to continue in the body, but to join the heavenly choir, and see God face to face.

From your affectionate father,

H. VENN.

———

At the beginning of the year 1793, Mr. John Venn removed from Little Dunham to Clapham. He was much oppressed by a sense of the responsibility attached to so important a ministerial charge. The next Letter was written to encourage and strengthen his mind under these painful feelings.

———

TO THE REV. JOHN VENN.

MY VERY DEAR SON,   *Yelling, Jan.* 17, 1793.

Though I wrote to you yesterday, yet the letter I received from you last night grieves me so much, that I cannot rest without immediately offering some considerations, which may, I trust, be useful.

i. I hope you will consider that you are no otherwise afflicted with a sense of your own de-ficiency, than the very excellent of God's servants were in their trials. One cries out, " I am undone ! I am a man of unclean lips !"—Another, " I am a child! I cannot speak!"—Ezekiel is called upon to guard against fear of the faces of men. It is a plain intimation, that if he gave way to such a fear, the Lord would confound him before them. St. Paul was in weakness, fear, and much trembling, lest he should not be able to fulfil his ministry at Corinth ; and was assured by Christ Himself, that a great door and effectual was opened, and there were many adversaries. From these instances, I hope you will see, my dear son, that it is a general method of the Divine proceedings to impress a very deep sense of utter insufficiency on the instruments He makes use of, in calling sinners to Christ. Be, then, of good cheer! as you stand now only in circumstances similar to these blessed and highly-distinguished servants of the Lord.

II. I beseech you to understand how very plainly has the choice and appointment of you to this service appeared. The judgment of all who consider it, is but one—that you are, if ever man was, called and chosen to the work. Moreover, all agree you are eminently fitted for the situation. Surely the conclusion, from both the manner of your coming to be Rector of Clapham, and your acknowledged fitness for the place, ought to give you boldness.

III. You are at liberty to write all your sermons, till you have both ability and freedom to speak. And when your whole time is devoted to the service of your profession, I think you must indeed greatly mistake the matter, if you think you are unable to do credit to your profession, and feed the church.

IV. Your hearers are much inclined to think of your trials, and wish you may not be discouraged.

Mrs. T —— told me, she felt very tenderly for you, and so did many more; and hoped a few weeks or months would make a great change in your mind.

v. The opposition in the appointment of Providence, respecting myself and you, is very striking. I was sent *from Clapham*, that at Huddersfield I might be taught the *plague of my own heart;* (and though, I trust, few are obstinate as I was, and need to be brought so near the edge of a most tremendous precipice as I was;) yet I have more reason to be *thankful* for what I gained by that temptation, than for any prosperous event I ever had in my temporal circumstances. *To Clapham* you are led, in order to be experimentally taught what is in your heart. And be not surprised (as if it were a strange thing) at being thus cast down; for whenever we are called to do a work for the Lord, if we are not humbled before we enter upon it, there is little reason to think we shall meet with any success.

vi. You would consult much your own comfort, my beloved son, if, after pondering the trials and difficulties you are to expect, and will doubtless meet with, you would ponder also, in some just measure (which I fear you have but a very little done), the usefulness, the comfort, the liberty, and Divine love you will be the means, which God our Saviour will make use of, to communicate to many souls. When I looked round about me, after Divine Service, only the last Sunday, at Clapham, my heart bounded within me, to think how different a sacrament, in half a year's time, there would be on that very spot.

One mistake in my poor life (which has been full

of mistakes), I have cause to regret, is, that, from
fear of pride, I never paid due regard to the numberless passages in Holy Writ which so plainly point out,
and extol, the high dignity of our office. Prophets
of God, abettors of His cause, His ambassadors, sent
by Him immediately after His ascension, to open
the eyes of the blind, to turn men, &c. &c.—oh! had
I, some forty years since, my dear son, given but
a little consideration to these passages, and many
like them, representing the authority, the dignity of
our office, I indeed believe (humanly speaking) I
should have had much more comfort in my own
soul, and more success, both in public and private
addresses to my people. Among the numberless
deplorable defects of my ministry, I scarcely can
find out one from which my usefulness hath been
more hindered, than from a total forgetfulness of
the highest honour of my office, and persevering in
continual fear lest I should be proud and lifted up.
Beware, I beseech you, my dear son, that your
ministry be not materially hurt by what has injured
your beloved father, and hindered his usefulness.

VII. I beseech you to assure yourself, you are
not to expect the help God will give you, *till the
exigency of the case requires it.* Abraham went out,
not knowing whither he went. Faith in all His
children, is of the very same nature, from the first
to the last—a venture, whether we shall sink or
swim, as shipwrecked mariners. Why, then, should
you not be content to trust—to be depending on
the promise with quiet expectation; though your
deepest feeling is, that you are not sufficient to
think so much as a good thought of yourself.

VIII. My dear son, I beseech you, consider, with all possible attention, how great a danger you are exposed to, which you do not seem, I apprehend, to attend to sufficiently—the danger of disparaging all that God hath wrought for you. You remember he brought a charge against Israel of old, that they did not serve Him with joyfulness of heart. I know, also, that the nature and subtlety of the Wicked-one works this way; especially with those who are of a modest and self-diffident cast (which never was mine, I confess): and till I saw how that cast has worked upon you, I the more lamented it was not my own cast. I pray you resist and oppose the suggestions of this malignant spirit: never reason, but pray against him: when he sees you engaged in reasoning against him, he is confident, and rejoices:—when he sees you upon your knees, he trembles; he will flee from you, a vile sinner, in utter despair of conquering; nay, in fear, lest you bruise his head.

So much for spirituals—all written in a coffee-house, among Jamaica captains, and in a great din.

I now give my opinion on your temporalities. But here I have little opinion of my own abilities. You tell me, in the *strictness* of the law, you have a right to much more than the other party will allow you. If, by the *strictness* of the law, you mean uncertainty whether it will be determined in your favour if tried at law, it may then be prudent to let them have their will; but if the law is clearly on your side, neither reason nor religion require you to take less than your dues, but the contrary. I am rather sorry I said a syllable about my papers.

So many are your employments, I ought not to have troubled you about such a matter. Forgive me! My love to your dear wife: I feel for her, as for a beloved child.

I am yet uncertain whether I can be able to come into Norfolk. My dear Brother Berridge is dying; as a letter received last night from Mr. Whittingham informs me—and, at the same time, how supremely happy he is in his God and Saviour. He goes a little before us : we shall very soon follow after.

From your affectionate father,

H. Venn.

TO THE REV. JAMES AND MRS. HARVEY.

MY DEAR CHILDREN,   *London, Feb.* 14, 1793.

——Dining this day with Sir R. Hill, and being in rather better health, I gladly embrace the opportunity of a frank, to send you an account of the last days of my dear brother at Everton; who was most affectionate towards all my dear children ; and his regard for me was very great indeed. His departure is to me a loss unspeakable, and not to be repaired! The country will appear very dreary, now I have no friend there, to whom I can unbosom my soul, as he was wont to do to me. You know that I had promised to preach his funeral sermon. My weakness of body, and of my mind, prevent my fulfilling that promise ; and I was, much against my inclination, obliged to refuse the application from Everton to perform the last office for this eminent man of God. After increasing weakness, he was, on the 12th of January, seized with a violent asthma, in which his

friends thought he would have died. He recovered, however, and lived ten days, unspeakably
favoured with the presence and love of his adorable
Redeemer, often expressing his full assurance of
being with Him for ever. Mr. and Mrs. Whittingham, Mr. Ellard, and Mr. Hewitt, were with him,
when he departed without a struggle or a groan·
His funeral was very solemn. Six clergymen bore
the pall. Mr. Simeon preached from the very
words I wished him to do ; and shewed how truly
Mr. Berridge might say, with Paul, 2 Tim. iv. 7, 8 :
" I have fought a good fight ; I have finished my
course ; I have kept the faith : henceforth there is
laid up for me a crown of righteousness, which the
Lord, the righteous Judge, shall give me at that
day : and not to me only, but unto all them also
that love His appearing." The church could not
contain more than half of the multitude who came
to the burial of their beloved pastor. Nor is it
easy to conceive what tears and sighs were to be
seen and heard, from those who had been called to
Christ through the word of the dear deceased. He
is gone, a very little before me. May I patiently
wait till I meet him above!—an event which I hope
is not far off.

From your affectionate father,

H. VENN.

In Letters written during Mr. Venn's absence from
Yelling, he frequently mentions the very gratifying
accounts which he received of the success of his curate,

Mr. Evans, who was the means of exciting many to a serious concern for their salvation, who had heard Mr. Venn's preaching without effect, or had relapsed into indifference, after having been once awakened. Such accounts evidently cheered his heart, and called forth fervent praises to God. I add, as a specimen, an extract from a Letter to Mr. Thomas Atkinson.

———

—— was absent from home when your liberal present to my poor arrived; and my servant is not the most exact in observing the orders given him. These circumstances must plead my excuse for not acknowledging, some weeks sooner, your kind regard to my poor people, whom you have helped to clothe.—Mr. Simeon, last month, was at Yelling; and has brought me such an account as will rejoice both *your* heart and your wife's. He says, " The people are as different as it is possible to conceive. There was a church-full on the week-day. They sang, they prayed, they heard, like people alive to God. They quite refreshed my soul."—From this account, you will see how highly favoured I am in the pastor my God has sent to supply, nay, abundantly more than to supply, my place. And I write to you, that you may know, that some of the objects of your liberality are the poor who *receive* as well as *hear* the Gospel.

———

After thirteen months' absence, Mr. Venn returned, with his daughter, to Yelling. He thus describes the joy which his arrival excited among the villagers.

Yelling, June 8, 1793.

——WE came here yesterday, after a pleasant journey, which did us both good. The people were glad and eager to see us. The bells rang, as soon as we came in sight in the field. Some were too much affected to come and greet us, at our arrival. Others flocked to the rectory ; and a testimony was borne, by every countenance, that their friend and pastor was returned. The faithful Ruth was over-come with joy.

TO THE REV. JOHN VENN.

(AT BATH.)

MY VERY DEAR SON, *Yelling, Aug.* 1793.

Your two letters afforded me great pleasure and comfort ; and we have abundant reason to be thank-ful that the Bath waters appear to do you so much good.

I am much reduced ; and have nothing but a decrease of bodily strength to expect ; for my appe-tite is almost gone ;—not that I have cause for com-plaint. You have been every day in my thoughts, as enjoying now one of the most delicious gratifi-cations below—travelling from place to place, visit-ing the excellent of the earth : yet, while you were in my thoughts, I accounted myself not less favour-ed, in silence, solitude, and much prayer. I have enjoyed the Word of God ; and " my meditation of

Him has been sweet. " I was never more happy.
This one thing I will desire of the Lord, and with
the prayer of faith require, that I may find grace
sufficient for me.

I have a sweet enjoyment of midnight hours,
when I cannot sleep. At three or four o'clock
I sit up in my bed ; and you and yours, and the rest
of my children, are before me, as in a picture; and
I am entreating my God for your growth in usefulness—for your living a bright example of your
Christian profession.

Many thanks to you for "Milner's Church
History!" Little did I think what a feast was prepared for me in my old age! When he describes
the state of the Church, and the martyrs of the
second or third century, what sound understanding, what boldness and vigour of mind, does he
display! Blessed be our God, for Joseph Milner
and his work!

From your affectionate father,

H. VENN.

TO MRS. RILAND.

Yelling, Sept. 1793.

——My daughter loves me a great deal too much
or her own peace. She would fain have her beloved
ffather exempted from the pains and penalties which
flesh is heir to—which the whole ransomed Church
are called to bear—which are not worthy to be
named with the sufferings we deserve—with the
glory ready to be revealed. I can, with great sympathy, say, as Jephthah did of old : " O my daughter,
thou art among those that distress me this day!"

How can I help figuring to myself a child exceedingly pained for the anguish my body may suffer without remedy, unable to find one moment's ease till the earthly house of this tabernacle falls;—and Ruth, like another daughter, no less agitated:—both of them without brother or sister, or one friend to cheer their spirits. Yet do not think, my dear friend, I am cast down, nor that my soul is disquieted within me. I pass my time in sweet serenity, and entire trust in my God and Saviour. I pray night and day, without ceasing; and frequently rejoice, in the full assurance that He who hath loved me as His own from the beginning, will love me to the end. Where I prayed one hour out of the twenty-four, I now pray three or four times as much.

——At times, indeed, my faculties are benumbed; so that I can neither read, nor think, nor pray at all, as I was wont to do; yet mercies abound in the midst of all. I have a sweet composure, a solid peace, a glorious prospect into our future and eternal inheritance. My soul has more dwelt upon the felicity of God's chosen this year, than all the years of my life before.——

TO MR. EDWARD VENN.

MY DEAR NEPHEW, *Yelling, Nov.* 12, 1793.

——I cannot but be highly pleased with your tender attention to my sister and her daughter; though I am, by that excellent conduct, deprived of the great pleasure of a visit. I must console myself— as I do—that I, and all those who are most dear to me, are all travelling in the King's highway,* to His own place, to "see Him as He is." There we shall enjoy the glorious realities—of which we here obtain a glimpse, and then we lose it. In our best estate below, how very feeble are the impressions of our future glorious inheritance!

What pleasure did I feel in reading, that, when you were at Clapham, on Sunday, you were well instructed before you met at the table of the Lord. My prayers had been warmly presented, that the name of the Lord Jesus might be magnified, and many might eat the flesh of the Son of Man, and drink his blood. Help your dear cousin with your prayers. Expect, and earnestly long for, a day of the Redeemer's Power at Clapham church. Oh, that my son may have no rest in his soul, till those arrows, which are very sharp, reach the hearts and consciences of the King's enemies!

I recommend to my dear nephew to buy four sermons of Dr. Caleb Evans, on Christ Crucified. The two first are very sensible, but not extraordinary. The two last are among the first, for excellency, that I ever read. I would venture my reputation on my recommendation.

Grace, mercy, and peace, be with us, till, dying in the Lord, we meet above!

Your affectionate uncle,

H. VENN.

---

* Mr. Venn was accustomed to give a beautiful illustration of this expression. "Things necessary and essential are all plain. The way to Heaven is not a bridle-way, winding, and difficult to be discerned: but the King's highway, is straight, and lifted up like a Roman road; itself a full direction to the traveller."

TO MR. ELLIOTT.

MY DEAR, MY VERY DEAR SON,   *Yelling, Oct.* 7, 1793.

You have largely contributed, for past years, ever since your union with us, to the comfort of myself, and every one of my children; for which we have all great reason to be thankful to our God. Next week we hope to see you all here.

I am still very highly favoured, though declining apace, but not faster than I would wish. "Come, Lord Jesus! O come quickly!" is, almost every hour, my prayer. And when, by reason of pain, I lie awake for hours in the night, I am favoured, not only with a quiet mind, stayed upon my God, but rejoicing in the glorious prospect of soon being without error or pollution, and of having the name of my God in my forehead, and serving him without defect—and waiting for your ascension, and I hope the ascension of your offspring, sweet dears!

My son's sermons, the two Sundays before last, collected a more numerous congregation yesterday than, I think, has been in our church for years. We had eighty at the table. I read the prayers. We sang that admirable Hymn, in which are these lines:

> "But when he groan'd, and bled, and died,
>   He ruined Satan's throne, &c."

After Service, with a triumphant voice we made the church ring with Hallelujahs—

> "Lives again our Glorious King!"

It was a glorious feast indeed! Glory be to God! —My love to all your sweet babes.

The Lord give you a prosperous journey, and much of His grace and heavenly benediction, when together!

From your affectionate father,

H. VENN.

TO THE REV. JOHN VENN.

MY DEAR SON,   *Yelling, Sept.* 21, 1794.

——What a load of misery is entailed upon us from our birth! Man inherits affliction and trouble; and there is no security of any blessings, except spiritual and eternal ones. We may certainly also conclude, that cleaving, as we do, to the earth, though full of disappointments and affliction, but for them we should all be bewitched to our destruction. I observed, as I generally do (except illness prevents) with exactness, my time for writing to you—a fortnight, to a day, last Thursday, and finished the letter; but it did not go till Saturday. Punctuality is an excellent thing, I have long been convinced; and I have practised it accordingly.

You will oblige me much by writing me the Clapham news. How much do I enjoy your present full employment, and the account of your church being so well attended! I have no doubt the Lord is with you, and will Himself testify of His grace. It cost me prayer without ceasing, for years, to obtain knowledge, and in any measure the tongue of the learned (the qualifications for my high office); and so it will every one.

The Lord Jesus help you, and be in a remarkable manner with your spirit, when you preach the Visi-

tation Sermon.   If a text is not chosen, suppose it
was this :—" Preach the word : be instant in season, out of season ; reprove, rebuke, exhort, with all
long-suffering and doctrine."—I never shall forget,
and hope ever to humble myself for preaching, my
sermon at St. Saviour's.   It was, thank God! the
only time I was not able to withstand temptation.
I was not bold ;—no offence was taken ; and my
powers, as an orator, allowed.

I am glad Mr. Grant will have no other house
but that on Clapham Common.   May you be more
and more united, and the sons of my old friend, and
Mr. Wilberforce ; and quicken and excite each other
to do much in the service of Christ, and evidently
magnify his name !

On Monday last, a gentleman came here, and
accosted me in these words :—" I suppose you do
not know me; as I should not have known you.   My
name is Hodson.   In gratitude, I was obliged to pay
you a visit.   Thirty years ago, I heard you at Huddersfield."—I recollected him with much pleasure.
He is one of the most amiable of men : he has made
his fortune in Jamaica.   What an indication of his
excellency will you think it, when I tell you, that, in
the mention of his slaves, and the great affection
they shewed him, tears fell from his eyes; and he said
he had doubted whether he should not have stayed
with them till he died !   He had heard of you ; and
perhaps may become one of your flock.   He is a
steady, sensible man—a native of Huddersfield.
Oh ! how extensive, and always upon the increase,
is the good done by preaching Christ, the Way, the
Truth, and the Life !—God bless you both, in a

degree far beyond what He hath done! and bless
your aged father, that he may be an example to
his children, teaching them how a Christian dies!

Yours affectionately,

H. VENN.

TO THE REV. JAMES STILLINGFLEET.

Yelling, Jan. 4, 1795.

DEAR, and for ever dear, Brother in our Lord!—
The day before yesterday, Kitty's letter told us that
your beloved wife was very dangerously ill. I shall
not be satisfied till I hear how the Lord of all Lords
deals with you, that I may remember your case, in
all circumstances, before Him.

One year and a half I have been nearly a prisoner
to my house:—soon shall I be (unless suddenly
translated) to my chamber, and then to my bed;
and then this body shall rest in the grave, and my
spirit " enter with boldness," (ever mine!) "into the
holiest, by the blood of Jesus!" For though my
eyes are, more than ever they were, opened, to see
my wickedness has indeed been great, and mine
iniquities infinite, and the overspreading depravity
in me not to be extirpated till my dissolution—do
all I can against it; yet this creates no bondage or
despondency;—the spirit of power, of love, and of
a sound mind, is given me from above. I pray,
much more then I ever did, for myself, my relations,
my friends in Christ; and particularly for my fellow-
labourers, in whose conversation, example, and
company, I have received so much benefit. I am
so infirm, as not to be able to pray with my own
family: nevertheless, " He that loved me will love

me to the end." One thing only I desire, without ceasing—that, for the sake of the thousands to whom I have preached "the unsearchable riches of Christ," and contended for His glory, I may, in the hour of death, look through an opened Heaven to a Crucified Saviour, smiling upon my poor guilty soul!

I told my invaluable Jane I must write to you, but no more than five lines. Upon seeing what I have written, she tells me I surely meant to have said five pages. She joins with me in wishing it may please our Heavenly Father to preserve your beloved wife; or, if not, to keep from excessive grief the survivor, under a blessed assurance of meeting, after a very short interval, in the eternal fellowship, with all the elect of God.

Not a single word for past silence!—In your present suspense, to expect more than one line would not be friendly; and for a directory to me, in my intercessions, it would be sufficient.

With fervent love to you both, we remember you.

From your affectionate,

H. VENN.

P.S. We wish you both a happy new year, in the fulfilment of the Covenant—the new and better Covenant, established upon better promises, which follow in the Father's declaration to Messiah, before His holy incarnation and nativity :—"All Thy Children shall be taught of me; and great shall be the peace of Thy Children. They shall be established in righteousness, and shall be far from oppression; and as for terror, it shall be far from them."—May you have this witness in yourselves, from the opening to the close of the year, or so

M M

long in it as you remain in the body ! and the kings and princes of the world, the most admired and most envied of men on earth, will be exceedingly poor, and wretched, and miserable, in comparison with yourselves.

At the close of a Letter to Lady Mary Fitzgerald (January 17 ,1795), the following noble sentence occurs :—

I HAVE not slept out of my house, or been farther than my garden and the adjoining fields, for more than eighteen months ;—yet I enjoy liberty. I soar to Heaven ; and mix in the society of Cherubim and Seraphim, and all the Ransomed of the Lord.

TO THE REV. JOHN VENN.

MY DEAR SON,   *Yelling, Jan.* 1, 1796.

Be assured I very sensibly feel your very kind attention to my interest ; and, placing confidence in your judgment, am well satisfied with the arrangement you propose.

I am not displeased with the opposition of the Huntingtonians to your preaching : their hatred is much to be preferred to their praise. You write, you are well satisfied ;—and you have cause to be so ; not only from the full approbation of your friends at Clapham, but from the whole tenor of the Word of God ; for you teach and preach as the Oracles of God. Every Prophet and every Apostle insists as much upon the fruits of faith, as upon faith itself, and the glory of Christ's Person. The sovereign and electing grace of God, by which alone we are brought to Him, bears no proportion in the Scripture to the continual mention that is made of the absolute necessity, beauty, and excellency of a holy life and conversation, in the sight of God and man— bears no proportion, I say, to the practical part of our holy religion. It is very remarkable, also, that our Saviour would not preach about Himself, the freeness of His grace, and justification by His blood, till He had first of all laid the foundation most emphatically of that holiness which these *Solifidians* deny. As remarkably, St. Paul had no sooner finished his triumphant accouut of grace reigning through righteousness, than he leaves the subject; and writes a whole chapter, by way of guarding against an Antinomian interpretation of his doctrine.

It therefore gives me great pleasure to see you stand in the place your father did—pelted on one side by ranters clamouring for sinless perfection, and on the other by Antinomian abusers of grace. Many of these last you will see like meteors of a day, and, by their bad fruits, too plainly attesting that all their wisdom and religion is from beneath. Look upon yourself as loudly called upon by the jarring sects to search the Scriptures, and study them, and *them only*—more devoutly, *more constantly*, in full assurance that, in doing so, you shall be led into all truth.

I have to tell you—and would, if it were with my last breath—that I can wish for nothing more than I now find Christ is to me. And though I discover, more than ever, most lamentable defects in my preaching, and cannot place the smallest confidence in the multitudes to whom God has been pleased to make His Word a blessing by my mouth and pen, yet I am absolutely certain that I have preached the very doctrine that Christ and His Apostles did. The *whole* Word of God is equally acceptable to me ;—not less those parts which are the fortress of Arminians, Perfectionists, and Antinomians, than the others ; so that I am, and have been for thirty-five years, in the happy state of not being tempted to wrest any Scripture, or pervert it, in order to make it favour my own tenets.

I wish you to be more zealous, more bright and shining in your life and practice, this year, than any before—that you may stand perfect and complete in all the will of God, putting to silence the ignorance and malicious prating of all opposers. I would fain hope to see you once more, for one Sunday. My daughter sends her love with mine. Love to all the little-ones.

From your affectionate father,

H. VENN.

The Letters of a subsequent date are too few and brief to afford any further additions to this selection. Here, therefore, the Chronological Series of Correspondence closes. The Editor feels, also, that the style and subject of the foregoing Letter render it peculiarly appropriate for the position it holds, as the last of that series.

PART III.

LETTERS ON PARTICULAR SUBJECTS.

PART III.

LETTERS ON PARTICULAR SUBJECTS, TOO LONG FOR INSERTION
IN THE PRECEDING SECTIONS.

TO JONATHAN SCOTT, ESQ.*

(DIRECTIONS FOR LEADING A CHRISTIAN LIFE.)

DEAR SIR,   *Nov.* 6, 1765.

I cannot leave Shropshire without giving you joy
on your knowledge of Christ, and determination to
live in His service. This connects us more closely
than if we had sprung immediately from the same
parent : for, in numberless instances, own brothers
will be separated from each other, far as Heaven
from Hell; but all who love the Lord Jesus shall
dwell for ever with Him. Love to Him and your
soul prompts me to lay before you a few hints, furnished from long service in the Church of Christ;
which, had I received on my entrance into it, might
have preserved me from many hurtful mistakes.

Your Christian calling is a warfare, where no
quarter can be given on either side. If you prove
faithful unto death, angels will receive your depart-
ing soul; eternal glory will be your crown; the
armies of the saved will receive you with transport,

* This Letter was printed many years ago, as a Tract; and has
lately been reprinted, in several different forms.

as a soul ransomed with that precious blood, to which they owe their all; and the Redeemer's presence will be your Heaven for evermore. Should you forsake His service, or hold secret correspondence with His foes, you must be punished, like them, with eternal infamy in Hell.

The enemies you have to oppose, and conquer, will probably be, first, your former intimates, friends and nearest relations, whose polite conversation and affection for you have been so pleasing: for till their judgment of sin, true religion, and man's chief good, are formed from Scripture, as your own now is, they must both despise and hate the way of life in which you must persist. With these opposers your corrupt nature will take part, and a subtle destroyer, long practised in arts and wiles, to compass the ruin of immortal souls. In this perilous condition you have joined yourself (effectually influenced by His grace) to Christ, as your Leader and Commander. Under His banner, diligently using the MEANS He, in tenderest love, enjoins, you are confidently to expect both protection and victory.

These MEANS are: Secret Prayer—Study of the Bible—Public Worship—Hearing faithful Preachers —Christian Society—and much Retirement.

1. *Secret Prayer*, at stated times, was constantly practised by our Lord. "At evening," says he, "and morning, and noon-day, will I cry unto Thee, and that instantly; and Thou shalt hear my prayer." All His illustrious saints have done the same. Indeed, stated times of prayer, where they can be had, are no less needful to make the soul flourish,

than stated meals to keep the body in health. Wilfully to neglect them, is to walk contrary to the example of Christ and His saints, which can never produce resemblance to them in our life. Yet stated times of secret prayer will grow tiresome, and prove of no use, unless you take pains to present yourself a worshipper before the Lord in spirit and in truth, by looking up, and begging the Spirit of grace and supplication may be poured out upon your soul. But, when you duly observe stated times of secret prayer, be not cast down because you will often find great stupidity of mind, and know not what to ask; or because you feel your faith very weak, much backwardness to pray, and a swarm of idle thoughts oppressing you. Do not, on this account, leave off your constant devotions, nor question whether they will profit your soul. It is much for your good, to feel you have no power to command your own thoughts. It is much for your good, that your own experience should confirm what the word of God and His people teach—that you are weak and poor, always standing in absolute need of the mercy of God, the grace of the Lord Jesus Christ, and the power of the Holy Ghost.

On the contrary, beware of being elated on account of great enlargement of heart, and spiritual joy, which you will find sometimes flow in upon your soul. Should this favour lead you to think highly of yourself, carelessness first, and then a miserable fall, will follow; for self-exalting thoughts always defile the soul, and grieve the Spirit of God; neither can any dependence, as to future safety, be

justly built on what has passed in our own minds.
Witness the noble confession Peter made of his
faith in Christ one hour, and astonishing repri-
mand he received the next : " Get thee behind me,
Satan ! thou art an offence unto me." These sweet
sensations of spiritual joy realize to us some of the
precious promises made to believers in Christ ; and
are designed to allure us, not to excite a conceit of
any thing good in ourselves.

2. To secret prayer you will join *devout study of
the Bible ;* because it is our infallible guide, and the
treasury of all truth necessary to salvation. But
the riches laid up there are not to be found by
proud or careless minds : none possess them, till
they dig for them as for silver, longing to know the
will of God, that they may do it. To superficial
readers of the Bible, it presents little more than
a great number of duties, which must be performed ; and sins, which must be renounced ; with
insupportable pains, in failure of obedience ;—passages of excellent use, when believed ; as they at
once rouse the selfish soul of man to seek reconciliation with God, and help from Heaven ;—and
sweep away every refuge of lies, under which love
of sin leads us to take shelter. But *earnest* and
devout readers of their Bible discover much more :
they discover the tender heart of Christ; the efficacy
of His blood, to cleanse from all unrighteousness ;
and a variety of spiritual blessings, which are the
present reward of being true-hearted in His service.
I am at a loss for words to express how much solid
knowledge, transforming your mind into the Divine
image, you will certainly gain by persevering in

diligent prayer, year after year, for the true interpretation of God's blessed Word, that you may be
made wise and holy. A pattern is plainly set
before us, in these memorable petitions :—may
they come from our hearts, and ever dwell upon our
tongues !—" I am a stranger upon earth (very soon
to leave it; therefore its riches and honours cannot
profit me) ; O hide not Thy commandments from
me, which will enrich me for ever!—Open Thou
my eyes, that I may see wondrous things in Thy
Law!—Thy hands have formed and fashioned me ;
O give me understanding, that I may know Thy
Law!" This method of reading the Bible must be
continued through life, especially whilst the capital
truths of the Bible are before our eyes. By this
means we have an absolute security from abusing
any part of the Word of God. And those who dare
despise persevering prayer to be taught by the Spirit
of God what is contained in His holy Word, as if
they knew enough, fall into pernicious errors; wrest
some passages of Scripture, to contradict others;
or grow violently zealous for doctrines ; but very
cold respecting that heavenly mind, those doctrines
are revealed to produce. Our profiting will then
only appear, when, after the example of David and
St. Paul, we pray from deep conviction that we
cannot be properly affected with what we believe,
unless we are divinely taught ; and that if any man
thinketh that he knoweth any thing as he ought to
know, that man knoweth nothing.

3. Secret prayer, and devout study of the Bible,
will prepare you to *worship* in the House of God.
—And here you must beware of a fatal error,

common among those who love to hear the Gospel.
Assured from the Oracles of God, that preaching the
Gospel is the appointed means to convert sinners,
and knowing they were themselves illuminated in
this way, not a few shamefully disparage public
worship;—as if all good to the soul was to come
through the speaker; none from calling, with one
heart and voice, upon the name of the Lord, in his
own House. Hence, whilst both minister and people
should be abased before God, in confession of their
vileness; should be pleading, in the full assurance
of faith, the sacrifice and intercession of Christ for
pardon; should be earnestly imploring more grace,
to serve the Lord to all well-pleasing; should, with
flaming love to all mankind, be recommending them
to the tender care of our Heavenly Father; and be
filled with joy, in returning ardent thanks for the
loving-kindness of God towards themselves and all
men; whilst this grand business should fill their
souls, a total inattention is visible in many countenances. Their entertainment seems only to begin
when the preacher has taken his text.—Gross ignorance! Impious indecency!—Professed believers,
can you imagine you shall ever receive profit in one
means of grace, while you pour contempt on another?
or that after passing through the time of divine worship without any exercise of repentance, love, and
devotion, you can be in a fit disposition to attend to
the things which shall be delivered from the pulpit?
Be undeceived! It is novelty and curiosity by which
you are pleased, in all the discourses you extol.
On the contrary, I would have you, dear Sir, raise
your expectations very high, of the good you are to

receive from first praying with the congregation, as a Child of God by faith in Christ Jesus, before you hear the pastors of His Church.   There is a necessity for this.   It is intended to prepare and soften the ground for receiving the good seed ; and to open the heart for believing and obeying the truth. Remember, though preaching Christ is ordained to gather in the outcasts; when gathered, they are to offer up prayers and praises, intercessions and thanksgiving, a pure offering in righteousness.   Remember, that hearing will very soon cease for ever : spiritual worship is immortal.   Had we therefore our choice, whether Paul should preach to us, or call us to fall low with him on our knees in prayer, we must prefer the latter; because every one had much rather come into the presence of his beloved Sovereign, to ask what he has promised to bestow, than hear another extol him ever so highly.   An itching ear is a disease dangerous and epidemical : and if hearing has not made us love the House of Prayer, it is hard to conceive it can have done us any good at all.

4. You will not misconstrue these remarks, as if they insinuated that *preaching Christ* is not of the utmost importance, and what all Christians must value and attend to.   This preaching conquered the bloody-minded persecutors in Judea, and brought thousands to adore Christ Crucified.   This subdued the Heathen world; and every Church of Christ owes its existence, preservation, and increase, to the Word of life preached.   Our Lord emphatically warns us against false prophets, by comparing all who expect advantage from their preaching to the foolish

hope of gathering grapes from thorns, or figs from thistles. Our Litany deprecates, almost in one breath—as three of the greatest curses to mankind —pestilence, rebellion, and false doctrine.

Much indeed are we to prize the faithful preaching of the everlasting Gospel! It is the good seed; which falling upon good ground, the believing heart, brings forth fruit abundantly. Only honour equally, in its turn, every ordinance of God. Esteem spiritual worship of Him, in His House, no less profitable than the dispensing of His holy Word.

5. To secret prayer, study of the Bible, public worship, and hearing the Word, you will add *the society of Christians* engaged in the same warfare as yourself. This is commanded by our God; and is of great advantage. We are social by nature; and our companions must be infectious, if destitute of faith; or greatly improving, if we make a right choice. Love unfeigned to our Saviour must give us invincible aversion to the discourse and company which pour contempt upon all His excellency and precepts: nor is it possible, where the duty of men, in their business or office, does not oblige them to be [in company with profane and voluptuous men, to consort with them and be guiltless. The command is peremptory: *Go from the presence of a man, as soon as thou perceivest the words of wisdom are not in him.* The warning is merciful, and very alarming: *A companion of fools shall be destroyed.* And, lest worldly interests, or a remaining love for the witty, enlivened conversation of profane people, should bribe us to believe we may sometimes associate with them, and yet receive no harm, the salutary

advice is, *Be not deceived; evil communications corrupt good manners.* Your society, therefore, must be with real, not nominal, Christians ; *for he that walketh with wise men shall be wise.*

But do not expect to find real Christians such as you may figure them in your own mind, nor scan their life with a severe eye. Judge of your fellow-soldiers by what you know of yourself, in earnest as you certainly are. Innate corruptions are very stubborn, and, though besieged, and doomed to death, make frequent sallies. Hard is the conflict to get the mastery over a besetting sin ; which is seldom obtained at once, or without many falls. Be jealous of the hypocrisy, natural to us all, of passing a favourable judgment on our own condition, faulty as we are ; yet condemning others as dissemblers, for the same things we find in ourselves. Alas! the very best have abundant cause to think themselves vile : for it is notorious (whatever some may boast) that believers in Christ, one and all, are polluted, imperfect, inconstant—impatient of each other's infirmities, and scarcely able to be at peace among themselves ; though they all experience, as they confess from day to day, the tender compassions of their Heavenly Father, under all their failures.

Be not stumbled, if you meet with many hollow professors, talkative, and full of confidence on account of their supposed conversion, and the knowledge they have attained in spiritual things. So it has been from the beginning. Upright followers of the Lamb are few in every age : you may know them by their disclaiming, with equal care, all trust in their own spiritual attainments, and the baneful abuse of imputed righteousness and the election of grace ; by their tender fear of offending God ; by their humility and meekness, their generosity and compassion ; and the great benefit to be derived from their discourse, full of a Divine savour. With persons of this excellent sort, cultivate an intimacy : they will build you up in your holy faith ; they will establish you in every good purpose. You will burn with desire to be like them ; and, upon leaving their company, you will find a spirit of prayer spring up in your mind.

6. But company, beyond a certain measure, is of bad consequence. *Keeping much retired*, and by ourselves, is most profitable for us all. Indeed, when our worldly business is attended to as it ought to be, and secret duties are punctually observed, there cannot remain a good deal of time for persons, in any station, to spend in company : and they who imagine that praying at certain seasons, hearing the Gospel, and then entering into a sort of general conversation about religion and religious people, will be sufficient, are grievously mistaken.   Unless we love (and contrive, as we are able) to be much alone, how can we often and solemnly call to remembrance the evil of our past life, so as to loathe ourselves ?—how feel contrition for the follies of our innate depravity ?— how, with the blessed Mary, ponder in our hearts the sayings of our Lord ?—how enter deeply into His agony and death, the price of our peace and eternal life ?—how weigh the value of our spiritual privileges, and the weight of the crown of glory laid up for the faithful ?—how feel the strength and multitude of our obligations to live in exemplary

obedience, constrained by love passing knowledge? Though the pastors of Christ's Church speak on these subjects, and they make part of every conversation, we must ruminate in private upon them, or they will never duly impress and fill our mind.

Hence the most distinguished saints, before they entered on any arduous work for the glory of God or the good of men, did not think their purity of intention, or the promise of God's Spirit, sufficient, without preparing by much retirement. Moses, Elijah, Daniel, the Baptist, and our Lord Himself, teach us, by their practice, the benefit and necessity of being often and much alone. Great and many evils grow in the Church, from its pastors and people neglecting to copy these infallible examples.

For want of being much alone, popular teachers are puffed up; thence become contentious, jealous of those they fear as their rivals, disputers, and abusers of their fellow-servants. For want of meditation in private upon the truths of God, professors of faith in Christ are arrant Pharisees, whilst they violently condemn pharisaism; formalists, though they know it not, in the midst of perpetual exclamations against formality;—for they can talk, without humiliation, of man's total corruption, and the sinfulness of sin;—they can talk, without gratitude of redemption by the blood of God, manifest in the flesh; and, without grief, on the hypocrisy and unbecoming lives of many who make profession of faith in Christ. Nothing, in their discourse on these deeply-affecting topics, strikes the hearer's mind as coming from a broken heart. This profanation of sacred truths, by talking of them with a careless, dissipated spirit, does much hurt; and we incur guilt, like those who take the name of the Lord in vain. Yet this must be the case with us, unless there be a due mixture of solitude with society, to gird up the loins of our minds, and effectually impress them, by much intercourse with God alone.

With respect to the multitude of ignorant and licentious men, you must expect their ridicule and censure; which by no means should gall or irritate your mind. You could not be a servant of Christ, were you approved by them. "If ye were of the world, the world would love its own: but because ye are not of the world, but I have chosen you out of the world, therefore the world hateth you." The light in your mind is a distinguishing favour, which you are ever to remember. No one can believe there are such "things prepared for them that love God," as you know, till the eyes of their understanding are opened, as yours have been; and their incomparable excellence felt, as it has been in your soul. Yet, in this case, love hopeth all things, and endureth all things;—hopeth the time will come, when they, who think you mad, will worship with you in Spirit and in truth. Meanwhile, love will enable you meekly to receive contemptuous treatment, and hard speeches against your faith, your conduct, and your friends. Be not eager to justify yourself, nor over-forward to make converts by much speaking: an irksome truth becomes more so by being unseasonably urged. Besides, wordy people are set down as loving to hear themselves talk; and novices are proud to gain proselytes, before they are themselves established in the Truth, or know their own religion.   But in victory over pride, anger, and all wickedness—in stead-fastly observing every rule of holy living laid down by our Saviour—in courteous behaviour to all men —in calmly urging the Word of God, when some favourable opportunity occurs of bearing testimony to the truth—in these things you cannot exceed. Wait patiently; and you will, by such irreproach-able and wise conduct, stop the mouth of prejudice, and win over some to come forth and live a Chris-tian life, as you do.

I wish you much of the presence and peace of God in your soul; in your practice and tempers, much steadiness and love ; and a gracious answer to your prayers for your friends, relations, and fel-low-sinners   May we remember each other before God; beseeching Him, that we may strongly re-commend His Truth and service, by great useful-ness, till we are for ever with Him!

From yours, &c.

H. VENN.

TO JOHN BRASIER, ESQ.

(DIRECTIONS FOR LEADING A CHRISTIAN LIFE.)

MY DEAR COUSIN,   *Yelling, Jan.* 23, 1777.

I regret the loss we had in not seeing you in your way to town; not merely as the visit would have given us so much pleasure, but as I should have had an opportunity of talking very fully upon a subject of the last importance, and on which I can write but very imperfectly—I mean, your set-tlement in life.   The whole family join with me in love to you both, and the most cordial wishes for your present and eternal welfare. This is what I am always wishing : and having, through the most adorable mercy and infinite condescension of God, been led into the way of peace myself—and to so much comfort every day as excites my astonishment—I would fain see all my fellow-sinners, and much more my friends and relations, brought into the same delightful enjoyment of life. I shall now, therefore, lay before you what I judge the sure and certain method of living a Christian life, profitable to men, and pleasing to God, in abundance of peace and hope, light and love from Heaven.

The first material point is, a conscientious waiting upon God in prayer ; not satisfied with bowing our knees, and beginning the day with devotion ;—but, *we must pray.* I used long to exercise an idle lukewarm way of praying (by which I got nothing, but deluded my own soul); as if it were a necessary consequence of my corruption, which all felt, and all deplored. But to pray without attention, or without importunity—to pray with our hearts asleep, and worldly thoughts intruding, as guests of every character do into an inn—is hypocrisy. If we are not grieved and afflicted at it, as our disease, and long for the Spirit's power, and confess our sinfulness, our religion is mere form. If we do lament it, we shall succeed ; and, generally, our secret approaches to the Throne of Grace will be refreshing, animating, and the sweetest hour of our life.

When secret prayer is thus performed, one part of our earnest request will always be, that the worship of the family may be solemn and spiritual, affecting every member of it, and offered up with self-abasement from a company of vile sinners before a glorious God—a means of creating mutual affection and unfeigned good-will throughout the day. I have had family worship ever since I kept house; but never, till within these five years, was concerned about carrying it on as it ought to be. Not that any one could discover irreverence in my manner, or that I had not some desire God should be honoured; but my desire was exceedingly small; and I did not intercede with God, that we might never meet together without the exercise of repentance, faith, hope and love, and without such a manifestation of His presence as He has promised to "two or three who are met together in His name."

When secret or family worship is thus performed, the blessing is to be confidently expected, in a recollected and watchful frame of mind, amidst trials, and preparedness for them; in a jealousy of self-will, which is ever working; and in a fear of every thing that savours of a sour, angry, hasty spirit, the bane of domestic felicity, and the great contradiction to the Christian temper. At noon-day, as you are not engaged in business, you must contrive to find a season for retirement, to be with your God and Saviour. Daniel and David did this, in the midst of all their great employments and numerous cares. Our Saviour did the same; for He is the person speaking, when he says, "At evening, and morning, and noon-day, will I cry unto Thee; and that instantly." Probably you will say, I am sadly at a loss what to pray for at each time. My rule

is this :—when I do not pray, at noon, with Mrs.
Venn, or if I do not find the Spirit of prayer
when alone—I read some Psalm, or some of St.
Paul's Epistles; and presently find matter suggested from those Lively Oracles, and generally the
Spirit of prayer too. And when you find you cannot
pray, rise from your knees, stand, or sit down, and
ponder deeply on the state of your heart: ask
yourself some such questions as these : " Have I no
sins to confess, no corruptions to lament ? Have
I no need of pardon, or of the Holy Ghost, that I
can be so stupid, so heard-hearted ? Oh, what a
sinful man ! how sunk, how fallen ! how unable to
help myself!"—"Lord, arise !" will follow: and if it
does not, this solemn consideration of your own
vileness will be exceedingly profitable to your soul,
and endear the name of a Saviour, and convince
you that you are saved through sovereign grace,
abounding in God's Son.

At evening, you must have a stated time for retirement, and preparation for family worship; which
I would entreat you always to have, in the morning,
before breakfast ; and at evening, before supper.
And never expect to prosper in your soul, if the
food prepared for the body, or the setting out the
table, bears any weight, compared with the spiritual
repast for the soul, which family worship ought
always to be, and regarded as one of the most
solemn things which occur in the whole day.

Make choice of serious servants ; praying to God,
who will, in such cases, direct and provide. And
then, by careful observation of these rules, you will
enjoy His peace, you will walk in His light, you

will receive what He published His Gospel to bestow, and be increasing with all the increase of God. Nothing higher, nothing greater than this, are you to expect. A family fearing God, working righteousness, obtaining promises, living in peace and love, is a picture of Heaven in miniature. Such I pray your family may be!

There are two points more, of great moment—company, and public worship. Nothing hurts the soul more than much acquaintance. The time is wasted—the attention is drawn off—an idle strain of conversation, even about religious subjects, is indulged—the spirit of the world creeps in, and a pleasure in entertaining, and appearing just as those who know not God. I believe more religious professors perish by this error than any other. Be therefore deliberate, and very discreet in the choice of your company. Always say to yourself: " Do I find either reproof, or exhortation, or comfort, or instruction in the great things of God, from their company? Otherwise, what loss must I suffer, and how to be thrown back, whilst I want every help to set me forward!"

With regard to preaching, never leave your own pastor, who preaches the Gospel. For as rain, without which nothing can grow, may fall so often, and in such excess, as to prove no less hurtful than a drought; so it is common, very common, for religious persons to hear, and hear, and hear, till they are very little alone—are utter strangers to meditation—are as ignorant of the Scriptures, and the interpretation of them by the Holy Ghost, as those who hear only ignorant teachers. Once in the

week, besides the Lord's-day, is certainly sufficient.
I had rather spend one hour with the dearest friend
I have upon earth, than hear him commended for
days together. Private prayer, and meditation upon
the blessed Word of God, is spending our time with
the Beloved Jesus. The sermon is the commendation of His excellency.

Some would now be apt to say : ' Must all this be
done? Surely it is not needful!'—Judge from the
shameful conduct of professors—from the complaints
resounding, on every side, of masters against their
domestics, and of servants against their superiors.
Judge, from the worldly compliances so common
amongst those who hear Christ's ministers, and can
scarcely, in any thing else, be distinguished from
natural men. Judge, from the few who are fervent
in love, active in zeal, judicious and animating in
their discourse, clothed in the heavenly robes of
humility and righteousness—whose words are as
goads, and their whole deportment a pattern. Judge,
from the very great scarcity of such characters ; and
see how absolutely needful it is to do more than
others, and to labour, in the way I have pointed
out, for "that meat which endureth unto everlasting
life." The general ruinous mistake of professing
Christians is, that justification by faith, imputed
righteousness, electing grace, and everlasting love,
are to be believed and extolled, and heard with
great eagerness ;—and then, alas! they stop. Not
so the Word of God : it teaches all these doctrines,
but as means of engaging our hope, establishing
our faith, spiritualizing our affections, conquering
the world, and making us long for the coming of

the Lord, to whom we are dear as the bride to the bridegroom, and whose presence without a veil can alone satisfy us. Oh, the deplorable apostacy from a Christian spirit, whilst the doctrine of grace is maintained with zeal! I pray God ever to preserve us from such abuse; and make us long to be well-pleasing, in all our ways and doings, to Him whom we call our Lord and our Redeemer!

I am so well recovered, that next week I purpose beginning my usual course of work, which has been for more than a month suspended. I ride every day; and God has been pleased to recruit my strength. I was so weak, as not to be able to pray with my family for near a fortnight. My son, by the help of Mr. Jenks, was my chaplain.

You cannot think how I rejoice to hear that the minister so justly dear to us both is again able to lift up his voice and cry, "Behold the Lamb!" Oh, may he run, and all of us who are now in our last stage, as racers always do, the swiftest—catch much of the fire from Heaven before we enter, and be evidently transformed and fitted for that world of the Redeemed!

If you and dear Mrs. Brasier are not dismayed at this long epistle, let us hear from you soon, and how you go on.

From your affectionate cousin,

H. VENN.

P. S. Mrs. Venn, as well as myself, hope to have the pleasure of waiting upon you and my cousin, in Yelling Rectory; but shall first, most probably, see you at your own house in the spring. It is a noble promise to the Christian Church, expressed rather darkly—" In that day shall there be upon the bells of the horses, ' Holiness to the Lord'; yea, every vessel in Jerusalem and Judah shall be, ' Holiness unto the Lord of Hosts ' " !   The meaning is, The whole family shall be holy; and all that is done in it shall be done from a pure intention to please God.   Such may your house be ! and "the eyes of the Lord be upon it for good," from the beginning to the end of the year !   Whatever comforts and blessings you enjoy together (and may they be many !) still may you both be looking forward to that grand immortal life with the Church triumphant, in the presence of the Lamb, for which your souls are forming !   There I hope to meet you ; and not yield to any one, in the whole armies of the saved, in acknowledging my marvellous deliverance, freely bestowed on the vilest and most abominable of men ! Then, how different from what we know now, our knowledge of ourselves, and of our sin—of our Redeemer, and His love ! How different our feelings, our services, and our delight !

> Could we leave our foolish dreaming
> Of a fancied heaven below,
> And see Jesus' glory beaming,
> How our souls would long to go !

TO LADY MARY FITZGERALD.

(ON THE DOUBTS AND FEARS OF UPRIGHT CHRISTIANS.)

Yelling, Nov. 25, 1777.

IT is nearly a week since I had a momentary interview with your Ladyship.   Since that time, you have been scarcely an hour out of my mind.

Base worm as I am, I yet feel much for every

one who has begun the glorious warfare of a Christian. I feel still more, when one is plucked from among the high ones of the earth, as " a brand out of the fire ";—when there is found in Cæsar's household an Honourable Lady, bold to confess the faith of Christ Crucified ; and returning to the ᵃArk of God, like Noah's dove, over a vast world of waters gaping to swallow her up.

Let this be my apology, if your Ladyship should think I need one, for sending you, unasked, this no short epistle. It comes from an aged servant of that ever-blessed Lord who has revealed Himself to you as all your salvation.

From the few words you dropped in the Chapel, I at once understood your case to be the same with the greater part of the family of our Saviour : for, strange as it may sound, it is too true, that few, comparatively very few, *upright* Christians are free from gloomy doubts and fears ! The universal cause, in these excellent persons, is a discovery of manifold sins and corruptions of heart, to which they were once strangers. They now feel prodigious unbelief, and often a brutish stupidity of mind. They often are devoid of the Spirit of prayer, of delightful communion with God, and of any sensible impressions from the love of Christ. They feel pride and sloth, and self-love, fighting for the mastery, &c. &c. &c. For these things they are sadly cast down.—But we may say, to such upright Christians ; How read ye the Scriptures ? Is it not written, that the " flesh," in God's Children, " lusteth against the Spirit ;" and that they even bear about with them what properly deserves the dreadful name of a " body of death"?

In every age, the most useful and excellent in Christ's Church, even when sure of eternal glory, have been compelled to cry out, "Oh, wretched man that I am!" Your soul, blessed be God! is athirst to resemble the chief of his saints. It is a Divine ambition;—yet you forget that the very complaints, so bitter to your soul, were found in them all—the same change in their spiritual frames—the same involuntary wanderings in prayer, and manifold deficiencies. On this account, even St. Paul concluded himself "less than the least of all saints," and had no confidence in himself.

Indeed, were not our case *here* thus deplorably defective, what need of atoning blood to cleanse the best—of "the righteousness of God, which is, by faith, unto all, and upon all, them that believe"—of mercy in its brightest display—of all the wonderful process in the salvation of the Church? every part of which supposes, in the heirs of glory, defects and stains, which have excited their tears and groans, in all ages. Besides, daily observation proves, that no sooner do we lose a sense of our vileness, than self-preference, or a conceit of our perfection, rises up in the mind. We should therefore be humbled to the dust, from the knowledge of ourselves : but so long as Christ is our only hope and our peace, and the supreme desire of our souls is to serve and please Him in newness of life, never let us one moment give place to a doubting temper, whether we are in Him, and He in us. This, I can have no doubt, is every day your aim. "Be, therefore, of good cheer!" is the command of all the Prophets, Apostles, and the Saviour—which you are to realise, as if addressed to you by name—" thy faith hath saved thee."

" Still," you may be ready to reply, " I am afraid, lest I should be deceived, and at last be found a hypocrite."—Against this ruinous self-deception there is an infallible security. Pray thus: " Try me, O God! and seek the ground of my heart; prove me, and examine my thoughts; look well if there be any way of wickedness in me, and lead me in the way everlasting!" When this prayer is repeatedly offered up, to suppose it possible our most gracious and loving Father should permit us to be imposed on to our ruin, is at once to deny His goodness, and all success in prayer.

Your Ladyship fears lest you should be found at last a hypocrite. No Child of God but has had this fear; some for a shorter, others for a longer time. It is often of great service, to excite to greater vigilance and diligence, till love casts out this uneasy fear. But I would have you fear, also, and pray against hard thoughts of God:—these are natural to us. Before we are awakened, and believe the Word of God, we think, foolishly, that He is such an one as ourselves; and then daringly live in the way of self-indulgence, and conformity to a world which hates Him: saying, " Tush! there shall no harm happen unto us!"—though all the penalties and pains denounced on the children of disobedience stand in full force against us. After the remembrance of this our wicked way is become grievous to us; and we even loathe ourselves, for what we have been, and what we have done against our glorious God : then we are beset with sad

apprehensions, as if He were implacable. Though
His nature be love, His mercies over all the works
of His hands, His long-suffering—as you and I
know—exceedingly great; though He swears by
Himself, He hath "no pleasure in the death of the
wicked;" we are still apt to fear He will be extreme
to mark what is done amiss in us. Though He
loved our persons when we were dead in trespasses,
and delivered up His Son for us when we were
enemies, we fear He does not love us, to save our
souls, after we are reconciled.

You should fear denying the tender compassion
of our Great and Merciful High Priest, and calling
His most faithful promises into question. You
should fear being guilty of entertaining low thoughts
of His blood, as if it only cleansed the most advanced in holiness—not Jerusalem sinners, who had
execrated His person, and shed His blood, with
blasphemous exultation over His agonies. You
should fear, also, disobedience to His repeated commands (though He knows all your defilement, and
just causes of complaint against yourself) of *rejoicing* in the Lord, whilst you have no ground of
confidence in yourself. You should fear grieving
the Spirit of God, who is the *Comforter* given to
make glad the Church of God, and vouch the perfection of the sacrifice offered by Christ, and accepted, as the full, perfect, and sufficient payment of
their debt who flee to Him for refuge.

I would now address your Ladyship upon another
topic.—Your choice and separation from the great
world, absorbed in gaiety and pleasure, must have
been, and often still is, the subject of much con-

versation among your relations and friends. It is
designed, by your Beloved Lord, as a call to them;
and will no doubt be, in some instances, the blessing you desire it should. Yet, humanly speaking,
the advantage they will gain depends on your re-
futing two errors, which they grasp with all their
might, and expect to see confirmed by your conduct
and feeling.

The first is, that imagination, not sound reason—
designing priests, not the word of the Living God
—have led you into this religious path. "Now,"
say they, "you will find we judge right; for you will
perceive in her Ladyship no steadiness, but a va-
riation continually in her judgment and sentiments.
First, this thing must be renounced, all innocent as
it is; then another. First, this preacher will be the
oracle; by and by, his sermons will be of no worth.
At one time, those principles will be insisted on as
absolutely needful, which, before the year ends, will
be discarded as erroneous. In a word, you will
observe her driven with the wind, like a ship at sea
without a compass."

The effectual refutation of these injurious sur-
mises will be your maintaining, with all perseverance, the substantial, never-changing difference
between the Children of God and the Children of
the Wicked-one; which is this—a sober, that is, a
vigilant, righteous, and godly life, from the knowledge of Christ, and love unfeigned to His name.
There is nothing greater, or higher, or more spiritual, than this. The heights of the soaring, greatly-
deluded perfectionist, or any peculiarities on which
devotees lay a mighty stress, are of no use, to say

the least. But, a constant study of Scripture, a
wise choice of a few heavenly-minded acquaintance,
a serious and earnest use of prayer, and love for
the House of God, where some faithful messenger
expounds the Scriptures—this cannot be censured
as the work of imagination, nor charged with levity.
And when the benefit of these means for spiritual
life and godliness is evidenced, in humility, and
meekness, and good-will to all who are in connexion
with you as friends, relations, and domestics, you
are a Christian altogether: you are—what the Bible
describes—a new creature, an example, a comfort,
a blessing: angels minister to you: God teaches
you: Christ is your life, and Heaven your everlasting habitation. You will be separate from the
world, as you should be; and they in vain will seek
to find any thing ridiculous or absurd in your conduct and principles. By persevering—without turning aside to any sect, or being at a loss to know
which is the way you should walk in—they will be
forced to confess you know the certainty of the
words of Truth, and are fixed upon the Rock.

The other error the world grasps, and which, by
your feelings, they hope to have confirmed beyond
a doubt, is, that the service of Christ has nothing
at present to recommend it: it is hard and melancholy, tending to bondage and despair. " The
very people," say the world, " who have got into
this religious way, are heartily tired, and would be
glad, with all their hearts, to get back again to us,
but for the terrors of their cruel superstition, and
the positive denunciations of misery thundered out
against them by their teachers, should they return

to us." Indeed, if such as your Ladyship, who have given up yourself to Christ's service, daily watching at His gates, and praying to Him for His grace—if such are not fully satisfied and established in peace, they will think themselves justified in rejecting the yoke of Christ as an insupportable burden, and will explode, as cant, the affirming that His service is perfect freedom, and an intercourse of dearest friendship and Divine love!

Now you will confute and confront this injurious conclusion, when you walk in light and peace, in hope, and a sweet sense of the Divine presence with you, as a duteous child. But you will answer: "This is not in my power, any more than to command the sun to shine." I reply: It is the will of God concerning those who are in Christ Jesus, that they should rejoice in the Lord, no less than be subject to His authority; that their joy should be full, no less than their lives be holy. Both are equally beyond their power to attain; but both are to be the matter of our repeated petitions, and urged with importunity. As children in our Saviour's family, we have a right to plead, in some such terms as these, with Him:—" Lord! I entreat Thee, not only for the comfort of my own soul, but for the glory of Thy Name, make me glad with the joy of Thy salvation! Enable me to express the blessings I enjoy under Thy government! O King of Saints! fain would I chase away the prejudices so many have against Thee, as a hard and austere Master! Oh, my Lord! forbid it, that I should ever prove a stumbling-block in their way! Following after Thee, I have come out from them, and am separate:

they narrowly observe me : they expect to see me wretched, and miserable, and melancholy. Anoint me with the oil of gladness! fill me with peace and joy in believing! make me abound in hope, through the Holy Ghost given unto me, that I may speak good of the Name of the Lord; and my heart dance within me for joy, whilst I tell of Thy loving-kindness!"

Such requests, persevered in, will and must be answered, in due time, and in the best manner. I shall share in your felicity; and, should we meet again, my soul would bless the Lord to hear you say, " I know whom I have believed, and am persuaded that He is able to keep that which I have committed unto Him!"

Though I have done my best, I know not whether you can read my writing without great difficulty. Our dear friends in St. James's Place will help you to decipher the character. May " every good and perfect gift" be multiplied upon you!

Yours, &c.   H. VENN.

It is necessary to state the circumstance under which the next Letter was written. A clergyman of Mr. Venn's acquaintance having taken up the notion that the English Translation of the Bible was very incorrect—and that it was of paramount importance, for obtaining right views of the Truth, to study the original languages—zealously urged his newly-adopted views upon his friends and hearers. Mr. Venn, therefore, drew up the following statement of his own opinion on the subject; and sent the Letter to the clergyman alluded to.

It must be carefully observed, however, that Mr. Venn's objections against the critical study of the Hebrew are to be chiefly applied to the cases of clergymen *engaged in the active duties of the ministry,* or other persons who have little time or talent for the study of languages. Mr. Venn was very anxious that his son, whilst at College, should acquire a competent knowledge of the Hebrew, which he thought was far too much neglected by Students in Divinity generally.

If the Letter be read with these preliminary remarks in view, it will afford much useful advice. And it proves, for the comfort of those who are ignorant of the original languages, the full sufficiency of Translations to convey the knowledge of the Truth to humble and devout inquirers.

———

TO A CLERGYMAN.

(ON THE STUDY OF THE HEBREW LANGUAGE ; AND THE SUFFICIENCY OF TRANSLATIONS TO CONVEY THE KNOWLEDGE OF THE TRUTH.)

Yelling, Jan. 3, 1780.

YOUR zealous endeavours, my dear friend, to make me entertain the same idea of the great use of Hebrew learning which now so fully possesses your own mind, is owing to the real regard you bear for me. But, as this subject draws us into debate, and diverts us from better things, I now send you my reasons at large, which compel me totally to differ from you in this matter.

First, I must premise, that I readily allow great masters in the Oriental tongues are well employed in their study ; because, *in general,* they are men evidently strangers to the life of God in the soul, whilst they possess fine abilities for verbal criticism.

Their works, therefore, I read diligently ; and when they bring satisfactory evidence for a reading different from the Authorised Translation, I adopt their corrections : just as classical men do those of Dacier, Francis, and Hurd, in Horace, without the drudgery of searching all the volumes they have done. Some places in the Psalms I have corrected by Dr. S. Chandler ; some in Job, by Mr. Peters ; some in Isaiah, I have done by Bishop Lowth ; &c. &c. Yet, before such eminent critics in the Hebrew tongue corrected our Translation, respecting several unintelligible sentences, the Sacred Books were, in their substance, no less profitable (saving in these few places) to every reader. And, upon the most exact inquiry, I cannot say that I have received from their labours one new spiritual idea, or any instruction in religious doctrines I possessed not before I adopted their emendations of the Text. These amount to no more, in my judgment, than taking away a few blemishes on the fingers or toes of the noblest statue the world ever saw; which, though it be a pleasing and desirable work, adds nothing to the grand idea the statue itself impresses.

I observe further, that even those excellent emendations, made by these celebrated critics, are still a *Translation*—not what you seem to lay such mighty stress upon, the Original Hebrew ; so that, when I adopt their corrections, in one place I receive Chandler's, in another Lowth's, version, instead of our established one. And the utmost the ablest Hebrew scholar can attain to, is no more than to prefer *his own interpretation* of the Original Text, as better than that of a number of scholars more deeply learned in the same tongue than himself. For what a prodigy of parts, and application too, must he be, and what a high conceit of his own intellect must he possess, who can think himself more able to *translate* the *Hebrew* than Forty-seven men skilled in that tongue, and therefore selected for the work out of all the divines then in the kingdom —men, who did not lean to their own understanding, but looked up to the Father of Lights for direction and teaching; some of them confessors for the truth—men who studied more hours in a week than modern scholars in a month—men who lived so truly the life of Children of God, and members of Christ, that none of us can keep pace with them ! These forty-seven men were diligently employed, near three whole years, about this great work, and conducted it by the best rules one can conceive. Now, is there the least degree of probability that any individual Hebrew scholar should have acuteness, learning, and judgment so superior to these forty-seven truly venerable scholars, as to be justified in calling their version "*lies*," but his own version the Word of God ?

I now extract, from a very valuable book (Dr. Fuller's Church History), the Rules our Translators observed in their important work :—

1. The Bible read in the Church (called the Bishops') was to be followed, and as little altered as the original will allow.

2. Every particular man, of each company, was to take the same chapter or chapters ; and having translated or amended them severally by himself

where he thought good, ALL were to meet together, to compare what they had done, and agree what should stand.

3. As any one company (the forty-seven were divided into six companies) has despatched any one Book in this manner, they shall send it to the rest, to be considered of seriously.

4. If any *one* of the comp any, upon the review of the Book, shall doubt or differ upon the places, they are to send the rest word of it, noting the places, and offering their reasons : to which if they consent not, the matter is to be determined at the general meeting, which is to be of the chief persons of each company, at the end of the work.

5. When any place of *special obscurity* is doubted of, letters, directed by Royal Authority, are to be sent to any learned in the land, for his judgment on such a place.

6. Letters to be sent from every Bishop to the rest of his clergy, admonishing them of this Translation ; and to move and charge all, who are *skilful* in the tongues, and who have taken pains in that way, to send his own particular observations.

7. The Translation by Tindal, or Matthewe, or Coverdale, Whitchurch, or [that of] Geneva, to be used, when they agree better with the Original than the Bishops' Bible agrees.

Besides observing these Rules, they compared the Italian, Spanish, and Dutch Versions.

Now, let any scholar, free from prejudice, consider all the learning and piety, the industry, judgment, and care, used by this assembly (who had also the help of the whole fund of learning in

Hebrew, at that time, in the kingdom); and then say, Whether there is reason to think any private person is likely, by his own pains, to translate the Text better than they have done? Strange! if even Vitringa, Lowth, or Kennicott, should be able to translate—I will not say the whole Hebrew Bible, but even a considerable part of it—with so few mistakes, as the most venerable assembly, probably, that ever sat in the world have made! The experiment, in many instances, has been tried, and confirms my conclusion; for Lowth corrects Kennicott; Kennicott, Lowth;—a third great critic corrects them both! So much did I observe of this, early in life, to my great grief, as to make me pay little deference, ever after, to critics, or their corrections in general.

The conclusion therefore is plain :—I must either hold, every Hebrew scholar is more to be trusted as a faithful interpreter of the Text, on the force of his own learning and abilities, than all our Translators : or, I must allow their version, *upon the whole*, is much more likely to be the meaning of the Text; which, in general, is the conclusion I hold.

When you call our Translation " *lies*," and not the Word of God, you bring no proof of your very crude assertion. Our Bible relates the Creation of the world in Six days—the Fall and its consequences— the Universal Flood—the Promise of Christ—the Call of Abraham—the history of his posterity— the character, life, death, resurrection, ascension, and offices of Christ—the exceeding great and precious promises of life through Him—and universal Resurrection and Judgment to come. Now, our souls need nothing more, for doctrine, than these great things, taught by the Holy Ghost: on these are founded our knowledge, faith, love, hope, peace —and our salvation is secured: and all these great things are *entirely independent* of every obscure passage which it is the work and joy of the verbal critic to set right. You should, therefore, my friend, either prove to me that these great things, in God's Law, are not every way, of themselves, when taught by the Holy Ghost, sufficient for all spiritual life and godliness; or prove, that our Translation gives a very deficient account of these matters, far different from the Original. Till this is done (which I never heard was attempted), I must conclude we have the substance of the Word of God as truly in a Translation as in the Hebrew Bible; and that every real Christian, who now devoutly ponders on his English Bible, has before his eyes the Oracles of God; and no less hears His voice, than if he could read the Hebrew, and understand it as well as Isaiah himself.

Further: when you contemptuously reproach the English Bible, and call it " *lies,*" because there are in it many faults, you seem to forget the Hebrew Text itself is very far from being absolutely pure or intelligible. The Arabic, the Syriac, the Chaldee Versions are often ransacked, in vain, to explain a word or sentence in the Text. How often, in one single book of the Prophets, does Bishop Lowth interpret the Hebrew, and correct it, by the Septuagint! whilst Bishop Warburton goes so far as to say, the Hebrew without the Septuagint would be as unintelligible as a cipher without its key. Again: how many words are left out! how many

are put in! How does Bishop Lowth lament the very
imperfect state (N.B. in the superlative degree) of the
Hebrew Text—" never (says he) to be recovered"!
Notwithstanding all this, you call the Hebrew
Scriptures the Word of God—and justly; because
all these errata and interpolations, taken together,
and made the most of which an enemy can, bear no
proportion to what is pure; nor at all affect either
the grand and marvellous facts, or the essential
doctrines of the Christian Faith. What bigoted
partiality then, and how cruel to English readers of
their Bible, to call it " *lies*," because it has many faults
—more, perhaps, than the Hebrew! The only
lawful conclusion from hence, as it appears to me,
is, that the Providence of the All-wise God has permitted these things, in order to humble men who
would exalt themselves on account of their Hebrew
learning, as if they had those superior advantages
over common Christians, which they are so ready
to claim. These things, being permitted, prove that
the great end, for which "all Scripture is given by
inspiration of God," is fully attainable in every Translation, no less than by the knowledge of the Original; and that both learned and unlearned equally
need the Spirit of Truth, without which neither the
Original nor a Version will do the soul good.

This leads to another remark: That our God
never prescribes a critical study of the Hebrew Text;
but a very different way, which every contrite spirit
always chooses. He commands—He repeatedly
commands—and urges us, to seek, with vehement
prayer, as a matter of life, and to *cry unto Him,* for
knowledge in Divine things. Whilst His Oracles are

before us, assuring us, that this Divine knowledge, of peerless excellence, is not the mere fruit of study and learning, but His gift: Prov. ii. 1—9. Should I therefore search indefatigably for a correct Hebrew Text, if I did not at the same time with importunity implore God to teach me, I should indeed be guilty of a sinful neglect; and God would say of all the pains I took to get Hebrew learning, "What is *this* to *me;* even to me? saith the Lord!" From Him I can never find the least intimation that His adorable Word would be sadly perverted by a bad translation;—though Christ and his Apostles knew perfectly well that the Scriptures could not possibly be read by the Gentiles (one in a thousand excepted), unless read in a version. They give not a single hint of any evil which was to arise to the Church from this; though Christ very plainly told the Pharisees, that they, by their tradition, made the commandment of God of none effect. And this remark is much to my purpose; as there is good reason to believe the Hebrew Text, in his time, had faults.—St. Paul, in his directions to Timothy and Titus, to choose pastors, never bids them be careful not to lay hands on any Christian who had sinfully neglected to read the Hebrew Bible.

Translations were early made; and these were used by the Primitive Fathers, who, it is notorious, understood not the Hebrew. St. Jerome was the first, eminent for Hebrew knowledge; not a Primitive Father:—and his (the Vulgate) Translation, though the most faulty perhaps of any, is yet proved, by the learned Professor Michaelis, to have been of great use to all succeeding translators of the

Hebrew Bible. Indeed, the situation of the Christian Church in the Apostles' days, and for more than three centuries following, made it impossible for them to read the original; for manuscripts were very dear, consequently very scarce; and the major part of the Christians were the poorest of mankind. All the Bible they could have was unspeakably short of what the very worst version contains: it was nothing but the Word of Life faithfully preached to them by the pastors of the Church, with the Holy Ghost sent down from Heaven: still they possessed the whole in its essence, sufficient to make them a pattern to all generations in the Church. The case, from that day to this, is nearly the same. Multitudes of the inhabitants in our land never saw the inside of a Bible;* yet, whilst preachers declare the substance of it, the Holy Ghost opens their understanding, reveals Christ, and brings what is needful to their remembrance sufficient to make them lead a new life, do credit to their profession, and die in peace. I reflect with pleasure, how many instances of this kind are registered in the Book of Life, through your preaching, to poor sinners, Jesus, and Him Crucified. From this indisputable fact, I consider your position, 'that the Word of God is only to be known by reading the Hebrew,' as a sinful attempt to limit the Holy One of Israel to *one way* of revealing His salvation, and making the soul meet

* At the time this Letter was written, neither was reading so general among the poor as at the present day; nor were Bibles so universally dispersed as they have since been, through the glorious instrumentality of Bible Societies.

for His presence, which He has not at all declared
to be so—a way which not one in a thousand can
ever put in practice.   So that all common illiterate
Christians, whose "delight is in the Law of the Lord,"
as they have it in the Translation, may say, ' Neither
Christ nor his Apostles ever hint that the Word of
God may not be savingly known, and all its benefits
fully enjoyed, by reading the Bible in our mother
tongue.—Why should any, who call themselves
Christians, peremptorily deny this?'

Further, it is the universal consent of all Divines,
with Chrysostom, Πάντα τὰ ἀναγκαῖα ἐστὶν δῆλα, " All
things necessary to be known, are manifest."   If
so, then whatever is not to be known but by scholars and masters in the Hebrew tongue, cannot with
truth be ranked higher than among matters of
curiosity and amusement, which may employ idle
men of a critical taste, as the whole system of plants
employed the attention of Solomon.   Yet he who
possessed the largest intellect ever given to mere
man had probably never been such a reproach to
the Israel of God, had he spent more of his precious
time upon τὰ ἀναγκαῖα δῆλα, and less in making the
wonderful discoveries he did in the creation of God!
Indeed he tells us so, when he was recovered, and
the right use of his understanding was given to him.
Then his conclusion is, what all real Christians,
however unlettered, make effectually as he did:
" Fear God, and keep His commandments; for
this is the whole duty," business, and happiness "of
man."   This very remarkable instance of Solomon,
and the practice of all the Scripture saints, certainly lead us to this conclusion, that when we

neglect what is of infinite value, through a passionate pursuit after things of little weight, we are guilty of sinful neglect, and are sadly deluded.

Further, the word of God, in Hebrew, Greek, and English, especially charges all pastors and teachers to be examples to the flock in the vigorous exercise of all zeal for the souls of men, and to see well to it that they fulfil the ministry they have received. Such pastors of the Church, all agree, are the glory of Christ. No blame need they ever fear from His lips, for giving themselves up so wholly to this work, as to have neither time nor inclination for a thing so immaterial as an accurate investigation of the Hebrew text; when it is allowed that all things *necessary to be known* are the same in every Version as in the Original. It is, to all intents and purposes, sufficient: by the English Bible their souls were converted ;—by that, through the Divine Spirit's influence, they have been quickened, comforted, established, and made ready to every good word and work. Blessed are those servants whom the Lord, at His coming, shall find in this state !

On the contrary, if the time and thoughts of those who are ministers of Christ are principally employed to become masters in Oriental learning (and such they certainly should be, who take upon them to vilify the Translation), their application to this business will leave but a fragment of time for secret prayer, devout meditation, or preparation to carry on family worship with any life or benefit or pleasure ; and still less will it leave of that frame of mind which is essential to true worship. For, after investigating a Hebrew Root, or endeavouring to elucidate a dark passage by the aid of Buxtorf, Pagninus, Gussetius, Cocceius, &c. &c. (a critic always consults these famous Lexicographers) — after this business, which has no relation to the devout exercises of the heart, the mind will still be running upon the reasons each different author offered for his sense of the passage, or derivation of the root, or aiming at some happier conjecture. Smitten with the lust of correcting an established version, and, imperceptibly to themselves, filled with the flattering idea of their own great ingenuity, such scholars will be indefatigable in searching for evidence to support their own interpretation — be exceedingly partial, through self-love, to their own important discoveries—very violent and obstinate in defence of them—and, narrow as is the human mind, and not made to pass, by a quick transition from things so foreign from all communion with God, to a profitable use of the means of grace, such pastors will grow cool to all exercises of the mind which are truly spiritual, and cease to do good to the flock of Christ—the Church He has purchased with His own blood. Now, for my own part, I do not see how any pastor in the Church of Christ can justify himself, if this be the effect of studying Hebrew learning intensely; and that no other effect is generally experienced, there are too many melancholy proofs.

Our Saviour tells us, doctrines are to be tried by their fruits. We may safely apply this to our studies, and to scholars of greatest note. Consequently, if we saw strenuous pleaders for the necessity and vast benefit of Hebrew learning go far beyond all others in compassion for perishing sinners—in zeal for enlarging the Kingdom of Messiah—and imitating his example, so that not a relation, friend, or acquaintance, could be with them without receiving good to their souls—we should then, without hesitation, allow they did well, and could never too highly exalt the usefulness of that knowledge which brought forth such good fruits. But, where are these excellent effects found to proceed from an indefatigable application to Hebrew learning? On the contrary, I know several Hebrew scholars, who no sooner came to the knowledge of themselves and of Christ, and were fired with an Apostolic desire to save sinners, than they relinquished their pursuit of Hebrew learning. Mr. Clarke, of Chesham Boyce; Mr. Stillingfleet, of Worcester; Mr. Berridge, and others, I have authority to say, did so. The same was my own case : and all for the same reason ;—we found that, in reading the Hebrew, our attention was called off to consult the Lexicographers, and very much of our time taken up in inquiring whether the Text was rendered best by such and such a derivation of the Root. Without therefore consulting at all together, we all gave up ourselves to our ministerial work ;—and I believe not one of us has ever repented.

I have many further objections against exalting the Hebrew Text as you do, to the utter disparagement of the Translation ;—first, with respect to infidels ; but still more, to the multitude of unlettered people ; and, most of all, to the faithful in Christ Jesus.

You observe what work Voltaire makes of the

Vulgate, to reproach the Scripture. Would he make less advantage of the assertion of learned divines, that the Bible, in the Translation, is a book of lies? Yet have the Scriptures never been known in the Christian Church, to one in a thousand, but in a translation.—What could that daring blasphemer have wished for more, than what Bishop Lowth and Bishop Warburton, and many more, allow to be the state of the Hebrew Text? Would he not cry out with triumph, "Nobody can tell what the Text is—so many are the errata and the interpolations! The Text is just what they are pleased to make it. I think they can say nothing more to their purpose against the Translation!"—But scoffers will be scoffers still, and never want a stumbling-block to take offence at.

The case of the illiterate deserves our consideration. They immediately (I have known many instances) conclude, that if the Translation is materially wrong in some places, it may be so in many more, and especially in what strikes directly at their favourite lusts. A gentleman of my acquaintance had a servant who had heard the English Bible not over-respectfully treated; and upon being admonished by his master, that servants were commanded not to answer again, when reproved—" O, Sir!" says he, " *that*, I am told, is a wrong translation." How often do I hear this, even among the common people! And the consequences of such a notion are bad enough. Yet there is still something worse and more cruel, in this matter, than what concerns infidels, or the unlettered multitude.

I am grieved beyond measure to see the Children

of God startled, and confounded, and distressed to
the last degree, from numberless and most peremptory accusations against the English Bible, as false;
—yet is it all they have!   And when their soul's
health depends on giving the fullest credence to it—
when, of themselves, they too slowly, alas! receive
the things recorded in the oracles of God—to have
it asserted, with the most solemn airs of assurance,
that the Translators are not to be trusted—what is
this, but to fill them with endless doubts, and lead
them to despise their English Bible, and think the
Christian Religion itself an uncertainty?—How often
have you observed to me, what strange interpretations the Rector of a church in London would give
of the Hebrew, and how unsupported! yet, to make
way for even such interpretations as these, forty-
seven men, who could " render a reason," are pub-
licly branded as fools, compared with himself. Oh! it
will neither please God, nor be of any use to men!

Thus, to use a proud word for such a man as
I am, you have my *ultimatum* about this matter.   I
wish you to be jealous over yourself, and, as in the
presence of God, ask yourself what real good you
have received to your immortal soul from so much
study, and such violent pursuit of Hebrew learning?
How different was your judgment, when we were
first acquainted!—how becoming your profession,
when you brought with you into Yorkshire, and
dropped them by the way, "A Word to a Drunkard,"
" to a Sabbath-breaker," &c.!—when your whole
soul was so engaged with the work you undertook
—when dear Mr. Grimshaw, Mr. Hervey, and others,
whose whole talk was of the power and glory and

mightiness of God's Kingdom, were so pleasing and profitable, as you then confessed! Their discourse was all to the purpose : it was the substance we were then all concerned about. Oh, may we be more and more so, the nearer the hour of our departure approaches! I have been lately ill; and found, as Dr. Watts says of himself, I had no comfort then, but from the plain promises—just as every common man, who can hear the Bible, has for his support.

From your affectionate friend,

H. VENN.

TO LADY MARY FITZGERALD.

(CAUTIONS AGAINST THE DISCOURAGEMENT WHICH SOMETIMES ARISES
FROM READING THE LIVES OF EMINENTLY HOLY PERSONS.)

MADAM,   *Yelling, March* 3, 1787.

Taking it for granted that your Ladyship, and the Christian Ladies, my very kind friends, who so often meet with you, would read the Life of that very extraordinary servant of God, Mr. Fletcher—I had no sooner finished it, than I was under some concern lest it should hinder your spiritual progress, though it was written to animate and press us forward in our heavenly race. I have frequently known the lives of most eminent saints to have had rather a bad effect, than otherwise. I intended, therefore, immediately to send you my thoughts upon this subject; but was prevented till now, by the correction of my Heavenly Father.

The first thing obvious in the account of very eminent saints, as generally given by their friends,

THE BEST, VERY IMPERFECT.

is the exhibition only of their excellencies;—not a fault is allowed to mingle with the description of their character;—you are led to judge, they go on conquering, like the Saviour, in the greatness of His strength.   But this is very far from being the case. We must remember to make a large allowance for partiality, and the fervent love of their persons, so strongly felt by those who have received inestimable benefit from their bright example and shining attainments.   We must remember, also, we have infallible authority to pronounce them polluted, offenders in many things, and defective also above all that we can conceive, "when judgment is laid to the line, and righteousness to the plummet."

I prove this by a most decisive instance.   St. Paul appears more like an angel than a man—a very flame of love to Christ and the souls of men—in labours more abundant than any of the Apostles— in affection to the saints so tender, that he compares his concern for them to that which a mother feels for her own child at the breast.   He appeals unto God, as well as to the Church, how holily, how justly, how unblameably he had walked.   And had he chosen to put himself off for better than he was, how easily might he have deceived the Churches, and led them to think he had no plague in his own heart to lament and bewail—no conflict with manifold corruptions—nothing, at least, similar to what you and I, my honoured friends, so often, to our shame and grief, feel moving within!   But this man of God (the first, many suppose, of the fallen race) will not suffer such a deception, respecting his own character, to be entertained.   Behold!

he opens a window into his own heart. He owns to all the Churches, that, notwithstanding he had once been a murderer of the members of Christ—notwithstanding the grace he had received—his constant preaching of humility—and his having been admitted into the third heaven—he owns he needed (lest he should perish by exalting himself above measure)—he owns he needed (what in mercy was given him) *a thorn in the flesh,* a messenger of Satan, to buffet him. What strength of depravity is here! —what evil, mixed with the most shining excellencies!—what cause for Paul to say, " Oh, wretched man that I am! who shall deliver me from the body of this death ?" Here the Apostle, the first of men, is sick with our malady. We stand together on a level, as fallen lost sinners; equally in need of the redemption of Christ, and the robe of His righteousness.

We are continually taught in Scripture, that there is none without deplorable spots and defects before God—no, not one! While, therefore, we glorify Him in His saints, for their excellent life and conversation, we must not forget, that, however they appear, they are not yet without sin, or less need the Advocate and the propitiation than other men.

Again : in reading the life of an extraordinary Christian, when his spirit and manner of life are highly to be admired, we are often tempted to despond. We compare ourselves with his shining attainments ; and feeling at so great a distance, we grow dissatisfied, and can scarcely think that what God has done for us deserves any consideration ; or believe that we are in a state of grace and salva-

tion.   Our pride (though we do not perceive it) is
hurt, and self-love is mortified, to see we are so far
outdone.   The good hope we were willing to entertain of our faith in Christ, and union with Him, is
ready to fail, because we are no better.   The spiritual riches, in which the saint seems so to abound,
makes our own poverty apparent and undeniable.
Consequently, we feel much uneasiness and vexation ; and are apt to conclude we are unfit to die,
and ought not even to be called Christians, till we
are exactly, or nearly, such as the blessed saint,
whose history is before us.

Herein we greatly err: we seem not to know
that a very great disparity prevails through all the
works of God.   In heaven there are many different
degrees of excellency; and, no doubt, a vast distance
between the powers and excellencies of the highest
and the lowest angels.   In our own bodies, how
does the head and the eye, and the tongue, surpass
in excellency many other parts!   In the Church, it
is the same: according to the ability which God
gives, and according to the measure of grace given
unto us, *we are what we are.*   Some bring forth a
hundredfold—more than three times as much as
others ever will do ; according as the same Spirit
divideth " to every man severally as he will."   And
though the three last lines of Mr. Fletcher's Life
affirm that *every one* may be exactly like him if he
will, I beg leave, on the contrary, to say, that a fowl
in a barn-yard, which mounts with great difficulty so
high in the air as the top of the barn, or into a lofty
tree, might as reasonably be expected to accompany
an eagle in its flight, as myself and the bulk of

Christians can be just what dear and blessed Mr. Fletcher was, in his spirit and manner of life. No! a natural cast, a great capacity, a vivid impression from every object, a very quick sensibility of affections, and a very uncommon measure of grace, must all concur, and be all diligently improved, before a vessel of honour, of such magnitude and brightness as he was, can come forth from the Great Maker's hand.

Yet why should this disquiet our souls? We are not accepted or beloved for our own excellencies, but for Christ's sake, from the goodness of God; and *two*, no less than *ten*, talents may be used, and will be most amply and gloriously rewarded. We ought to be comforted and animated from the consideration, that whatever the most eminent saints possess, it is received from the same inexhaustible Fountain, of which all the Children of God partake; and that there is in reality, though in miniature, every feature in the least and lowest Child of God, which is so prominent and beautiful in the fairest of the saints.

To exemplify this, I will go through several of the graces with which dear Mr. Fletcher was clothed.

His *humility* was so unfeigned, and so deep, that, when I thanked him for two sermons he had one day preached to my people at Huddersfield, he answered, as no man ever did to me, in a way the most affecting I can conceive: with eyes and hands uplifted, he exclaimed, " Pardon, pardon, pardon, O my God!" It went to my very soul: I shall never forget it! Great grace was then upon this blessed servant of Christ;—yet a measure of the same is

in our souls, though it be but a very little. We
unfeignedly beg for mercy. We put not our trust
in any thing we do. We utterly abjure our own
righteousness; and the same Spirit that wrought,
in Mr. Fletcher, that cry, so vehement for pardon,
by His mighty power keeps up in us an abiding
sense of our sad defects; and our supplication, with
godly sincerity, is, " Enter not into judgment with
thy servant, O Lord !"

Love to man, and bowels of mercies, displayed in
Mr. Fletcher a noble imitation of his Incarnate God.
He indeed thought the day lost, and could find no
rest in his soul, unless he was doing good to the
bodies and the souls of men. The whole family of
Christ are of the same gracious temper, in some
degree—they are merciful, loving, and righteous.
Their prayers, their constant wishes, their endeavours—their watching for opportunity, by letters, by
books, by discourse, to instruct the ignorant, and
to remove prejudices against the Gospel of Christ—
their conscientious retrenchment of foolish expenses
—their good-will to promote every good design—
proves that God hath given them the spirit of love,
and to be kindly-affectioned towards their fellow-
sinners.

Love to the Lord—how did it govern, and flourish
in, dear Mr. Fletcher! His admirable consort tells
us, he scarcely was awake, in the night, a moment,
without lifting up his soul to God in holy aspira-
tion. And all who are taught of God, and born
from above, have their heart where their treasure
is. Their souls truly " wait still upon God, from
whom cometh their salvation." They have spiritual

wants, urgent and many, to be supplied;—more grace they covet;—mercies vouchsafed, and growing discoveries of His adorable excellencies, excite their praise. Stated times for prayer, therefore, and religious exercises, never satisfy any whose souls are alive to God through Jesus Christ our Lord. They see Him in His works of creation—in His Providence—in His Gospel. He hath so won their hearts, that they can be happy in Himself alone; and look upon every thing besides as emptiness and mere vanity.

I have seen Mr. Fletcher, for six weeks together, under a hectic fever, sometimes spitting blood— when, night after night, he could rest very little— *well pleased to suffer*—never complain, never but be cheerful. Once, when I asked him how he did, " Oh!" said he, " how light is the chastisement I suffer! how heavy the strokes I deserve! I love the rod of my Heavenly Father!" Now, all the Children of Christ feel so too; or, if they do not, it is their additional burden and grief, lamented and confessed with tears; nor can they forgive themselves, till they feel they are reconciled to the will of God, and can take pleasure in suffering what it pleases Him to lay upon them.

Once more, which particularly applies to myself.— Dear Mr. Fletcher had such a sense of the weight of his office, that, like his Saviour, he could continue in prayer, in the wood, all night long; and, like Him, lie prostrate on the ground, pleading for grace to fulfil His ministry. Oh, how admirable! how rare such a spirit in such a degree! Yet every pastor and Teacher, who hath the grace of Christ dwelling in his heart, feels a constant desire to be found faithful, and is a daily supplicant for the salvation of his hearers. Every true pastor appeals to his Lord: " Thou knowest all things—Thou knowest that I love Thee, and desire to live only to gather in more outcasts, to feed Thy lambs and Thy sheep, and bring glory to Thy name." This resemblance, real, though faint—this sameness of disposition and temper, found in the least and weakest of the flock —proves that they are in Christ, and Christ in them, no less than believers who very far excel them in their fruits of righteousness and true holiness.

Still further: we are in much danger of being hurt and hindered in our spiritual progress, by reading the life of an eminent saint, when we think we must do the same things we find set down, and use exactly the same methods as he used;—and, most of all, we are hurt when our hearts are turned off from Christ Crucified and interceding with the Father for poor sinners, to the spiritual graces dwelling in us. For these will ever be imperfect, ebbing, and flowing; and the more light and tenderness of conscience we receive, the more we are sure to find we cannot rest our hope upon, or enjoy comfort from, our internal grace. The fulness there is in Christ—the work He has finished—the work He is now every moment performing—the love of His heart, intense and ever active—and His faithful promises, understood, blessed, and embraced—must be the way of our comfort and sanctification, turning our eyes only to these things.

But, my dear friends, using proper caution, and guarding against the mistakes I have now pointed out, we may read, with great encouragement and profit, how the chief of saints have fought our common enemy, prevailed over the corruptions of nature, adorned their holy profession, and left their name and memory to be a blessing to the Church. How delightful to see in them the Scripture promises fulfilled—" The righteous are preserved for ever"—" The path of the just shineth more and more, unto the perfect day"—" They who wait upon the Lord shall mount up, as on eagles' wings ; they shall run, and not be weary; they shall walk, and not faint"! Viewing these fair examples, we may joyfully exclaim : " As we have heard, so have we seen in the city of our God (which is His Church), God upholdeth the same for ever !" Are we ready to loiter, or be idle, from the unprofitable conversation and life of professors in general? How useful, to mark the fervent love, the persevering zeal, with which *they* ran the ways of God's commandments, who were men of like passions with ourselves! The success of *their* faith in Christ—of their prayer, vigilance, and self-denial—do, in a forcible and pleasing manner, recommend the same graces to us. The consolations they enjoyed by the way, through a single eye to the glory of God, and their hope and triumph in death, demonstrate to us the wisdom of their sober singularity ; and call loudly upon us, " See how blessed, in life and death, are they who diligently seek the Lord !"

My much-honoured friends and sisters in Christ! I will conclude my address to you on occasion of dear Mr. Fletcher's Life, with an observation, confirmed by the experience of the Church of God, and built upon His own promises : it is this :—Whosoever desires to persevere and increase in the fear of the Lord, and in the comfort of the Holy Ghost, to live and die in hope that maketh not ashamed, must be *diligent in secret prayer;* must constantly *read God's Word*, begging Him to explain it, and give faith in it; and must *walk with those who walk conscientiously before God*—who are always aspiring to what they have not attained—in whose manners, spirit, and discourse, there is what reaches the heart, and tends to humble, quicken, and comfort the soul. In all my reading and acquaintance, for forty years, with religious people, I never saw an instance of one decaying and coming to nothing, who observed these rules—never saw one who presumed, on any consideration, to give over attention to them, who did not fall away.

Let us then, notwithstanding all obstructions, use these means. Whatever our frames or our complaints, our sins or fears, may be, diligence in secret prayer, and cries for knowledge of God's Word while we read it, and society with His children, will, in due time, heal all—sanctify all, till we are taken out of this evil world, and join the armies of the saved, who are gone before us, who wait for our coming; to testify, as we shall each of us do for ever, that God, our Covenant God, was faithful, and would not suffer us to be tempted above what we were enabled to bear, to the glory of His name, and the honour of our holy profession. Amen!

H. VENN.

The following Paper was drawn up by Mr. Venn, for the use of his son, about the year 1792. It was entitled—

THE MISTAKES INTO WHICH YOUNG MINISTERS ARE APT TO FALL.

I HAVE too much reason to think the success of my ministry was much impeded from the following causes :—

1. Several bad consequences, I judge, might have been prevented entirely, or in a great measure, among my people, had I taken care frequently to let them know how greatly I stood in need of their prayers, that the Spirit of God might be given to teach me so to preach as to do them good, and to make me feel more love for their souls;—if I had also often pressed them to consider how great a charge was laid upon me, and what a solemn account I was to give of the doctrine I delivered to them, and of the awful relation there was between them and myself. These things I did often allude to, and even briefly mention. It would have been better had I dwelt often upon these subjects; because the flock listen, with peculiar attention, when their pastor proves the care and affection which he owes them ; and when he solicits their prayers, that nothing may be wanting, on his part, which may promote their present and eternal welfare. At the same time, a full explanation of the duty of a pastor towards his flock is the means of raising their esteem for him, and a more earnest attention to his word.

2. I should have set before my people the com-

mand, addressed to all believers, " to esteem very
highly in love" those who labour among them in the
word and doctrine, " for their work's sake ;" and
have shewn them what they owe to them, as the instruments, in the hand of God, by which their souls
are saved ;—and proved from hence, that they would
go directly contrary to their duty, if they should
slight their ministry ; much more, should they forsake it.

I did not choose to treat on these subjects, from
an apprehension that I should be thought to aim at
pre-eminence, and at bringing them into subjection
to myself. But there would have been no difficulty
in proving the good which would follow from a just
esteem for the minister of Christ—the wise ends
for which he had required it : and a behaviour void
of all arrogance and self-exaltation would have
shewn plainly to them, that I aimed at nothing but
their profit and salvation.

3. After my hearers began to taste the good
Word of God, and the powers of the world to come,
I neglected to point out to them the several ways
in which spiritual pride and self-conceit will begin
to work—how ready they will be to conclude they
have much grace, when it is not certain they have
any ; how highly they will think of their own gifts,
if they can pray with fervour and fluency, and speak
with great readiness of utterance ; how soon they
are tempted to behave themselves unseemly, by
abounding in their own sense of things—obstinately
contending for their own opinion, and their own
way in every thing, in opposition to old disciples,
and their own teacher, who have had so much

more experience;—with what a hasty and uncharitable spirit they will censure this or that person, for any thing they happen to dislike in them;—whilst they are little humbled for all the evil they have done, or the manifold corruptions of their own hearts. If I had particularly pointed out these things, they might have been stirred up to watch and guard against them; and others would have perceived the wrong spirit working in them, when, as novices, puffed up by their fleshly mind, they were speaking to corrupt others.

4. I was no less to blame for not pointing out, how men, enlightened, but not converted, are always the first to create disturbances about things of no importance, instead of confining their attention to the grand and fundamental doctrines of Christ, and the fruits they are to produce. I should have proved that it is sloth, and love of sin, and a dislike to take pains in the mortification of every corrupt temper, which really, though imperceptibly, lead men to make trifles appear great matters. Thus, the points in difference between us and Dissenters—whether a Form of Prayer in Public Worship always the same, or one left to the minister—whether persons are to be admitted to the Lord's Supper without giving in their experience, or not—are made subjects of debate, which unsettle men in their judgments, draw off their attention from the evil of sin, the Salvation of Christ, and the necessity of holiness; make men captious in their spirit, so that they lose their love for each other, and the concern they began to feel to walk worthy of the Gospel of Christ. I should have marked the rise and

progress of this bad spirit, as the effect of pride, and
the device of Satan; and appealed to their own consciences, whether these things did not hinder their
communion with God, and destroy their peace.

5. I neglected to be large and full in describing
the lamentable consequences of division and separation, amongst a people awakened, and called
to the knowledge of Christ, by His minister—how
separation and division lead men to conclude no
one can certainly determine what the faith of Christ
is; and that they serve no better purpose than to
cause variances and janglings without end—than to
perplex and stumble the weak in faith—and give
the ungodly occasion to boast, that passions and
prejudices are nowhere less subdued than among
the most religious. By these means, the Gospel is
judged to be of little use to mankind; though so
much extolled by those who preach, and those who
profess to receive it, as the Gospel of peace, which
transforms men into the image of the God of peace
and love.

6. I was guilty also of a great neglect, in not
instructing my people more frequently and fully
concerning the danger of preferring and exalting
the ordinance of preaching, to the spiritual worship
of God in the congregation, which is the great end
the Gospel, when received, should produce—how
men deceive themselves, and grieve the Spirit of
God, who are eager to hear, and expect a blessing
from hearing, when they have been idle and lukewarm in confessing their sinfulness, or in their petitions for grace and knowledge; and without importunity, and bowels of mercy, in making interces-

sion; and void of all gratitude to God, when praise is offered up to Him for all His mercies—that the exercise of these affections, habitually and comfortably, is much beyond hearing the best sermons, and a full proof we are born of God. Yet how evident is the want of this spiritual worship, in those who call themselves believers in Christ! What a manifest drowsiness and stupidity, and hardness of heart, prevail amongst professors in general! Hence, God being so little honoured in the worship offered to His Divine Majesty, His Spirit is withdrawn; the word preached is not made effectual; but generally is a dry, insipid thing to the greatest part of the hearers, after the novelty ceases, as they themselves confess.

7. I am conscious, also, that I did not press, as I ought to have done, upon professors, how much it was their duty, as they received the knowledge of the things of God themselves, and had ability, to begin to work together with their minister. I ought to have told them plainly, and constantly, how little good, in comparison, could be done by one man, as a teacher of the Truth; or by his conversation, or visiting the poor, the ignorant, or the afflicted;— that this ought to be regarded, as it was in the Churches planted by the Apostles, as the common and indispensable duty of every man professing godliness; that they be diligent among their neighbours in these works and labours of love;—that the minister is to be considered as the officer, indeed, who gives the word of command, and takes the lead in all good works; but that all the people of God, like soldiers under him, must fight against the

common enemy—must take pains in diffusing light
and knowledge, and shewing all compassion towards
those that are ignorant and out of the way, and in
endeavouring to bring them to the knowledge of
the Truth. I should have shewn them, that, on
many accounts, private Christians are fitted to exhort, and instruct and reprove, those of their own
age and condition;—as this is an affecting proof
of love for them—is more likely to stir them up to
seek for knowledge, when they see others besides
the preacher are acquainted with Divine things,
even men who have had no better education than
themselves;—whereas the greater part excuse their
ignorance, supposing the poor, and all who work for
their bread, have no time to gain knowledge. The
very few who have love and zeal thus to come forth,
to help in promoting the salvation of souls, find that
God blesses them for their good-will to their fellow-
creatures, and with such sacrifices He is well pleased.

8. I shall mention only one mistake more; which
was, in my way of talking to persons always full of
doubts and fears and uneasiness, and never comforted. I too readily concluded this arose from a
right and deep sense of their corruptions, and of their
great defects in obedience, and from not putting their
whole trust in Christ. But generally, as Mr. Baxter
observes, such persons are indolent, and not fully
persuaded even of the certainty of an eternal Heaven
and Hell—that their souls are at stake, and they
must be up and doing. I ought faithfully to have
put the question to them, whether the love of money
did not rule in their hearts, and was their confidence;
whether they were not shutting up their bowels of

compassion towards their distressed and suffering fellow-Christians; and whether this was not the cause of their walking on in darkness. This, I am persuaded, is generally the case; because the promise of light, and great consolation and joy in God and prosperity of soul, is made to those who are of a loving and bountiful spirit.—See Isai. lviii. 6—11.

THE END.